# Likely Lads *and Lasses*

# 'PARENTS, GIVE YOUR SON A CHANCE'

*'Let your boys join their fellow Britons beyond the seas.*
*They will be welcomed by people who speak the same language,*
*share the same traditions, and are heirs to the same history, literature,*
*ideals as the citizens of the mother country.*
*The flag above them will be the same old Union Jack,*
*plus the five stars of the Southern Cross -*
*the symbol of Australian nationhood.*
*Your boys need Australia: it is their opportunity.*
*And Australia needs them.'*

Appeal to British parents by (Sir) Richard Linton,
founder Big Brother Movement (1925),
later Agent-General for Victoria in London.

# Likely Lads
## *and Lasses*

Youth Migration
to Australia 1911-1983

Alan Gill
Author of 'Orphans of the Empire'

Likely Lads *and Lasses*
Youth Migration to Australia 1911 – 1983

Includes index.
ISBN 0-646-45327-0.

First published in 2005 by BBM Ltd

www.bbmyouthsupport.com.au

Printed by Southwood Press
80 Chapel Street, Marrickville 2204 N.S.W.

Design and typesetting by The Visible Word Pty Ltd
Sydney, NSW

This book is dedicated to
the late FRANK MANSELL and CAROLYN NELSON

*Also to the many 'young' people – young in spirit even if chronologically elderly or middle aged – interviewed for this volume, and to the greater number whose stories are known only to their families and to themselves.*

*Special thanks for their assistance to Barry Coldrey, Stephen Constantine, Chris Makin, Leonie Peake, Michael Rakusin, Geoffrey Sherington, Eddy Steele, Alan Taylor, Peter van Gessel.*

*This book was published with support from the Big Brother Movement.*

Alan Gill  2005

# Contents

# PREFACE

Several years ago, while I was working as a reporter for the *Sydney Morning Herald*, an elderly man visited the Fairfax building, brandishing a large sheaf of papers. He told the receptionist merely that he had a story to tell.

It was a busy day and no one was keen to see him. He wore a clerical collar, which was the determining factor. I was, after all, the paper's religion writer, so I was landed with the job.

His name was the Rev Arthur Brawn. He was a retired Methodist minister, and the story he told threw new light on an unsolved mystery concerning the disappearance of some 1,500 Australian prisoners of the Japanese in World War II.

Arthur Brawn's story, and his own role in this extraordinary affair, is told in Chapter 12. In the course of our conversation the visitor mentioned that he was a 'Dreadnought Boy'. He spoke the words with obvious pride. The name at that time meant nothing to me. Now it means a lot.

By coincidence, a few weeks later I met and interviewed another Dreadnought Boy, Norman Monsen, who had just been elected Moderator of the Presbyterian Church in New South Wales.

This well-known Sydney clergyman told me about his departure from Tyneside when he was still only 14. His mother had been too upset to come to the station, but his father and a brother did so. I imagined what it must have been like – dad with his arm around the other boy, perhaps both choking back tears, as the train pulled out, gradually enveloping them in steam.

He told the story matter-of-factly. I suspected he had blocked part of it from his memory. I was more moved by it all than he was.

Norman Monsen departed for Sydney, on the *SS Benalla*, on 19 August 1926. It was to be 45 years before he returned to England again. I thought at the time: 'How many others must there be?'

He was, in fact, one of several thousand young people of school leaving age or a little older, who came to this country from Britain as sponsored unaccompanied youth migrants in the first half of the 20th century and beyond. The Big Brother Movement, which I heard about later, performed a similar role on a larger and better organised scale. As the sole survivor of the original sending and receiving organisations, it nowadays fulfils a valuable (if unexpected) social service role, with which the ghosts of its founding fathers should be well pleased.

Common to all the migration schemes was a requirement – which lapsed in later years – that boys should work on the land and the girls go into domestic service. Pre-war arrivals, in particular, have a shared experience of loneliness, courage, humour and adversity bravely born.

At a reunion luncheon a Dreadnought Old Boy mentioned that in his first two years in Australia he had slept only in stables. To which another octogenarian replied: 'That was luxury. I had to build a humpy.'

As a journalist, and British-born adult migrant, my curiosity and compassion were aroused. It was a story, I thought, that not many people knew about and which had to be told.

The best of plans sometimes go awry. I had just begun research when I came across another group of expatriate Britons (though all would now consider themselves dinkum Aussies), worthy of attention. These were the former child migrants, sent from orphanages and institutions in the United Kingdom to be raised in orphanages and children's homes in Australia.

The situation of the child migrants (as opposed to youth migrants) involved basic issues of justice and demanded immediate social action. Many, as adults, were still suffering trauma resulting from childhood experiences of separation, physical, sexual and emotional abuse. By the mid-1990s their situation had become a public concern in Australia, overtaken in interest only by the removal of Aboriginal children, which has an obvious parallel.

I decided to make the child migrants my priority, and in 1992 set out to research and write my first book, *Orphans of the Empire*. It was followed, in 2004, by *Interrupted Journeys*, about the reception of young refugee migrants from Hitler's Reich.

Feeling guilty about my sins of omission, I decided to tackle once more the saga of the youth migrants and their place in Australian society. *Likely Lads*, a term used by Norman Monsen's local vicar to describe young people with the "right stuff" for migration, is the result.

# 1

# Farm Lads for a White Australia

# 1

# Australia bound for Empire's sake

―――

*'A young man left his native shores*
*For trade was bad at home*
*To seek his fortune in this land*
*He crossed the briny foam.'*
Doggerel, supplied by a Dreadnought Boy.

IT HAS BEEN SAID that Britain is the only nation to export its children. Thanks to the TV mini-series *The Leaving of Liverpool*, a Senate Inquiry and various books on the topic [1], most Australians, as well as Britons, are now aware of the traffic commonly known as child migration.

Less well known, though the numbers involved were greater, were schemes to bring out school leavers and older teenagers – the boys as 'farm lads' (the preferred term) and girls as domestic servants. After a brief induction program – one such course involved milking an artificial cow – youngsters of both sexes entered directly into the Australian workforce. After World War II the rules insisting upon rural employment were gradually relaxed

Formal youth migration schemes began in the early years of the 20th century, influenced by improvements in sea transport, and continued for over 70 years. Some 30,000 people were brought to Australia in this way.

Young people brought out under the schemes came from a variety of backgrounds. Most, but not all, would have considered themselves working class. The majority, particularly in later years, had trade skills. A scheme confined mainly to Victoria [2] sought to recruit upper class boys from English public schools (ie. private schools) as future gentlemen farmers.

Organised youth migration once formed an important plank of Australia's immigration policy. It was bolstered by an appeal to patriotic sentiment, the idea being to 'seed the empire' with yeomen farmers of 'good British stock'[3]. Nor were community organisations slow to respond. It is not generally realised, for instance, that the Sydney Club, now unfortunately defunct, was originally the Millions Club, formed by zealous businessmen with just such a purpose in mind.

It should be stressed that youth migration, unlike the traffic in younger children, has basically an honourable history, except for claims of exploitation of labour, examples of which are contained in this book. While alarming by modern standards, in the context of the time they were not too serious. At any rate the public didn't much care

Being older, and not having to endure institutional life, youth migrants were virtually free of the physical and sexual abuse encountered by the child migrants. Some teenage girls were subject to sexual advances from their employers. Youth migrants, by and large, were able to look after themselves.

This is not to suggest their lives were without trauma. For the early migrants, in particular, there was the curse of extreme loneliness, resulting from isolation and the hardships common to all who lived in the bush.

Participants in the migration schemes were genuine volunteers, though some were hazy about which organisations were sponsoring them, and came with the blessing of parents or guardians. They were led to believe – some later concluded they had been conned – that it was an honour to have been selected. Their motives were to better themselves or find excitement. Poverty – except in the very earliest years – does not seem to have been a factor.

The emphasis on farm workers meant that there was a lesser interest in recruiting girls, who were seen as potential farmers' wives. The Fairbridge Farm Schools even had a line in the school song about it[4]. Young female migrants were expected, on arrival, to go 'into service'. Even this was portrayed as having a certain buzz. Only in the 1960s did new arrivals challenge the convention that work 'below stairs' was inevitably to be their lot.

The migration schemes were intended primarily for British youngsters. Attempts to bring out youths of other races and nationalities received short shrift. There were a few exceptions, notably schemes to assist Jewish refugees from Nazism[5].

The schemes were operated, with some exceptions, by secular patriotic associations without religious affiliation. They were, in effect, agents of the federal Government. In the early years State Governments also directly recruited young migrants, the South Australian Government (1913) being the first to do so. Later migrants under this scheme were known as Barwell Boys, on account of the role played by Sir Henry Barwell, Premier of South Australia from 1920 to 1924. In 1914 (a traffic interrupted by the Great War) 1,082 boys of school leaving age were directly sponsored by the NSW Government.

The first non-government body to enter the youth immigration scene is thought to have been the Salvation Army, which, unlike other religious bodies, put the needs of school leavers and young adults above those of unaccompanied younger children.

Empire loyalty and – more importantly – the Army's highly developed work ethic prompted this concern. An emigration department was established at the movement's London headquarters, paving the way for young migrants to be sent to the 'colonies' (meaning Canada and Australia, as well as countries in Africa) as early as 1908.

No one could accuse the Salvos of doing things by halves. In 1925, and again in 1927, 1928 and 1929, the Salvation Army chartered an entire ship, the SS *Vedic*, to bring migrant youths and some married couples to Australia.

The charisma of men such as Kingsley Fairbridge, founder of the Fairbridge Farm Schools, who featured in school textbooks on a par with the Reverend John Flynn, gave to youth migration the topic the feel of a missionary enterprise.

Kingsley Fairbridge was a South African-born Rhodes scholar, whose exaltation of 'Empire' led him to take children from English slums to imperial frontiers. His first such expedition took place in January 1913, when he took a party of 13 youngsters to a homestead – by modern standards unbelievably primitive – between the townships of Pinjarra and Coolup, about 86 km south-east of Perth.

The advent of World War I only temporarily curbed his ambitions. When the conflict was over he went back to London, seeking support wherever it could be found. The Government of Western Australia gave

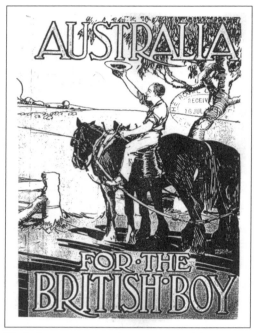

*Typical pre-war recruitment poster (about 1925).*

*Advertisement in British Scouting magazine (1924).*

*Left: In 1913, the Australian States combined to advertise widely in Britain for boys to go to Australian farms.*
*Source: Royal Commonwealth Society Library Pamphlet Collection.*
*Right: Plea to young Britons.*

*Front cover of Australia's Heritage*
*Magazine (1925).*

him a living allowance and an office in the Agent-General's building. His arrival was opportune as imperial unity was in vogue, and convinced imperialists such as Lord Milner and L.S. Amery were dominant at the Colonial Office. Milner was to call the Fairbridge scheme: 'the finest institution for human regeneration that has ever existed'[6]. Certainly, the founder's 'hands on' approach lent a mystique to the organisation which outlasted his death at the unexpectedly early age of 39[7].

The first party of Dreadnought Boys[8] arrived in Sydney in April 1911. They were officially aged 15 to 18 at the time of recruitment. This colourful body, with equally colourful members, inspired the original desire to write this book. The Dreadnoughts were to play an important role in the story of youth migration.

The Sydney Millions Club began its activities in 1921, coinciding with a renewed migration programme by the South Australian Government – the previously mentioned Barwell Boys scheme. In August of that year, amidst Labor Party opposition, the state government formally passed legislation for a British Boy Apprentice System, with the aim of attracting 6,000 British boys, aged between 15 and 18 years. A more modest scheme was announced the same year by the Government of Tasmania.

The South Australian scheme got off to a good start with a launch (actually re-launch) in Britain by Barwell himself in 1922. The scheme had the support of the Boy Scouts and similar movements, and caught on with the British public. More than 14,000 boys – many more than could be accepted – applied[9].

The first Barnardos Girls[10] – teenagers who would enter directly into the workforce – arrived in 1923. In the same year the Fairbridge scheme was re-instituted in Pinjarra.

All these operations, with the possible exception of the Dreadnought Scheme, were shortly to be overshadowed by the arrival of the Big Brother Movement (nowadays known as BBM) which brought out its first group of some 100 migrants in 1925. 'Little Brothers' were a little older than the Dreadnoughts, with an age range on arrival from 16 to 20 years, and occasionally (in later years) 21[11].

The Big Brother Movement and Dreadnought Scheme were to become the best known of some 40 groups involved over the years in youth migration. Both groups were fired with a passionate desire to fill Australia's 'empty spaces' with young migrants from the mother country. They advertised in newspapers, popular magazines, and in boys' comic books. Publicity material had an appropriate get-up-and-go, empire-building ring. Photographs depicted bare-kneed, flaxen haired youth; they might have been senior scouts[12].

There are stories of boys secretly responding to ads in the way other adolescents wrote for information about body building courses[13] – then badgering their parents to let them go. Certainly, in the case of the Big Brother Movement there were more applicants than places available.

Though they co-operated closely, a degree of friendly rivalry developed in the early years between the Big Brother Movement and the Dreadnought Boys. Better staffing and supervision, plus the fact that it preferred to recruit youths who had already completed apprenticeships or trade training, gave to the BBM a slightly higher 'edge'. It was (and is) perceived as holding the blue riband among youth migration bodies.

The Big Brother Movement had as its basis the idea of a 'big brother' – a settled or long-term resident, or perhaps the organisation itself, helping a 'little brother' (the young migrant) settle and adapt to the Australian way of life. The concept was quickly 'borrowed' by other organisations, namely the South Australian Barwell Boys scheme, which recruited a further 1,557 'farm lads' in the period 1927-1928[14].

Actually, the idea of a 'Big Brother helping a little Brother' did not originate in Australia. It is possible the BBM's Australian founders got the name from the larger (and pre-existing) Big Brothers of America[15], whose interests did not, however, include migration. The US body, now the biggest of its type in the world, is not mentioned in early literature of the Australian movement.

Certainly, the Australian ideal, like the American one, was highly successful, and was copied in various degrees by many of the organisations mentioned in this book. A typical example is that of the Young Christian Workers' Movement[16], whose migration objectives included: 'To provide a well-established "Friend" who will take a personal interest in each new arrival, and, as far as possible, take the place of absent parents and friends.'

In theory, young people sponsored by the various bodies were supposed to keep in touch with the organisations and its officers until they were 21. Many failed to do so, forgetting even to submit a change of address, resulting in loss of contact, not just with 'head office', but often with friends and family as well.

## THE DEPRESSION

The Great Depression (1929-1934)[17] brought youth immigration to a virtual standstill, with no Government funding being made available.

In 1937 the economy improved sufficiently for child and youth migration to resume. In that year a second Fairbridge farm school was established at Molong, near Orange, in NSW. A farm school run on similar lines was opened in Victoria by the trustees of the Lady Northcote Emigration Fund. Other farm schools were established in Tasmania and South Australia.

However, the earlier impetus had been lost. R.H. Wheeler, a senior officer at the Department of Immigration, wrote a memo (now in the Australian Archives) giving his view why, despite the economic upturn, it would be harder to obtain suitable youths for immigration.

Wheeler offered five reasons for his pessimistic view. They were a declining birth rate in Britain; better employment opportunities for boys in the UK; the extension of social services whereby unemployment benefits were given at an earlier age; the grave international situation, and the disinclination of parents to grant permission to their sons to emigrate.

It seems he was correct in his assessment. The Dreadnought Scheme, among the more seriously affected bodies, resumed migration activities in March 1939. However, the respite was temporary. Despite the trustees' best endeavours a total of only 76 youths were to arrive in the six months remaining until the outbreak of war in September.

## WAR AND POST-WAR

During World War II military priorities meant that both adult and juvenile migration virtually ground to a halt, an exception being the influx of a small number of Fairbridge youngsters and several young Britons as wartime evacuees[18]. A consequence of the Allied victory was that the need for new migrants was now perceived as greater than before.

In late 1944, while fighting was still in progress, the Federal Government announced a scheme for the introduction to Australia of 50,000 child and youth migrants, the majority of whom would be 'war orphans'[19]. The youngsters were to be brought in at the rate of about 17,000 per year 'during the first three years of peace in Europe, or as soon thereafter as practicable.' Like many such intentions, it proved wildly optimistic.

A conference of Commonwealth and State Officers was held on 9 January 1945, to cost these proposals. However, victory celebrations brought in their wake a greater realism. Transporting the juveniles would provide a problem. One of the original suggestions had been for a 'sea lift' using ships of the Royal Navy or RAN. This was deemed impracticable – 'bringing home the troops' had to have priority.

During the first year of peace no juvenile migrants, or for that matter adult migrants, came at all. Australia's post-war immigration program – for both adults and children – formally came into effect on 31 December 1946. A new assisted passage scheme was approved, in which 'assisted' adults could travel for £10, and certain categories (including child and youth migrants) for £5 or, in some cases, free.

To show that he meant business, Arthur Calwell, Minister for Immigration, announced a schedule of priorities for assisted migrants. There were 11 categories, with child migrants (the term is understood to have included youth migrants) at the head of the list. Second were 'nominated migrants, who can be accommodated by their nominators and are classed as essential workers for Australian industry'. Third were 'nominated migrants who can be accommodated by their nominators and can be readily employed'.

The Minister gave no ceiling on numbers for unaccompanied youth and child migrants, suggesting the problem lay not in Australia's capacity to absorb, but in the availability of shipping and the numbers of youngsters available.

It was proposed that, as with pre-war arrangements, child migrants should go into institutions and orphanages rather than live with Australian families, and that youth migrants should go into training farms. A fostering program, with various options, was proposed by the (London-based) Overseas League and rejected by the Department of

Immigration as unsuitable. A similar scheme worked well in New Zealand, where fostering was the usual practice for younger children[20].

The traffic in juveniles actually resumed, later than expected. It was kick started by the arrival of the *Empire Star*, in Melbourne, on 19 August 1947, whose passengers included 17 'Little Brothers'. However, the arrival created less publicity than that of the *Asturias* in Fremantle, on 22 September 1947, with 1,698 migrants, including 150 'war orphans',[21] bound mainly for Catholic orphanages in Western Australia. The children were aged between four-and-a-half and 14. Recipient bodies at that time were the Christian Brothers, Sisters of Nazareth, and the Swan (Church of England) Homes.[22] Catholic children – but not Protestants – were finger printed.

Two months later, on 17 November 1947, the *Ormonde* arrived in Sydney with children to be raised in orphanages and institutions in New South Wales. The 93 young people who disembarked included 38 children (20 boys and 18 girls) to be raised by Barnardos and 27 children (15 boys and 12 girls), bound for the Fairbridge Farm School, Molong, near Orange. There were also 20 older youths sponsored by the Big Brother Movement.

February 1948 saw the arrival of the first organised group of post-war Jewish youth migrants. They had survived the Holocaust and were welcomed as heroes by the Jewish community[23].

Perhaps sadly, the Dreadnought Scheme – formerly second only to the Big Brother Movement as provider of youths for immigration – decided not to re-enter the fray. The Salvation Army decided to confine its activities to unaccompanied adults or young people travelling with or coming to join relatives.

Among the sponsoring organisations that remained, changing community attitudes and shifts in the economy brought about an end to the insistence on rural occupations. Girls were allowed to take up occupations other than domestic service. Pro-British sentiment remained strong. Patriotic migration movements flourished, including the 'Bring Out A Briton' campaign[24].

By 1952 most of the 'caring' organisations were also looking after Australian children. Barnardos was the odd one out – concerning itself exclusively, until the 1960s, with the migration and welfare of youngsters from the United Kingdom. Likewise, the role of the Big Brother

Movement, which dealt exclusively with British migrants, was regarded in some quarters as anachronistic.

In the 1960s, ironically as child and youth migration was drawing to a close, the various sending and receiving organisations decided that future parties of young migrants should come by air. The last Barnardos party to travel by sea sailed from Britain on the *Oriana*, arriving in Sydney on 6 June 1964. According to the annual report the group comprised 12 children, an obviously disappointing figure[25]. The year before (1963–64) there had been 40. Only the Big Brother Movement, among the major players, continued to use sea transport, which it did (also using air travel) until 1966.

In December 1965, it was announced that the Fairbridge Farm School at Molong would cease taking British youngsters from the end of 1966[26]. The announcement coincided with rumours that the British and Australian Governments were losing interest in child and youth migration. Other organisations found themselves in similar difficulties. Air travel did not prove the success anticipated. In 1966–67, according to the annual report of Barnardos: 'Our migrant intake has been the lowest for many years with only three individual children arriving from Britain. Prospects for the future, are, however, a little brighter[27].'

Child migration – though not, strictly speaking, youth migration – formally ended in 1967. By this time most of the organisations bringing out youth migrants had also faded away. Only the Big Brother Movement carried on largely as before. Youths brought out under its auspices were now older than previously. Most had completed apprenticeships. Some were as old as 20.

The organisation continued its work until mid 1983, when the Hawke Labor Government forced it into virtual redundancy[28]. The intervention caused a stink at the time, but, contrary to expectations, the Big Brother Movement did not fade away. It continues to operate, nowadays in a different – but not inappropriate – role.

## GETTING THE NUMBERS RIGHT

Throughout the history of the schemes newspapers and broadcasting media often lumped the youth migrants with the 'child migrants', making it hard to provide accurate information concerning numbers. The inclusive term 'juvenile migrant' was sometimes used.

To add to the confusion the Government itself treated the youth migrants sometimes as children[29], and at other times as young adults. In fact, many of these 'adults' were as young as 14, the school leaving age in Britain at that time. A survey by Australia House, in London, unintentionally included some 80,000 British youngsters who had migrated to Australia with their parents. These youngsters were not the 'unaccompanied minors' for whom the policy was intended, but were simply young people adding to Australia's population[30].

Some groups – eg. Fairbridge, Barnardos, and to a lesser extent the Christian Brothers – had a foot in both child and youth migration. They took in *child* migrants, assuming responsibility for their care and education, but kept them after the minimum school leaving age in farm or trade schools, thus assisting them to find future employment[31].

As with the child migrants, the former youth migrants now have unlimited access to their personal records and many are now seeking this information, if only to meet passport and citizenship requirements. Ben Mohide, a former 'Little Brother', recalls, as a boy, submitting his birth certificate, school reports and reference to the Big Brother Movement. Recently – more than 50 years later – he received them back, held together by the original pin, which was now rusty.

In today's Australia few people – even those whose parents or grandparents were among the 'new chums'[32] – are more than dimly aware of the manner in which so many young people came to these shores, and how they fared when they got here.

It's an important story, which has been sadly neglected. The clock is ticking away. The youngest Dreadnought Boy, for instance, is now in his 80s. As a reader[33] wrote to me in another context: 'This is probably the last opportunity not having to rely on hearsay or historical notes only.'

This chapter contains material researched by Dr Brother Barry Coldrey, author of *Good British Stock, the Australian Archives Guide to Youth and Child Migration*; and Professor Michael Roe, author of *Australia, Britain and Migration, 1915-1940*.

---

# 2

# White, British and 'Racially Pure'

———

*'If there is one gift of Providence for which, beyond all others, Australians should be proud yet humbly thankful, it is the preservation by our country of its racial purity.'*

From *The New Australian*, magazine of the Victorian Big Brother Movement. May 1928.

YOUTH MIGRATION, as with adult migration, was based on the premise of a 'white' Australia. Also – a situation so axiomatic that it hardly needs stating – a British one. The topic was promoted in a *Boys' Own Paper* style, with English lads as young 'empire builders', participating in an exciting (and affordable) adventure.

This attitude was particularly prevalent in the years between the two world wars, a period that included the founding of the Big Brother Movement, the largest migrant body of its type.

An article in the July 1928 issue of *The New Australian*, magazine of the BBM's Victorian branch, referred, without embarrassment, to 'young adventurers' setting sail for 'this newer England'. An article in the English newspaper *The Times*, reprinted in the same journal, lauded the work and goals of the Big Brother Movement, but wondered if England really 'can afford to lose all her best lads'.

The newspaper left the question unanswered, but offered the comforting thought: 'Happily there are still many of the best [lads] who have in their hearts that spirit of voluntary adventure that has built up the British Empire... These are the boys to whom the call is made and the great opportunity given of prospering in the great farmlands of Australia.'

A publicity bulletin, produced in Melbourne in 1928, used similar language. 'The strength and foundation of the [youth migration] movement is character. Already the results have shown that the qualities of grit

Making fun of the "New chum". From Smith's Weekly Magazine. (May 1926).

*Making fun of the young British migrant. Bulletin cartoon (1924).*

and tenacity which have made the British race such great colonisers are still dominant in the youngest descendants.'

Government agencies also pumped the empire cause. The same magazine's March 1929 issue contained an advertisement – presumably paid for by the South Australian Government – which stated: 'Selected Little Brothers are warmly welcomed in Sunny South Australia, where the population is 98 per cent British'.

The ad listed employment opportunities in the state, ending with the sales pitch: 'Parents of Little Brothers ask for and insist on getting products grown by your sons and kinsfolk under the British flag.'

Other media took a similar line. Cinema newsreels, aided by breathless narration, presented a clean-cut, outdoor image, of healthy, fit and contented English lads. The German film maker, Leni Riefenstahl[1], could not have done better. Youth migrants were also romanticised in verse, most notably in the poems of a West Australian literary figure, Lillian Wooster Greaves (1869-1956). Intensely patriotic, she believed passionately in immigration as a cure for Australia's ills and idealised 'British boyhood' in a manner bordering on obsessive[2].

> *'Australia, land of promise,*
> *A prize the wide world knows,*
> *Is envied by her neighbours,*
> *Is coveted by foes;*
> *But she's waiting, waiting, waiting,*
> *With her rich rewards and joys;*
> *She is waiting to bestow them*
> *On the heads of British boys.'*

From *British Boys*, Lillian Wooster Greaves

The Victorian Big Brother Movement went further than other youth migrant organisations, warning darkly of threats to 'racial purity'. *The New Australian's* May 1928, issue carried a long (2,000 words) article by a supporter[3] who had recently visited North America. The article highlighted racial problems in that country – 'Cities overrun with Negroes' – against a warning of what might happen here.

According to the opening paragraph: 'If there is one gift of

Providence for which, beyond all others, Australians should be proudly yet humbly thankful, it is the preservation by our country of its racial purity.' The article went on to state:

'One of the greatest inducements which this country can offer the new settler from England is that it is racially the purest country in the world, with the possible exception of New Zealand. Australia is actually more British than England itself. Here is no helot race threatening white standards of civilisation. Here is no alien people to threaten the purity of our blood. Please Heaven there never will be!'

After reading the above one is tempted to shout: 'Sieg Heil!' Material of this type does not appear to have featured in the literature of the organisation's NSW branch, whose more thoughtful style reflected its professed 'non-political, non-commercial and non-sectarian' credo. However, it, too, promoted a concept of the 'old country' helping the new, and saw empire settlement as a quasi-spiritual endeavour. This would have been the normal view of community leaders at the time, and commanded widespread popular support[4].

As with child migration, proponents of (British) youth migration saw it as a means of keeping undesirable intruders out. Victor Courtney, a prominent advocate for youth migration in Western Australia, wrote of his friend J.J. Simons[5], founder of the Young Australia League:

'With his usual far-sighted vision, he could see the day when land-hungry people of other countries would cast covetous eyes on the natural wealth of this huge continent. He realised that our only hope for continued possession of our heritage lay in our sustained efforts to populate it to its maximum and work it to its capacity.'

The advent of a Nazi state in Germany, in 1933, led to pressure from Jewish organisations for a compassionate approach towards Jewish (youth and adult) migration. The demands increased as the nature of Hitlerism became evident. The generosity of the government's response was – and still is – hotly disputed. Jews were 'white' but perceived generally as an alien group, hardly in the 'kith and kin' category.

World War II strengthened existing prejudices. Henry Gullett, MP for Henty (Vic)[6], probably spoke for many at that time when he said in Federal Parliament (27 November 1946): 'Whilst I am not a prophet, I believe it to be quite certain that within the next 10 years very heavy pressure will be put on us to accept unlimited numbers of coloured migrants... Australia is white today, and we support that policy.. simply because we have to support it.'

He continued: 'The preservation of every standard that has been built up in this country is conditioned by the maintenance of a white Australia. Let us have a little less humbug and pious expressions about what white Australia means. It means no more nor less than our existence, and that is the way we must regard it.'

A week earlier, in a now famous policy speech[7], Arthur Calwell, had outlined the country's post-war immigration policies. He stated inter-alia: 'No country needs immigrants of the right type more urgently than does Australia. And no country has taken more energetic steps to secure them...

'We Australians are a young and virile people and our national heart beats strongly. But the body, of which that heart is the motivating force, is a huge land mass, an island continent of some three million square miles with 12,000 miles of coastline. Before a body of such vast dimensions can be operated at full efficiency, its heart must beat strongly and be fed by the extra life-blood which only new citizens can supply.'

Drawing direct on the perceived 'yellow peril' threat, widely held at that time, he continued: 'There was a time just four years ago when Australia faced its gravest peril. Armies recruited from the teeming millions of Japan threatened to overrun our cities and broad hinterland. They were so many. We were so few.

'Today we are at peace. But, while all of us must work to perpetuate that peace, let us not forget that armed conflict remains a grim possibility, both in the New World and in the Old – a possibility against which we must guard with all the intelligence, all the realism, and all the energy that we can muster.'

There is a tendency to depict Calwell as a clumsy racist and bigot, remembered for his famed 'Two Wongs don't make a white' remark and similar quips. Many insist this is an injustice. While he stuck to the white Australia policy, as did most Australians at that time, he did not insist that they be British, and is criticised in some quarters for opening the floodgates to Balts, Slavs, 'Ities' and 'reffos' from all corners of Europe.

In the 1950s a rare breach occurred in the 'British only' attitude towards youth migration. Following pressure from Catholic sources a small number of unaccompanied Croatian youths were allowed to settle in South Australia. The sales pitch was their role in the fight against communism.

In the 1960s and 70s – almost as a last gasp – suggestions were floated to expand the migrant intake to include young people from the Republic of Ireland, other British Commonwealth countries and continental Europe. It makes interesting reading, but never truly materialised.

## CHEAP LABOUR?

*'I had a few lines from my boy; he doesn't seem to be satisfied with his wages…
if he had taken my advice he would still have been at home.'*
Letter of complaint to the Queensland Department of Immigration (1925).

It is generally assumed that 'youth' migrants had a softer time than the *Leaving of Liverpool* kids. But did they? Imagine the situation of the average pre-World War II youth migrant, who perhaps turned 15 on the voyage out. Within a few weeks or even days of his arrival, he was likely to be whisked off to a remote rural backwater – deprived of the company of his friends – to work for an unspecified period on a farm property.

Some employers were benevolent, treating the newcomers as members of their own family. A few of the 'lads' ultimately inherited the properties on which they toiled. Other employers displayed social attitudes unchanged since the time of Dickens. On 29 November 1921, Sydney's *Sunday Telegraph* ran a slightly defensive article, headed 'Barnardo Boys Not Slave Labour'. The examples given seemed to suggest otherwise.

In those early years living and working conditions for 'farm lads' were, by modern standards, extremely primitive. The following account by James Hill (Barnardos, 1924)[8] says it all:

'On my 17th birthday I was sent to a 27,000 acre Hunter Valley property. The owners were from the old British style of aristocracy. I lived in an old unlined tin hut, with two round saplings cut from the bush, nailed to the wall and covered with chaff bags, with a chaff bag stuffed with straw for a mattress. I had my meals, mostly bread and mutton, in the laundry among the dirty washing. I had to wash in the creek and there was no furniture in my quarters.'

The Barwell Boys in South Australia fared little better. Philip Norton[9], aged 16, was assigned to the property of a certain Mr J.F.W. Schultz of Morgan, Waikerie. For a start the boy would have had difficulty finding the place. A note from the farmer to the Immigration Department stated: 'Send the lad along to Robertson Bros (Morgan, Waikerie and Loxton mail service). This is all the lad got to look for at Morgan...'

About a year after starting work on the property a disagreement arose with his employer. Philip went to see a neighbouring farmer, Mr W.A. Blight, who also employed a Barwell Boy. Blight, who considered the lad poorly treated, wrote to the Director of Immigration, Victor Ryan, in the following terms:[10]

'He [Philip] has never complained to anyone. All the conversation in [the] Schultz [household] is in German...He slept in part of the chaff shed. He would have his tea with the family then retire to bed [with] no one to speak to. So I sent my lad up to tell him to come up here any time he wished but he never came...I find out now the reason. They would never allow him to have a horse. Another thing he has never learned the lad anything. He has been cutting bushes and stick picking ever since he [arrived]. He can't drive a horse or use an impliment [sic] of any kind.'

The Immigration Department reacted by moving Philip Norton into the employment of James Matthews, a disabled fruit grower, also in Waikerie. The orchard produced stone fruit and grapes, for drying as muscatels, sultanas and currants. Philip wrote a thank you letter to the immigration department: 'I am quite satisfied here as I have got with nice people and have got the life which I have always wished for'. In a further letter he stated: 'It is a treat to get with someone that speaks English.'

Further correspondence in South Australian Government files indicate that the lad changed his mind, pointing to long hours of work for which he was not paid overtime. In December 1925 he wrote an article about his experiences in his old school magazine.

'I get up before sunrise and get the horse out of the paddock and feed him. Then I put the horse in the sledge and carry two tubs of water up to the end of the block where the "dip" is. I next have to fill the boiler, light the fire underneath and get it boiling by 7. After that I chop enough wood to last for the day (all the fires here are kept going by wood, and it takes a good time to chop enough). I then go to breakfast. At half-past seven the two pickers start work...I help to load [the dip] and then go on picking.. I can pick up on my own 100 buckets a day, which is about a ton of fresh fruit, and when dried about 4 cwt...The pickers knock off work at 5.10, but after they have gone I have to cut food (lucerne) for three horses for next day, stack the peaches, box two or three cwt of currants, get in a quantity of wood for morning, and do divers odd jobs. By this time it is dark, and when I have had tea and a bath it is bedtime.'

Regardless of which organisation had sponsored them, grievances over workplace wages and conditions were common. A Barnardo boy of a later generation told me that unhappiness at their conditions, rather than the generally ascribed motives of patriotism, explained the high volunteer recruitment rate among former youth migrants at the beginning of World War II.

Despite comments such as the above, the young migrants were, at the time, generally uncomplaining, regarding tough conditions almost as 'adventure'. Parents were less understanding. Many wrote angry letters to the sponsoring organisations. The Australian National Archives have interesting examples of such missives.

An anguished father, J. Mole[11], complained to the Queensland Government: 'You ought to look after him better. I am an old man myself, but will save every penny I can to get him home again...They told my boy such things about Australia.' Another parent complained: 'It breaks my heart to think of him being so far away and not happy.'[12]

There was also criticism from farmers. A file in the Australian Archives has a letter from a Burnie farmer, C.B. Elliott, seemingly indignant at the youth and inexperience of 'farm lads' recruited for Tasmania.

According to the letter: 'Many boys are not up to standard; not long out of school [and] should be at home with their parents. Older boys, 17-18 year-olds are wanted.[13] The [boys] know nothing of farm life.'

It seems the criticism was taken seriously. The Chief Medical

Officer, Hobart, wrote to the Prime Minister's Department, on 1 November 1923: 'Owing to complaints received from employers of the boys, it has been decided to discontinue the shipment of further parties.'

These and similar letters were written before the economic depression, which, of course, only made a bad situation worse. Case histories during this unhappy era[14] are described in some of the following chapters. Boy farm workers who had come to Australia for 'self-betterment' now found themselves' working without pay, merely to have food and a roof over their heads. And they were the lucky ones!

As previously noted, Government funding to assist youth migration ceased in 1932, because of the Depression, bringing most such activity to halt. The decision was not welcomed by proponents of migration. Canon David Garland, director of the Church of England Immigration Council in Queensland, wrote to the Prime Minister, stating: 'The temporary difficulties in which Australia finds herself should not be allowed to obliterate the still greater problem of keeping Australia white, by filling it with our own kith and kin.'

He added that in the previous two decades Queensland had received many thousand farm apprentices, and the scheme had been 'an unqualified success'. The Government was unsympathetic. The letter was minuted: 'Unnecessary to pursue the matter further.'

Bill Wilson, later to become president of the Dreadnought Old Boys' Association, feels the sponsoring organisations could have done more to help their young charges at this time. He says the Dreadnought trustees were 'miserly', and 'sat on' the trust's assets in the Depression years, when funds might have been spent on assisting those already in Australia.

He says that when the trustees did assist other welfare bodies, which was permitted under the charter, this was done 'under pressure from these organisations – they never initiated anything themselves'. A result of this saving was 'a great deal of loss through inflation, the full effects of which only became apparent at the end of the war'[15].

However, even outside the Depression years the grievance that farmers (and possibly Government agencies) considered the teenage farm workers 'cheap labour' was widespread, and cannot be easily dismissed. It was common, for instance, for youths to be dismissed from their jobs on reaching adult age, because industrial awards prescribed higher wages thereafter.

A report commissioned by the South Australian Government said a group of boys 'felt much anger' when, after serving their terms, they applied for a £300 loan – which was apparently granted by statute – to enable them to become independent farmers; only to learn that financial stringency delayed honouring of that promise.

A Tasmanian bureaucrat admitted – after a scheme in his own State was terminated – that there were various abuses and shortcomings. He wrote in an officially sanctioned report:

'The scheme for nominated boy farm labour was very far from satisfactory. In a large percentage of cases it was only used as a means to get cheap labour. The treatment that the boys received was regrettable. Many of them were required to work from daylight to dark seven days a week. The cash payment that was due in some cases was withheld. The boys – discouraged by their hopeless position – left the person who had nominated them at the first opportunity, going to other employers, getting work on the roads, or coming to the cities for work in the factories.'[16]

The complaints were not all one way. It appears some migrant youths were 'bookish' and by nature unsuitable for farm work. A Queensland farmer said of an English lad in his care: 'As soon as my back was turned he would sneak back to the house and read...I took the whole of my books – a considerable number – and burnt them, thinking to give the lad his chance, by removing temptation.'[17]

A Government bureaucrat involved in NSW immigration alleged that many youths were 'cheeky and lazy', insisting that the Government 'look after them' till they turned 21. Others 'broke all restraints', yet were not prosecuted, lest that 'provide ammunition for opponents of migration'.

Certainly, many of the young migrants were unhappy. Bed-wetting was common, just as it was among child migrants. Some youth migrants were surprised to find – contrary to the image conveyed by Australia House – that they were not universally popular. A British Member of Parliament who visited Australia in 1922 noticed 'dislike and hostility towards the new settler – almost a wish that he should not succeed'.

A Sydney urchin, whose sport was to stand at the docks where he could abuse 'new chums' disembarking, called out to a just-arrived new-comer: 'Fuckin' well go back there ya pommie bastard.'[18]

It seems Britons were – and are – unduly sensitive to insults. 'Many Australians do not feel bad language used towards them as Englishmen do,' remarked a Minister in charge of the South Australian migration scheme.

A disillusioned Scot in Melbourne wrote to the Overseas Settlement Office in London: 'Why in God's name do we from the motherland find such a well of prejudice against us? Chinamen are Chinamen here, Greeks are Greeks, Italians are Italians, but we from the Old Motherland are con-sidered "dirty pommies" and by no less than those who were recently "pommies" themselves.'

The ambivalent attitude of the media did not help. The popular press, whilst strongly supporting youth migration, tended to make fun of the 'farm lads' and depicted them as stupid.

A cartoon in *Smith's Weekly* (May 1926) shows a farm boss exclaim-ing to no one in particular: 'Where th' 'ell's th' milkin' machine?' To which the 'choom' inside the shed calls out: ''Ere I be, Sir!'

# 3

# When the Ocean Liner was King

---

*'All the while it was calm*
*I felt quite gay and frisky;*
*But Oh! How pale and ill I looked*
*When on the Bay of Biscay.'*

Norman Monsen, passenger on the *Benalla*.

SHIPS AND SHIPPING have a close, almost romantic association with 20th century migration to Australia. It was a time when the ocean liner was king. The long sea voyage provided novelty, adventure, a holiday (for some travellers maybe their first and only such experience), even, depending on the vessel and level of service, a touch of luxury.

Of course, not all travellers found their journey fun-filled. Young European refugees on rust buckets such as the *Derna*[1], and C-category enemy aliens on board the *Dunera*[2], hardly saw themselves as beneficiaries of a holiday cruise.

However, even for those whose recollections of the voyage are tinged with sadness, the very nature of the experience made it memorable as a kind of hiatus, or forced interlude, between the past and future directions of their lives.

Probably the greatest send-off was given to those travelling under the auspices of the Salvation Army. Brass bands escorted the departing passengers to the quayside. There were rousing speeches, prayers, and a 'quiet time' for the voyagers to bid goodbye to loved ones prior to departure.

From the early days all would-be migrants underwent a medical check. A file in the Australian Archives, setting out conditions for recruitment of Barwell Boys, said 'teeth and urinary organs' were to receive close attention; boys wearing glasses were not acceptable. Insurance cover (against accidents, sickness and after-care) were to be features of the South Australian scheme.

---

27

Youth migrants, unlike child migrants, were not press-ganged and at least knew where they were going[3]. Most found the voyage at least pleasurable, a few irksome, depending on such factors as the emphasis on studies, the location of their quarters, pocket money (or the lack of it), and the degree of freedom they received.

Ben Mohide, who travelled out as a post-war Little Brother on the *Asturias*, says he found the voyage eventful and uneventful at the same time.

'Uneventful as far as sensation is concerned, but to me, a 16-year-old lad who had never been anywhere, it was absolutely eventful in the sense that every day was colossal. There was the experience of being on a ship for the first time, seeing menus[4], having people waiting on you, even making the bed for you every day.

'Then, of course, there were lots of girls on board. Young nubile girls, and we made the most of that. There were also the ports of call. Places like Malta, Port Said. Oh, it was wonderful.'

Bill Wilson migrated to Australia in July 1928, at 17, under the Dreadnought Scheme. He still vividly recalls the journey in the P. & O. liner, *Baradine*. 'We slept in cabins of eight, which were grouped around an open area called a hatch. The cabins looked like temporary structures which could be dismantled when the hatch was used to store cargo.'

His cabin mates were from Liverpool, London, Scotland and Northern Ireland. 'By a miracle we could understand each other's dialects.' Because of the strong Scottish presence 'a lot of the impromptu dances which took place around the deck piano were eightsome reels. They were sometimes rowdy.'

He recalls the weather was very rough in the Bay of Biscay and many passengers didn't turn up for meals. 'We called at Las Palmas in the Canary Isles. Longboats laden with fresh fruits and fabrics were rowed out. There was a lot of huckstering and goods were sold to passengers and crew.'

Norman Monsen, a youth migrant on the *Benalla*, was similarly impressed. 'Here was a phenomenon new to us with rowing boats coming out to our anchorage brimming over with all sorts of goods – tropical fruit, items of clothing, souvenirs.' Vendors approaching the ship in small boats put fear into the hearts of some travellers, who thought they were about to be attacked by natives.

---

Not all spent their money. Bill Wilson recalls: 'I bought nothing. My stepfather had given me a pound for pocket money on the journey, but I figured I would need that in Australia.'

The last port of call before reaching Australia was Cape Town. According to Bill: 'We spent two or three days there. Thomas Sedgwick[5], who accompanied us, had a sister who lived on a farm in Cape Province, and he very kindly paid for a coach tour around the vineyards in the region and we had lunch at his sister's farm.'

Here Bill managed to spend most of his precious one pound. 'We called at Fremantle, Adelaide and Melbourne on the way round the Australian coast. At Port Adelaide I had a haircut for which the price was one shilling and sixpence, whereas I had only sixpence in my pocket. This was the cost of a haircut in Wallasey. The hairdresser accepted my sixpence with good grace but I was embarrassed.'

Two former youth migrants told me of their pain at witnessing a sea burial – the deceased being placed on a wooden platform and tipped into the ocean. Others remember the thrill of seeing flying fish and an albatross 'showing off' its enormous wingspan.

Len Rushton, a Little Brother who came out on the *Orion* in 1951, found himself – and the ship – in a war zone in the Suez Canal. It was 1951 and an uprising had occurred in Egypt against King Farouk. 'There were lots of gunboats and men in uniform came on board, some of them firing. It's a good story; I shall never forget it.'

Despite the inconvenience – the journey took two weeks longer than usual – Len reckons 'We had a marvellous time.' As a bonus the two thousandth Little Brother was on board. A party and ceremony were arranged in his honour.

Sea air and 'dashing around the ship' created voracious appetites. The lucky ones encountered friendly stewards who would sneak them in to a second or even third sitting at lunch and dinner[6]. A post-war adult passenger on an Italian vessel, travelling first class, recalls smuggling cakes and other goodies to young migrants, after telling them to station themselves by a doorway. She imposed one condition – that the same faces and hands did not reappear at the following day's handout.

The boys' appetites prompted Thomas Sedgwick to write a memo to the Dreadnought trustees. In it he detailed what others had hinted – that, having their first experience of leisure and supplied meals, many young migrants 'ate to suffocation', and in the absence of exercise and work[7] 'became constipated and liverish'.

In another memo Sedgwick observed that many of his boys had out-grown their clothes. This view was confirmed by an adult on the same voyage, who wrote to a friend: 'I have increased a lot and my wife is as fat as a bullock.'[8] Of course, seasickness could effectively kill the best of appetites. Norman Monsen was one of several victims. He wrote a little poem about his experiences (See beginning of this chapter).

The claim of 'lack of exercise' seems to have applied mainly to pre-war migrants. Ben Mohide says of his August 1949 journey on the *Asturias*: 'There was a Grenadier Guards sergeant on board, who offered to give the lads some "fitness". 'He organised PT for us every morning. We were all volunteers, and it was great.

'Most of the boys on our trip were city kids. Some had never been close to a cow, sheep or horse. We knew we'd be going into physical labour on the farms, so it was right to start getting into shape. We also used to run around the ship. I think eight circuits made a mile.'

Len Rushton's group also had daily gymnastics – not from a Grenadier Guardsman but from a female schoolteacher, in her twenties, who was paying her way home. Again there was no shortage of volunteers, though perhaps for a different reason. 'She was very friendly with a lot of us. She was very strong, and gave us quite a time.'

Accommodation was generally cramped, which situation fuelled per-sonality clashes and other disagreements. Brian Bywater travelled out as a Little Brother in 1956. He recalls: 'Our ship, the *Otranto*, had previously served as a troop carrier. There were eight youths to a cabin, which was too much. Of course, there were fights and brawls and all the rest that goes on where a lot of fellows are put together.'

Nearly 30 years earlier, Bill Wilson had witnessed similar fights on board the *Baradine*. 'In our time they were strictly Marquis of Queensbury – except for bare fists. They were held in our hatchway before a crowd of cheering boys supporting one or other of the contestants.

'I nearly got involved in a fight myself. There was a sudden flare up between me and a boy called Geordie. A challenge was issued and a time set. Fortunately for me, Geordie slipped on a stairway and twisted his ankle before the appointed time. He was bigger than me and I had short arms, which was a handicap in boxing, so I probably would have got the worst of it.'

The big passenger ships, as already noted, observed the usual class distinctions of their day. Maxine Goodman, a young post-war migrant[9] on the *Asturias*, recalls her frustration at being unable to use the swimming pool, which was in the first class section, and cordoned off from the hoi polloi. When the ship was near the equator buckets with holes punched in their sides were strung up and filled with water to provide substitute 'fun' for sweltering passengers.

A company rule was that officers could only fraternise with first class passengers. Maxine recalls several officers secretly partying with her parents and their friends – a condition being that the captain not be told. The captain was, in fact, a 'decent bloke' who probably would not have minded. Child migrants on an earlier journey recall that he offered two guineas – then a sizeable sum – to the first in their group who saw the Australian coast.

Sometimes first class passengers swelled the prize-funds for the migrants' social activities. On the *Beltana* in late 1923, according to Michael Roe,[10] a passengers' sub-committees attended to the needs of both adults and juveniles. This included concerts, dances, deck games, even education for those of school age. Games included Darby and Joan, Apple Bobbing, Collar and Tie, Candle Lighting, O'Grady Drill, Snake Face. It is not clear what these actually involved. At night, according to a passenger, bright young things could 'dance in worship of jazz music, their god'.

Sea voyages traditionally lead to romance. A Dreadnought Boy, then aged 17, was smitten by the daughter of a fare-paying passenger, who was nearly three years his senior. The age difference and other factors (including distance) created problems which to others might have been insurmountable. But true love will find a way. They were married after a courtship by post which lasted 10 years[11].

In the late 1940s many of the ships bringing child and youth migrants also carried a number of war brides (strictly speaking war fiancées). A young woman on board the Asturias caused consternation by declaring, half way through the voyage, that she no longer wished to link up with her Australian 'intended', having fallen in love with a European migrant on his way to work in the Tasmanian hydro-electric scheme.

On the same voyage were 270 Polish migrants, members of Poland's 'free' army in exile who had fought with Australians in North Africa. A cinema newsreel of their arrival suggested they were 'bachelors all' in search of wives. Disembarking child migrants were far more concerned with the fate of the Poles' military mascot, a rhesus monkey, which they had kept since leaving Tobruk. The animal was smuggled off the ship, while quarantine officers were distracted, but was captured on the quay-side, and, to the horror of onlookers, seized as a 'prohibited immigrant' and destroyed.

As stated previously, the long sea voyage was for many youngsters the source of much excitement. Others quickly felt the pangs of separa-tion. Bill Steele, a Dreadnought Boy, who came out in 1928, spent much of the next decade trying to work his passage on a ship 'home'. He told the writer: 'I was unable to accomplish this. Then the war came and I enlisted, hoping I might be put me on a ship for Plymouth by mistake. That didn't happen either, so I studied for the Christian ministry and became chaplain on a migrant ship.'

Probably the least comfortable ships were those which travelled from continental European ports, with the cargoes of (mainly Jewish) refugees.

Rita Newell is one of a number of young people who migrated twice – from Germany to Britain on a *Kindertransport*,[12] then (when peace returned) on to Australia. Unlike others on her 1947 voyage, she is tol-erant about standards on the *Johan De Witt*. 'I think the older generation probably found it a bit of a hardship. The young ones, we seem to have had a good time.

'Of course, it isn't the sort of cruise you would want to take these days. It had been used as a troopship. The men and women were separat-ed. There was no privacy for ablutions. There were wash basins; but I don't remember about showers. The toilets didn't have doors. You had to use the loo in front of all the other women.'

She remembers one incident with wry amusement. 'It was a hot night and some of the girls decided to sleep on deckchairs up on deck. I woke up quite early – it was just getting light – to find one of the Malay crew kissing me. When I complained they had a line up and I had to identify him. They all looked the same.'

Another teenager recalled her gratitude when a sailor offered to rig up a temporary shower with canvas sheeting to provide privacy. While dousing herself she looked up to see a dozen sailors gazing at her from above.

## ESCORTS AND WELFARE OFFICERS

From 1923, supposedly at the behest of the YMCA, most ships carrying assisted migrants had a welfare officer, with a responsibility towards both adult and juvenile passengers. Organisations sponsoring youth and child migrants also brought their own 'escorts', whose roles overlapped.

Welfare officers had control of order and discipline, while escorts – many of them women – seem to have had a more 'caring' role, and were more popular with their young charges. Both groups seem to have been recruited on an ad hoc basis. Often the task of escort was given to homeward bound Australians – one was the diver, documentary film maker and photographer, Ben Cropp – who were glad to have their fares paid in exchange for not very arduous duties.

Schoolteachers and ministers of religion were among those most commonly selected for this task. Wilf Bennett,[13] a Dreadnought Boy, recalled 'the wonderful old Christian minister who was in charge of the boys on our ship. When he found out some of us hadn't been baptised, he asked us whether we would like to go through the ceremony, which we did.'

As stated above, both child and youth migrants were under the care of escorts. General Eva Burrows, who retired in 1993 as international leader of the Salvation Army, was an escort to child migrants on the *Otranto* in 1952. 'I had been in England for two years. The Army said I could come home but they wouldn't be paying my fare. So the Commissioner for Migration said he could get me a free trip to Australia if I would look after some youngsters.

'Another young woman and I looked after 12 children for the Fairbridge Society. There were 10 boys and two girls, aged from about five to 14. The two older boys were very difficult, but the others were beautiful kids and we had tremendous fun.

'The other escort, I can't remember her name, was an Australian teacher. There were lots of British migrants on board – people coming for £10, with their families. Each day we'd have a singsong and play games. It proved very popular. We ended up with not just our own kids, but every kid on the ship, and not a few grown-ups.'

The Rev Alan Sir Walker, later to become Superintendent of Sydney's Central Methodist Mission,[14] and his wife, Winifred, also looked after a group of Fairbridge youngsters. The couple travelled on the P&O liner *Orama*, in January 1939. According to Win: 'We were glad to be able to give them lessons, which was one way of keeping them occupied. Of course, it was not real classroom stuff. We talked to them about Australia, and what they should expect.

'I remember there was a boy called John Ritchie. He was older than the others, about 15.[15] He had run away from home in Scotland and presented himself one day at the door of the Fairbridge people in London, saying that he wanted to go to Australia. They said, "You're too old, we only take children up to 13". He badgered them, and eventually it was arranged that he should join our group.

'We liked him and found him a great help. He helped us bath the little ones and was a friend to all. When we arrived back in Australia Alan was posted to Cessnock. Goodness knows how long had elapsed, but one day there was a ring at our front door and there was John. He had run away from Fairbridge, joined the Army by falsifying his age, and run away from that too.

'Alan got in touch with the Army, told them he was under age, and they let him off. We got him a job on a farm near Cessnock. He wasn't there very long before he ran away again. The last thing we heard he had joined the Merchant Navy, and jumped ship in Western Australia. We never discovered what happened to him after that.'

In the 1970s, Roger Climpson compered a *This Is Your Life* program on Alan Walker. Guests included four of their former Fairbridge charges – regrettably not the one who had run away – now grown up with families.

Teenagers coming to Australia with groups such as the Big Brother Movement often had escorts who were little older than themselves, and whose approach seemed cavalier.

Bill Hudnott, who came out with the Big Brother Movement in 1960, recalls: 'Until my visit to Australia House [to be processed as a migrant] I had never met an Aussie. So what was my first impression when we met our escort officer for the five-week voyage on the *Fairsky*? He turned out to be Paul Hogan's Paul Hogan.

'When we sailed out of Southampton the first thing he said to the 17 of us was "Boys will be boys – Do what you like, as I am only here with you 'cause I run out of money in England and the only way I can get myself home to Australia is to take you lot there back with me".

'We had an absolute ball on the ship but got into a bit of trouble with the Argentinian captain and the Paraguayan crew. Every time we got into trouble they would front him and he would say "yep" to everything and off we would go again.'

Welfare officers – as distinct from escorts – were often quite severe. One young migrant was punished for misbehaviour by being made an unpaid cabin boy. Other staff 'adopted' him as their mascot – so the 'punishment' was quite pleasurable, with extra rations and interesting company.

On board some vessels youth migrants took paid jobs in defiance of regulations. On the *Sophocles* in October 1925, a party of Dreadnought Boys were officially signed on as stokers and deckhands when the crew went on strike.

On landing in Melbourne in November 1926, the welfare officer on board the *Baradine* complained of general disorder among the teenage migrants. He labelled a group of Dreadnought Boys 'degenerates' and 'verminous reptiles'.

His report, generally dismissed as exaggerated, said older passengers exercised a bad influence on the lads, encouraging them 'to break every regulation in the ship, and to flout the authority' of the officers and himself.

He said gamblers and crooks of both sexes met in the bar and the smoking room, and the Dreadnought Boys went there too. Men and women 'drinking, gambling and smoking cigarettes' were 'an attraction for the lads, who apparently had money to squander'.

According to this officer the English boys joined with left-leaning crew members in singing *The Red Flag* and gave welfare officers 'a warm time'. 'I warned the offenders that their conduct would be regarded in

Australia as that of degenerates and undesirables but they heeded not, and gloried in their shame.'

He said the girls on board (it is not clear what sending organisation was responsible for them) were no better behaved than the boys.' From my experience of those in the foreward section, where I ate and slept, I cannot report otherwise than that a number were utterly lacking in morals, devoid of decency and displayed moral depravity.'

Reports such as the above may almost certainly be discounted. Female youth migrants, according to most accounts, were much smaller in number, and generally well behaved. While some teenage girls probably disliked the outward voyage, or found it boring, others clearly had the time of their life. 'Could you please tell me when the *SS Benalla* is due at Outer Harbour,' wrote a ladies' maid to a South Australian departmental officer in 1926. 'I would like to go down and see it again.'

A BASHING

Not all escorts have rose-tinted memories. In June 1961, David Paris was hired by the Big Brother Movement to escort 38 Little Brothers on board the *Orsova*. David, 23, had sailed to Australia before, as a Little Brother on board the *Otranto*, in April 1955.

In 1959 he had returned to Britain, to meet his parents and to travel in Europe. When the extended holiday was over, and being short of funds, he welcomed the chance to be an escort for the organisation that had once sponsored him.

David, who had already seen commissioned service in the Royal Australian Navy[16], seemed the ideal type for such a role. At first all went well. 'I got on fantastically with the lads. I started by setting guidelines on how they should behave and what they should do. One was that they should do gym work every morning. I also told them that if ever they found me still asleep in bed when they got up, they could throw a bucket of water over me. They were always trying to win. It never happened.'

Soon after the start of the voyage some of the boys came to him and said they had been sexually propositioned by members of the crew. 'I was really concerned about this. Some of the lads were pretty young. I advised the purser and asked him to convey to the crew that such attentions were very unwelcome. I also held a meeting with the lads and told them that this type of thing might happen, and if it did, to report it to me.

'A few days later I was on deck with friends, and we decided we would go for a swim. I went to my cabin to get my swimming trunks. From then on I had total loss of memory. Someone or a group of people had bashed me severely. I had a brief period of semi-consciousness, dimly recalling being lowered in a stretcher over the side of the ship.

'I didn't fully recover consciousness for four days. I was in the Princess Elizabeth military hospital in Aden. I discovered later that I had been put ashore to die. I had multiple skull fractures, contusions to the whole body, damage to my eye, broken and missing teeth and a whole range of troubles.'

David was in hospital for a month, then allowed to continue his journey – there was an argument with P&O about who should pay [17]– on board the Greek passenger ship, *Patris*. 'My original plan was to go to Sydney where I had some management jobs organised. But I was in such a state, with stitches across my face and one eye totally closed, that I couldn't consider them.

Instead, I got off the boat in Fremantle and became a stockman in Geraldton.' I finally went to Sydney some six months later and took up one of the jobs previously offered[18].

### SHIPS AND SHIPPING

Until about 1960 virtually all unaccompanied juvenile migrants came by sea. The traffic was at its highest in the years following the two World Wars, when the Government sought to dramatically increase Australia's white population.

Youth migrants from Britain in the early 1920s probably would have sailed on ships of the Aberdeen Line, the 'All Red Route to South Africa and Australia'. These modest vessels of 12,000 to 15,000 tonnes were named after such Greek heroes and travellers as *Demosthenes*, *Themistocles*, *Euripides* and *Diogenes*. They carried both first class passengers and migrants on third class tickets.

Those departing in the mid to late 1920s probably travelled in the Commonwealth Line 'Bay' ships such as the *Largs Bay*, *Hobsons Bay* and *Esperance Bay*, or P&O 'B' ships – used extensively by Dreadnought Boys – such as the *Ballarat*, *Balranald*, *Baradine*, *Barrabool*, *Beltana*, *Benalla*,

*Bendigo, Berrima* and *Borda*. These were slightly larger, but basically converted cargo or troop ships and often one class only.

In the 1930s, there were the more up-market P&O liners *Strathnaver* and *Strathaird* (launched 1931), and the Orient Line's *Orcades, Orion, Oronsay, Orontes, Otranto* and *Orama*. The *Orama*, which brought many juvenile migrants to Australia, was the first British liner to be built without a second class between first and third.

Many P&O vessels served as troopships in World War II. *Orama* was sunk by the German heavy cruisers *Gneisenau* and *Scharnhorst* while attempting a rescue mission in Norway in 1940. *Oronsay* was torpedoed and sunk by an Italian submarine one year later. Their sister ship *Orontes* compensated for these defeats by landing the first wave of troops on the beaches of Sicily, being straddled by a stick of five bombs as she withdrew.

Juvenile migration was discontinued during the war, but as previously stated, a number of British children (many of whom later returned as adults) were accepted as temporary wartime evacuees. They were brought to Australia in three ships, the *Batory, Nestor* and *Diomed*, which left Liverpool in August and September 1940. While the ships were at sea, two sister vessels, the *Volendam* and *City of Benares*, which were taking children to Canada, were torpedoed, the latter with heavy loss of life.[20] Some weeks earlier, a German U-boat had sunk the Canada-bound *Arandora* Star, whose survivors, mostly Category C enemy aliens, were transferred to a new ship, the *Dunera*, and a new destination, Australia.[21]

Post-war migrant vessels included the re-built *Orcades* and *Oronsay*. In 1957, the majestic *Oriana*, the last liner built for the Orient Line, replaced the now defunct *Strathaird* and *Strathnaver*. She was able to accommodate more passengers than these two ships combined. Ironically, this and other big ships came into service as juvenile migration was decreasing. Another Orient line vessel, *Ormonde*, was heavily involved in the child migrant traffic.

Some ships left an indelible imprint on their passengers. There is a tendency to invest the ships themselves with human characteristics. The *Dunera*, whose title was adopted by her most famous passengers, and the *Asturias*, which brought the first post-war child migrants to Western Australia,[22] are examples that come to mind.

The latter's association with the child migrant traffic led to a cameo role (with the name altered from *Asturias* to *Austuras*) in the TV series *The Leaving of Liverpool*. However, it is not generally realised that there were actually two ships called *Asturias*, both owned by the Royal Mail Line, and both with remarkable histories.

The first *Asturias* was built in 1907 for services to South America and to Australia. In World War I she became a hospital ship, was torpedoed in the English Channel, and much of the stern blown off. She ran aground off the coast of Devon and was abandoned as a wreck. In 1919 the Royal Mail Line bought her back from the British Government. The Harland and Wolff shipyard rebuilt her into a cruise liner, re-named Arcadian. In 1933 she was sold to shipbreakers in Japan.

The second *Asturias* was built in 1925 by Harland and Wolff for the Royal Mail Line's South America run. In World War II she became a troopship and – like her predecessor – was torpedoed and ran aground, this time off Freetown, Sierra Leone. The British Ministry of Works towed the vessel back to Britain, and re-fitted her in the final months of the war for use as a troopship.

In July 1949 – still technically owned by the Government but managed by the Royal Mail Line – the *Asturias* began services to the Far East and Australia, mainly for the migrant trade. Sometimes the entire ship, other than the first class section, was used for this purpose. The *Asturias* was sold for scrap in 1957 – her last duty being to serve as a floating set for the film *A Night to Remember*, about the sinking of the *Titanic*.

By the early 1960s air travel had replaced shipping as the normative means of transport for youth and child migrants.

The 1964/65 Annual Report of Barnardos Australia expressed matters thus: 'Ship life is unrealistic for many of our children who do not find it easy to settle down to more orderly living. It does also cause considerable boredom for the latter part of the journey and is not without its hazards for young teenagers travelling in our group.

'The journey itself places immense strain on the escorts who try to keep a large group of children occupied, in good health and properly disciplined throughout the long voyage... In future, our children will arrive within 48 hours of leaving London and should quickly settle in their new environment...'

# 2

# Girls for Hire

# 4

## 'Breeders and Nurturers'

**Y**OUTH MIGRATION from Britain – perhaps because of the spartan lifestyle – is assumed by many to have been exclusively a male preserve. In fact, about one in five unaccompanied teenage migrants were female.

In the early years of the 20th century women in the workforce were still considered a luxury. From the British point of view there was little need to emigrate. Those who wished could find jobs as domestic servants; it was assumed that most young women would 'marry and settle down'.

The situation in Australia was a little different. The desire for population growth meant, inevitably, that women were required as 'breeders and nurturers', if not to join the paid workforce. In Australia, unlike in Britain, there was a shortage of domestic staff – such work being considered demeaning by a people who had only recently thrown off their convict yolk.

To facilitate the traffic girls of school leaving age were sponsored directly by State Governments and other official agencies. Church organisations and patriotic bodies were also involved.

Statistics are confusing, since immigration figures for females, unlike those for males, do not distinguish between adults and juveniles. A general pattern may be gleaned from a letter to the Governor General, Lord Forster, from the Secretary, Church of England Immigration Committee for Victoria, the Rev F.A, Ray, dated 12 December 1923. The letter states:

'Knowing the keen interest that you take in immigration, I venture to bring under your notice the activities of the Anglican Church with reference to this important matter. A committee, consisting of His Grace, the Archbishop of Melbourne, as president, and others,[1] has been formed to facilitate migration to Victoria, and has decided to bring out to this State a monthly quota of 30 lads, 14 to 18 years of age; 20 men, 18 to 20 years of age, and 30 domestic servants.'

The letter says the migrants would be selected in London by the Church Army,[2] and would be subject to medical inspection, also some form of vetting (to what extent is unclear) by Australia House.

'These lads will be drawn for the most part from the Church Army Training Farm and from the rural districts of Great Britain and will, therefore, have had some little farming experience. The domestics also will have received training by the Church Army under their agreement with the Overseas Settlement Department of the Colonial Office.'

The Dreadnought Scheme and Big Brother Movement, the two major private 'importers' of youth migrants, were not interested in recruiting girls, at least officially. The BBM was in the process of changing its policy when the Government axe on its activities fell.[3]

Nevertheless, the traffic in teenage girls was considerable. It is known that in 1928 Australia recruited 3,240 female domestics.[4] NSW led the field, with 1,200, followed by Queensland (720) and Victoria (600).

## AN ISLAND, A MAN AND A CIGARETTE

Fears were expressed – seemingly justified – about the young female migrants' exposure to moral danger. A journey on the *Ballarat*, in 1925, seems to have surpassed even that of the *Baradine* [5]in regard to improper behaviour.

According to Professor Michael Roe,[6] historian and respected writer on immigration matters, members of that particular party experienced a 'fantastic voyage' in which sex was an ingredient. The symptoms began at the initial boat-drill, when a girl was heard to proclaim: 'Oh, to be wrecked on an island with a man and a cigarette.'

Stewards made passes at girls who took their fancy,[7] providing special cabins for their favourites. Officers too had fun, beguiled by a lady who dressed in a nun's habit.

In Cape Town the *Ballarat* became entangled in a world-wide seamen's strike, which lasted seven weeks. The crew joined the strike, and received encouragement from their sweethearts. There was more singing of *The Red Flag*, this time with female participation. Some of the girls befriended black Africans. The ship's welfare officer tried unsuccessfully to impose 'rules', but received little support from the Captain, who was pursuing his own adventures.

In the years before World War II, and possibly after, there were tensions on most vessels between full fare-paying and assisted fare passengers. Senior officers generally ignored all third class passengers, whatever their status. Swearing, drinking and gambling were par for the course. On one voyage, according to Michael Roe, there were reports of a 'gambling gang', whose activities caused some passengers to arrive in their new homeland penniless and in fact minus their own clothes.

There was also a view that the very nature of seaboard life meant a relaxing of conventions. Lady Mary Masson and Lady Elizabeth Mitchell, two women of Melbourne's high society known for their work for migrant welfare, considered the long sea voyage inherently 'dangerous' for domestics,

The two women were concerned not merely about direct threats to the girls' chastity, but that undesirable traits, such as assertiveness, independence and a general fondness for hedonism might might develop and 'grow too strong'.[8] Lady Masson demanded that migrant ships employ matrons 'trained in welfare and in discipline'; that single men and women travel in different ships, and that male stewards not be allowed to service women's cabins.

## 'SKIVVIES' AND FARMERS' WIVES

As stated previously, both the Fairbridge and Barnardos organisations ran farm training schools, which enabled young migrants of both sexes to learn rural occupations.[9] However, both groups saw the role of women primarily as home makers.

The Fairbridge Farm Schools had a rule against taking anyone whose schooling was completed[10]. Barnardos, which was more flexible, accepted – in addition to child migrants[11] – school leavers of both sexes, who were considered sufficiently mature to enter directly into the workforce. For reasons which are unclear, Barnardos (other than in the early stages) tended to send boy school leavers to Canada and girl school leavers to Australia.

Teenage girls brought out by Barnardos had little or no choice about their future. They were to be 'in service' and that was that.[12] Nor was their lot easier than that of the boys. The following anonymous account was given to Anne Howard, co-author of *After Barnardo*:

45

'I came out to Ashfield[13] on 3 December 1936. On the eighth, five or six of us were put on a train to Canberra, like sheep; you just went. I was picked up and taken to a grazier's property miles from anywhere. The cook left, then the children's nurse left, and I was left with everything.

'They had two children aged four and six. I grew quite fond of them, but I never had a day off unless she took the children to a birthday party and then I went with them. I had to put wet newspaper on the floor, then sweep it with a millet broom, clean the silver tureens, wash the clothes in a copper and iron with a flat iron off the stove. I served at table and always ate in the kitchen.

'I had seven shillings and sixpence a week, with five shillings banked by Barnardos and two shillings to pay off my uniform. My afternoon dress was yellow, crossed over and tied at the side, with a filly muslin apron. I wore a hat tied at the back with ribbons. Miss Wedlock [a Barnardos staff member] came to inspect the situation every six months.'

Publicity to attract teenage girls was unsubtle, at least in the early years, and drew deserved criticism. Cartoon strips were among the methods used. In one example, from the 1920s, a series of illustrations shows the young domestic's progress in the home of a wealthy landowner.

The first frame shows the girl dusting and doing housework in a genteel way. The second frame shows the squatter's son paying attention to the maid, hinting at a future marriage. In the last frame the mother-in-law is shown seated by the fireside with her knitting, while the new mistress of the house attends to the household affairs.[14]

(Whilst researching for this book I was told of a Barnardo girl, whose employer – who was seeking a companion rather than a maid – paid for her to attend a business college. After completing the course she became secretary to a bishop in charge of home missions. The lady continued to have the girl living in her home and, when she died, left the house and the bulk of her estate to her.)

Lily Hooper (neé Blomfield) offers an interesting example of the 'old style' approach. Lily, who came to Australia in April 1923, was a long term Barnardos resident, having been placed in the organisation's Barkingside homes when she was five.

Her two elder sisters, who were in the same group of homes, went into service when they were 15. Lily, who was missing them, assumed she would follow suit, and was disappointed when – despite having been fitted out with a maid's uniform – a doctor declared her unsuitable.

Then came the opportunity, when she, too, turned 15, to join a Barnardos group to Australia. 'When I had the offer, I just lapped it up, if only to get out of these four walls.'

Her group of about 50 was the very first party of Barnardo girls, as distinct from boys, to come to Australia. The British and Australian authorities, in line with the empire leanings of the day, regarded the occasion as significant.

Certainly, their send-off from London was grand. They were farewelled at Buckingham Palace. In Lily's own words: 'We shook hands with Queen Mary.[15] They gave us a cup of tea.'

Lily found the journey on the *Euripides* disappointing. 'We were kept right down at the bottom of the ship, and were strictly supervised. I had left school but we still had to do lessons every morning.'

On arrival in Sydney they were welcomed at Government House, then lodged in a hostel owned by Barnardos at Sandringham. 'I had only been there a few days when I was introduced to this lady who said I was going to work for her as a domestic.

'She had a nice house in Turramurra. The lady was quite nice really, but I used to cry and cry. In particular I missed two girls from the boat, who were like my family. They were working in other houses in Turramurra. I cried so much that the lady I worked for used to ring up the places where they worked and say 'Can I send Lily over?'

Was she happy there? 'It's hard to say. I wouldn't say it was unbearable. The places I went to after that were much worse.'[16]

## ROMANCE

As previously noted,[17] the various sending and receiving organisations employed escorts to accompany those in its care on the long sea voyage to Australia.

Most escorts were home-going adult Australians, but at least one English Barnardo girl, whose two brothers were already in Australia with Barnardos – performed this role.

On the *Maloja* in June-July 1950, 19-year-old Melita Hewitt assisted an older woman, remembered only as Miss Poole-Connor, as temporary guardian of a group of Barnardo children bound for Sydney.

Melita, who was not much older than some of her charges, found the work enjoyable, but for an unexpected reason. Also on board was Neil Molineux, 26, a home-going Australian who was escort to a party of Fairbridge children. Romance blossomed.

More than 50 years after the voyage, the couple still remember every detail. Neil, who had gone overseas to attend a Rover scout meeting in Norway, says that he was initially 'too busy looking after the kids' to notice Melita, who was likewise occupied. Things changed when the ship reached Aden. Neil had taken his charges on a shore excursion, and on return saw Melita and some of the Barnardos children on deck, arm wrestling with the Aden police.

'I thought, I can beat this girl. I'll have a go. Actually, I think I beat her the first time and she beat me the second. I said to myself, "She's not bad".'

Was it love at first sight? 'She took my fancy all right. Of course, the children in both groups guessed something was up. They'd run to tell me where Melita was, and run to her to tell her where I was.'

After landing in Sydney Melita went initially to Barnardos' Picton farm, where she was reunited with her brothers, then took up a child-minding job – arranged by Barnardos – with a doctor and his wife in Mosman. 'They were nice people, and treated me as one of the family.'

Meanwhile, Neil had returned to his parents in South Australia. About a year later – with permission from Barnardos – Melita herself moved to South Australia, where she worked in a home for unmarried mothers and their babies. She was surprised – but accepted in good grace – that as a minor she was still required to report regularly to local welfare officials.

They married when Melita turned 21. For many years she and her husband ran a family business, a delicatessen, in Port Augusta. Neil and Melita Molineux now live in the Barossa Valley. They have four sons, 11 grandchildren and two great grandchildren.

Of her time as a Barnardos escort, she says simply: 'We had a lot of fun.'

## SOCIALLY CHIC

Young female domestics – like their male counterparts on the farms – had little or no choice in the matter of who would be their employer. Indeed, some were recruited into jobs pre-arranged in the UK. This was supposedly for their own 'safety' but led to exploitation by hirers who saw them as cheap labour.

In Sydney society, as late as the 1950s, it was considered socially chic for people of a 'good family' to employ a Barnardo girl, and to let slip the information in conversation with one's peers. A titled woman, who also served on the Barnardos committee, was in the habit of going to England, visiting Barnardos homes there, and recruiting her own servants.

A titled Melbourne society matron took two Barnardo girls into her home. She declared herself satisfied, allegedly telling her friends at afternoon tea: 'At present they are more work than help, but in a few months I expect them to be a real comfort.'

Barnardos' management were, and still are reluctant to criticise the motives of these 'top drawer' employers, many of whom gave generously to the organisation. Stan Allen, the first Barnardos Old Boy appointed to a management role within the organisation, had no such hesitation. 'When I was in charge of [the home at] Normanhurst, some of the people on the committee were only involved because it was "nice" to be there. It really got me. They'd say things like, "I've come [to the children's home] to see the tree that Lady Slim planted." They were not interested in the kids.'

Not every employer acted from selfish motives. Bishop Donald Robinson, formerly Anglican Archbishop of Sydney, recalls a succession of Barnardo girls passing through his parents' rectory. 'We treated them like family.'

Many girls enjoyed working in 'posh' homes, and disliked it when they were called 'skivvies'. A girl wrote to a friend: 'Since landing in Australia I have never looked back. I have been in the same position for four years to date. Since my arrival I have been joined by my two brothers and later by my parents, and quite recently by a married sister, her husband and three children...I am studying opera singing and may branch out as a professional before long.'

*Wanted – Domestic Girls (1922).*

Others felt very differently. Tom Price, formerly Australian general manager of Barnardos, told me: 'One of the girls phoned me up and said she was unhappy, being ill treated and so on. It was a very upper crust home. I went over there and had an awful blue with the lady of the house, who felt that I was siding with the children. I said, "Well, why shouldn't I? I'm their guardian".'

Another girl wrote to the authorities: 'It is so lonely. It's 10 miles to go to church. I shall never be able to go. Before I go mad will you please get me another place.'

Domestic service had advantages in the workforce. There was an excess of demand which meant that a girl who fell out with one employer could fairly easily find work with another. The passage of 'selected' migrants, as early Government-sponsored juveniles were called, was absolutely free, unlike others, who had to pay at least a modest contribution towards their fare.

Gladys Pott, a member of the Overseas Settlement Department in Britain, reported the practice among some girls of calling themselves 'ladies' helps' rather than domestics. She also considered some of the girls to be uppity. 'The girl whose obvious object is to "stand up for her rights" rather than assist in duties not actually specified in her contract of service is neither a credit to Britain nor to herself. Such an attitude often brings unpopularity on the British migrant.'

Some employers complained of lack of competence – that they were being asked to employ 'shop girls' and 'mill workers' with little idea of domestic chores. A Queenslander complained that the girl she had hired couldn't wash clothes, make a bed or even sweep the house. 'I must look out for a dark girl. These new chums want too much.'[18]

One of the largest importers of young women in the early years of the 20th century was the Salvation Army. Though valuable records have been destroyed,[19] it is possible to gauge much of the extent of this activity through pages of the Army's newspaper, War Cry. The following was reported in the issue of 6 January 1923:

'In a steady downpour of rain a party of girls from England, and another smaller party of boys, landed in Melbourne on Thursday afternoon from the steamer Balranald. The band of new settlers had originally numbered 153, but 50 had landed at Fremantle, to be housed temporarily at the Salvation Army's new Immigration Lodge recently opened by Commissioner Richards to meet a very pressing need.

'Others had disembarked at Adelaide, so that the remainder, except for a handful bound for Sydney, who came ashore at Melbourne, numbered 84. Of these, 62 were widows with their children, and girls who had come out with the intention of entering domestic service, and 28 were lads, whose ages ranged from 15 to 19 years, who came to work as "farm learners", and who will leave almost immediately for the country.'

Girls brought out as domestics were required to remain in such employment (though not necessarily with the same employer) until they were 21. The obligation was waived if they should marry – as many did – before reaching this age.

The main complaint among the girls was of low wages. A potential employer described an incident when she and other ladies came to interview four girls newly arrived off the boat. The usual rate of wages – 25 shillings to 30 shillings a week with board – was offered, at which point the four 'looked at each other and broke into rude laughter, saying that Australia House had had told them nothing but lies, and that it was disgraceful that girls should be brought out for such wages.'

After World War II changing social attitudes put an end to the widespread employment of servants by Australian families. Barnardos – somewhat reluctantly – allowed girls under the organisation's wing to take other employment, including office work[20].

Here, as before, there were complaints – rejected by Barnardos – of low wages. According to Tom Price: 'They [employers] would have to pay what the award rate was. We abided by that as everyone else did. The unions were by this time [the mid-1950s] very strong.'[21]

Many Barnardos Old Boys and Girls remain sceptical. Shirley Ronge, who organises the annual reunions, recalls: 'I used to look at the ads in the newspaper, and could see that you could get paid twice as much if you were not a Barnardos kid.' Stan Allen[22] echoed this comment: 'There was no union to help us.'

As anticipated by their sponsors, many former domestics did find fulfilment in marriage. They raised large families, responding to the roles desired for them by their sponsors.

A girl wrote to a friend in England: 'I got married early in 1922...I married into the bush life and wherever we pitch our tents there is home... The glorious sense of space and freedom in the bush districts of Western Australia can only be truly realised by those who have lived and worked in large cities and disliked them, all clatter and smoke.'

And another: 'I was married in Sydney to my Aussie Boy and we are very happy. My luck in Australia has been the best.'

# 5

# 'Below Stairs' at Government House

**B**ALLYPOREEN, TIPPERARY, in the Republic of Ireland, is a modest village whose main claim to fame is as the birthplace of the ancestors of former US President, Ronald Reagan. Some of his relatives still live there.

Our story is concerned with another human export, Bridget (Bridie) Leonard, née Creagh, who was born there in 1935. To a child growing up in the village it seemed a small, unprepossessing place, populated mostly by 'farmers with very large families'. Bridie herself was one of 12 children, two of whom died at birth.

Her parents, like almost everyone else in Ballyporeen, were poor. 'Dad was a labourer with the local council. He had a horse and butt[1], fixed holes in the road and worked in the quarries, breaking stones.' As with many Irish families, the dominant figure was her mother, a woman of fixed ideas, which was to lead to conflict over her daughter's desire to emigrate to Australia.

Early memories are of the village school, unsympathetic priests and nuns, and constant illness. At the age of about eight she developed osteomyelitis. She spent three-and-a-half years in the one hospital, undergoing numerous operations; her mother steadfastly denying the demands of surgeons to amputate. A presumed recovery, involving a spell in a convalescent home, proved short-lived and it was back to the former hospital for a further year.

Bridie was nearly 14 when she was considered fit enough to return to school. The nun in charge was horrified at her inability to recite the catechism, and called in the parish priest. Together they admonished her and she went home that day in tears.

'Mum was furious. She said: "That's the last day you'll spend at school. You're not going back to those nuns". She was also angry because I had two sisters, both very clever, who had won scholarships to a boarding school. But the nuns wouldn't let them go. They gave the places to daughters of big farmers who were better off.'

Having abruptly left school, a place was found for her – she's not sure how – on the domestic staff of a hospital in Wales. It was a complicated journey, for someone who had hardly left home, made more so because it was an isolation hospital, situated on a hilltop far removed from the nearest town, which was Bridgend. It took patients suffering from TB, diptheria, scarlet fever and other infectious diseases.

Bridie's job was to look after the staff, rather than the patients, which was just as well, given her own precarious health. 'Matron was very nice to me. They were always saying that I was too thin and should eat more. Rationing was still on – it was 1949. We used to get an ounce of butter a week, and an ounce of sugar. Tea was also rationed so we only had a cup of tea a day. Matron was worried about herself being too fat, so she gave me her butter ration which made the cook jealous.

'We had fish and chips four nights a week for tea, and you'd get sick of it. One day I'd eaten up my butter ration with jam and bread, and I told cook I didn't want their fish and chips. I was threatened with the sack over it.'

Trouble of another kind arose when it was realised that at 14, she was too young to be legally employed in the British Isles – though not in the Irish Republic. Happily, Bridie had a sister in Wales, with whom she went to stay for the requisite period before resuming her employment at 15.

In 1952 Bridie began to get itchy feet. 'I'd been in Wales just over three years. It was always damp, cold and foggy, and I was often getting sick. I wanted to work in London, but my mother knew Matron was looking after me so well and didn't want me to go.

'Anyway I got a newspaper and looked for something residential, possibly looking after kids. I answered three advertisements, which gave limited information. One of the replies said the job would be at Government House, in Tasmania.'

The letter, was, in fact, from Lady Cross,[2] wife of the then Governor, Sir Ronald Cross.[3] 'I hadn't a clue what it was all about. I asked one of the hospital staff: "Where's Tasmania?" And she said: "It's an island off Australia," I said: "Where's Australia?" Anyway, it sounded good and I decided to have a go.'

Bridie was asked to provide a photograph of herself and three references. One of those she approached for a reference was the Ballyporeen parish priest, with whom she had crossed swords earlier. He obliged, albeit with reluctance. 'He said: "You're going out to Australia. There's no religion out there. You won't see a church for years." I said: "That's OK. I'll go to church when I come back." He said: "There are Aborigines out there. You could be attacked in the back".'

'I sent it all to Lady Cross, who said the photo looked nice and the job was available if I wanted it.' [4]

Her mother's reaction was 'as bad as that of the priest'. 'I gave her a little book that Australia House had sent me, all about Australia. She said: "It's full of animals and Aborigines. They're in the main street. You can't go out there, I won't give my permission".'

Bridie next had to take a medical examination. 'I had to go to Cardiff for this. I knew Australia had strict health standards for migrants, and I was worried. My sister in Wales came with me. She said: "You won't pass". My mother had already written to them about my years in hospital and osteomyelitis. But the x-rays were all clear and I passed. I really think it was because I was going to Government House.'

There was still the problem of my mother. 'I tried a new tactic. "If I can't go to Australia, I'll go to London and I won't come home for years either." But she still wouldn't give her permission.'

'Happily, my mother was friends with a midwife who used to deliver all the babies in Ballyporeen. Nurse Hennessey had been out to Australia many years earlier. She said to my mother: "Let Bridie go. She might never get that opportunity again. And she'll be in safe hands with the Governor and Lady Cross".'

'So my mother gave in and let me go. She signed the paper and I was on the next bus.'

## DEPARTURE

A few weeks later – with no time to change her mind – it was time for Bridie to say her goodbyes. She bought a sturdy trunk and carefully packed her meagre belongings. It added a note of finality – there was now no turning back.

Her troubles were not quite over. Unwisely, she sent a telegram to a brother, Michael, in London, suggesting he meet her train at Paddington Station. He had not previously known about her intention to emigrate, and he definitely did not approve.

As Bridie tells it: 'It was my last night at home. I had gone to bed, and suddenly someone was in the room shaking me. It was Michael. He had come all this way just to stop me. I told him it was no use. The next morning he tried again, following me as far as the railway. The train came æ as I put one foot on, he was pulling me back. This went on for several minutes until he was forced to let go. I got to Paddington all by myself, then took a taxi to Sir Ronald Cross's place at Kensington.'

It was a four-storey house; the servants' quarters, with tiny windows, occupying the uppermost storey. 'That night one of the staff showed me around London. I saw Buckingham Palace. It was wonderful.

'The next morning, 1 August 1954, was our departure day. Another girl arrived at the house. She was coming out as well. The Salvation Army had been looking after her. I remember Lady Cross walked into the room. I happened to be standing up for some reason, and she told this other girl: "Where's your manners? When I walk into a room you all stand up. Just take heed of Bridget".

'An hour later a man came from Australia House, I can't remember his name, but he was very nice. He took us to the station, and came with us on the train to Tilbury. All the time he was saying how big Australia is and that you could put England two or three times in New South Wales.' When I saw the *Strathnaver*, I got frightened. I said: "It's huge, I don't think I'll get on that". But he came on the ship and even had lunch with us. He was Australian, he seemed to know a lot of people.'

When the ship sailed Bridie quickly lost her timidity. 'Everyone seemed very happy, the weather was lovely and I made several friends. We were served with fruit first thing in the morning. We had silver knives and forks and beautiful china plate. I lapped it up. And, of course, the food was delicious.

'There were two young girls in my cabin [of four] and we used to go to the dances every night. We used to play cards and guessing games. The boys we danced with would join us. There were some nice lads, but I wasn't much interested in boys at that time.

'The only time I felt lonely, in fact very lonely and apprehensive, was when I got off the *Strathnaver* in Melbourne, and said goodbye to all the people I knew. And I had to go on another ship, the *Taroona*, to Tasmania. That's when I felt very much alone.

'The ship went to Burnie, from where I got a train to Hobart. I took a taxi to Government House.' The first sight was impressive æ a magnificent old building, completed 1857, with views towards the Botanical Gardens and the [old] Tasman Bridge. It was 'the sort a girl like me could only dream about.'

Bridie found less to dream about in the housekeeper, Mrs Neal, a stern disciplinarian, who had formerly been housekeeper to the Queen's aunt, Alice, the Princess Royal, and had been part of the Queen's entourage in the royal visit that same year.[5]

'I think it was because of her having worked for royalty that she gave us an awful time. She sort of crawled around, wore soft shoes and would creep up behind when you least expected it.'

A housemaid's routine began at six in the morning and finished at 10 or 11 pm. 'We started before breakfast. First we'd clean the drawing rooms. There was all that cigar ash; I'd feel sick from the smell. We cleaned and dusted very thoroughly. Mrs Neal would purposely go round putting her fingers on something to see if we had missed it.

'It was a like that old TV series, *Upstairs Downstairs*, only worse. It was a lovely old building, but a bit primitive. They didn't have proper-showers. We had to clean each bath two or three times a day until it shone. This was just in case it might be used.'

Dinner parties were held frequently, causing staff to work back until 1 am. or later. Custom dictated that conversation overheard could not be repeated. And Bridie admits to having overheard a few choice snatches, some of them distinctly politically incorrect, from the Governor himself.

Staff were allowed a break in the afternoon, subject to other commitments. Wages (in 1954) were £4 for a supposed 60-hour week. Servants had a day off on alternate Sundays.

Bridie found that she soon got to know every room in Government House. 'The state rooms, the Governor's or Queen's bedroom. Each had a different name. I knew them all.'

One day, after she had been there a few months, Bridie and her roommate, another housemaid, were skylarking. The other girl pulled a mat, causing Bridie to fall awkwardly and break her arm. A bone was actually protruding. Bridie struggled to her feet, and was taken in to see Mrs Neal. The housekeeper was unsympathetic, as usual. 'She said: "Serves you right. I heard you laughing 10 minutes ago". I fainted in front of her.'

Bridie was told, somewhat reluctantly, that she could have time off to visit the hospital. There were three cars in the garage, but the chauffeurs were off duty and no one offered her a lift. She walked three miles to Hobart General Hospital, only to be told that the x-ray section was closed – it was Sunday – and that she should come back the following day.

The next morning she was up before six as usual, and made to clean the drawing rooms as if nothing had happened. 'The pain was something shocking. I didn't have any tablets or anything.' Her appointment was at 10 o'clock. 'I walked to the hospital again and they plastered me up. Two or three days later I put my arm down and the plaster fell off. That's how swollen my arm was.'

Despite the above  – she doesn't know if her employer was ever informed – Bridie considers Lady Cross a 'decent employer', though she didn't actually see much of her.

Her tasks included serving drinks at receptions. She was young and pretty. Protocol demanded that she could reply, if spoken to, but not say more than a few words. 'We weren't allowed to talk normally with anybody, and I mean anybody, other than a fellow servant. If someone spoke to us at a party Mrs Neal would be hovering around to see what was going on.'

Sir Ronald and Lady Cross then had two daughters, addressed as Miss Susanna and Miss Karina, living at Government House. They were aged 16 and 12 respectively at that time. Bridie remembers Karina, the younger daughter, as 'the biggest tomboy you ever met'. Another two daughters remained in Britain.

The two girls, in particular Susanna,[6] would sometimes engage her in conversation. Probably they were unaware of the 'rule' against talking. The housekeeper, who had amazing powers of hearing, would 'sneak up from behind' and say, 'Pleae leave the room. I told you before you're not allowed to talk to the young ladies.'

Bridie's duties – another before breakfast task – included waking up the girls. 'At seven o'clock I'd go in and pull back the curtains, wake them, put their slippers by the bed and help them with their dressing gowns. Of course, I had already prepared the bathroom and made sure there was hot running water.'

(Susanna Sitwell nee Cross, contacted by the writer in Britain, has her own recollection of these events. 'Although Bridie may have woken my sister and myself in the morning by drawing the curtains, we were not helped with our dressing gowns and slippers, although she would have helped guests in this manner. Certainly, we were not pampered, rather the reverse. We always had a cold shower too in the morning. We did all our own washing and ironing, and made our own beds. Our governess was a very strict disciplinarian in the old-fashioned sense and stood no nonsense!')

One day Bridie's chores seemed to be less than usual. She thought fate had been kind to her. 'There was a cloakroom and toilet just inside the main entrance. It was the only thing I had to polish that morning.

'There was a box with all your equipment in it and I just pulled out the rag, opened the tin and rubbed the rag on the polish. It's only a small floor; I gave it a good shine. Then I went into the drawing room, where Mrs Neal came in. She said: "Why haven't you polished the toilet this morning?" I said: "I did." She said: "No you haven't." I repeated: "I have." She said "Don't tell me lies." I said: "I'm not telling you lies, I've polished it."

'She said: "I've looked in your box and there's no polish in there." I said: "That doesn't mean I didn't do it." "Anyway," she said, "I'm going to report you to Lady Cross." I said; "OK." At eight o'clock we went for breakfast. I couldn't eat it and went to my bedroom.

'Who should barge in but Mrs Neal. She told me off again and said: "You'll have to go and see Lady Cross." I said: "Definitely I'll go and see Lady Cross and tell her about you." I said: "What year do you think this is? It's 1954 not 1854. And you can't speak to me like that. I'm going to tell Lady Cross what you're like; the way you sneak around behind us and that you never speak nicely to any of us."

'To my surprise, and to her own credit, she apologised and said: "We'll forget it." So I never saw Lady Cross, but I made sure to curtsey whenever she or her husband walked past.'

Soon after that incident Bridget Creagh left the staff of Government House to work variously in a pub, chocolate factory, repatriation hospital and in various other occupations in Hobart, Melbourne, Sydney and – during a three year home visit – London.

Back in Melbourne, she met her husband, Cec, a refrigeration engineer, at a St Patrick's Day dance at St Kilda Town Hall. They were married in 1959, had six children, and now live in St Hubert's Island on the NSW Central Coast.

When looking back on her life and experiences, she often tells her friends: 'They sent us out here as if we were convicts. But really they sent us to paradise.'

# 6

# 'Cybergranny'

"If I've been good, why am I going?'

*Barnardos (then Dr Barnardo's),[1] the British organisation principally known as an operator of children's homes, provided Australia, Canada and New Zealand with child migrants and also with school leavers – mainly girls who were recruited for domestic service. The following is the story of one of them.*

S HE WAS BORN KATHLEEN REDSTONE, in Folkestone, Kent, on 17 January 1912. She was the youngest of seven children.

Her father died when Kathleen was two. The following summer, whilst the mother was working to support her much loved but troublesome 'tribe', the oldest girl took the others to the beach. When the older girl's back was turned, one of the younger ones, Barbara, 'a determined child', ran into the sea and nearly drowned.

Someone reported the incident to the authorities. Clearly, the mother 'couldn't cope'. Which explains how, on 25 May 1915, Kathleen, aged three, and the two next youngest – twins Barbara and Norah, aged five – were put into the care of the famed Dr Barnardo's Homes, headquartered at Stepney Causeway, in London's East End, and placed in a facility known as Babies' Castle.

Kathleen has vague memories of a staff member, Sister Mackie, who was kind to her and kept her photo on her desk. She assumes her time there must have been happy, for 'why was I sad at leaving?' This occurred, two years later. Sister Mackie told her: 'You're going for good.' To which the child responded: 'If I've been good, why am I going?'

It was time for the five-year-old and her sisters to go into foster care. In Barnardos parlance this was 'B.O' (boarded out).

Kathleen and Norah were sent to a Mrs Grace in the Bedfordshire village of Aspley Guise. Barbara stayed behind, to have her tonsils out. It was a picture postcard spot not far from the Duke of Bedford's estate at Woburn Abbey. Apparently, there was an 'arrangement' with Barnardos, as several other children were fostered in the village.

The stay was a short one. Kathleen has no memory of her first foster mother, though she does recall there was a fowl yard next door. After leaving Mrs Grace, Norah and Barbara – who was now also in the village – were briefly cared for by two 'lovely rich spinsters' until a place for all three could be found.

'One day my sisters were at school and I was at home with a cold. One of the women was brushing my hair and told me to sit down afterwards and do breathing exercises. I had other things on my mind – perhaps making a doll's dress – and forgot. I had to go without my dinner and watch the others eat, whilst I did the breathing exercises.'

After a few weeks the two spinsters found coping with the children too hard. It was Barnardos policy that siblings, as far as possible, should be kept together. The twins were taken in by a family, but there was not room for Kathleen, who was placed with the couple next door. Their own children had died – one in the Great War, the other from pneumonia , and they were clearly lonely.

Kathleen recalls: 'I grew to love Mrs Masters[2] and was glad she was my foster mother. 'She treated me as her own and asked me to call her "Mummy".'

It was a period of confusion in the child's life. 'I couldn't understand why other children lived with people called parents. For us living with someone else had been the natural thing to do.'

Kathleen was to stay with the couple for about six years. 'I went to church and Sunday school. Because of my good memory I was given the main part in Sunday school plays.'

Partly her happiness was due to the attitudes of the local population. 'We were never snobbed.[3] We couldn't have had more kindness. They treated us better than their own people. There was goodness in their hearts.'

The physical surroundings added to her joy. 'Aspley Guise was a lovely place. I remember being led through a spinney; there was this lovely English country atmosphere. I've often dreamed about it. I was given a hoop – I don't suppose modern children know what that is – and bowled it along with a large stick.'

The village also took in boys from a workhouse. One of them, having grown up, achieved moderate success. She remembers being surprised when he told her: 'You put your money in the bank and it grows.' 'We had never heard of *money* banks. We thought he must be digging his money into the bank at the side of the road.'

When she was 11 her idyll came to an end. Her two sisters, who were 13, were considered old enough to be trained for work. Because of the policy of not separating siblings, all three had to be sent to the Barnardos Girls Village at Barkingside, Essex.

When it was time to go, Kathleen heard Mr Masters tell his wife that he did not wish to take the girls to the station, as he had previously taken other Barnardos children and he felt he 'could not stand the crying'. Instead, the children were taken by the two rich spinsters.

Kathleen, mindful of what she had overheard, was determined not to cry. 'But as the train came into the station I broke down. Later I was glad that the two rich spinsters had reported this to my foster mother.'

The Barkingside community had its own school. Kathleen shone in lessons and was regularly top of her class. However, the headmistress disliked her, which feeling was reciprocated. About a year after they arrived at the village, she received news that her sisters were to be sent to Australia. She was not allowed to see them off, but will remember the 'goodbyes' in the school playground until her dying day.

She studied extra hard to compensate for her loss. A feature of school life were the crushes on various female teachers to the extent that a girl would deliberately get into trouble in order to stay behind and receive a 'talking to' from the favoured one. Kathleen believes this was less burgeoning sexuality than a desire for mother love.

She had no such feelings towards the headmistress, who 'didn't like me because she considered I had been spoiled. She thought she might put me in a B class, but would try first the A class, and when I got to the top, it made a fool of her.'

Grudgingly – on account of her obvious prowess – the headmistress made her a prefect. Kathleen was proud of her badge and the extra responsibilities, which included ringing a large bell. She also occasionally assisted another teacher, whom she 'adored', in class preparation.

Barnardos at that time had its own company of Girl Guides. Kathleen joined the movement and was thrilled when invited to go to camp with a non-Barnardos group from the London borough of Tooting. She was surprised to meet two sisters who shared a bed. 'At Barnardos we have our own,' she said proudly.

There was a canteen at the camp which sold sweets and refreshments. The guide captain asked if she had any money. She had all of one halfpenny, therefore truthfully answered 'Yes'. Alas, it wasn't enough. She had to stand by and watch the others make their purchases.

From time to time Kathleen was visited at Barnardos by her mother. The daughter savoured these visits. 'It was like living in a dream world. She seemed such an ethereal person. I was proud that she always dressed very smartly. She brought various goodies which, of course, I duly shared.'

Coming and going was a constant feature of life at Barkingside. One day it was her turn. She was sent for by a governor.[4] 'Did I want to leave school?' 'No, I didn't. I would like to train to be a teacher.' 'Oh well, you'll have to give up that idea. You're going to Australia. There's a party leaving next February.'

Then followed a succession of tests, interviews and a medical examination. Her report card noted: 'Good behaviour, continually near top of her class'. 'I thought why did I have to have such a good report, when all they want is someone to do housework. It was blindly assumed that I was not fit for anything else. In my own mind I was determined that when I got to Australia I would go to evening school as well.'

Meantime the girls' cottage mother, who was liked, had been transferred to a new position, and they were given a new one, which caused resentment. They decided to make things difficult for the newcomer, who was disliked anyway.

According to Kathleen: 'Not being that type of girl, I was not part of the discontent, but in any case I could not afford to risk losing my chance of migration. Still, it was quite a surprise when on the last day our new cottage mother invited me into her room for breakfast, and a private chat. She told me how sorry she was that I was leaving, that if it hadn't been for me she could not have stood what she was taking on. I felt very guilty about my private thoughts.

'Then she took me down to our meeting place and I was hurriedly placed into line with the other girls. To my further delight our old cottage mother came rushing up to me with tears in her eyes to say goodbye. As we boarded the coach the present cottage mother grabbed me. "Kathleen," she said, "you never said goodbye to me," and hugged and kissed me. Once again I felt guilty. I generally found in those days that the people I loved were unaware of it, and the people I didn't love loved me. Why?

'I did not cry, on leaving England, as I knew I was going to join my sisters.'

The P&O vessel, *Berrima*, with some 40 Barnardos girls among its passengers, departed Tilbury on 14 February 1926. The average age of the youngsters was 14. As already noted, they were not child migrants, but 'workers' who were expected to take up employment within weeks of their arrival.

For Kathleen the journey was the ultimate excitement. In fact, she still dreams about it, more than 75 years on. Interestingly, in her dream the vessel never actually reaches its destination.

Eating in the ship's restaurant was another thrill. 'The uniformed waiters, the food, silverware – just everything.' Adding to what she considers her good fortune, an outbreak of measles on board meant that the journey had to be prolonged, taking eight weeks instead of the usual five. 'The ship was our home and it was really the end of my childhood.'

## CHILDHOOD'S END

After disembarking in Sydney, followed by a reception with the local Press, the new arrivals were taken by bus to the organisation's hostel in Ashfield. As the youngsters climbed down from the vehicle, a voice called out 'Kathleen, your sisters are here.' 'My heart nearly leapt out of my body with joy.'

They were there for a week while jobs were found. The young people themselves were not consulted. Rules were strict and the matron carried them out to the letter. Kathleen was discovered by matron in the dormitory during the daytime – one of the greatest of breaches. She had gone there to brush her hair. 'I had expected a severe reprimand. Incredibly, she put her arms around me and kissed me. She warned me not to follow the ways of my sister Norah, whom she considered "a devil", but to follow the example of my other sister, Barbara.

'Matron's kind treatment of me continued for the rest of the week. All this loving spoiled me for the work ahead. From being treated with great kindness I was to spend the next 11 years as a practical outcast in other people's kitchens.'

Her entry to the paid workforce began in Young, a thriving but 'gossipy' country town. She was to be 'in service' to the manager and his wife of the local branch of the Bank of NSW.[5] It was a convenient arrangement, as sister Barbara worked for the Anglican rector, and Norah worked for the manager of another local bank.

As with most rural branches the office and family home shared a single property. At initial meeting her employer – Kathleen regarded the wife, rather than the husband, as the boss – was almost too welcoming. 'She seemed a very motherly lady, boiled me an egg and made me a cup of tea. To show me what to do meant that she had to do it herself. This meant that she was up at six to demonstrate.'

The work schedule – which rarely varied – was severe. 'My first job was to light the fuel stove, then upstairs to sweep the long veranda which stretched the length of the bank. Then downstairs at the front of the bank to do the same job. We used straw brooms with long handles; we didn't have those in England. They were taller than I was. I felt like a witch. At the end of the first week I thought my back was breaking. Of course, all that was just for starters.'

Prospective employers had to complete an application form, which included 'sleeping accommodation'. Many years later Kathleen was to see the one filled in by the bank manager's wife. It said: 'Room indoors, comfortable and well furnished'.

'That's interesting,' she says with hindsight. 'I remember just a curtained corner of the room for my wardrobe, and a washstand with jug and basin. To get water I had to go down a dark back staircase. I was not allowed to enter the family bathroom.

'There was a small room at the top of the landing, about 4 ft x 4 ft in which was a round, galvanised bath tub. I had to heat a kerosene bucket of water on the fuel stove and carry it up these stairs, stopping half way to move the candle to the next stopping place. Afterwards, I had to empty the water back into the bucket and carry it downstairs. I was small. The bucket must have been about half my size. And the manager's wife wondered why I didn't bathe every day.'

In the town itself many middle class people employed servants, which was a symbol of status. 'The maids were one of the chief objects of discussion. They loved to pull you down. Everyone knew what a bad girl you were.'

There were other matters of concern. 'I was 14 and my wage was 10 shillings a week, 2s and 6d of which was to be deducted and remitted to the Barnardos office[6] where it would be banked for me as compulsory saving.

'Actually, ten bob a week wasn't too bad. One of the girls told me that in England she'd been paid five shillings, and I think had to pay half of that in board. On the other hand I remember getting a lecture from the head of the homes, when I asked if I could have some money to pay the dentist. She said: "You should save your money". I thought how the hell can we save out of 7s 6d. Mind you, I didn't talk like that in those days. I didn't say "hell".'

A large part of Kathleen's duties involved kitchen work. 'I was scared to death the whole time of doing the wrong thing. One day I cut my finger. Some blood got on to the meat dish, and I was not game to admit it. I lied about it when challenged, and got into awful trouble.'

One day the manager's wife, with a friend, was going to a function. 'She asked if I could look after the friend's daughter. who was duly brought to the house after school. I took her to play in the dining room, while I sat there doing some knitting. When they came home my employer had a fit. Me seated in her dining room!'

Worse was to come. 'One night I lay on the bed to read my Bible. I fell asleep with the light on. It had to be off by nine o'clock. Even more damning was that I had gone to bed with my clothes on.'

## A GIRL CHEAPLY

After about five months the bank manager and his wife concluded they'd 'had enough' of Kathleen. 'Probably it was all she could take from an inexperienced girl like me. I don't particularly blame her. Everyone was thrilled at getting a girl cheaply. But they expected professional services in return.'

People who donated to Barnardos had priority in obtaining servants. Kathleen's next job was with a family at Bribbaree, a tiny hamlet about 25 miles from Young. To the young English girl it seemed the ultimate in remote living. She could only see her sisters occasionally, and greatly missed her old friends from Barnardos. She had been told in England that Barnardos domestics would be treated 'as part of the family'. In Bribbaree that part of the claim was true. She had to share a bedroom with the couple's children.

Her duties were less arduous than in the previous house. The main enemy was boredom. 'One day, being bored, I brought the cows home.'

She spent about six months in Bribbaree, followed by a string of postings which read like screen credits or names rolling off a computer. She thinks there were 14. Or maybe 15, or perhaps more.

One job, back in Young, was with a family who also had a female lodger. The young woman was a teacher at the town's technical college and gave her the incentive for self-improvement. The employer's husband, who was sympathetic, endorsed this plan to the extent of obtaining a typewriter, for which I paid in instalments, and Pitman's shorthand manual. The proviso was made that she hide the items away and only practise when his wife – who would have considered it treachery – was not around.

Alas, some months later she had to quit the job – she cannot now recall the reason – and was too nervous to keep the typewriter. 'I think he took it back for me.'

More jobs followed, one of which was with a doctor's wife. Kathleen's mother came to Australia, got a job in Sydney, and came to Young to visit her. Kathleen was given time off to go out with her, a proviso being that she had to be back in the house by nine o'clock. Alas, she returned late, her mother having begged her to stay a bit longer. For this she was severely reprimanded and told that, from then on, her mother was to come to the house, and conduct meetings with her daughter in the kitchen

Another job was with the Mayor of Young and his wife. 'I got quite fond of this lady, though she hurt me quite often. She'd say things like "You're only a Barnardo girl".

'One evening I took supper into the lounge room and her two boys were sprawled out on the floor in front of the fire, listening to the wireless. My whole being wanted to be part of a family and sprawl on the floor as if you owned it.'

A craze in Young at that time was miniature golf. 'It was a game of challenge; you had to get that ball out of all sorts of difficulties. I used to play on my afternoon off, and so on one of the occasions the Mayor and his wife were going to Sydney, I asked permission to go there after the drama class was over. Normally I was required to be home by 10 pm. It was about 20 minutes walk from the town, a distance I would not dare walk at night by myself now, but in those days we had "minnie golf", not drink and drugs.

'They gave me permission to go there, also after choir practice, from which I had to leave early.' After one of these visits her sister told her that she had been spotted by the rector's wife, who considered her guilty of 'a sin of all sins'. The next day, as anticipated, the phone rang and Kathleen answered it.

'I want to speak to your mistress,' she said in a haughty manner. 'What were you doing at minnie golf the other night?' 'I told her I had had permission, but she did not believe me. Feeling very righteous I brought the mayor's wife to the phone telling her the trouble. It gave me great pleasure to hear her telling that busybody where to get off.'

At about this time Kathleen developed an interest in the opposite sex. The object of her affection was the local dentist. 'We were all in love with him, including my sisters. He was the only decent young man in the place.'

After a routine visit, Kathleen was told that 'something special' needed to be done to a tooth and that it would take longer than normal. Instead of being annoyed, she was delighted. 'A whole hour in that chair. It was the nearest thing to heaven I could think of.'

When the time came for the appointment, the Mayor's wife said she couldn't go, as they were expecting an important visitor – the local MP – and the girl's presence was required. Kathleen insisted: 'I have to go. It's booked.' At which point the woman rang the dentist and cancelled it herself.

'That was it; I'd had enough. I put the dinner on and then decided I was going to "escape". I didn't know where I was going or how I was going to get a taxi without using the phone. But that was beside the point. As my sister had taught me, "First things first." I went into my bedroom to pack. I was not supposed to be in there during the day and the wretched woman saw me.

'I see you've been packing,' she said. "Well, you can go tonight. I'll pay your fare to Sydney and you can go back to the hostel." She gave me no chance to say good bye to Barbara and arranged with the MP to keep an eye on me as he also was returning to Sydney. But this was not in my plans.

Kathleen devised a complicated plan which involved getting out of the train at a half-way stop, supposedly to stretch her legs, and buying a ticket to some other destination, where she hoped to move into a hostel and find secretarial work. The scheme backfired. Plain clothes police – somehow alerted to her scheme – took charge of her and sent her back to her original employer.

A confrontation followed in which Kathleen was told she would be sent to the Ashfield home, this time under police escort and in a locked carriage all the way to Sydney. As it turned out, there were no police and the carriage door was unlocked. Also to her surprise, when she arrived at Ashfield station (at 6 am) the train was met by a smiling Matron, 'who grabbed me and kissed me'. Two lads were also present to carry her luggage. When they got back to the hostel there was still no reprimand. Instead, Matron gave her a welcome breakfast and suggested that, because it was Sunday and the girls did not have to get up until nine, she might like to go to bed for a lie in.

Now that she was back in Sydney, even Barnardos decided it was time for a change, and Kathleen was sent to the organisation's Picton training farm as a cook.

It was only a short stay, but she quite enjoyed it. Though social contact was forbidden, she met various Barnardos boys – mostly much younger than herself. 'They were lovely kids, who went through the same hardships as we did. I remember one young fellow was put in the barn to sleep. There was just hay on the floor and holes in the roof. Birds pooped on him during the night.'

A variety of short term jobs followed, mainly in the City area, but also in Bowral, where she made many friends. By this time she was legally adult, in fact in her mid-twenties, and Barnardos could no longer control her movements.

She took a room in Glebe and started to think seriously about 'something different'. A leaflet caught her eye advertising a business college in George Street. She went to see the principal, who said to her: 'Start this afternoon.' The course cost £13 and subjects included book-keeping, typing and shorthand, arithmetic, and English. To save money she had to do the whole course in half the normal time.

She not only did the course, but came top. It was then time to seek employment. Her first job was in the Sydney markets, but her handwriting was too small and there were other difficulties. The college principal stepped in to help, and secured her an interview with a master plumber in Chatswood.

Kathleen was not very keen. In fact, she didn't even wear make up for the interview. With some reluctance she accepted the job – at £2 per week. The premises were shabby, but the boss was pleasant. 'On the first day he brought some cups, a billy can, and invited me to light a fire under a kerosine bucket so we could have a cup of tea.'

There were just five other employees. She was shocked by some of the plumbing terminology – male and female pipes etc – but took to book-keeping 'like a duck to water'.

Slowly the business expanded. 'The war came and we spent hours quoting for Government jobs. We moved to new premises; even employed a cleaner.' Kathleen's own responsibilities grew. She found herself running the office alone, while the boss was in the country. The staff now numbered 100.

She had been there about 11 years when 'the unforgivable happened. At least my boss thought so. I fell in love.' Kathleen and her husband

'Horry' (Horace) were married in April 1949. She was now Mrs Rourke. Their son Dennis was born the following year.

Kathleen gave up her job – she was then 39 – to concentrate on raising their son. Life was initially hard. The first family 'home' was a garage. Things gradually improved. The time came when she had the satisfaction of seeing her son sprawled out on the floor, in the manner she had envied at Young. When he called her 'mummy' the word had that special ring.

Eventually she returned to the workforce, holding a variety of jobs in accounting and book-keeping roles. Her plumber boss called her back, finally making her a director and company secretary. She was there, before and after her marriage, for a total 25 years. She took her last job – with The World of Wood, a manufacturer and supplier of doors and timber products – when she was 73. She stayed 14 years.

Her husband died in 1983. At about that time a leaflet arrived in her letter box. It said: 'Computer lessons will be starting at Narrabeen Learning Centre...' She thought: 'Why not?' Like the book-keeping course, it was a challenge. She was the oldest, and most favoured pupil. It was the beginning of a new interest.

Her sister Barbara died in 1991. Norah, the surviving twin, died of cancer two years later. It was an agonising death. Visiting her sister for the first time in hospital affected her profoundly. 'Norah lived at Epping and I was on the North Shore and didn't have a car, so we hadn't seen each other for a while. When I entered that ward I nearly walked out, thinking it was somebody else. I started feeding her, but couldn't stand it any longer. I put my spoon down and went outside and burst into tears.

'The shock of it all altered me. I used to sing and was always in the choir. Suddenly I couldn't sing any more.' A childhood stutter returned.

At about the time of her sister's death, Barnardos introduced its 'open files' policy. It was October 1986. Kathleen and others were allowed to inspect their personal records. She found the experience an eye-opener. 'The thoroughness was astonishing. Every letter I had ever written to someone at Barnardos, either from England or Australia – they were all there, and copies of their replies. There was a letter from my mother, pleading – unsuccessfully – that I be allowed to take on something other than domestic work.'

There were also reports from her employers and local Barnardos representatives. Some of them were unflattering. Many were untrue – overstating the amenities or exaggerating her 'happiness' in a particular household.

Kathleen Rourke is 93 (at the time of writing). Her home is now an 'independent living unit' on Queensland's Gold Coast. She enjoys regular visits from her son and keeps her brain alert by pounding away at her computer keyboard. When the author first spoke to her he asked if he could call her 'Cybergranny' She fancied the name and now uses it to sign off her email correspondence.

# 3

# The Dreadnought Experience

# 7

## 'Fear God and Dread Nought'

———

"Australia for Boys 5,000 Lads Wanted in Australia."
NSW Government campaign poster, about 1913

**A** SPRING MORNING[1] in the historic Rocks area of Sydney. Tourists are everywhere, but show little interest in the knot of about 50 people, standing on a street corner, waiting for a ceremony to begin. They had gathered to pay tribute to one of Australia's more unusual clans.

It started to rain buckets, and many of those present were in their eighties. But the Dreadnought Boys are made of stern stuff. Ralph Wood, then president of the Dreadnought Association, spurned even the loan of an umbrella.

The purpose of the meeting was to unveil a plaque in honour of the 'Boys'. It was actually the second unveiling; the plaque having been moved (slightly) and renovated, since its first unveiling on 20 April 1984. The downpour did not dampen the fervour of the speeches by, among others, State politicians Michael Photios and Jim Small, nor the warmth emanating from the very nature of the occasion.

The plaque, at the corner of Kendall Lane and Argyle Street, was paid for by the 'boys' themselves, which seems unfair. Four generations of Dreadnought families were present. The unveiling was performed by Robert and Tanya Elder, whose great-grandfather, George Elder, had come to Australia under the Dreadnought scheme in 1922.

The ceremony ended with the impromptu (and unaccompanied) singing of *Advance Australia Fair*, the singers having to do battle with the wind, rain, and tourist buses trundling by. Eden Thompson, 85, chided those present for not knowing the second verse.

During the singing, the older Dreadnoughts might have been forgiven for imagining they heard their own footsteps some 70 years earlier.

At that time, having disembarked in Walsh Bay, the young migrants

———

would have marched past the site of the present memorial, or very close to it, on their way to the old Empire Service Club in George Street North, where Dr Mary Booth[2] and the ANZAC Fellowship of Women served them tea and buns – their first meal in Australia. From there they marched to the Department of Labour and Industry, where they received a pep talk about jobs.

That night they would again sleep on the ship. After breakfast the next day, with bags packed, they would leave the ship for the last time to be conducted – possibly by British Empire idealist, Thomas Sedgwick[3] – to Central Station, where they were given tickets to whatever destination (probably a farm school) their mentors had in store.

The Dreadnought scheme, as its name implies, has nautical origins. The very word has overtones of empire, strength and resoluteness, which in a sense is what the scheme was all about.

The concept dates back to 1903, two years after Federation, when the Australian Government, lacking a Navy of its own, voted to pay £200,000 a year towards the expenses of the British Imperial Squadron in the Pacific.

In 1909, the Lord Mayor of Sydney, Sir Allen Taylor, motivated by the same concern and influenced by the threat of German naval power, convened a meeting in the Town Hall for the purpose of establishing a fund to purchase a *Dreadnought* class battleship, then considered the ultimate weapon in the Empire's defence arsenal.

The meeting passed the following resolution: 'That, in the opinion of this meeting of citizens glorying in the traditions of the British race, of which they are a part, the time has arrived for the Commonwealth to take an active share in the naval defence of the Empire.

'That, in view of the expressed determination of Britain's rivals to challenge her naval supremacy, Australia should present a *Dreadnought* to the British Navy as an immediate expression of her invincible resolve to stand by the Mother Country and take her place in the Empire's fighting line.'

Within four months of the Town Hall meeting, some £90,000 had been raised – an enormous sum by the standards of the day.[4] However, before the money could be handed over, it became known that the Federal Government had decided to establish an Australian Navy.

Clearly, local needs should take priority. Hence new purposes would have to be sought for the Dreadnought fund.

The organising committee subsequently decided to split the money raised into two, roughly equal, parts. A new Navy must have facilities to train its officers. The sum of £40,000 would be given to the Government to help establish a Naval College at Jervis Bay. The larger sum – a little over £50,000 – would be used to support the goal that 'every attempt should be made to encourage immigration from Great Britain'.

In pursuit of this aim the trustees of the Dreadnought Fund took over a farm at Pitt Town, near Windsor, north-west of Sydney. The trustees, who included such notables as Sir Allen Taylor (former Lord Mayor) and the retail magnate, Sir Samuel Hordern, simultaneously entered into an agreement with the Government to bring out British youths between the ages of 16 and 19 'of good character and physique at a rate of about 20 every fortnight, and to pay the Government £5 for each of the lads sent to the training farm'.

The Government and the Dreadnought trustees stated as their common aim that of 'securing the practical training of British youths in Australian farming methods, in order to encourage the best class of immigration to this State and assist in developing its resources and providing for its defence' Youths selected should be of 'high moral character and from the rural districts of Great Britain'.

The first Dreadnought youths – 12 in number, aged between 17 and 20 – left London on 3 March 1911, and arrived in Sydney on 20 April 1911. They travelled on the SS *Tainui* to Hobart, changing to the SS *Paloona* for the final leg to Sydney. They were followed by a party of 27 others on 15 June. *The Sydney Morning Herald* described them as 'fine, strapping young English fellows'[5]

The farm at Pitt Town has an interesting history, which predates the arrival of the first Dreadnought Boys. It was founded in 1893 as a co-operative village settlement. About 100 families participated in what was subsequently described as 'an early form of communism'. The venture failed within five years, and it became a casual labour farm where the unemployed could cut wood and get a bit of money.

## SCHEYVILLE

At this point one of the remarkable men in turn-of-the-20th century Sydney enters the scene. William Schey was a former union leader, active in the formation of the Railway and Tramway Employees Association, who was elected Member of the Legislative Assembly for Redfern, and later for Darlington, on the strength of the unionist vote. In 1900, the New South Wales Government appointed him Chief Labour Commissioner. In 1905, his title was changed to that of Director of Labour for the newly formed State Labour Bureau. Though criticised for holding a sinecure, he quickly proved himself a capable and most remarkable administrator.

Schey re-established the Pitt Town farm as the Government Agricultural Training Farm for Sydney Youths.[6] Though well patronised, numbers were insufficient for the farm's large size (1,000 hectares). It was considered tailor-made for the activities of the newly created Dreadnought Scheme.

Schey was an Orangeman, and prominent Freemason, whose personal philosophy was in tune with this new role. That the farm itself came to be known as *Scheyville* illustrates his strength of conviction and interest in its development.

Early Dreadnought Boys (all now deceased) described him as 'round faced, with neat, small beard' and as a man of 'amazing energy'. Schey, who died in 1913, personally welcomed the first group of boys at a ceremony at Challis House, in the city. He told the newcomers, who were straight off the ship, that Australia was 'a great country' and if they had any problems they should go straight to him. He said each boy would be given a rifle and should 'learn to shoot straight'. He added that in his view all young Australians should undergo military training.

Scheyville was not the only training centre to which Dreadnought Boys were sent. There were a limited number of places at other farms run by the NSW Department of Agriculture. These were more specialised – fruit, sheep or cattle – experimental farms, and were located at Wollongbar, near the Queensland border, Grafton, Glen Innes, Arrawatta, Cowra and Yanco.

In selecting boys, the Dreadnought Trustees in Australia relied initially on various British-based organisations, including the somewhat bluntly titled Central Unemployed Body, formed in London under the Unemployed Workmen's Act of 1905. The Act provided financial assistance to charitable bodies engaged in emigration.

The NSW Government promised to do what it could to find employment for the boys when they left the training farms, but this could not be guaranteed. It accepted no legal responsibility (after training) beyond 'conveying the boy to the town nearest to the training farm'.

Scheyville had 'rules' similar to an English boarding school. Youths – most aged between 15 and 17, but some as old as 19 – slept in dormitories with lights out at 9.30 pm. A memo on a file in the Australian Archives says dormitories were under the charge of ex-AIF sergeants, and that domestic arrangements were maintained 'to conform with those the lads will experience subsequently in employment'.

During meals in the communal dining hall, and in the reading and writing rooms, conversation was restricted. No liquor was allowed anywhere on the farm.

Schey had, sensibly, limited the period of training to three months. Even this – in view of the rather severe lifestyle – was not to the liking of many of them. Schey himself, in his initial report to the Dreadnought trustees, said that of the 61 boys so far received, only six had stayed for three months, although many others had satisfied him as being sufficiently trained. Happily for the boys, demand for labour was at that time intense. Employers were particularly eager to take on a Dreadnought Boy.

Unfortunately for the Dreadnought trustees, the advertised intention of sending fortnightly shipments of 20 lads quickly proved optimistic. In 1911 and 1912 – the first two years of operation – there were a total of 202 and 233 boys respectively. There is a story that one of the shipments contained teenage girls, who also went to Scheyville, but were sent home when a number of them became pregnant. The Dreadnought Association says the entire episode is 'a myth'.

There were other problems. There was an 'understanding' that, after a reasonable passage of time, Dreadnought Boys should be required to refund the cost (or part thereof) of their passage to Australia. In the 1920s this was £11 sterling for lads over 17 years and under 19 years, and £5 sterling for those under 17 years.

The duty to repay the money was inadequately conveyed to some of the boys. Albert Page was alarmed – while working on a remote rural property – to be visited by a trooper demanding £4 as part payment towards this sum. The trooper came back twice more until the £11 was paid off. A further unwelcome surprise came when he turned 21 and the same trooper summoned him to Court for failing to register for the vote.

'Youth is what Australia represents to the whole world.
She is young herself; to the young she is especially alluring.
The Boy, above all, Australia particularly understands and wants.'
Advertisement by Governments of Victoria and NSW, 1913

It is said that imitation is a form of flattery. In 1912, the New South Wales Department of Agriculture, impressed by the Dreadnought Scheme, directly recruited youths from England for its agricultural colleges. During 1913, NSW and Victoria combined their immigration offices in London. An advertising campaign was launched to attract 5,000 lads on to Australian farms. A typical advertisement stated:

'Australia is a fine country for everybody, but above all for young people. Its sunny freedom, its unlimited offer of opportunity, its enormous natural wealth, its undeveloped condition, which calls for energy and muscle and confidence – all this appeals to the Boy, nay, claims him.

'Youth is what Australia represents to the whole world. She is young herself; to the young she is especially alluring. The Boy, above all, Australia particularly understands and wants.'

In 1913/14, before the tides of war put a stop to immigration, the Dreadnought trustees widened the net of their recruitment programme, which now included boys from all parts of the British Isles, with a good mix between rural and industrial areas.

A number of Jewish boys were recruited, via Jewish organisations in London, for agricultural training at Scheyville. Whether or not they technically formed part of the Dreadnought Scheme is unclear.

There was also an attempt to attract 'young lads of superior education', an idea later pursued by the Big Brother Movement,[7] which led, in turn, to an emphasis on boy migrants as empire-builders rather than as fodder for farms and factories.

In 1913 there were 148 Dreadnought arrivals in New South Wales, and in 1914 there were 175. World War I put a stop to immigration, but not to the activities of the Dreadnoughts. By 1916, many of the Dreadnought Boys who had come out in the first four years of the scheme (1911-1914) were old enough to fight. Almost all did so. By 1916 at least 200 former Dreadnought Boys were back in the old world – this time in the trenches.

The Dreadnought Scheme recommenced in 1921 and the first post-war migrants came in October of that year. Many of the Dreadnought lads were – by Australian standards – well educated. A party of 40 Dreadnought Boys, who arrived on the *Themistocles*, in 1922, included 14 boys who had attended English public schools.[8]

The Dreadnought Scheme started as a New South Wales initiative and remained so. In 1923 a British Oversea Settlement delegation arrived in Australia to inspect the early results of Empire Settlement. The delegation was impressed with the work of the Dreadnought Scheme, leading to suggestions that the British Government would endow it financially. By 1925, the scheme's funds were running low,[9] creating a dilemma. While financial support was welcomed – from Australia as well as Britain – there were qualms among the trustees about the political influence this would bring.

In particular, there were fears about the unknown attitude of the NSW Labor Government, and its maverick leader, Jack Lang. The trade union movement at the time was highly suspicious of the Dreadnought and, indeed, all migration schemes, regarding them as an attempt to get and control cheap labour for farmers. The Lang Government, while sympathetic to this view, did not intervene decisively. Interestingly, more assisted immigrants were to arrive in NSW under Labor than under the previous non-Labor Fuller Government.

By 1925, the Australian and British Governments were jointly paying two-thirds of the £33 pounds fare, whilst the New South Wales Government was paying the full cost of training at Scheyville.

The Dreadnought Scheme was by now well established and had acquired a very good image. Applicants required at least two references and a medical certificate. There were boys from middle class as well as working class families, some of whom, as previously noted, had attended (but been forced to leave due to change in parental circumstances) minor English public schools.

As numbers of youth migrants increased – including those sponsored directly by the New South Wales Government – more elaborate arrangements had to be made for their reception. The YMCA, Boy Scouts, Church organisations and numerous smaller groups all had a hand in welcoming and settling in newcomers, and sending them on their way to farm schools or direct to places of employment.

There were internal feuds – on matters which now seem petty – between many of these organisations. In 1927 scandal was caused when an official of the YMCA was heard counselling Dreadnought Boys (who had just stepped off the ship) to have nothing to do with the Empire Service Club. At about this time the Empire Service Club, through Dr Mary Booth, hit on the idea of producing a monthly magazine, *The Boy Settler*. It was intended to help Dreadnoughts (and others) keep in touch with one another and to provide information on farming and life in the country. Its faded pages have provided valuable information to present day researchers.

By the late 1920s, only about half the newly-arrived Dreadnought Boys were being sent to *Scheyville*. The remainder went to the other experimental or training farms or, in some cases, direct to rural employment.

## WOODEN COW

Training methods at *Scheyville* were primitive. Lessons in milking were given on an imitation 'cow' – a Heath Robinson device of bladders and wooden supports. In 1926, a British High Commission representative in Australia, W. Bankes Amery, visited *Scheyville* and reported to London: 'The boys complained somewhat of their meals but the food is of good quality and is ample in quantity. I myself had lunch there and had the same food as was being supplied to the boys and saw no reason for complaint.'

Apart from hard work there was not much else to do at *Scheyville*. Some boys walked into Windsor or other nearby settlements to buy food, go to church or for simple amusements. In the late 1920s, a group of ladies from Windsor, who called themselves the Scheyville Entertainment Club, occasionally visited the farm. The boys themselves sometimes organised entertainments such as boxing matches.

An incident in 1925 caused concern in British and NSW official circles when the father of a Dreadnought Boy complained to Australia House, in London, about the way his son was being treated. The lad was employed by a boarding house keeper who also ran a small farm near Moss Vale in the Southern Highlands. The boy was required to do dirty work around the boarding house as well as farm labour, and living in dirty quarters he caught scabies.

## 'Work here is not labour, it is slavery, pure and simple.'

Resulting from the scabies incident a circular was sent to Dreadnought Boys whose addresses were held, asking for their views on the scheme. Of a surviving sample of 46 responses sent to London, only five openly admitted to dissatisfaction with the scheme or the way in which they had been treated. The clearest complaint came from a boy working on a dairy farm, who stated: 'Work here is not labour, it is slavery, pure and simple.'

Officials in London also became concerned at a number of suicides among juvenile farm workers, which seemed to indicate severe problems of loneliness and isolation for new arrivals. Between 1923 and early 1925 there were six suicides of Barwell Boys (a farm school broadly similar to *Scheyville*) in South Australia, also one Queensland farm apprentice and a Dreadnought Boy who shot himself reportedly after being 'moody' and saying that he was lonely.

An investigation found that the rate of suicides among youngsters, aged 15-19, arriving under the various juvenile migration schemes was 1:532 compared to 1:5,955 among the Australian male population as a whole in the same age group. Another two Dreadnought Boys committed suicide in 1925, while from September 1925 until mid-1926 there were reportedly nine accidental deaths through drowning amongst juvenile migrants throughout Australia.

Promoters of youth migration – and certainly the lads themselves – had as their eventual goal that the young migrants should take up land on their own account rather than be permanently working for someone else.

In 1927 the New Settlers' League asked the Land Settlement Committee, NSW, to investigate the matter since, under an agreement signed in 1923, certain Dreadnoughts were eligible for grants.

The Dreadnought Boys' 'lack of capital' was the crucial issue. Correspondence now lodged in the Australian Archives shows that there were, at the time, 20 blocks in the Murrumbidgee Irrigation Area soon to be available. Four Dreadnought lads had applied, but only one possessed the £300 capital qualification, even 'before character references are considered'.

The reply by a senior public servant is tart. 'The £300 minimum capital is too low; the settler must have something to live on while trees grow and crops mature – and to make improvements. The boys cannot make a success on the capital stated. In view of these statements and the great uncertainty of the boy being successful, my executive has decided that it is inadvisable to encourage the boys to take up blocks upon the conditions offered ... share farming opportunities are best.'

The Great Depression was to seriously defer all such ambitions. The intake of young migrants was halted. Dreadnought Boys already in Australia, most of whom were still in low paid rural jobs and among the 'battlers' of society, were seriously disadvantaged.[11]

In July 1938, with the Depression easing, the Dreadnought trustees met once again after a break of over six years, and agreed to sponsor the monthly nomination of 25 boys. As stated elsewhere, only 76 Dreadnought Boys were to arrive under the new arrangements.

## THE LAST DREADNOUGHTS

The Dreadnought Scheme, which originated due to the desire to strengthen Empire defences against the threat from the Kaiser's Germany, ended in 1939, when Britain and Australia went to war against the Germany of Adolf Hitler. It was a victory of sorts for the Hun. The last party of 10 Dreadnought Boys sailed from England in August, and arrived in Sydney on September 9; six days after the formal declaration of hostilities.

*The Boy Settler*, still in existence in the 1940s, maintained a roll of honour of all known to have joined up. By February 1944, it had a list of 145 former Dreadnought Boys in the Australian military services.

Fifty years on, about 100 people attended the 1994 reunion lunch, in the presence of the movement's then patron, the NSW Governor, Rear

Admiral Peter Sinclair. A pianist played *Wild Colonial Boy* and *When You're Smiling*. When the time came for the 'Boys' (as opposed to their guests) to stand to take a toast, barely 20 struggled to their feet.

At the time of the luncheon the youngest Dreadnought Boy was 75 and the oldest 100. To compensate for its thinning ranks the Dreadnought Old Boys' Association decided to drop the term 'Old Boys' from its title, and to admit widows, sons and daughters, grandchildren, and other supporters of the movement, to full membership.[12]

The association's vice-president for 1994/95, Bill Wilson, who was then 83, told me: 'The last remnants of our old timers are fading away and we've barely got enough to run the show.'

Four years on, in April 1998 a motion was put to disband the Dreadnought Association. Members were reluctant to take this final step and voting was deferred until the following year, when it was decided, amidst some confusion, to try to keep the organisation going. However, there was a problem in finding office holders – an offer of assistance from the Big Brother Movement[13] was considered and rejected – and in April 1999 the association formally folded. At least, so it was thought at the time.

There were some nice speeches at the 'final' meeting. Ian Vernon, chairman and newsletter editor, whose father, Reg, came out on the *Athenic*, in 1927, said: 'They might have a change of steering, but they'll never change the history of the Dreadnoughts.'

Bill Wilson, who had regarded the disbanding of the association as inevitable, said he was not personally saddened. 'We served our function which was to bring together the fellows who migrated under common circumstances and had a common interest, common experiences and very strong friendships.'

Actually, the movement did not totally disband. The Sydney-based organisation had long had an affiliate in northern NSW, known as the Dreadnought Association, Far North Coast. This autonomous body, in a region where many Dreadnought Old Boys worked and settled, continues to exists, and in February, 2001 took over the general running of the Dreadnought Association.[14] The NSW Governor, Professor Marie Bashir, followed her predecessors in agreeing to become the revamped association's patron.

A newsletter produced in 2001 had photos of the annual reunion at Wollongbar Agricultural Institute. Among those present was Wall Roberts, 93, who arrived in 1924 on the *Sophoces*, and 'mere youngster' Sandy Richmond, 77, who arrived in 1939 on the *Oronsay*, as part of what may have been the very last Dreadnought contingent.

The Far North Coast Dreadnoughts have produced a book of memoirs, *They Passed This Way*, and are planning a sequel, provisionally titled *These Also Came: More Stories of the Dreadnought Boys*.

Altogether, nearly 7,500 lads came to Australia under the auspices of the Dreadnought Scheme. To be precise 1,787 boys between 1911-14 and 5,669 boys between 1919 and 1939.

## RING OF PRIDE

The badge of the Dreadnought Association depicts, appropriately, a battleship on the high seas. Admiral Sinclair, in his speech to the 1994 reunion, said there was a ring of pride about the very name *Dreadnought*, and it was fitting they had chosen it as their emblem.

He told the gathering: 'You who wear [the badge] are, like the battleship, "tough and strong, able to withstand stormy seas". You have been steeled and strengthened by your experience.'

The *Dreadnought* class battleship was, in its heyday, way ahead of its rivals and established the pattern of the all-big-gun warship that dominated the world's navies for nearly 40 years.

The *Dreadnought* and the lighter *Invincible* class battle cruiser were the brainchild of a remarkable Englishman, Admiral John Arbuthnot 'Jackie' Fisher, who joined the Navy at 13, served as a midshipman in the Crimean War, and rose to become First Sea Lord. Fisher is also credited with introducing the torpedo and submarine.

First built in 1906, *The Dreadnought* had four propellers driven by steam turbines and displaced 21,845 tons. It was capable of a speed of 21 knots (23 miles per hour) and mounted ten 12-inch guns in five turrets.

The name *Dreadnought* is said to have come from Admiral Fisher's use of the phrase 'Fear God and dread nought', which was used as the title for a published collection of his letters.

# 8

# Hard Times, but few Regrets

———

'Are you pleased that you came out to Australia
under the Dreadnought Scheme?' '
Oh yes, it was the best thing I ever did.
I wouldn't have swapped my life for anything with anybody.'
Ralph Wood, Dreadnought Boy

THE HARD TIME EXPERIENCED by so many of the youth migrants form a common thread to many of the stories told in this volume. Hard times, but many say they have no regrets and would do it again.

Linda Rose, daughter of Harry Jackson, a Dreadnought Boy, says the first farmer her father worked for housed him in an unlined corrugated iron shed. When the lad complained , his employer sneered 'So long as it isn't a fowl house I can house youse how I like.'

According to his daughter: 'I asked dad why he had never mentioned that before, and he said it doesn't do to dwell on negative aspects, and a lot of Aussie lads were treated just the same.'

Bill Wilson, the last president of the (Sydney-based) Dreadnought Association, dissents from the generally rosy view.

'It was an ill-conceived scheme of migration. The boys were too young and naive to be the targets of the romantic literature which Australia House used to recruit them. They were recruited for an industry which, over a long period, had been shedding its labour force under pressure of technological progress and market forces.

'The printed material implied that the boys, after gaining experience and saving their money, would be able to buy their own farms. In the circumstances of the 1920s this was unrealistic. When farm prices collapsed in the 1930s, it became a bad joke.

'All the Dreadnought Boys were literate and some had secondary education, but at the age they migrated they had not had a chance to acquire any worthwhile occupational skill. Their total initial capital was

89

in most cases not much more than their two pounds landing money.

'Yet despite these initial handicaps a great many Dreadnought Boys did succeed in establishing themselves as solid citizens of Australia. In fact they branched out into a truly astonishing variety of careers and occupations.'

Catholic social historian, Brother Dr Barry Coldrey, who has almost clinically examined[1] youth migration records in the Australian Archives, with special attention to the Dreadnought Boys, says there was 'a culture shock involved in youth migration, and it comes through on just about every file.'

According to Coldrey: 'It is moving stuff because these lads had travelled so far. Backpackers were not then in vogue, and there wasn't the instant means of communications that exists now.

'They came from London, or crowded midland cities to wide open spaces and often rough and ready accommodation. Some probably hoped to make their fortune. Others had simpler goals. Many were pathetically young. You can get a very mature 15 or 16-year-old and you can get a very immature one.'

One example of 'culture shock' is shown in the unsuitable clothing which many of the young people brought with them. Coldrey tells the apocryphal story of the youth who arrived in the early 1930s with a small suitcase carrying virtually his total possessions – two clean shirts, a change of underwear, and silk pyjamas. When he got to the farm the farmer pointed out a hay shed and said basically: 'This is your bedroom.'

His bed was, in fact, a palliasse, with straw coming through. When he went to bed that night, he found the straw was penetrating his silk pyjamas, and in very embarrassing places.

It seems others were aware of this situation. A cartoon of the period, located by Coldrey in the Australian Archives, has an English boy, arriving at his place of employment, in spats and a bowler hat, with golf clubs and lunch basket.

In the case of the Dreadnought Lads promotional material exaggerated the attractions of the Scheyville training farm. The much vaunted swimming pool, which would have had strong appeal to English youths, turned out to be an unhygienic muddy dam. According to Bill Wilson the philosophy was 'Take a farm dam, stick a diving board on it and call it a swimming pool.'

Coldrey comments: 'It was a poorer world, in which people had to make their fun with a lot less money and sophistication. So a swimming pool might often be just a country dam where local kids swam bare-arsed without a care in the world. If you had a storm maybe the dam blew away, and you had to build it again. The same hole did for the beasts to drink out of as well as the kids to swim in.'

Certainly, the difficulties faced by the young migrants – as revealed in their stories – were very real.

Many left England to avoid the ravages of the Depression. They found an even worse situation in Australia. According to Coldrey: 'We talk about the Depression as if it was a short period. But for many of these youngsters it lasted right up to the outbreak of war. Life was hard, but not necessarily always miserable. As I have said, people had to make their own fun, but they didn't have much money to do it with. And not much sophistication.'

## ON THE DOLE

'Towards the end of November I ran out of money. The Salvation Army had an institution for destitute men in Foster Street, and I moved in there. I felt a strange feeling of relief when I did so.

'I had hit bottom. The Salvo refuge provided clean beds, showers, and two meals a day in return for the dole ration coupons. These were issued once a fortnight to the city unemployed from an office on Number 7 Wharf, Walsh Bay.

'The dole coupons were valued at seven shillings and sixpence a week. For breakfast at the refuge we were given two great slabs of bread, thinly smeared with melted butter, two sausages and a mug of tea. Dinner was stew or casserole, bread, a piece of fruit and a cup of tea.

'Everyone had to be out of the refuge by 9 am and the doors were closed until 4 pm. The bulk of the "guests" at Foster Street at that time were not drop-outs. Most of them nursed an inner pride and they tried to keep up appearances. The social atmosphere reminded me, in some of its aspects, of the debtors' prison in Pickwick Papers.'

*(High School-educated Dreadnought Boy, Bill Wilson, describing life on the dole.)*

## MEMORY LANE

The surviving Dreadnought Boys are getting on in years.[2] Many are now in nursing homes and find their memories are fading into the mist. Some have recorded their memoirs on tape, others in typed manuscripts. All are anxious that their grandchildren and future generations should know of their experiences.

For many youth migrants the goodbyes with their parents were traumatic. Long gaps before reunions were normal. Some even feared problems of recognition. The sister of one young migrant was worried that she wouldn't recognise him again. She said: 'You'll be black.'

Probably the most vivid memories retained by surviving Dreadnought Boys – apart from sad farewells – are of the sea voyage[3] and the few weeks spent at a training farm.

Like a national serviceman's experience of 'boot camp', the initiation into farm life was unforgettable. Passengers for Scheyville alighted at Mulgrave railway station, from where they were conveyed – at first by dray[4], later by a motor truck – to the farm. Many were met by an Irishman, Andy, whose joke was to point out crosses and trees along the way, claiming they were memorials to boys who had died on the farm.

Andy was an expert horse handler despite his small stature. He slept in quarters attached to the stable, and when he lost his temper with one of the boys he would yell 'Scum of the earth – 2/6.'[5] However, he was generally regarded as a good fellow.

Wilf Bennett,[6] who came out on the *Beltana* in 1926, recalled: 'Andy controlled the stables and horses. He carried out his job with an iron hand. Absolutely nobody argued with him. He was a law unto himself and knew more about horses than most horse trainers.

'I found under his gruff manner, however, that he was always ready to explain any points that we brought up. It was different if one tried to be smart with him. I learnt a lot the week I trained under his guidance, as did most other boys. The problem was nearly all the boys came from city areas and didn't have a clue about handling and managing horses.'

Harry Jackson, who came to Australia in 1929, found another reason to remember Andy. 'He retired while we were at Scheyville and I took him to the station. I think that was the first time I saw a grown man cry.'

To Wilf it was a big adventure. 'On arrival at Scheyville we were taken to one of two dormitories and allotted our beds. Our gear was kept beside our bed. The dormitory was large and airy and the beds were comfortable. There was a row of beds down each side and I think about 40 boys in our hut.'

Harry Jackson discovered that sleeping accommodation was arranged in an interesting manner. 'There were dormitories for various age groups and groups of arrivals, also a "scallywags" dorm – to which I was moved for upending one of the folding beds whilst the lad was in it. There was also a dorm for boys who snored badly.'

A boy who arrived in 1922, gave a less attractive account. 'The dormitories were large, but we found that the first night we had other occupants – bed bugs – thousands of them.'

According to Wilf: 'After settling in, we were taken to the dining room and kitchens which were about half a mile away from the sleeping area. We had our first meal – the food was plain and the bread was baked on the farm. We had our first insight into the Australian way of calling golden syrup "cocky's joy". We found that a cocky wasn't a parrot but the slang name given to farmers.'

It appears hygiene was noticeably absent. Another boy recalls: 'The cook's name was "Dirty Dick". He had a battery of wood burning stoves and we took it in turn to help him. He or a boy would place sticks on bread on the stoves to make "toast" and if there was a gap between slices, he would spit tobacco and stained spittle between the gaps. He could drown an insect 10 feet away.'

According to another boy: 'After our first meal we were shown the notice board which listed our daily work routine and also shown the window in an office where we could buy stamps and post letters. We were also told that we would also receive a weekly allowance of one shilling and threepence. We spent the money on stamps and also were able to buy little round biscuits with sweet icing on the top.'

Farm training began the next day. In the dairying class Harry Jackson was introduced to Scheyville's famed artificial cow. 'This was a fake cow's udder at which we sat to learn how to milk by hand. It was actually a leather bag with four rubber teats and much more difficult to milk than the real thing.' A punishment for minor misdemeanours was to have to 'milk' two gallons of water from it.

From artificial cows to the genuine article. According to Wilf Bennett: 'Training involved learning to milk cows twice a day, which meant starting work at daybreak. We were taught how to feed the cattle and process the milk and clean the equipment. Whilst we were on this job a giant of a blind Clydesdale horse was used to pull machinery up to the silo. I was told he lost his sight when he was over-strained pulling a heavy load.'

Boys from city backgrounds had to cope with the heat and hard manual work. In his second week Wilf was introduced to timber cutting. 'The man in charge was an old bush man who had lost a leg and was a real character. He seemed rather surly and was a hard man.

'We drove horse drays out into the bush. It was a stinking hot day and we were given axes and had to cut down the trees he pointed out, then cut them into lengths and load them into the drays.

'It was a mystery to me that nobody was hurt with trees falling down. I did notice that we were instructed which way to fell the tree and we had to call out "timber" when the tree started to fall.

'When we arrived back and unloaded the drays, we were a very sorry lot of boys who had badly blistered hands and were worn out. We weren't allowed to slack on the job and most boys had never had physical work like that before. The next day we were put on cook house duty. I think we were given light duties to allow us to recover.'

The course at Scheyville also included training in piggery work. As Wilf tells it: 'My brother Fred [also a Dreadnought Boy] and I were on piggery duty, which was a filthy job. One thing we had to do was scrape the meat off all the bones and offal. The bones were sent away for processing. It was not only filthy but smelly. In the midst of it someone told us that VIPs had called to visit. When we met them I noticed that they kept well to windward of us. They didn't stay very long.'

A more pleasant task involved orchard training. 'We spent three weeks working in the orchard, picking the biggest peaches – nine to a case – which were sold at Central Station. We were told we could eat as many as we liked. Boy! What a tummy ache! I couldn't look at a peach for 10 years after that.'

Training include learning how to slaughter animals. Wilf Bennett again: 'One of my last memories of Scheyville and the worst one was when four of the boys, including myself, had to report to a shed and we were instructed how to kill and dress sheep.

'I had to pull a sheep's head back over my knee and push a knife through its neck and turn the knife round and cut out then hold the animal while it bled to death, then skin it and disembowel it. I think I was then sick from the shock. I'm sure a more humane method could have been used.'

Wilf and his brother found little time for hobbies or leisure interests. 'We had brought our box Brownie camera with us, also some film and chemicals to process and print the photos.

'We found we could develop the film in the wash basins at the end of our dormitory and we were able to print the pictures by the light of an Aladdin light on the table which ran down the centre of our hut. We also processed film from some of the other lads until the warder in charge of the dormitory found out what we were doing and that finished that.'

## FIRST JOB
Next in line on the newcomers' list of memories is taking up their first job. The very remoteness of so many farm properties meant that just getting there was often an ordeal. Wilf Bennett offers a fairly typical example.

'My brother Fred and I were sent to jobs in the Nowra area. We travelled by train from Sydney, arriving at Bomaderry Station about midday. Fred was met by Mr Barron and he worked for him for five years and was treated as one of the family.

I waited on the platform for about an hour and nobody turned up to meet me.

'I had the address of the farm and I made enquiries and found out I had to take the bus to the other side of the Shoalhaven River to Nowra, then found I had about six miles to go to the property.

'After making enquiries, I was directed to the road I had to take. It was February and very hot; I was carrying a suitcase and kit bag. I came to a post office and asked whether I could leave my kit bag there. The people were very kind and gave me a drink. Then they told me I wasn't on the direct road and was walking the long way round. I set out after being given the right road and had only walked about 100 yards when a man in a sulky pulled up and asked where I was going. He said "Hop in, I have a property near there and you are very lucky as they are a lovely family." I was very happy to hear that.

'We arrived and Mr Borrowdale looked at me and because I was rather small, he didn't know whether I could do the job but said he would give me a go. After about two days my wrists were very, very swollen. Mrs Borrowdale sewed tight bandages round my wrists and said "Stick it out, you will be all right." I was with the Borrowdales for five years and was treated as one of the family.'

The 'one of the family' reception was not universal. Many of the young British migrants – whose heavy workloads gave them big appetites – were upset at being told to eat their meals separately, often being given inferior food. In one case history given to me, the farmer's daughter smuggled food to the English lad, and eventually left home because of her father's 'meanness'.

Barry Coldrey says this should be taken within the context of the time. 'I don't want to be the old Australian defending anything and everything. I am saying that, while it wasn't very charitable, the idea that kids of 15 or 16 had the same rights as family members was not sustainable, at least at that time.'

Sectarian attitudes in employment were also common. Bill Wilson recalls a man 'asking me questions about whether I believed in the miracles at Lourdes and so forth. I replied in terms which didn't please him and consequently I didn't get the job.'

Many of the newcomers experienced loneliness, though hard work gave little time for contemplation. Bill Steele, who arrived in New South Wales in January 1928, had a novel experience. 'When I first arrived I wrote to my parents regularly. But then, I regret, I dropped off. One day I was working on this property and this ancient vehicle came up to the main gate. Out steps a policeman, who asked: "Are you so-and-so?" I told him I was, and he said: "I've been ordered to give you a reprimand for not writing to your parents".'

## AUSSIE WIVES

At a function in 1997 the then New South Wales Governor, Gordon

Samuels, said he had been told the secret of the success of the Dreadnought Boys was their Australian wives.

To this a shaky, elderly voice responded: 'One of the greatest things that ever happened to me in this country and in all my travels and trials was coming on the scene of my dear one. She's an Australian, a bloody Australian. Same as we used to be called Bloody Poms.'

Amidst laughter, a female voice – presumably his wife – chipped in: 'I didn't know at the time that he was a Dreadnought Boy.'

As with other juvenile migration schemes, the bond among the Dreadnought Boys is very close, and has extended to their wives and families.

Rita Neame (born Rita Jones) has married two Dreadnought Boys. Her first husband, Bill Moseley, from Wigan, Lancashire, came out on the *Demosthenes* in 1922. They met in Sydney in 1942, when, over a period of several months, they found themselves sharing the same tram – he on night work coming home, she on her way to 'war work' at Standard Telephones and Cables.

They were married on VE Day. 'I was 21. It was a marvellous day for a wedding; there were streamers everywhere, people out celebrating. We took the ferry to Manly for our honeymoon at the Pacific Hotel. It was only two days but it was lovely.' After the war the couple acquired a large house in Bellevue Hill, formerly a private hospital, and converted it into a guest house, which they called *Fairweather*. 'We had such interesting people, Naval officers, and people from Europe who had lost their entire families.'

Bill Moseley died in 1975. His widow tried to run the guest house alone, receiving support from, among others, Bill's friend, Clifford Neame, a Dreadnought Boy from Tonbridge, Kent, who had come out on the *Vedic* in 1925.

Cliff, a widower, returned to Britain in the late 1970s – sadly, too late to see his mother, who had also died, but in time to see a sick brother, who 'hung on' until his arrival.

After about four years Cliff came back to Australia. As Rita tells it: 'He thought I needed a break, and used to take me to a show and that sort of thing, and we decided to marry.' Clifford Neame died in 1992. The twice-widowed Rita continued to attend Dreadnought reunions, where she partied like a teenager. 'It gave me a really happy feeling,' She told me.

# 9

## Old Boys and Older Boys

—

*'I am getting along A1 and like this life though it is rough... I live with the*
*boundary rider in a tin hut and I've had to make my own furniture. This con-*
*sists of a wash-stand made from a Sunlight soap box, a table, seat and book*
*shelf made from kerosene boxes.*
*'My bed, which is the only thing I have not made, rests on boxes for fear*
*that some fine night when the moon shines bright*
*it might fall to bits...*
*'A lot of my time is spent in the saddle*
*and I reckon my legs are like hoop iron. If they do not*
*come up to that mark in strength they do in shape.'*
Letter from Dreadnought Boy, George Elder, to a friend (1925).

D READNOUGHT OLD BOYS have followed a variety of callings
from dairy farmer to dance band leader, Member of Parliament[1]
to master builder, plumber to policeman.

A notable Old Boy was the late Sid Black, long-time illustrator for
*The Bulletin*, one of whose cartoons is reproduced in this volume.

Another was the Rev Arthur Brawn, a former president of the association, whose personal crusade on behalf of 1,500 Australian war dead
inspired the writing of this book.[2]

One of the better known Dreadnought Boy had a profile very different to the Empire-loyalist, pro-establishment image commonly associated with the movement.

Ernest Thornton was born in England in 1907 in the old wool textile city of Huddersfield, Yorks, the son of a tram driver and an Irish
domestic servant. He was left motherless at two and raised by his father.
He attended local board schools and, still only 14, worked in factories and
on construction sites where he became interested in radical politics.

An old Scottish socialist advised him: 'Always ask for a rise or you'll never get more pay.' He did and he got the sack. Thornton migrated to Australia in 1924, age 17, under the Dreadnought Scheme.

Thornton settled in Victoria where he took jobs as a farm labourer, road construction worker; also working in the Geelong saltworks and a Northcote pipe plant. He was sacked from a road construction gang during the Depression, apparently for encouraging Italian migrants to speak up for themselves and demand award wages.

He became involved in the Unemployed Workers' Movement, a 'fraternal' of the Communist Party of Australia, and in 1931 joined the Party proper. According to his wife, Lila: 'Ernie used to go along to the bank of the Yarra for meetings on a Sunday. He came home one Sunday and told me he had joined the Communist Party. I was horrified.'

His wife's misgivings did not last for long. She said the Communists spoke about what things could be like under Communism, with no unemployment and plenty of food and clothing for the children. 'At that time we were renting a room in Clifton Street, Richmond, and I was worried about how I was going to get some shoes for the boys to wear. I thought to myself wouldn't it be good if we didn't have those worries?' An official came over to their room that night and enrolled Mrs Thornton as well. It was to become a life-long commitment for both of them.

Ernie Thornton quickly rose to positions of influence in both the Communist Party and the trade union movement, becoming, in 1936, general secretary of the Federated Ironworkers Association of Australia. That union was considered the jewel in the crown of the CPA because of the industrial strength it brought to the Party.

## RED CZAR

Politicians feared and loathed him. Others grudgingly admired him. He was called the 'Red Czar of Australia'. Physically, he was an amazing looking character. He had beetle black eyebrows, wore his hat pulled down over his eyes and (according to his enemies) 'looked like a thug'. His admirers were hardly more flattering. One of them described his smile as 'like that of a sabre toothed tiger'.

Thornton's reputation was not confined to Australia. He was a leading Communist internationally, being active in the Moscow-dominated

World Federation of Trade Unions. This activity alone led many Australians to consider him a traitor.

There were others within the Australian union movement anxious to topple him. This was very nearly accomplished in 1949, when, after a battle of more than 15 years, Laurie Short, Thornton's chief opponent and rival for power, beat him in the battle for secretary of the Ironworkers Association.

Defeat was not immediate. Amidst charges of fraud and forgery, Short was deprived of his victory until the Arbitration Court, after wrangling lasting nearly two years, found in his favour and declared Short to have been elected.

By that time Thornton, who had anticipated the outcome, had left Australia to become full time liaison officer with the World Federation of Trade Unions. In 1953, he returned to Australia, and tried to rejoin his old union but was refused membership.

He later joined the Federated Engine Drivers and Firemens Association, but was not active in union circles. From 1957 to 1967 Ernie Thornton was a full-time employee of the Communist Party of Australia. He suffered a heart attack in December 1968, and died the following June.

In union journals Thornton sometimes mentioned his Dreadnought roots, describing the conditions faced by himself and his companions in terms of 'slavery'. It would be fair to say that, nowadays, he is not among the most honoured of Dreadnought Boys, and his name is rarely mentioned.[3]

## REFUSED PAY CUT

*'A stranger I came to this land,*
*Leaving a land of rain and of snow.*
*There I was given the warm hand,*
*Of a people who helped me to grow.'*

Eden Thompson, from Newcastle-on-Tyne, turned 17 on the voyage to Australia in the *SS Borda*. It was 1927. Although he already had a job, he had been lured by adventure and the fact that his mother, a socialist, would not let him join the Army.

'You'll ne'er come back again,' his friends and neighbours told him, and they were right. After disembarking in Sydney, he was sent to a training farm near Yanco. One day the manager asked all the boys to be outside the office. As he tells it: 'When we were all there the manager and a well dressed man, wearing a business suit, walked among us, looking us over. The man pointed to me and the manager called me over.

'The fellow asked if I would like to work for him on his farm about 20 miles away. He said he'd give me one pound a week and keep. The work would not be hard, looking after cattle and sheep, so I said yes and went in to pack my bag and later left with him in his big Fiat car.

'We arrived at his home, which was not the usual farmer's house. It was made of weatherboard, but the walls and ceilings were plastered, and it was lit by acetylene gas. As the car rolled to a stop a lady came out and stood alongside. My employer introduced me and said his wife would set out my work for me. We then went in for lunch and I found myself sitting at a table in the corridor just inside the door. There were two other employees sitting with me. The family ate in the dining room.

'After lunch the lady told me that I would be working for her, milking the cows and working around the house. A week passed. The job was not a hard one and she was a thoughtful boss and we got along very well, until one day when she said her husband wanted to talk to me in his office.

'When I went in the owner said he had a problem; they had put an advertisement in a Sydney paper a few weeks ago through an agent. They had heard nothing from him so he went and got me, but they got a telegram to say that a boy was to leave Sydney the following day to take the job that I had. Was I happy here, did I like the job and would I like to stay?

'If I wanted to stay, that was good. He would then tell the agent not to send the boy from Sydney. But there was one thing which had to be settled. Would I take the wages they were going to pay the Sydney boy which were half what he was paying me? "No," I said. I had been told that the wages I was receiving were the usual and I did not intend to work for less.

'The next day he drove me back to the training farm and left me at the gate and then drove away. I walked into the dormitory and was greeted by the boys. What brought me back? I told them and they all wondered if that was going to be their experience. Then the manager came in and hearing my tale, he said I had no right to come back. I said I was told before I left home that I would be given a job with reasonable wages and that the job he had given me was not up to that promise, and when he found me a job which was as it should be, I would leave.

Eden then took a variety of jobs as a farm labourer. He met his wife-to-be, Nella Catherine, while working on a farm near Leeton, and 70 years on still refers to her as 'my lovely'.

'I took a fancy to her and she took a fancy to me and we both said yes, and it has been yes ever since,' he said. Eden described their courtship in one of many poems about his experiences:

> 'It was Saturday night in Leeton;
> down there in the Riverine...
> Dancing was of my delight,
> and mostly with my girl.
> I danced with her so often
> and with others had a whirl...'

After 12 years on the land, Eden Thompson gave up farming to work as a machinist for 18 years. He then had a milk run for 17 years. In the 1980s the couple moved in retirement to Edgecliff, Sydney, where Eden wrote more verses about his years as a Dreadnought Boy.[4]

## A DIPLOMAT'S 'MINDER'

Bootmaker, engineering worker, Government House kitchen hand and chauffeur to the US Consul-General. Few, if any, Dreadnought lads have led a more varied life than Ralph Wood.

Ralph was born in 1911, into an Army family in Aldershot. His earliest memories are of the family's move to Ireland, where his father, a colour sergeant in the Leicestershire Regiment, was sent during 'the troubles'.

In 1919, having survived the hell of trench warfare in France and Belgium, he was stationed in India, where the family was allowed to join him. It was a huge adventure for a small boy, including the troopship passage through the Suez Canal and a two-day journey by hospital train from Bombay to Delhi.

The constant moves hampered his education, and other factors prevented him from taking up a scholarship – a pity, since he was usually top of the class. He remembers a proud moment when he was commended for spelling, and for knowing the meaning of the word 'accoutrements'.

At 14, Ralph left school and got a job in one of Leicester's many boot and shoe factories. He didn't really like it. 'It was my background of travel. I was mechanically inclined, and got a bit restless.' A variety of other jobs followed, including one in a marine engineering workshop which more suited his aptitude.

Ralph's real ambition was to be a sailor, specifically an engine room artificer. Unfortunately, the Navy rejected him – for flat feet. At about this time his employer sent him and a young companion to the annual engineering exhibition at Olympia. It was intended as a reward but it backfired.

'We were in London for the first time. We were goggle eyed at all this huge machinery and thought 'There's a big world out there.' We were coming back to Colchester quite late at night, and into the railway carriage gets a bloke who'd had a job on a banana boat to South America. He told us all about it and Arthur and I looked at each other and started thinking about broadening our horizons. A few weeks later we saw a bit in the newspaper about the Dreadnought Boys and thought we'd give it a go.

A local shipping agent, who also acted for the Dreadnought Scheme, helped the boys fill in the forms. Ralph recalls: 'The day came when Australia House sent some papers to be signed by our parents. We hadn't told them anything, but they didn't mind, which was a relief. We also had to get references from various people.'

Arthur Jefford and Ralph Wood left England in a party of about 25 Dreadnought Boys on 26 January 1928. 'Mum didn't come to the railway station. Dad did. My grandmother came all the way from Leicester and gave me a few silver coins. We sailed from Tilbury in the SS Baradine.'

Having already travelled by sea to India, Ralph found the voyage to Australia less of a novelty than did most other boys. On arrival in Sydney, he remembers the walk from Walsh Bay, down Argyle Street to the old Emigration Department. He was given a bank book with two pounds in it – 'I think the Government might have put that in.' He kept the same bank book for over 50 years. Somewhat unsportingly, the Commonwealth Bank recently changed the number.

His early years in Australia were spent at various farms near Leeton, in northern NSW. He recalls his introduction to the rural life. 'To milk a cow, my feeling was, well, I had to be introduced to that cow, and apologise for what I was about to do to it. I sat down and made myself comfortable. The cow had its head in the fodder, and turned round and looked at me as if to say "Get on with it, boy." This was in the darkness of the early morning, of course.'

Sleeping accommodation ranged from very bad to appalling, but was accepted without complaint. Did he, like other English migrants, have to sleep in the stables? 'Ah, that would have been home from home, you'd be lucky to sleep in the stables. The worst you could have was just a sheet of tin over you on the ground.'

Ralph checks himself. 'Most of the lads were pretty self-reliant. You'd soon knock yourself up a humpy or something like that. Wheat bags were sewn together for blankets. A few sticks and kerosine cans could be put together to make a table and chairs. All that was par for the course. Of course, you never lived in the house. That was for the farmer and his wife.'

After about five years Ralph decided that enough was enough and he would try his luck in the big smoke. The Depression was in full swing. It was not an ideal time to return to Sydney. According to Ralph: 'It was the world of soup kitchens and doss houses. I did all sorts of lowly jobs, anything at all. I scrubbed out baths, peeled potatoes in cafes just to get a feed. Very rarely were you paid in cash. There were gardening jobs on the North Shore and in Vaucluse and places like that. By the time you'd allowed for your tram fare there wasn't much left.'

Ralph found accommodation in a hostel for the unemployed run by the late Canon R.B.S. Hammond, the famed Rector of St Barnarbas', Broadway. They were nicknamed Hammond Hotels, superior to the usual doss houses, and aimed to help the unemployed person to retain his dignity while he looked for work. Ralph says of Hammond: 'He was a real man as well as man of the Church and I admired him greatly.' Ralph not only lived in a Hammond Hotel, but did odd jobs for Hammond and became his driver. It was the start of things to come.

Hammond was a personal friend of the NSW Governor, Sir Philip Game. One day Hammond got a call from Government House saying there was a vacancy for a temporary worker. 'It was a one night stand. I was asked if I'd like it and, of course, I said "Oh yes, with bells on".'

The work involved moving furniture and fittings, and other odd jobs for a royal jubilee. Later, Ralph had the call once again, this time on a semi-permanent basis, to work for the new Governor, Sir David Anderson. He was officially a scullery man, and also had to maintain the large and very temperamental boiler. 'I enjoyed it, I had a ball. I was getting a reasonable wage and all I could eat. I could even buy myself some clothes out of a shop.' Unfortunately for Ralph, Anderson died in office and the temporary incumbent , Sir Philip Street, declared him redundant.

For Ralph this meant back to a depression-hit workforce and an uncertain future. To his advantage was the fact that he had a driving licence with 'Government House' stamped on it. Ralph got a job with a garage, which catered for top business people. The cars were serviced and washed at night, and collected by the client in the morning. The cars were top of the range models. Ralph did a deal — he washed the vehicles, slept in them, and got a modest wage.

After a while Ralph Wood graduated to the status of a full blown motor mechanic, earning enough to pay rent and lead an improved lifestyle. One of the customers was the US Trade Commissioner, who admired Ralph's competence and brought in business from other expatriate Americans. One day the Consul himself called. He explained the post was being upgraded to Consul-General, and that there was a new man on his way, who would be bringing his own car and would probably be seeking a driver.

Ralph didn't need to be asked a second time. A few days later he personally collected the newcomer off the ship and drove him to his suite in the Hotel Australia. The next day Ralph saw the American again, who made him a job offer.

'He told me: "You'll have to wear a uniform". To which I replied: "It depends on what you mean by uniform, but if you mean a peaked cap and a double breasted coat with buttons down the side and leggings, I don't think I could be in it." He said: "Oh No. You've been looking at too many American movies. What I have in mind is a dark double breasted coat and I'll require you to wear a cap and sometimes gloves. After all we have a position to maintain".'

Ralph found the Consul-General, Thomas Murray Wilson, a friendly bloke, and liked the sound of the 'we'. He also liked the car, a swank Lincoln Zephyr. The American was a bachelor – one of the most eligible in town – and Ralph found himself playing a variety of roles. 'I had to take possession of a house, a mansion, that he'd rented for two years. It was in Ginahgulla Road, Bellevue Hill, and belonged to Sir Adrian Knox, Chief Justice of Australia.'

The American asked Ralph to occupy the house. But there was a surprise: 'There was to be only me in it. He said: 'I'm going to stay at the Rose Bay Golf Club.'

'It was an odd situation, almost unbelievable. It was like being Lord of the Manor as well as "Minder". If people asked me what I was I'd say "butler-chauffeur".'

## LADIES' MAN

The American never married, and remained – at least whilst in Australia – much sought after by unattached eastern suburbs women. One of Ralph's jobs was to 'sort wheat from chaff'. 'I remember one day the boss was invited to speak at a function at Farmers in George Street. I was lurking, as usual, not far away. He came flying out of the door and said: "Quick, quick, they're after me." I thought perhaps the ladies had proved too much for him. He never enlarged on it.'

Thomas Wilson was replaced by another diplomat and the post upgraded to Ambassador. The newcomer explained that to keep the job Ralph would have to move to Canberra and find a wife, who would be employed as housekeeper. Ralph wasn't so keen on that idea – though later he married happily – and decided reluctantly to quit the post, reverting to his first love of engineering.

World War II came along and Ralph answered a Government advertisement for young men with engineering experience to apply for adult apprenticeships. Classes took place at night time after the normal students had gone. Each session was eight hours – four hours theory, four hours machining.

The Japanese entered the war and bombed Darwin. 'Like many people I thought it was a phony war until the Japs came in. I decided it was time to have a go. I presented myself to the RAAF and like a fool told the truth, I said I was a fitter and turner. I was told: "Go back to work. You're in a protected industry." A few weeks later Ralph successfully joined the Army, this time describing himself as a labourer. He soon found himself in the Royal Australian Electrical and Mechanical Engineers, rising quickly to the rank of sergeant.

Whilst serving in the forces, he met his wife, Kathie, at a celebration in The Rocks.

After the war he spent 10 years running an oil pumping station for the fuelling of ships at Woolloomooloo. He also spent 10 years working on the Warragamba Dam, and 10 years with the engineering company, Hardy's.

In 1953, Ralph was visited in Australia by his father. After his father died, he travelled to England to meet his mother. Then in the 1960s, accompanied by Kathie, he returned to England once more, via India. A highlight was when he retraced his footsteps from Delhi Railway Station to Delhi Fort, a journey he had last taken, with soldiers and their families, in the middle of the night, when he was just eight years old.

Ralph was the last-but-one president of the Sydney-based Dreadnought Association, and its most enthusiastic member. On the eve of a Dreadnought reunion he had an eye removed in a surgical operation. He told me: : 'I always looked after the photographic and recording side, and I'm also into video. I was bringing everything together and then, whammy. What should happen but this disaster?'

The *disaster*, it seems clear, was in missing the reunion as much as having the operation. When I saw him a few months later he was philosophical. 'Next year I'll be cameraman with this one eye.'[5]

# 10

## A 'Passiona' Romance

*'It was getting near to Christmas and I said to him, "When are you going to
pay me?" And he said, "I can't pay you, I haven't any money."'*

FRED WOLSTENHOLME, from Blackburn, Lancashire, sailed
from Tilbury on board the *Barrabool*, which departed on 23 June
1927. For 60 years he kept the receipt issued by Australia House for
his portion of the passage money.

A P&O brochure, which he also retained, praises the ship's features
– 'All Steamers Fitted with Wireless Telegraphy' – and notes that 'as there
is but the one class, passengers are not restricted to a certain portion of
the vessel, but have the full run of the ship.'

Fred thought the ship's virtues overrated. 'There was absolutely no
entertainment on board.' In addition to 40 Dreadnought Boys there were
about 50 Barnardos Boys whom he found 'a bit reserved. They had an
escort, a schoolteacher, who was very strict. They didn't mix much with
us on the ship.'

The other passengers were all migrants and their families from various parts of England. He took particular notice of a girl of 19 called Beryl
Lord. Fred himself was 17. 'I fancied her, but I thought maybe she felt I
was too young for her. There was also the risk her parents wouldn't
approve.'

A more pressing consideration was food. 'There was this long dining room about the size of a town hall. There were great long benches
and it was all rather spartan. The meals weren't up to much and we were
always hungry. I remember the kitchen staff would put rolls on the tables
for breakfast. We'd nick down and pinch them, and, since there was no
supper, eat them at about nine o'clock at night.

'We had two pieces of fruit twice a week, on Wednesday and Sunday.
They had these great big cow pumpkins, about a metre wide.'

Seas were rough, particularly through the Bay of Biscay. Everyone was seasick. The ship had no stabilisers. 'Between Cape Town and Adelaide we had a very rough time; mountainous waves came right over the top of us. Once the vessel nearly overturned. They told us we were saved because of an item of cargo – a huge piece of metal which was to form the "knuckle" of the south side of the Sydney Harbour Bridge. This prevented a list, providing balance on the other side.'

Coming into Sydney Harbour, a sailor pointed out construction work on the bridge, which had begun in 1923.

The *Barrabool* berthed on 16 August 1927. The Australian Government showed its pleasure (so he thought) at the arrival of the Dreadnought Boys by giving each a cash gift of 10 shillings as they land-ed on Australian soil. Fred and his companions were marched up George Street North to 'a big hall' (the Empire Service Club) where, from a stage, 'a man barked out requests such as: "Six boys wanted for Wagga, five boys wanted for Grafton."

'I said to my mate: "I don't even know where these places are." He replied: "A friend of mine is up in Lismore; we'll go there." So when they called out Wollongbar, near Lismore, I put my hand up.' It was an exper-imental training farm, where Fred and several others spent nine 'glori-ously happy' weeks.

His first permanent job was on a Jersey stud farm near Binna Burra. 'Binna Burra is about 20 miles out of Lismore. I got on a goods train and sat with the guard. He told me when to get off. He said, "There's no lights there. Just walk along the platform and cross the line. There will proba-bly be someone to meet you."

'In fact, there was no one. It was pouring with rain. I saw a light in a house about half a mile away, and made towards it. I had an overnight bag, and just my working clothes. It was the local post office. The woman was singing away; she asked me where I was going. She said the farm I had to reach was about six miles away over the mountains.

'She rang the farmer, who arrived about two hours later in a sulky. I slept that first night on the floor. I was eaten alive with fleas. It rained for two months solid and I was absolutely fed up. If anybody had offered me a trip back home I'd have gone back. But I was way up in the mountains, five miles from the nearest town, and I didn't even get to see that for another month.'

That first visit to the town came when Fred sought time off to get a hair cut. Permission was grudgingly given, albeit with a list of errands – from delivering cream to getting the horses shod – which would have taken the average man all day. Fred had to do it all, plus numerous tasks on the return journey, and be back at the farm by 3 pm.

Fred stuck it for several months, then found work at Bangalow – the second of 11 farming jobs he was to have in a seven-year period. In another job, where the pay was supposed to be one pound a week, Fred was passed over in favour of a youth who was prepared to work for 10 shillings. 'I suppose you might say the pay in all these jobs was better than may at first appear, since the work involved a seven-day week and consequently little, if any, opportunity for spending any of my wage.'

At another farm the farmer did pay him the agreed one pound plus keep. But not for long. The Depression set in and after a few months the man ceased to pay him. 'It was getting near to Christmas and I said to him, "When are you going to pay me?" And he said, "I can't pay you, I haven't any money." We ate well there and the accommodation was quite good so I put up with the situation.

'This went on for several months, until, after lunch one Sunday, I just pushed my chair back and said, "Goodbye, I'm off now." He said, "Where are you going?" I said, "I'm leaving." He said, "You can't leave, you'll have to give me a week's notice." I said, "I don't have to give you a week's notice; you haven't been paying me for six months." He said, "Who's going to milk the cows? There's only me and my wife." I said, "I don't care if they all die".'

Fred quit the property, summoning as much pride as he could muster. He settled down by the roadside in a large covered container used for carting cream and waited for the carrier to come by. It could have been a long wait – possibly until the following day. However, another farmer saw him and offered him temporary accommodation which was to lead to greater things.

Fred's 11th and final rural employer, by now back in the Lismore area, was Charles Cottee, a member of the Cottee foods' family. 'I spent

18 months with Charlie who was a bonzer fellow.' He left with a fabulous reference – which he wrote himself – having decided, after seven years, to quit country life and try his luck in Sydney.

Fred had another reason for wanting to live in the big Smoke. All these years he had corresponded with Beryl, the 'wonderful' girl he had met on the ship coming to Australia. With his return to Sydney in 1934, a sharp drop occurred in the revenue of the Postal Department since 'on the spot' courtship now became possible.

Fred began job hunting. As he tells it: 'I prowled around everywhere. I went into every big store, Nock and Kirby, Woolworths, Coles, you name it I was there. "Have you any positions?" "Sorry, no positions what-soever." I went to one chap in one of the stores and he just looked at me and said, "Look, I'm fed up with you people coming looking for jobs." I replied, "Look mate, Have you ever looked for a job?" He said "No." I said, "I hope you do one of these days".'

One of the men visited by Fred was Harold Warwick Cottee, man-aging director of the Cottee organisation, who immediately offered him a job. Fred became the first male employee in the Cottee factory. At that time the entire personnel of the firm, which came to be regarded as an Australian icon, comprised Harold and Ernest Cottee, one female clerk and three girls under the supervision of factory manager, Mr Alan Cottee.

His first task was preparing Passiona. Although it later became well known, Australians at that time hardly touched the stuff. 'At that time practically the whole output, 600 gallons monthly, went to fill a London order. We put it into four gallon jars. There was also a large export order to India.'

Did he ever tire of Passiona? 'Not at all. It was a beautiful drink – pure passion fruit and a very health giving drink. The present stuff isn't the same at all.'

From Passiona Fred (and Cottee's) graduated to making jams, syrups and cordials, spreads and soups. He also prepared peanut butter and salt-ed peanuts, a task passed on to his brother, William, whom he sponsored as a migrant and who became known as 'Peanut Bill'.

Fred became the company's first salesman, and soon afterwards, transport manager. In August 1937, now with a secured income and prospects, Fred and Beryl were married. It was 10 years, less three days, since their arrival in Australia on the *Barrabool*.

In the war years Fred received military call up papers three times. 'Each time my employer applied for exemption on the grounds that we were engaged 100 per cent in supplying fruit juices for the Army.' The wartime petrol shortage provided a new outlet for his talents. 'I was sent to a Cottee property in Kulnura to burn charcoal to provide a new fuel source for our delivery fleet.'

In 1961, Fred Wolstenholme took long service leave and returned to Britain with Beryl and their daughter, Margaret. It was 26 years from the day in 1935 that Fred had taken charge of the first sales delivery panel van, and 34 years since both of them had come as migrants on the *Barrabool*.

Both travelled in considerably greater comfort than before – receiving VIP treatment on board the *Willem Ruys*, with stops at Auckland, Tahiti and Panama. They made two subsequent visits to the old country.

From having eight people on its pay-roll, the company now numbered about 900 people based in all the mainland capitals. In 1965 Cottee's was taken over by the American company, General Food Products. They in turn sold to Cadbury Schweppes in October 1986. In 1969, Fred resigned from the company, which he had served for 35 years.

Beryl Wolstenholme died in March 1994. They had been married for nearly 57 years. Fred told me philosophically: 'We had marvellous times together. I was looking after myself at 16, so I reckon I can look after myself at 85.' Fred himself died in 1997.

## THE 'PROPAGANDA' WORKED

As a boy of 16 Noel Fidler visited the 1925 British Empire exhibition at Wembley. On an impulse he went inside the Australian pavilion, and liked what he saw. He made application to emigrate and still has the rather wordy letter received in reply.

Noel was raised in Clacton on Sea, Essex, but his parents had a wine importing business in London. He attended fee-paying schools, but his future plans were hit by the Depression. 'I had matriculated and wanted to go to Cambridge University to study engineering. Now everyone was broke, even the public transport had stopped.

'Then I saw this sign. It said, "Come to sunny New South Wales, the land of opportunity and prosperity. Australia offers wonderful opportunity to the British boy." It was just propaganda but it worked for me.'

Noel came out the following year, going straight to the training farm at Scheyville. While many of the boys considered Scheyville a hell-hole, Noel remembers it fondly, particularly the Saturday nights when girls, accompanied by their mothers, came from Windsor for a dance.

'My first job was in a place called Texas on tne border of New South Wales and Queensland. It was 100 degrees and a dry climate. It was the best thing I could have done. I had this spot on the lung. But it just dried out.' Noel Fidler went on to own taxis, a cycle shop, run a bus service and dabble successfully in real estate. Does he regret coming to Australia? 'Not at all. I was always a weak, skinny little runt, and if I had stayed in England I'd have died of TB years ago.'

He went back to England 'just for a holiday' in 1954. 'It was the year rationing was taken off.' He has been back 13 times since.

## CATHEDRAL WEDDING

His mother said, 'What are you going to do with your life?' Her son said, 'I'm going to Australia.' On the basis of that spur of the moment response Tom Bromby became a Dreadnought Boy.

In June 1928, Tom, who was 15, left his native Hull to sail to Australia on the *Berrima*. He did the standard training at Scheyville. 'We were treated very well. The food was good and there was little or no bastardry.' It was the first time he had seen oranges growing and when the time came to do his week at the orchard got a good bowel clear out from being somewhat greedy.

He found work on a sheep farm near Moree. He was a station rouseabout, or 'cowboy', whose tasks included milking cows, chopping wood, feeding chooks, slaughtering and butchering.

About this time the Scullin Government raised the postage rate for a letter from one-and-a-half pence to two pence. Tom remembers the stir this caused. By now the Great Depression had set in, and jobs for Australians, 'let alone Pommy bastards like me,' were well night impossible. Tom was by this time unemployed, and found himself joining the bands of men roaming the banks of tributaries of the Darling River, living off handouts and the fish they caught. 'If you caught a good one you'd try and trade it with the butcher for meat.'

He and his companions were like gypsies – 'The dole was 6s. 6d. a week and you couldn't get it in the same town twice. You had to keep moving.' On Christmas Day 1930, he and his friends found a bit of flap (a cheap cut of mutton from the lower rib cage), which was 'distinctly on the nose' and a soggy damper, which had been cooked in the ashes. In his own words: 'There's nothing like having to eat one's own cooking to improve one's standard.'

In 1932 he got a learner's pen at shearing, and managed to shear 44 in one day in his first week. The award rate was 27 shillings per 100 sheep (about $2.75). 'From then on shearing was my main job, but all was grist to the mill in the need to find a few bob.'

When war broke out Tom joined the 2-3rd Battalion, 6th Division AIF. He got part of one lung shot out, but declined repatriation and 'soldiered on'. When peace returned he won a block of land in a soldier settler land ballot. It was 40,000 acres at the back of Bourke; the rear of his property was the Queensland border.

Tom returned to farming and went tank sinking (excavating farm dams), 'doing pretty well'. In 1950 he proposed to Jane Maxwell, a 'country girl' from Byrock. On the day planned for their wedding Tom was taken seriously ill with what was at first thought to be anthrax, a disease caught from sheep. He was hospitalised and the ceremony cancelled. When he got better he and Jane borrowed a car and drove to Sydney, taking the wedding gown she had never worn. They were married in St Mary's Cathedral, but within days were on their way back to Bourke.

About 1954, Tom drew a block of land called Kingbolt, which had an old boundary rider's hut where he and his bride lived for about 18 months. 'It was a wreck.' He recalls that dust would rise up through cracks in the floor.

'While living there, we built a house for ourselves. It shocked the locals as it had a concrete floor, then almost unknown. It was comfortable, with 32 volt electric lighting and water laid on. It had a long, wide verandah out front. We were very pleased and it was our home for many years.'

The couple's circumstances continued to improve, with Tom running about 4,000 merino sheep on their property, weathering the difficulties of the mid-1960s, when the pastoral industry experienced a recession.

A noted outback identity, Tom for years kept a jumper with holes in it which he said was 'for interviews with bank managers'. Largely self-educated, he wrote letters to friends and contacts in the big city (including a 14 page missive to his Bank), using a dictionary to aid him.

Tom Bromby died, aged 83, in December 1995. He stated in a note to me, a few weeks before his death: 'To be accepted as a Dreadnought Boy you had to be physically fit, and prepared to work hard. It didn't do us any harm. They talk about people getting depressed and all this nowadays. That's newfangled talk; in them days you just went plugging along.'

## SHIPBOARD PRANKS

At school in Bury, Lancashire, birthplace of Sir Robert Peel, founder of the London Police Force, they taught Harry Jackson about Australia. 'It wasn't very much and what there was turned out to be misleading.'

He left at 14, finding work in the textile industry. But times were hard and this employment dwindled to one day a week. He saw a newspaper advertisement for the Dreadnought Scheme and applied through a church-based organisation, without first consulting his parents.

On 6 June 1929, he received notification that he could join a group sailing on June 22 – a mere fortnight away and only three weeks after making his original application! 'There was no such luxury as a briefing. I'd never met an Australian, nor even anyone who had come out here and gone back.

'My decision was not greeted with much enthusiasm, although my employer thought it a good opportunity. My mother and grandmother were broken-hearted. My father simply commented that I wouldn't be able to swim home from Australia.

'We sailed on the *Oronsay*. It was a magnificent ship, maintained to a very high standards. The other boys and I were third class passengers. An Australian adult was to watch over us throughout the journey. At various ports we were given guided tours by officials who had something to do with the scheme.'

Harry remembers the journey as 'a wonderful experience', punctuated with various pranks. 'There were some Italians on our deck and we would tie rope to the cabin door handles on opposite sides of the corridors, knock, and then cheer madly as they each tried to open their doors.

'We would also rub the polished floors in the corridor with soap so they became slippery. On a personal front, I climbed the ship's mast, got caught and taken before the Captain who put me on "assistant steward" duties for most of the journey as a punishment.' This turned out to be no punishment, as the miscreants got to mix with the crew, ate better, and even sat in on their concerts and entertainment.

Though their destination was Sydney, the lads disembarked temporarily in Melbourne. 'As we walked down the street a group of local youths abused us as "Pommy bastards" here to take their jobs. One thing led to another and we had a fist fight. When we returned to the ship we went to the Australian looking after us. He had warned we would be called names, but it hadn't occurred to us that we would be unwelcome. He told us not to worry, as we would be working as farm hands in the bush and wouldn't affect local jobs.'

Their Australian escort offered much advice – some novel, some useful. 'I recall him saying that everything in Australia revolved around a kerosene tin. For example, animals were fed in measures of say half a kero tin, that the tins were used in many ways on the domestic scene, and even the wooden packing case was converted into stools. He was also proud of the fact that margarine was unavailable in Australia and scorned the British for selling it.'

The *Oronsay* reached Sydney on 1 August 1929. The Harbour Bridge was still under construction at each end and there was a gap in the middle. 'We were taken to a building for further briefing about life in Australia and what we had to do under the scheme. Our only requirement to that point had been to have a clean change of clothes and ten pounds.

'Most of us had given our money to the ship's purser for safe keeping. He gave a lot of us a gold sovereign as part of the money when we left the ship, and he told us it would be valuable in years to come and not to spend it. Unfortunately I didn't heed his advice and exchanged it for a pound note from an employer some years later.'

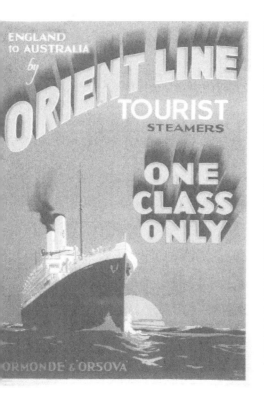

The Great Adventure

*Government Training Farm, Scheyville (September 1911)*

*Class in sheep shearing at Scheyville (about 1911)*

*William Schey*
*established Government*
*Training Farm*

*Happiness is milking time.*
*From magazine of Big Brother Movement*
*(1928)*

*Feeding calves at the Government Training Farm (1926)*

*Dreadnought Boys – January 1926.*
*Photo published in Sydney Mail with the caption*
*'Determined to be Good Australians'*

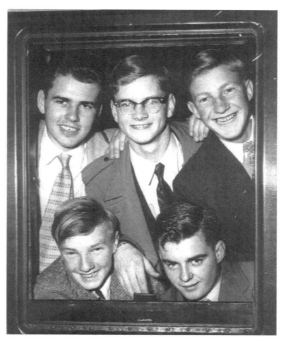

*Little Brothers en route for Australia (1950s)*

*Young female migrants 'adopted' by Bondi Lions Club,*
*after their arrival in Sydney on the Fairsea (10 March 1960)*

*Bridie Leonard*
*(nee Creagh) aged 17.*
*New maid at Government House.*

*Kathleen Rourke*
*(nee Redstone)*
*'Cybergranny'*

*'Wistful thinking'*
*Evocative cartoon by Dreadnought Old Boy, Sid Black.*

*Kathie and Ralph Wood (1994)*

*'A diplomat's minder'*
*Ralph Wood as chauffeur to US Consul-General*

*Ernie Thornton*
*'Red Czar'*

*Harry Jackson*
*Shipboard pranks*

*Tom and Mary Bromby*
*Cathedral wedding*

*Nathalie Higgs (age 7)*
*at Dreadnought Memorial,*
*The Rocks*

*Noel Fidler (left) and Fred Wolstenholme at 1994 Dreadnought reunion*

*Certificate of farm competence given to Fred Wolstenholme*

*Fred Wolstenholme's
first pay packet (August 1934)*

*Noel Fidler
The 'propaganda' worked*

*Bill Wilson
'Fireworks for the
War Effort'*

*Bill Wilson
at age 17 (1928)*

*Noel Fidler (left) and Eden Thompson*
*re-visit the old Scheyville Training Farm (1995).*
*Sydney Morning Herald Photo*

*Rev. Norman Monsen at Dreadnought*
*re-union (1994)*

*Norman Monsen*
*'Likely Lad' on embarking for*
*Australia (1926)*

*Rev Arthur Brawn – life-long quest to find missing men*

*Frederick Lambert-Carter: 'Bring Out a Briton'*

*J.J.Simons (right) 'on parade' for the Prince of Wales*

*Les Waddington, age 10, as mascot of the Young Australia League*

*Sir Arthur Rickard*
*'Crusader for immigration'*

*Les Waddington*
*climbed Harbour Bridge at 80*

*Millions Club / Sydney Club*

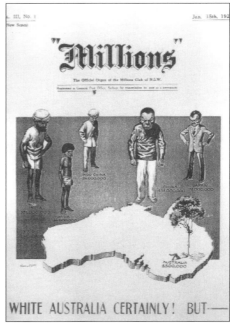

*Cover of Millions magazine (1922–1924)*

*Australia House, London where the journey began*

*First group of Little Brothers arrive in Sydney, 14 December, 1925*

*Sir Richard Linton*
*formulated notion of*
*'Big Brother-Little Brother'*

*Big Brother Movement War Memorial*
*Training Farm (1948)*

*Wide open spaces*
*BBM Training Farm*

*Hungry lad –*
*mealtime at the training farm*

Harry, who was not yet 17, was sent with others to Scheyville. They were met at Mulgrave railway station by the famed Irishman, Andy. Harry sat next to him – the boys had to wait whilst he slipped into a hotel to 'wet his whistle'. 'At Scheyville we were greeted by a man called Captain Harper and shown our quarters. Whilst we carried our gear from the carts a man astride a beautiful racehorse watched us. He introduced himself as the manager, a Mr Scully. He referred to us as "pommy vermin", and said that if we had a problem we were to go to him, but that he didn't want to see us as he knew it would mean trouble.'

Harry's hardest and most unpleasant experience in training was having to kill a sheep. 'We were given a demonstration of how to hold the sheep between our legs, pull the head back to expose the throat, insert the knife near the ear and slice out in one quick action. When it was my turn to complete this task I summoned up all my courage and inserted the knife, but I couldn't continue.

'The chap in charge was very angry and took over, but I was bluntly told I would have to do it to complete my training. I managed to do so the next time, but I have never killed an animal in this manner since.'

Harry's first official job was on a dairy farm at Shellharbour. The work was hard, but fairly routine, and the pay was one pound a week. He bought a Speedwell push bike for 12 pounds on a hire purchase scheme. When he left, his employer decently paid off the balance.

'I left about March 1930 and went back to the Immigration Office to tell them I had come to work in the bush and the Shellharbour area was too civilised. The officer was not very impressed and told me I was extremely foolish to leave such a good job.'

The next day he was given a job at Dorrigo – which all parties agreed was sufficiently 'bush'. By happy coincidence two lads already working there were Dreadnoughts. Harry remembers that journey and several others.

'One thing that struck us boys when we travelled on the trains in rural Australia was how slow they were compared with British trains. It took over 12 hours to reach Glenreagh, north of Coffs Harbour. It took a further eight hours to travel from Glenreagh to Dorrigo (less than 50 miles) as the train stopped at each small timber mill siding. At one point the train driver stopped and made a pot of tea. I was the only official passenger – although as the train crawled along the door crashed open and some freeloaders scrambled in. I remember being excited over this at the time.'

It was dark when Harry reached Dorrigo station and his new employer was waiting in a 1928 Chevrolet. 'I had my push bike with me, which he would not put in the car. I was told to follow his tail lights as he drove to his farm some five miles away. The road was gravel and mud and it was difficult to negotiate in the dark. When we arrived I was immediately told to go to the milking shed and assist the other two boys already working for him.

'We were paid 10 shillings a week – half what I was getting previously – and expected to work from dawn till well after dark six days a week. Sunday was free (between milkings) but we were expected to attend the local Plymouth Brethren meetings. The food was scarcely enough and appalling. Plenty of pumpkin, I recall.

'Towards the end of my third week there I was given a dog. The Boss shot it. So I left. Fortunately, when I reached Dorrigo township another farmer called Ted Jennings offered me work. He and his family treated me very well.

Harry Jackson remained in farm work in Dorrigo until about 1935, then returned to Sydney and soon worked his way to foreman of a textile mill. He volunteered for war service but his factory position was considered essential and he had to stay there.

After the war, during which he worked six days a week on 12-hour night shifts, he had stomach ulcers and doctors advised him to find another occupation. He had been married about six years by then and so returned to Dorrigo to work on the land, at first share-farming and then buying his own farm.

When he left Dorrigo some 18 years later, the Chamber of Commerce presented him with a painting and a plaque thanking him for his services to the local community. Harry Jackson died, aged 83, on 15 December 1995. Says his daughter, Linda: 'Dad always put 100 per cent effort into whatever he was doing and I think he has been an asset to Australia.'

# 11

## Farm Boy to Church Leader

I F HE HAD BEEN ASKED to fill out a CV, the Very Rev Norman Monsen could have listed among his occupations farm hand, scrub cutter, fencer, wheat lumper and general labourer.

Interesting qualifications for a man who subsequently became Moderator-General of the Presbyterian Church of Australia,

When interviewed by the author, Monsen, then 83, reckoned he had preached in more than 450 churches, whose congregations had included Premiers and Prime Ministers, Governors and Lord Mayors. Despite this, the impression he gave was of a humble man who had not forgotten his working class 'Geordie' roots, still less his migration to Australia as a Dreadnought Boy.

Norman Monsen was born on 10 September 1911, in the grandiosely named Tynemouth Victoria Jubilee Infirmary. His Norwegian-born parents had settled in Tyneside, his father working as a shipping agent servicing Scandinavian ships plying in and out of the River Tyne.

Milton Terrace – the family later moved to the slightly more upmarket Cleveland Terrace – was not in the category of the affluent. It was a short street of brick tenement style houses joined together with families living one on top of the other; their front doors side by side opening right on the street without the luxury of a front garden.

Close by this drab street, the undertaker's black draped carriages slowly wound their way up to the cemetery, always with the horses black plumed and a silk-hatted, frock coated attendant striding in front. The mourners, most of them with black armbands on the sleeve of their coat, solemnly took up the rear.

The cemetery in contrast was for many families a pleasant spot in which to have a Sunday afternoon stroll. For older youths it was a place to pursue the opposite sex; walking discreetly behind the object of one's desire, showing just enough attention to them to make the afternoon interesting and enjoyable.

At the age of five Norman was enrolled in the Infants Department of the local King Edward School. It was 1916, and the Great War was in progress. On Empire Day (May 24) various lads were chosen to march around the playground illustrating the various Commonwealth countries. One year he was chosen to head the march, with the word 'Australia' emblazoned across his chest. It was perhaps a portent of things to come.

He left school at 14. It was 1926, year of the General Strike. His father's business was just about defunct, which situation precluded proceeding on to the Tynemouth High School, though his school reports were good. 'Schooling at that level in 1926 had to be paid for. No money, no high school. It was as simple as that.'

He looked for work, but also enjoyed boyhood pursuits. One of his haunts was the fish quay on a Saturday morning. Other recreational activities included silent films in Howard Hall on Saturday afternoons. There was also the fun of following – and sometimes assisting – the lamplighter. In summertime there were excursions to the Long Sands (a wide stretch of sand, a mile long) where youngsters could play, build sand castles and swim.

Life for the young Monsen was not all rosy. His father took to the bottle, aggravated by his work situation. Norman would be sent to search for him in the numerous pubs in the area. Later, his father curbed his addiction, which was greatly to his credit. Witnessing his father's behaviour, and the unhappiness caused to his mother, caused Norman to abstain permanently from alcohol.

The idea of migration was raised by a visit to the town of a man giving lectures on Australia as a 'land of opportunities'. He had been a migrant himself and had 'done well'. Norman attended two meetings on his own initiative and was suitably impressed. 'With my parents' consent I signed up.'

He was to say later, with the wisdom of hindsight: 'The removal of oneself to another country on the other side of the world is a matter not to be taken lightly... I think I saw migration as just a temporary phase and that I would be absent for three or four years, at the end of which I would return home with a fortune in triumph.'

The particular scheme offered to Norman Monsen and to other

youths in Tyneside was presented as the 'Dreadnought Scheme for the Migration of Boys to Australia.' His brother Moritz also became bitten with the bug, as did three friends.

The next step (at 14 years and 11 months) was to get a passport photograph, which he kept for nearly 70 years.

LIKELY LAD

He also bought a Box Brownie and two rolls of film, total cost 14 shillings and 10 pence. The local vicar, the Rev R. E. Holmes, supplied, unsolicited, a letter of introduction. It said: 'I can confidently recommend him as a lad likely to do well. He is strong and healthy and in every way likely to make a good colonist.'

Monsen later considered it significant that the word 'likely' was used twice in the one paragraph. He was to keep the letter in his wallet for the remainder of his life. 'Likely lads' became a term often used as a catch-phrase for the Dreadnought Boys and other youth migrants.[1]

On the evening of 18 August 18 1926 the group of 52 youngsters assembled in Newcastle Town Hall for addresses by, among others, the Lord Mayor, Anthony Oates, who presented each lad with an inscribed and signed Bible.

Leaving the town hall they marched in the middle of the road preceded by a kilted kettle drum band to the Angus Watson Hall, where they were given supper. They then marched to a cinema to see films about life in Australia. This was followed by time alone with relatives until 11 pm and departure of the night train for London.

Nearly 70 years on, Norman Monsen was to say of that experience: 'For my part, of course, it was an adventure. My mother, like me, could not anticipate it would be 24 years before we would see each other again.'[2]

Norman Monsen, with his brother and the other 50 migrant lads set sail from Tilbury Dock in the *SS Benalla on* 19 August 1926. He had his 15th birthday on board, September 10; one day before the ship docked in Cape Town.

The ship arrived in Port Jackson on October 15. 'It appeared to us a beautiful harbour', an impression confirmed as the *Benalla* sailed up the few miles to dock at one of the wharves adjacent to Circular Quay.

There was the usual mustering of newcomers at the Empire Service Club and Department of Labour and Industry. Norman's brother, Moritz, was assigned to an employer in Mummulgum in the Far North Coast of NSW, some 547 miles from Sydney. Norman was allotted a place as a farming trainee at the Government Experimental Farm at Grafton.

The journey to Grafton was long and unpleasant – at least 20 hours in a train pulled by a coal-burning engine belching smoke and gritty soot all down along the dog box carriages behind it.

In due time, the train chugged into Koolkhan Station, some 440 miles from Sydney, the nearest point of disembarkation for the Graftom Experimental Farm.

That first night he and other newcomers were victims of an elaborate practical joke. They were told they would be participating in a fox hunt. In reality it was an initiation. Dire warnings were uttered about the perils of treading on snakes and such like, thus 'putting the fear of God into us'.

After dark the newcomers were taken into the fields, through barbed wire fences, walking for what seemed miles. 'In fact, we were being guided in and out of the same two fields not far from our dormitories.

'Two by two we were posted and told to be on the look out for foxes for they, the older boys, were going into the scrub to beat out the foxes with banging and shouts. We were supposed to catch them or bash them with the clubs we carried. What really happened was we were simply left at our posts and the perpetrators of the hoax went back to bed.'

Norman Monsen's first paid job was with a dairy farmer at Argent's Hill in the upper reaches of the Nambucca River. Tom and Maggie Boorer treated him as one of the family, giving him his own room, a luxury in those days. They were church-going Presbyterians, whose influence was to shaped the young man's future.

The nearest shops were in Bowraville. There were two cafes on opposite side of the street. One café had been bought by Italians; the owner of the other had the unsubtle message painted along the front awning 'Come here before the day goes'.

After three years with the Boorers, Monsen thought it was time to move on. His brother had stayed only one year in the countryside farm-ing and had got a job in Sydney as a bus conductor. Norman decided to join him, but found city life not to his choosing and he decided to return to farming. His next job was on a wheat farm at Mirrool in the far west of NSW. He had a shock when he saw his sleeping quarters – a partitioned off area of the stables.

'On one side of my "bedroom" was the chaff room – feed for the horses – and on the other was where the horses were fed. The aroma was just what one would expect from horses' stables.' His 'mattress' was two layers of bags of oats.

Hardly surprisingly, the new employee stayed only for the harvest-ing season, then got a job with a dairy farmer in Griffith. This time his accommodation was a tent!

He returned to work for a while with his friends the Boorers. But the Depression was setting in and by mutual consent he left their employ, this time to work with a farmer at Bowraville.

By now the crunch had set in. Farms were going bust. Employees were working for their keep without pay. Norman received a letter from Mrs Boorer's mother, offering work on a farm at Gloucester. It proved a blessing. He loved the countryside and befriended the local Presbyterian minister, becoming leader of the kindergarten Sunday school.

On one occasion, in the absence of the minister, he preached the ser-mon. The minister moved away, and the parish could not afford a replace-ment. Norman Monsen found himself called upon to regularly conduct services.

'The preparation of sermons was not an easy matter for me for I lacked study experience and a library. Nor was I exactly adept at public speaking.' He practised in the paddocks at night. 'The quiet solitude of the night was helpful and I would preach aloud to the stars. There was no one around to hear me – I hoped.'

He felt a calling to the ministry, and contacted church authorities in Sydney, only to be told that his education was insufficient.

It was a blow, but fate lent a hand in that Norman got a job with a farmer whose sister-in-law was an accomplished scholar and teacher. She devoted much of her spare time to helping him, with the result that, in

1937, he began formal training as what was then known as a student home missionary.

Army service, in which Norman Monsen became an officer in the Royal Australian Artillery, temporarily interrupted these activities. In 1943, the Government decreed that young men studying for the ministry in the various Christian denominations were performing an essential service. Monsen was discharged from the Army in order to return to his studies. He began as a Student Minister of the Presbyterian Church, at Brighton-le-Sands, on 29 December 1943.

His was a varied ministry spanning – including duties performed in retirement – some 50 years. Much of it was as Superintendent of Home Missions (the name was later changed to Department of Home Mission and Evangelism), from which he retired, also from the active ministry, in June 1978.

In 1974-75 Norman Monsen was elected Moderator of the NSW Presbyterian Church. No more 'difficult' year could have been chosen. It was a year which saw a key poll in which the Presbyterian Church of Australia officially resolved to become part of the proposed Uniting Church. However, a substantial minority – including a majority of the presbyteries and congregations in NSW – voted to remain Presbyterians.

Theological differences over the formation of the Uniting Church led to practical differences, including lawsuits, over the distribution of property. Monsen, who was for 15 years a member of the NSW Presbyterian Property Trust, found himself involved. Time has now mellowed the once strongly held emotions. All sides regard him as having been a force for fairmindedness, commonsense and moderation.

Formal retirement proved to be nominal. In September 1981 – the day after his 70th birthday – he received an invitation to accept nomination as Moderator-General of the Presbyterian Church of Australia. Though diminished in size as a result of Church union, the 'continuing' body was undiminished in vigour. He was duly elected – 'one of the proudest moments of my life' – and served for three years from 1982 to 1985.

One of his first self-imposed duties after that – using a typewriter made in 1937 – was to 'write up' his personal memoirs, which he called, appropriately, 'One of the Likely Lads'.

Monsen was helped in his life and ministry by his wife, Alison, who died in May 1992, not long after the couple had celebrated their golden wedding anniversary.

In retirement, Norman Monsen continued to attend reunions of the Dreadnought Boys and spoke of the scheme with affection. He told the author: 'I have in retrospect no quarrel with the scheme even though it was sold to us in terms somewhat more glowing and extravagant than the reality. But is this not so with every prospectus and proffered transaction?'

He recalled with affection the vicar in Tyneside who gave him the two 'likely' commendations. 'I am honoured that he found me "likely", and hope that I lived up to his expectations. For my part I have found that nothing is surer than that God's ways are mysterious but nonetheless wonderful.'[3]

## 'FIREWORKS' FOR THE WAR EFFORT

Bill Wilson came to Australia for family reasons, and to better himself, when he was 17. The year was 1928. His parents had divorced when he was younger, and his father was now dead.

He was hostile towards his step-father, which attitude he now regrets. 'He was a good man. If I saw him again I would apologise. But I never did see him again.'

As for bettering himself: 'Before I left England I was doing well at school, I had matriculated, and was thinking of aiming for a professional career. Then I quarrelled with my step-father; the family atmosphere became unpleasant. At school we heard about the Dreadnought scheme, and it sounded good. But I should not have emigrated to Australia to take on labouring work, which is what happened. My headmaster gave me bad advice.'

For Bill, as for other young migrants, the actual departure was traumatic. 'My older sister broke down [at the station] which was upsetting. My mother came to London with me. I went to Australia House for a final pep talk, then went back to the place where we were staying. The next morning we had breakfast and both got on a bus to Tilbury Dock. I shall never forget the sadness in her face during that short journey.'

The journey out on the P. & O. liner, *Baradine*, was eventful, as was the final arrival – after stops in Fremantle, Adelaide and Melbourne – at Sydney's Walsh Bay.

'We were given a cursory medical examination on the boat. Then we were assembled on deck, where a press photographer took a group photo, after which two gentlemen in felt hats made speeches at us. I have no idea what they said.' Then followed a march to the Empire Service Club, and an introduction to Dr Mary Booth.

While having tea and buns at the club he became aware of a youth circulating and asking if there was anyone from Merseyside. Bill called out that he was from Wallasey. It transpired the youth was a Dreadnought Boy who had arrived a couple of years earlier, but whose father considered he was leading a harum scarum life in Sydney and had paid for his passage home.

The lad was hungry for news of home and of English football. Bill found the conversation disquieting. 'He warned me that I would be disappointed in Australia. He said that Australian Cockies[4] – this was the first time I had heard the word – were tight fisted exploiters, and that many Australians did not like English migrants, for whom they had coined the name Pommies, thus showing their contempt and dislike.

'When I asked him if there weren't any English farmers, he said they were worse than Australians. I found all this disturbing but consoled myself by reflecting that he had probably been a sorehead and not a good worker.'

After three months at Scheyville Bill was sent to a wheat and sheep farm in the south-west of NSW, about 60 km from West Wyalong. It was November 1928, and the wheat harvest had just begun. 'From then until the end of January we worked from dawn to dark every day except Christmas Day. It was over 100 degrees F. in the shade. The pay was one pound a week.'

He found the farmer and his wife a pleasant couple, with five children living at home. The young teacher at the district's one-teacher school also boarded with them.

Employees included several farmhands and contract workers. Among the latter was 'Clearer Jack – I don't think he had another name – a strange silent man who did bag sewing during the harvest. Every three months or so he would go off and stay in the township and there he would get very drunk and remain that way until his cheque ran out. Then he would stoically resume work.'

Bill's special role task during the harvest was to sit on the seat of the wheat harvester, and control the height of the 'comb' which ran through the crop just below the heads of wheat, cutting off the heads and passing them to a threshing drum and subsequently through a system of sieves and blowers which separated wheat from husk and sent the wheat to a wheat box.

'Every acre or so the wheat box would fill up, the tractor would stop and I would jump down and empty the wheat box into jute cornsacks, bales of which were dumped at intervals around the paddock. The filled sacks of wheat, each weighing 180 pounds, were subsequently sewn by Clearer Jack and loaded onto the wagon for carting off to the railhead.'

After the last bag was off, at the end of January, the pace of work slowed down, but Bill still worked six days a week.

A succession of seasonal tasks started with the grading of seed wheat for the next year's crop and treating of the same wheat with a powdered copper compound to eliminate a seed-borne fungus known as bunt. Routine jobs included burning of the stubble, ploughing, milking the cows (twice daily), feeding the working horses, hoeing out noxious weeds and setting traps for the rabbits which were in plague proportions.

Bill studied those who worked alongside him and felt he didn't fancy any of them as role models. Few people he met owned their own farms. Even his boss, an established farmer, had won his 1500 acre block in a land ballot.

'I concluded that there was no future in farm work for a boy without capital and that I should try to see if my matriculation certificate would get me a start on something better in the city.' One thing worried him – the stipulation that Dreadnought Boys had to spend a minimum two years on the land before branching out onto something else.

Bill was wondering how and if he should give notice, when his problem was solved in an unexpected way. He had written a letter to a friend in England, in which he had mentioned the long hours and lack of opportunity. Somehow he left the unfinished letter lying around. It was found by one of the boss's daughters, who showed it to her father. 'Relations were somewhat soured after that and about a fortnight later he gave me notice, also a cheque for 18 pounds which I cashed at the local hotel where I stayed overnight.'

It was April 1929. The dismissal was actually to his advantage. Bill took a train to Sydney where he booked into the People's Palace, a temperance hotel in Pitt Street. There he heard about a Scottish gathering in the basement of the Presbyterian Assembly Hall in Margaret Street. He went along hoping to meet some young immigrants. Sure enough, he was befriended by a youth who shared tips on employment and arranged for him to have cheap board and lodging with a former Dreadnought supervisor.

Bill heard about a cadetship with the NSW Department of Agriculture, which would include university studies and a paid job. This first attempt was unsuccessful. Instead, he landed a job as a laboratory assistant with the then newly-formed Council for Scientific and Industrial Research (CSIR)[5], and commenced a biology course at Sydney Technical College.

The office was transferred to Canberra, where he stayed two years. Towards the end of that period he was offered the cadetship for which he had initially applied. But the offer was conditional upon his raising a bond of £200, which he didn't have.

Bill immediately thought of the Dreadnought Trust, which probably would have acted as guarantor, but was unable to supply the address of the trust, nor to name, let alone locate any of its local representatives. The offer lapsed. For many years he was angry about this. 'The trust and its officers were totally invisible; that was their great defect. They hid themselves from the boys. They never fronted us; they did everything possible to avoid meeting up with us or making themselves known in any way.'

The story had an odd sequel. Bill stayed with the CSIR another year, then decided to take a two-year course (reduced in his case to one year) at Hawkesbury Agricultural College. There was a problem about raising the course fee. A philanthropic organisation in Canberra – or so he thought – made a cash award of £15, which, with £40 he had already saved, met both his course fee and modest extras such as hair cuts and cigarettes. Some 50 years later, while reading Dreadnought records in Sydney's Mitchell Library, he discovered that the donor was, in fact, the Dreadnought Trustees.

Bill Wilson was dux of the class throughout the year, but in the final examinations was failed by two marks in practical butter making. He was told he could take the examination again after one year. 'I said, "What about a job? I'm practically broke". I got the reply: "That's your business".'

It was 1933, the Depression in full swing, and jobs were hard to get. 'I managed to get myself a job picking apples in New England with a very nice family called Adamson. I was there three months. Then the apple picking finished. I went to Sydney to try to get another job, but the employment situation was even worse. I got more work picking apples – at 10 shillings a week – and drove sheep for a man called Booth. I missed out on the exam, which had been moved forward without my knowledge. I went back to droving for a man in West Wyalong – a very decent family – then finally re-took the exam, which I passed.'

From then on things started to look up for Bill Wilson. His diploma in primary dairying helped him get a job with the Dairy Farmers Milk Company, which was across the road from the Sydney Technical College. He resumed the course he had started with the CSIR, passed it, then began a chemistry diploma which he obtained after a further five years.

By this time World War II had begun. Bill was contacted by men from the Department of Supply and soon found himself in war work of an unusual kind – 'producing fireworks'. They were not party fireworks but heavy duty pyrotechnics. 'We made rockets and very lights, smoke generators and detonators of various kinds.' There were frequent accidents; possibly because workers were inclined to take less care than they would have done with bombs and more dangerous explosives, such as TNT.

Bill worked at two explosives factories – at Maribyrnong (Vic) and Salisbury (South Australia). He stayed in this occupation until late 1944. At one point, tired with civilian life, he offered himself for aircrew training with the RAAF. After a series of tests, he was accepted; only to have this overruled on the grounds that his present work was more important to the war effort.

In the last few months of the war Bill and several colleagues were switched from pyrotechnics to food technology. It involved a three months' training course at the CSIR – this time at government expense – and was to change the course of his life.

He became proficient in food preservation, drying and canning, and was responsible for quality control in three canneries in and around Griffith. The factories supplied canned food for many thousands of American and Australian troops, as well as civilians, which made Bill aware of his responsibilities.

When peace resumed Bill continued in the same line, but was fed up and sought a change. In a Sydney café he got into conversation with an elderly man who said he was the accountant at Crago Farmers in Newtown. 'He said they were looking for a cereal chemist and it might be worthwhile to apply. I got the job, which looked permanent.

'Crago developed flour mills and starch processing, and went into stock feed in a big way. The poultry industry was being more or less mechanised and stock feed was prosperous. So with all this development my job prospered and I did quite well there, and I stayed there for the rest of my working life.'

Bill Wilson waited 35 years before his return to Wallasey, in Cheshire, in 1963. His mother was still alive to greet him, but the house they had occupied at the time of his departure was no more, having been blown up by a German incendiary bomb. His step-sister died in the blast.

'Mum survived, and helped look after other survivors. There were so many people killed in that raid that they couldn't afford the dignity of private funerals. They dug a great hole in the park and put all the bodies in there. There is a notice on one of the seats[6] recording the event, but nothing very elaborate.' Bill and his mother sat on the seat and uttered a silent prayer.

# 12

# Without a Trace – 'Guilt' at Pacific Tragedy

I N JUNE 1992, a group of well-wishers, encouraged by an elderly man in a wheelchair, stood in front of a plaque in Parramatta, read from the Scriptures and sang aloud Psalm 107. The psalm has references to prisoners, to men who 'went down to the sea in ships' and to God's sovereignty over the waves and 'stormy wind'. It is often used to remember shipwreck victims.

The modest ceremony marked the 50th anniversary of a major, but little known, tragedy in World War II, in which nearly 1,000[1] Australian servicemen and over 200 Australian civilians, many of them missionaries, 'disappeared', shortly after having been taken prisoner by Japanese forces on Rabaul.

General belief – though this theory has many critics – is that the captives were being taken to internment in Japan on board a ship, the *Montevideo Maru*, which was attacked and sunk by an American submarine.

The man in the wheelchair, former Dreadnought Boy, the Rev Arthur Brawn, had a key role – perhaps the key role – in the drama, even though he was not involved.

In the late 1930s Brawn was a Methodist missionary at Malalia and Nakanai in New Britain. The men who were to die were his fellow students at theological college and his companions and neighbours in the islands. However, malaria, and not the threat of Japanese invasion, caused him and his family to return to Australia before the outbreak of hostilities.

For over 40 years after the war's end Brawn suffered a sense of guilt about 'why I was spared and my friends died'. At our first meeting[2] several years ago he expressed astonishment that the sinking of the *Montevideo Maru* and the tragic loss of life was not better known. 'Over 1,000 people went down, equivalent to the entire population of an Australian country town, yet hardly anybody seems to know about it.'

Those who lost their lives included men of the 2/22nd Battalion AIF (known as Lark Force), plantation owners, public servants and missionaries[3]. Public servants included the deputy administrator and government secretary, Harold Page, and eight heads of government departments. There was also an entire Salvation Army band.

After being taken prisoner, in June 1942, the prisoners were herded into compounds. It is thought that at about 8 am on June 22, non-officer soldiers and civilians were marched down to the harbour, where the *Montevideo Maru*, on charter to the Japanese Navy, was waiting.

About a week after its departure, the ship was sighted off Luzon, in the Philippines, by an American submarine, the *USS Sturgeon*, which tailed it throughout the night. At dawn on July 1, the sub closed in, firing four torpedoes in close succession. US naval records show that the *Montevideo Maru* sank, stern first, in about 10 minutes. It is assumed that the prisoners, if they were indeed on board, were trapped in the hold.

Nobody knows for certain if the men were actually on the *Montevideo Maru*. There is another theory: that the captives were marched to a nearby village, made to dig their own graves and then either shot or beheaded.

The former Catholic Bishop of Rabaul, Leo Scharmach, was the most outspoken exponent of this theory.[4] Indeed, he doubted the existence of the Japanese vessel (although the ship is listed in Lloyd's Shipping Register for 1930). The bishop's belief was that the prisoners were taken by truck, probably to the village of Matupit, made to dig mass trenches, then mowed down by machine-guns and buried.

While researching this topic I received letters from former servicemen in Rabaul with gruesome accounts of finding human remains in the areas mentioned by Scharmach. One correspondent stated: 'The Army intelligence unit was called in, also the War Graves Commission. They identified these bodies as soldiers of the 2/22nd Battalion. I don't know how many there were as we were kept out of the area…'

The bishop's theory about a massacre gained credence through claims attributed to New Britain tribesmen that they had met and spoken to the missionaries a year or more after the departure of the *Montevideo Maru*.

The view that the men did meet their deaths on board the

*Montevideo Maru* is supported by testimony from a former military padre and fellow prisoner, Chaplain (later Canon) John May, who, because of his officer status, did not travel with the other captives.

May, contacted by the writer in Tasmania, said: 'I saw and heard them leave, but I did not see them go on board the ship, neither did I see it sail. However, there were Methodist and Army nursing sisters held prisoner at Vunapopo Mission, about 20 miles away. One of them said she saw a ship leave Rabaul Harbour, and I assume it was the *Montevideo Maru*.'

Before the men marched out of the prison compound, May conducted a brief religious service, which included the reading of Psalm 107. The last sounds he heard were their marching feet.

The sinking of the *Montevideo Maru* went unreported until the war's end. The news appeared in the Australian press, in a few brief paragraphs, on Victory Day. It put paid to the joy of many a Sydney and Melbourne family. May himself wrote to next of kin. It was some consolation to learn that women prisoners, who had been sent to Japan on a second ship, had mostly survived. But the living may have envied the dead. They suffered appalling indignities[5] – for 'sport' they were made to eat food retrieved from a cesspit.

According to Japanese sources, two Japanese officers and 15 men – of a total of 20 officers and 68 men – survived the attack on the *Montevideo Maru*. They took to the lifeboats, which had capsized, and after a nightmare journey lasting nearly 36 hours made it to the shore, landing near an area known as Cape Light. While trekking inland they were attacked by natives and guerilla forces, and the officers were killed. A handful of survivors, led by one Quartermaster 3rd Class Katsushi, were said to have reached Manila and finally returned to Tokyo.

In the early post-war years some relatives of the dead Australians visited New Britain to pay homage to their loved ones and to examine the rival theory put forward by Bishop Scharmach. Among those who made the trek were the former West Australian Labor Parliamentarian, Kim Beazley (Snr), whose brother was a victim,[6] and the Rev Arthur Brawn. Brawn spoke to tribesmen who supposedly initiated Scharmach's reports. His verdict? 'Mere rumours … utterly false.'

In the years which followed, Brawn conducted a personal crusade to make sure the dead Australians, and particularly his fellow missionaries, were not forgotten.

Until a stroke rendered this impossible, he conducted his own 'very private' memorial service, either on June 22 (when the ship departed) or July 1 (when it sank). He held it in churches, school halls, a retirement village and RSL clubs. Sometimes the only other person present was the caretaker. Always his Bible was open at Psalm 107. He knew every line by heart.

For a few years after the war, relatives of victims of the *Montevideo Maru* laid wreaths at the cenotaph in Martin Place, Sydney. In 1967, a service, marking the 25th anniversary, was held in Sydney's Central Methodist Mission.

In 1955 a modest tablet in honour of the martyred missionaries was erected on the wall of a Methodist missionary training institute in Haberfield. The building was sold and the tablet removed. In June 1992, largely through the initiative of Arthur Brawn, the tablet was restored and re-located in the Uniting Church's newly-opened Centre for Ministry at North Parramatta.

There is a memorial to all those who died on the *Montevideo Maru* near Rabaul harbour, close to the old Rabaul Travelodge. It is in the form of a large rock with a plaque on it. According to a local resident: 'Unfortunately, it is slightly buried and every now and then we have to dig it out, due to the blockages of all the drains in Rabaul from the 1994 [volcano] eruption.'

## OPEN ALL HOURS

Arthur Brawn's decision as a boy to migrate to Australia was based on practicality. His father managed a group of boot and shoe shops in North London. The sign over the entrance said 'Nothing over 10/9d'.

Though his future seemed assured, the lad was not satisfied with conditions. 'We were open all day Saturdays, and our half holiday was Thursday.' It meant he could not play sports with his church youth fellowship on Saturdays.

The 17-year-old got into the habit of going to Australia House in the Strand on Thursday afternoons, seeing films of life in Australia, looking at their displays and reading the publicity material.

'On Christmas Eve 1923 we had opened shop at 9 am and I served my last customer at 11.45 pm. I remember going outside and saying to a friend who worked in a shop nearby: "I've had enough. This is my last Christmas Eve in a shop". "What are you going to do?" he asked and my reply was: "I think I will go to Australia".'

Arthur was accepted as a Dreadnought Boy and sailed from Tilbury with 59 others on 26 April 1924. On arrival in Sydney they were taken to the Garrison Church, in The Rocks, where women from the Empire Service Club formally welcomed them and gave them morning tea.

'They handed us each a sprig of wattle, and when we were walking through the Argyle Cut, on our way to see the City, locals chatted to us about "Wattle Day". I don't think any of us knew what this meant.'

After training at Scheyville, Arthur was rostered to a farm at Wilson's Creek, near Mullumbimby. If he expected to be met on arrival, he was disappointed. After waiting an indeterminate period at the station, he went into the town, where a local cream carter offered him a lift. A journey in a horse-drawn wagon followed, with Arthur perched precariously on empty cream cans. After the most uncomfortable ride of his life, his companion stopped abruptly, and said: 'This is where you get off. It's the other side of the creek.' He looked for the house, but couldn't see it.

Clutching his meagre possessions, Arthur set off down the track, and came to the creek, wondering how he was to get across. Suddenly, a 'wild looking man, with beard, flannel shirt and trousers, an old hat, and smoking a pipe, appeared at the other side, and with a broad Scottish accent, called for me to use the stepping stones and come across'.

It was his introduction to the McKean family. 'I had a very happy time with them. Les [the wild man] practised all sorts of pranks on the new chum, all in good fun, and helped me to settle in.' The newcomer took to farming naturally, and was passed from one local employer to another, with all of whom he enjoyed good relations. He took pride in acquiring various skills, and considered it a great day when, 'Mr East [his second or third employer] asked me to "plough up that paddock" and left me to my own devices.

'The paddock was close to the main road, and it was a challenge to "plough a straight furrow". We used to criticise farmers whose furrows were crooked, "like a black snake crawling up the paddock". On a hot day, Harry [a farm hand] would come over with a watermelon – cooled by immersing it in the creek – and under the shade of a tree there was a welcome rest.'

From the time of his arrival in Australia, Arthur sought out the nearest Methodist church for Sunday worship. He was proud when a training course was started for local preachers, and he was invited to attend. He did well, but was embarrassed at the thought of 'a young farm labourer [himself], having the temerity to stand up in front of these farmers, their wives and families, and preach to them'.

His preaching activities meant that Sundays were as busy as weekdays. He was required to visit two, maybe three churches in a day. Some were far apart. 'We rode together; in those days most country ministers still used horses, either riding or driving a sulky.' One day a travelling companion said to him: 'Have you considered offering for the ministry?' 'My reply was that I did not think I had the educational qualifications.' 'He said: "We will soon attend to that".'

The matter was resolved by the intervention of nature. Spring 1926 was very dry and by October the district was in the grip of a severe drought. 'Mr East told me one day that he could no longer afford to pay me "until the rain comes". He said I could stay on, without wages, as there would always be a bed for me.

'My reply was that I had not had a holiday since coming to Australia, and, if I could leave my horse on the farm, I would take a holiday until the drought broke.'

After completing three years at Leigh Theological College, Enfield, Arthur Brawn was ordained in 1932, and served briefly in Milton, NSW, before volunteering for missionary service in the Nakanai district of New Britain. He returned to Lismore to marry Jean Hewitson, daughter of a local motor dealer, and the couple spent three years in Melanesia as missionaries.

After furlough in Australia the couple were unable to return to the islands because Brawn had contracted malaria. As stated elsewhere, he resented this, which was to change the course of his life for ever. As a minister, he served subsequently in country and city parishes and was involved in youth work and evangelism, including the Christian Endeavour movement.

In 1974, he helped form the Dreadnought Association in order to gather the scattered remnants of the youth migrants for a yearly reunion. He was its secretary from 1974 to 1978,[7] and president from 1979 to 1991.

His wife, Jean, died in January 1993. Arthur Brawn himself died three weeks later.[8] His daughter and son-in-law, Edna and George Oakes, subsequently took on major roles in running the association.

# 4

## Filling the Empty Spaces

—

# 13

## Mary Booth – Ultimate 'Immigrationist'

EMPIRE LOYALTY and a desire to help fill Australia's 'empty spaces' motivated a number of men and women, and the organisations which they served, to give practical support to youth migration and to lobby others to do the same.

Regarded as heroes in their day, many of these 'immigrationists', as they were known, would nowadays be considered 'eccentrics' or 'oddballs'. Their contribution to the nation's growth was very real.

Dr Mary Booth, founder of the Sydney-based ANZAC Fellowship of Australian Women,[1] was among the better known crusaders for the cause.

The Empire Service Club, the base of many of her activities, was established initially to welcome soldiers returning from World War I. The modest, two storey building in The Rocks provided a place where they could relax in company of their own kind without going into a pub.

After the soldiers had all come home, Mary Booth and her friends began to focus on the young post-war migrants who were starting to arrive from Britain, and to do this they converted the premises into a migrants' club.[2] The rented building quickly became the first port of call in Sydney for many newly-arrived teenage migrants.

Booth was an early woman graduate of Sydney University (BA 1890). After two years as governess to the children of the Earl of Jersey, Governor of NSW, a legacy from her maternal grandmother gave her financial independence. She travelled with her sister to Edinburgh, where she obtained a further degree in medicine, and gained practical experience in infirmaries.

Returning to Australia in 1900, her medical career became subsumed in a myriad of worthy social and patriotic causes in which she became totally involved. Strongly feminist, she was a founder of the Women's Club in 1901, and secretary (later vice-president) of the National Council of Women of NSW.

Among her more prominent projects was a nation-wide program to train women in nutrition, cooking and home management, so as to promote the 'stability and fertility of Australian marriage'. In 1913 she represented the Australian Government at an international conference on infant mortality, in London.

On the outbreak of the Great War, she launched herself into a host of support activities from sewing guilds to fund-raising for war widows. She campaigned vigorously for conscription. An offer to supervise refugee camps in Egypt was refused. Apparently, she was too well qualified.

When peace returned, she tried unsuccessfully to gain a seat in the NSW Parliament as an independent feminist candidate. A similar bid for a Senate seat (in 1922) also failed.

The ANZAC Fellowship of Australian Women, which she founded in 1921, was the only civilian organisation permitted by the Prime Minister, Billy Hughes, to use the name 'ANZAC'.

Like others of her day, Mary Booth saw immigration – specifically the importation of young, white settlers from the mother country – as essential for the country's welfare. She was an office holder in the New Settlers' League of Australia, and founder president of the Women's Migration Council of NSW.

She took a specific interest in the welfare of youths who arrived under the Dreadnought Scheme, maintaining personal contact with some of them for 20 or more years. From 1925 to 1944 she published the monthly magazine, *The Boy Settler*. She saw it as a contribution to maintaining 'our own British stock' and counteracting communism. On a practical level, the magazine helped young migrants to keep in touch with one another, as well as offering practical information on farming and country life.

It has to be said that for many of the young migrants the first impressions on meeting her were not favourable. At a time when women's fashions were changing radically, she wore dowdy and old-fashioned clothes and looked distinctly eccentric.

A story told to me by a Dreadnought Boy was that she was travelling home late one evening and was alone in a compartment of a corridor train. She was very tired so she stretched out and reclined on a seat. A conductor came round to check tickets and pointed out that it was not permitted to rest feet on seats. She explained that she'd had a heavy day. She also said she was Dr Mary Booth. The conductor made an elaborate bow, saying: 'And I, Madam, am the Prince of Wales.'

The advent of old age did not blunt her activities. Among the organisations of which she was president or prime mover were various League of Nations auxiliaries, the English-Speaking Union and a campaign to combat venereal disease. At age 70 she gave land adjoining her home for a College of Household Arts and Science (its credo being that 'good wives make good husbands'). Three years later she persuaded others to stage a historical pageant beginning with Richard Coeur de Lion and ending with the creation of the Commonwealth of Australia.

Mary Booth died on 28 November 1956. A scholarship in her name was established for women economics students at the University of Sydney.

## GOLF CADDIES FOR EXPORT

Another keen supporter of youth migration was Thomas Sedgwick,[4] an Englishman who seems to have divided his time equally between the mother country and the new Dominions.

Sedgwick , a prominent worker in boys' clubs in London, came to wider attention in 1910 when − following an encouraging response from the New Zealand Government − he promoted a scheme to bring 'Town Lads' to that country for farm work.

A circular letter, prepared by Sedgwick, said youths would be apprenticed under regulations of the New Zealand Labour Department, and would receive one shilling a week pocket money. Their wages would be banked for them until the end of their apprenticeship, when they would receive payment due less the 10 pounds passage money.

His promotional material painted a far from rosy picture. 'The life will be found hard, rough, monotonous and dull,' he wrote. 'There are no lighted streets, shops, [nor] theatres in the country districts, and the nearest neighbour is sometimes 10 miles off.'

Potential migrants were told: 'Work begins at 4 am, and much farm work has to be done on Sundays. A day all alone on a hillside is very different to a few hours in a workshop.' He warned: 'The lads will have to do the HOUSE WORK as well as FARM WORK [his use of capitals] for their employers'

As a result of Sedgwick's endeavours, 50 'working class youths' – 25 each from London and Liverpool – duly sailed from London in January 1911. In a letter delivered to them two days before departure, he gave the following directive:

'Be at Fenchurch Street Station in full rig out. All should have a bath and hair cut tomorrow, and the tufty ones a shave as well.'

Before sailing, the whole party – with Sedgwick himself heading the signatories – signed a pledge to abstain from alcohol for one year from landing in New Zealand. A telegram of good wishes from King George V reached the ship when it touched at Plymouth.

The scheme had the support of farmers and their representatives in New Zealand , but had some opposition in political and union circles. Sedgwick noted in a letter to an admirer: 'If I can only break down the Labour opposition the farmers and manufacturers will cause the Government to expand their emigration policy before the November [1911] election.'

A personal visit and speaking tour in both the North and South Islands seems to have produced the desired favourable response, and several more shipments of youths followed. One who was not impressed was the Mayor of Christchurch, T.E. Taylor, who said youth migration meant bringing out 'the failures of the large cities of the Old Land' to become 'white slaves' on the farms.

After his successful speaking tour in New Zealand, Sedgwick returned to Britain and lobbied the various Australian states, requesting that they undertake similar schemes. The Government of Queensland, New South Wales and Tasmania responded favourably. The Queensland Government offered assisted passages not merely for farm workers, but for youths involved in ironworking, building, furniture making, carriage building and cycle trades.

While appreciative of his efforts, the youths recruited for Australia at that time were sponsored not by Sedgwick, but by the state governments.

Nevertheless, by now (1912) somewhat carried away with his own vision, he concocted a scheme for recruiting golf caddies, post office messenger boys 'and others in blind alley jobs' for rural employment in Canada, Australia and New Zealand. It is not known how many 'golf caddies' and 'messenger boys' applied.

Ever the optimist, he wrote to various celebrities, including the King and Archbishop of Canterbury, soliciting support for the above and similar schemes.

At the other end of the social scale, he wrote to the (newly formed) Public Schools Emigration League, endorsing that body's desire to recruit 'better class' boys for the colonies.[5]

Undeterred by what he considered a luke-warm response, Sedgwick broadened his interests, writing to the Governments of Ontario, Quebec, Victoria and Nova Scotia, seeking support for broadly-based youth migration programs to Canada. A commission of Inquiry into the matter was supportive. A letter from an onlooker stated: 'The farmer witnesses were unanimous that a forward immigration policy was absolutely necessary, as the farmers are greatly handicapped from the dearth of labour...'

In September 1912, Sedgwick took a party of 100 English boys to Canada. He wrote upon his return: 'I hope to get out 1,000 next year.'

However, none of this was to be. In 1913 his work was criticised in various newspaper articles and Sedgwick himself, who was inclined to be bombastic, crossed swords with Government Ministers and civil servants in Britain and Canada. Then came World War I, which put an end to all youth immigration for the immediate future.

Youth (and child) migration recommenced in 1921. This time Sedgwick – having had the pleasure of seeing so many of his schemes adopted – took a back seat. He became an escort, shepherding groups of Dreadnought and other sponsored youths from Britain to Australia and New Zealand.

He is fondly remembered by older Dreadnought Boys in this role, which continued until his death in 1929

## 'SUPER BOOMER'

Newspapers in Brisbane called him the 'Super Boomer', superlative form of a now obsolete slang word,[6] loosely translated as 'livewire'.

The Rev David Garland was born in Dublin in 1869 and came to

New South Wales with his parents as a boy. He originally sought a career in law, but felt a call to the Anglican ministry and was ordained in Perth as a missionary priest in 1892.

His 'mission' work almost immediately took back seat when his skills at launching and financing scattered bush parishes were realised. Within three years – at age 25 – he was made diocesan secretary and registrar.

In 1902 he moved to Queensland, where he was made Rector of Charters Towers and Canon of St James's Cathedral, Townsville. Again, almost immediately he was appointed administrator and registrar of the diocese.

After a disagreement with his bishop, he resigned from parish work to promote a controversial, but ultimately successful campaign for guaranteed religious instruction in Queensland state schools. He was also made Director of the Church of England Immigration Council in Queensland, which was to be a lifetime appointment. His reputation as a 'boomer' had begun.

From the time of his ordination Garland had been a chaplain to volunteer militia forces, and on the outbreak of World War I co-founded the pro-conscription Compulsory Service League, as well as becoming Senior Army Camp Chaplain for Queensland and director of the Soldiers' Help Society. He himself saw active service in the Middle East and, after the expulsion of the Turks from Jerusalem, was the first military chaplain to celebrate the Eucharist in the Anglican chapel at the Church of the Holy Sepulchre.

After the war ended, he remained in the Middle East, and was in Egypt during the 1919 Rebellion, providing liaison between the British military authorities and Oriental Christians. For this he received a knighthood with an appropriately exotic title[7] from the Patriarch of Jerusalem.

Returning to Queensland in 1920, he became Rector of Ithaca and resumed – now with greater urgency – his immigration and other interests. He was Queensland president of the New Settlers' League from 1926.

In the period 1925-1930 the (Queensland) Church of England Immigration Council,[8] headed by Garland, brought out some 1,600 people for work in Queensland, of whom about 900 were 'farm lads' (also called 'farm learners') in the parlance of the day.[9]

According to the Council's December 1930 half-yearly report: 'These farm lads have been an immense aid to the agricultural industry, and have proved an asset to the State in other ways.'

A letter from a farmer in Kingaroy, in the files of the National Archives, supports this view. 'I am very fortunate in that the majority of the boys sent to this district ring true and so they make it easier in finding work for others. It is surprising though what a lot of damage can be done by a boy who is not the right type.'

At a time when sectarianism was rife, Garland's (Church of England) Council had an ecumenical approach. In the words of the 1928 Annual Report: 'The Council assists immigrants of any denomination ... we want contented settlers ... we note with satisfaction the courteous acknowledgement by the Roman Catholic Archbishop of Brisbane, Dr J. Duhig, of our including in our nominations members of his church.'

(As a 'super high' churchman, Garland did, indeed, have unusually good relations with the newly-appointed Roman Catholic Archbishop of Brisbane, James Duhig, as well as with members of other faiths.)

With the onset of the Depression, the Federal and State Governments halted all migration. Garland was unhappy about this, stating in his newsletter: 'The temporary difficulties in which Australia finds herself should not be allowed to obliterate the still greater problem of keeping Australia white, by filling it with our own kith and kin.'

In the same newsletter Garland expresses a highly personal view about immigration, unemployment and Britain's 'excess' population. He wrote: 'The prosperity of the Empire depends upon the solution of the problem of the transfer of this excess population to where there is unoccupied land. But it is no use bringing the unemployed from where they belong, to remain unemployed where they do not belong.

'The problem can be dealt with only on a large scale. Perhaps the best suggestion we can make is that land should be prepared and farms got partially ready for those who, having had experience, would be suitable for taking up land immediately on arrival, or for those who, after some testing in England, would be willing to undergo training on their arrival in Australia.'

An inveterate letter writer, Garland badgered politicians with letters on immigration and numerous other topics, obtaining mixed results. Like so many others with similar ambitions, Garland's dreams of a mass migration by young Britons into Queensland were largely dashed by the Depression. A shift to the political left in national politics also meant that his philosophy concerning immigration came to be considered outdated. He also lost financial support.

According to Catholic social historian, Dr Barry Coldrey, who has studied Garland's and similar movements: 'As seen by the bureaucrats, youth migration – specifically the freelance efforts of groups such as Garland's – was good in its way, serving an obvious need, but also wasteful. They took in smallish numbers, and because they depended on volunteer labour, put in a great deal of effort to get those numbers.'

In time Garland and his friends came to be regarded as nuisances, even by those on the conservative side of politics. Senator Robert Wilson, who had been Health and Immigration Minister under Prime Minister, Stanley Bruce (1925-29), described him as a 'pest'. In 1935 Garland was snubbed at a dinner addressed by the then Attorney-General, Robert Menzies, even though the latter had declared in his speech his intention 'to urge [increased] migration as part of a grand imperial plan'.

The then Prime Minister, Joseph Lyons, repeated the snub – on the eve of a visit to Britain – by refusing a nomination from Garland for several farm lads and relatives of earlier migrants. This was despite the fact that a purpose of the visit was to stimulate migration.

Not that Garland was without other interests. He was the architect and originator of ANZAC Day[10] ceremonies in Brisbane, initiating the march and returned soldiers' lunches, the two minutes silence, wreath laying ceremonies, church services and even the badges.[11]

Among his minor pursuits – possibly dating from his encounter with the Patriarch – was a passion for obscure Orders of Chivalry. An enthusiastic Jacobite, he held various ranks in the Order of King Charles the Martyr.

From 1927 Garland broadcast Sunday services on public radio from his parish church of St Barnabas. When in 1937 the Australian Broadcasting Commission barred politicians from broadcasting for three months before the federal election, Garland challenged what he called the Commission's 'dictatorship of opinion'.

He invited the Queensland Premier, W. Morgan Smith, to be the principal speaker at a Communion breakfast, and when the ABC objected enlisted the private station 4BC. The result was a major furore and questions in Parliament.

David Garland died in October 1939, still promoting immigration and several other causes.

NEW SETTLERS
Reference has been made to the New Settlers' League, in which many of the key figures in youth migration held office.

The League's stated objectives were 'to prepare the way for settlers, to welcome them, [and] to assure them they are not strangers in a strange land'.

The League was most active in Victoria, at one time claiming 247 branches there. At the Melbourne Royal Agricultural Show in 1923, it exhibited what it called 'makeshifts' (do-it-yourself furniture) which the ideal migrant farmer should create. The items were wardrobe, wash stand, settee, ottoman, sideboard, bookcase, writing desk, kitchen dresser and cupboard – all constructed from kerosene cases. Old kerosine tins had been also turned into buckets, food bins, dishes, shower bath and dust pan.

In Western Australia the League was responsible for after-care of youth migrants in association with the Ugly Men's Association, a prominent service association in that State.

Pamphlets produced by the New Settlers'League had a slightly hysterical ring, with titles like *Keep Australia White*, *The Menace of an Empty Continent*, and *Youth – The Invaluable Factor in Migration*.

## BRING OUT A BRITON

'YOU can build Australia. Bring out a Briton,' ran the slogans in a style reminiscent of the World War I recruiting posters.

The Bring Out a Briton campaign, sometimes confused with the Big Brother Movement, was one of the success stories of post-war migration. About half a million British migrants arrived under its auspices. In one year alone (the financial year 1959-60) the scheme 'brought out' some

40,000 Britons out of a total British intake of 65,000. In that year the number of migrants from **all** nationalities was 125,000.

The campaign, which ended in 1965, was a Commonwealth Government initiative, under the control of the Department of Immigration. It operated a form of sponsorship, in that volunteers living in Australia were invited to contact the local Immigration Office if they could 'accommodate a British family' and/or help provide a job.

The scheme had the support of Protestant Church groups, who saw it as a response to disproportionate migration by nominally Catholic southern Europeans.

Its specific aim was to encourage the migration of families and young adults, but a number of unaccompanied teenagers got in through the net.

The Rev Frederick Lambert-Carter, until recently Minister of St Andrew's Congregational Church, in the inner Sydney suburb of Balmain, knows more about it than most. He came out under the scheme from Yorkshire in 1960 – but as a 'worker' ministering to fellow migrants on the P&O liner *Himalaya*.

Once in Australia, his brief was to be a port chaplain, by coincidence also based in Balmain.

As a port chaplain, with special responsibility for youth, he said he had 'seen them all' – Fairbridge kids, Barnardo Boys and the 'Bring out a Briton' migrants nominally in his care. The chaplaincy acquired five houses as live-in communities for young single migrants, with Lambert-Carter himself as 'foster father', who took pride in setting them on their feet.

'Some were successful, others not. They moved on; rentals were cheap, no one talked about a bond. You could buy a house in this district for £500.' Many were homesick and returned to the UK. Some came out a second time. His former charges visit him, even today.

One scene will stay in his mind 'for ever'. As Frederick Lambert-Carter tells the story: 'It was wharf 13 Pyrmont; I think it was about 1963. There was this lad, a huge fellow, standing quite alone. He was about 6 ft, and looked 18 stone. He was there with his baggage and no one at all to meet him. When I approached him I saw that there were tears dribbling down his cheeks.

'I talked to him, he'd just got off the ship. I discovered it was his birthday. His name was Michael Ware. I brought him over here to Balmain. My wife was away for the day. I went out and bought him some fish and chips and a big sponge cake and put a candle in the middle of it to celebrate his birthday.

'I found him a job at Callan Park as a gardener, but he didn't like that because the fellows were loitering a lot. He said, "I want a job where I'm going to work. Not where you're supposed to start work at eight and don't get started until nine." I remember he moved across to work in the stores there.

'He sort of drifted into church, and took part in its activities. He was also a great sportsman. We organised migrant teams, we won the cup in what they called the Protestant Churches League in football. I've still got the banner. The teams travelled about; it helped them to settle because so many of them were suffering from homesickness.

'One day, after a particular service, Michael said he would like to 'go into' the Church, by which he meant become a minister. This came out of the blue; he had no Church background. So I encouraged him, and pushed him forward to be accepted here as a candidate.'

Sadly, Michael was rejected for training. 'He was just a blunt boy from a rural district, a farm labourer's son, big, rough; they were not interested.' But Michael was still determined. Lambert-Carter pulled strings with friends in the UK and got him accepted into a theological college in Britain. Members of the Balmain congregation organised a collection and paid his fare.

He turned out to a very successful student, and was ordained as a Congregational Minister. During the turbulent 80s, Michael was based in the West Riding of Yorkshire. When Margaret Thatcher clashed with the miners he achieved a name as a man of compassion, providing a soup kitchen for those out of work and practical support for their wives and families.

In 1988 he was appointed to take charge of the parish at Selby, near York – the self-same parish from which Frederick Lambert-Carter had left to come to Australia.

---

# 14

## Bands, Banners and Patriotic 'Homilies'
## The Young Australia League

---

OF ALL THE LARGER-THAN-LIFE FIGURES associated with youth migration and patriotic movements, none stands out more than John Joseph Simons – Perth identity, newspaper owner and founder of the Young Australia League.

He was born in Clare, South Australia, in 1882, but moved to Fremantle, Western Australia, at the age of 13, and got a job as an office boy.[1] Lack of formal education was to prove no handicap. The lad read widely, went to night school, and within a few years had risen to office manager.

However, his real interest lay in 'social improvement'. While barely out of his teens, he gained a reputation as a strong and controversial debater on a variety of issues. He was knowledgeable about Australian politics, history and literature, and a powerful advocate of military, naval and industrial self-reliance.

Physically, he was tall – 6 ft 4 in. (193 cm) – but gangly, with ill-fitting clothes, tie and hair awry, and an outlandish taste in hats.

Although a fierce nationalist and organiser of 'Buy Australian' campaigns, he supported the goals of Empire, but believed Australia and Australians should act independently and put their own interests first. This makes him difficult to 'label' and explains the contradictory assessments of him by commentators in later years.

In Western Australia in those days a high proportion of schoolchildren had British-born parents and thus soccer was their favoured sport. The young Simons thought this was wrong and pushed for 'Aussie Rules' to be played in schools.

As secretary of the Western Australian National Football League (1905-1914) and founder of the Young Australia Football League (1905) he consolidated Australian Rules football in his own State and influenced growth of the sport elsewhere.

---

In 1905 – while still only 23 – Simons and a few friends established the Young Australia League, a youth movement, whose chief object[2] was to 'develop an all-round type of Australian boy'. It sought to achieve this via various means, including, what Simons and his friends called 'education by travel'. The League developed rapidly as a patriotic, independent, (officially) non-political and non-sectarian organisation, which, in its heyday, had an active membership exceeding 6,000.

Loosely modelled on the Boy Scouts, the Young Australia League, known by its initials YAL, was open to boys aged 12 to 17, and offered participation in team sports, bands, debating, theatrical and other 'home grown' entertainment of a kind which allowed Simons to demonstrate to the full his showmanship abilities.[3]

These talents had been demonstrated a year earlier by his organisation of a pageant to commemorate the 50th anniversary of the Eureka Stockade. His suggestion that the event should be marked with a public re-enactment prompted a howl of protest from conservatives, who considered it a 'celebration of treachery and rebellion'. Simons saw it as celebrating 'the triumph of justice over colonial tyranny'. As in more modern times, the resultant publicity ensured its success.

His height and confident manner – his gait and dress sense had by this time considerably improved – impressed the youngsters, who addressed him throughout his life as 'Boss'.[4] Yet the atmosphere at meetings and even on inter-state and overseas tours was relaxed, with first names or nicknames – the president, Lionel Boas, was called 'Pop' – as the general rule.

On tours prefects and a head prefect were appointed among the boys. Simons said the conduct of a contingent on tour should be 'like a college on the move'. Alcohol and tobacco were banned for all members until they reached 21.

In 1907, in line with the credo about 'travel', Simons organised the first such tour – a three months' visit to the Eastern States by young (Australian Rules) footballers, with himself as team manager. Its success led, in the following three years, to similar tours by non-footballers. Altogether, some 1,000 lads participated in the three trips. In those days, with no air travel and when many rural Australians had not even visited their own State capital, such a mass exodus, with the glamour of departure on a ship from Fremantle, created enormous interest.

In 1910/1911 the League went one better when some 40 boys toured the United States, Britain and Europe with their own brass band and 'minstrels' performing in various cities. They were away nearly 12 months. It was the first time most Americans had encountered Australians, and the lads were a hit. Revenue earned from musical performances helped meet costs, which would otherwise have to be borne by the boys or their parents. A highlight was a meeting with the US President, William H. Taft.

In Britain the boys were received by King George V and Queen Mary at Buckingham Palace. In typical style Symons made the boys march into the reception room with two standard bearers at their head. One lad carried the Union Jack, the other the new Australian flag, which greatly interested the King, who inspected it closely.[5]

Despite the absurdity of such a charge, Simons was accused by political and other opponents of being 'anti-British'. The accusation was based in part on such trivia as his rejection of 'British' football and an incident where he forbade boys on an inter-state tour from buying chocolates imported from Britain when a locally made brand was available.

Another factor was Simons's reference in his speeches to the need for closer ties with the United States, which opponents saw as being at the expense of Britain. In 1914 Simons organised a second YAL party to visit the United States and Britain. War was declared on August 4 – a few days before the group was to leave. Simons and his committee agonised over what should be done, but eventually decided to go ahead with the American leg of the tour, though not, of course, the British.

The decision aroused criticism but, according to the YAL, was the right choice. The US was at the time still neutral and the presence of the young visitors, with their brass band and singers (whose repertoire included folk songs from several US States) worked marvels at countering German propaganda against the Allied cause.

Simons, with his flare for publicity, staged a stunt that gave the Allied cause a big publicity boost in New York. The boys were officially invited to visit the British Embassy and Simons so arranged the route that the party should march past the German Embassy on the way. As they got level with the Embassy the band, flying the Australian flag and the Stars and Stripes, stuck up '*Rule Britannia*'. The Gemans could not resist rushing to the balconies and windows to see what was happening. The incident got big headlines in the papers the following day.

Also in 1914, Simons founded a monthly journal, *The Boomerang*, devoted to Young Australia League affairs. It started as a four-page effort, increasing, as interest and modest advertising revenue grew, to some 20 to 30 pages. It lasted into the 1960s, making it one of the oldest papers published by a youth organisation in Australia. For years the entire contents were collected, written and edited by The Boss in his spare time.

The period also marked the dawn of The Boss's political aspirations. Simons – unlike most 'immigrationists'[6] – opposed conscription and campaigned against it in the plebiscites of 1916-17.

In the 1917 Federal elections he was an unsuccessful Labor candidate for Fremantle. Opponents vilified him not merely as 'anti-British' but as a 'shirker'. He received a white feather and other calumny, which was grossly unfair since he had served in the militia and was twice rejected for overseas service on medical grounds. War hysteria forced his resignation in 1917 as paid secretary of the Western Australian State School Teachers' Union.

After peace returned, Simons resumed his work for the YAL. Inspired by the example of Kingsley Fairbridge in his own State, and by the Big Brother Movement in NSW, he took on youth migration as a further plank in the League's activities (see description below).

In 1921 Simons won the Legislative Assembly seat of East Perth for Labor. It was an uneasy alliance because of his support for youth migration, which many unionists saw as against their interests, and his links with another journal, the *Call*, which he had founded in 1918, and which had labelled strikers 'Trade union trash'. (Simons promoted advertising, while his friend Victor Courtney was editor.)

A row with the party executive caused him to resign his seat in November 1922, after which he stood unsuccessfully as an independent. Meanwhile, he and his friend Courtney founded another newspaper, the weekly *Mirror*, which outsold *The Call*.

The weekly *Mirror* featured sport and sensation, combining scandalous headlines – 'Nakedness at North Beach' – with pious editorials. Simons apparently saw no dichotomy between this and his youth work.

Loss of his seat in Parliament gave him more time to devote to the Young Australia League, which continued to develop rapidly. Branches of the YAL were established in New South Wales, Victoria, Queensland and South Australia.[7]

The NSW branch, formed in 1922, got off to a good start when a party of 100 boys visited Western Australia. Enthusiasm then flagged a little, but was boosted in 1925 when the movement's national secretary, Ted 'Wap' Marie, was sent from Perth to run the Sydney-based organisation.

'Wap', whose nickname, pronounced to rhyme with tap, was somewhat of a mystery, headed the Sydney movement for 11 years. Probably his proudest moment was when the NSW League Band was chosen to lead the procession at the official opening of the Sydney Harbour Bridge.

In addition to inter-state branches the movement by this time had auxiliaries for parents and an active Old Boys' Association.[8] Girls were also (somewhat reluctantly) admitted into membership.[9]

Popular entertainment, as well as marching bands, was (and still is) a prominent league activity. Show business personalities who gave their first performances as members of the YAL included Rolf Harris (then still in short pants), Terry Scanlon (straight man to Roy Rene), Bill Kerr, Colin Croft and George Nicholls.

In 1924 the League's headquarters, costing £32,000, were opened in central Perth. Much of the money was given voluntarily. Like many things associated with the YAL, the circumstances were unusual. In what was rightly considered a great honour, Walter Burley Griffin, no less,[10] had offered to supply a design, free of charge, but this took so long to arrive that the Prime Minister, William Hughes, laid the foundation stone before this was received.

When the plans did arrive, The Boss and others at the YAL were delighted. However, they were complicated as well as ambitious, and the City Council, as well as local architects, considered them 'impracticable' and unsafe. There was possibly a touch of jealousy on the part of the Architects' Association. Prominent contractors refused even to tender for the scheme, arguing that some of the special materials were not available within the State.[11]

Simons found himself in a 'no win' situation and was forced to discard Griffin's grand plan and to seek the services of a local firm of architects. In a letter to Griffin he stated inter-alia: 'I am fully conscious of the absurdity of a position under which we find that while Chicago, Sydney and Melbourne rank you as a great architect, you do not, in the minds of the experts of Perth, measure up to the standard of this comparatively little Western Village.'

The return of peace had allowed a resumption of overseas tours. In 1924 there was an 'Empire Tour' and, in 1925, Simons's grandest tour ever, when 140 boys[12] visited the United Kingdom, France, Switzerland, Italy and Belgium. They were received by, among others, King George V, the Prince of Wales, President of the Irish Free State, King of Italy, the Pope, President of the Swiss Federation, and the King of Belgium.

Another 'world tour', in 1929, was particularly memorable. Thanks to The Boss's organising skills, the group found itself in Washington on the day of the inauguration of Herbert Hoover as US President. Some of the boys noticed that from where they were stationed they had easy access to one of the flagstaffs of the Capitol. Within minutes the Australian flag was run up alongside the Stars and Stripes. It is not known if The Boss was party to the escapade.

US law decrees that one flag, and one flag only, the flag of the United States of America, shall be flown from public buildings during a presidential inauguration. Officials were horrified, but Hoover, who was notified, seemed to find it amusing and he let the flag stay. Subsequently, he invited the tour group to the White House, and presented them with the traditional laurel wreath under which he sat during his inauguration.

Inter-State branches, like their parent body in Perth, adopted a quasi-militarist style, with uniforms, bands and parade ground hype. There is a photo of a YAL contingent, dressed in a manner resembling Naval officer cadets, being inspected in Paris by Marshal Foch.

While 'on parade' the youngsters were given pep talks – his entry in the Australian Dictionary of Biography calls them 'homilies' – by Simons and his guests on matters deemed to be of importance.

Simons himself wore a specially designed uniform, in a style befitting the 'commanding officer'. A photo exists of The Boss standing stiffly to attention, walking stick under his arm like a drill sergeant's swagger stick, talking to the Prince of Wales, later King Edward VIII,[13] who is wearing a top coat with bowler hat.

## NOT 'BROWN SHIRTS'

Neo-fascist movements were at that time gaining currency, and to modern eyes it may smack of a 'private army' or worse. However, the League were not 'brown shirts' nor Mosleyites,[14] and it seems likely that Simons and his subordinates were just capitalising on the appeal of marching bands (then very much in vogue) and dressing up.

Certainly, the boys themselves did not regard the movement as political. To parents the League probably seemed a 'sound' organisation, promoting old-fashioned values like loyalty, patriotism and discipline. (Simons himself described the movement's guiding principles as 'Love, Service and Tolerance'.) These factors, and the opportunities for their children to travel, would have been attractive to middle class voters.

Concerning 'patriotism' it is worth noting that a number of 'League lads', having reached military age, died fighting for Australia in both world wars.[15] Nearly 500 'Leaguers' served in World War I, of whom 89 made the supreme sacrifice. Three boys of the League won the Military Cross and six were awarded the Military Medal.

In 1929 Simons came across a valley deep in the Darling Range, which captured his imagination as a potential 'garden of Eden' for recreational use by his lads. He purchased the 59-hectare site for £600 (the original asking price was £2,200) and cleared the land, using voluntary labour. Cottages and recreational facilities were quickly established, also a 'Grove of the Unforgotten' to commemorate the war dead. Simons did not believe in half measures. The grove was built in the shape of a giant lyre with a view to musical performances. A waterfall descended its full length. There were 89 steps and 89 cypress trees – one for each of the fallen.

In the 1940s the site, near Roleystone, on the Canning River, fell into a delapidated condition, but was restored in the 1990s after being bought by the State Government to avoid a threatened development.

A genius at self-promotion, Simons was inclined to be cheeky in his demands. In November 1926, having heard about an invitation to the Boy Scouts, he wrote to the Acting Prime Minister, Earle Page, suggesting that the League be invited to supply an honour guard at the opening of the Federal Parliament building, in Canberra, by the Duke and Duchess of York (later King George VI and Queen Elizabeth).

He wrote: 'We would suggest that the delegation should number say 50 – just half the strength allowed to the Scouts. We would make an endeavour to supply a band with a complete instrumentation and carrying a set of silk national flags, and moving with the same discipline and precision as marked the trained bands which we have sent out on world tours at different times.' His letter was passed to the event organiser who gave him a curt 'No'.

Simons attended personally to every detail of YAL activities, in particular the tours. On a later visit to Canberra an unknown Minister or public servant ordered ice cream for the boys, who had been waiting in the sunshine and 'looked hot'. Unfortunately, by the time the ice cream arrived the boys had returned to their hotel.[16] A 'paper war' broke out – recorded meticulously in the Australian Archives – about the mystery donor's identity and which Government department should pay the bill, totalling four pounds and five shillings.

In 1935 Simons and Courtney, with others, bought Perth's *Sunday Times*. With Simons as managing director, Western Press Ltd and Country Newspapers Ltd quickly expanded, owning three metropolitan and over 30 country newspapers.

Reflecting Simons's own sentiments, the *Sunday Times* reversed its former secessionist stance, depriving that movement of its mouthpiece. From 1943 the paper supported the Federal Labor Government and its attempts to win greater Commonwealth powers.

By 1939, when World War II again interrupted recruitment, some 50,000 West Australians, and a smaller number in other states, had at some stage in their lives been involved in a Young Australia League activity.

A key to the movement's success was teamwork. As Simons stated in a letter now housed in the Australian Archives: 'We desire to point out that practically all the work of the League is carried out by voluntary workers, and the tours are conducted by adults, who not only sacrifice their salary during absence from employment, but also pay their quota of cost for the various tours.'

In 1941 Simons assigned his interest in Western Press in trust for the Young Australia League. This yielded over £50,000 after his death from hypertensive heart disease on 24 October 1948.

In life, and even in death, The Boss's character and personality remained somewhat of an enigma. He never married, and lived with his mother until middle age. His friend and colleague, Victor Courtney, pointed to a romance in Simons's earlier years.[17] His entry in the Australian Dictionary of Biography[18] describes him as a man 'of temperate manly habits and strong-willed'. It says he was inclined towards 'gutsy humour issued in a roaring laugh and invective, which sometimes gave offence'.

He is buried in the Catholic section of Karrakatta cemetery, where his epitaph reads: 'I am the Spirit of the League'

## THE LEAGUE AND 'BOY SETTLERS'

The Young Australia League's involvement with youth migration began in 1923, when J.J. Simons had long and earnest talks with the then Premier of Western Australia, Sir James Mitchell, a proponent of immigration.

Simons sought an all-out effort to encourage the migration of British lads, aged approximately 15 to 17, for farm work.

According to Simons, 'a feeling of strangeness' and general homesickness were inevitable among young migrants. The League, with its large number of Australian lads in a similar age group, and the families from which they came, could play a decisive and positive role by welcoming the new arrivals 'into their hearts and homes', thus making the break from the United Kingdom less severe.

Simons spelled out his views in a letter to the (British) Overseas Settlement Office in London, in which he wrote:

'If satisfactory arrangements can be made with the Imperial, Commonwealth and State governments, our organisation will undertake the work of placing the boys in suitable positions and take responsibility for their aftercare. The method of procedure would, in brief, be as follows:

'The League would undertake the proper placing of a given number of boys per annum – say three groups of 40 each – for a period. Prior to the boys embarking from England, positions would be already be bespoken with farmers, orchardists, pastoralists etc of assured standing. The latter would be vouched for by the League parents in various parts of the State before the home was designated as being suitable for a British boy.

'On arrival at the port of embarkation, the migrants would, after official formalities had been complied with, be received by the parents of our City. A welcome function would be organised by our City mothers. The new arrivals would, for a short period of say three or four days, be billeted in the homes of our parents, the idea of this being to give a kindly home touch at the beginning which would create a feeling in the mind of the boy that Australia wanted him.

'The experience of the other schemes has been that the absence of everything but the cold official touch filled many boys with an inexpressible home sickness and loneliness which left a morbid impression on their minds which deprived them of any possibility of being happy in their new surroundings.

'After a short stay in the City, each boy would be transferred to the farm for which he was designated. On arrival at the country station, he would be met by our League parent, who would again manifest a kindly interest in him. The farm for which he was intended would probably be from 10 to 40 miles from the town at which he detrained. It would be the duty of the local League parent meeting the boy to make him happy between the time of his arrival at the station and his arrival at the scene of his work. The home of this League parent would be a sort of halting place on the way to the boy's destination.

'At each centre a committee of League parents would be responsible for the aftercare of the lad, including safeguards such as visits etc, relative to his housing, social facilities and general happiness.

'It will be seen from this that the boy from the time he lands up to the time he reaches the farm will have established two points of friendship; the one with parents in the City, the other with parents at the town where he detrains. Therefore from the outset he will feel the touch of friendliness which means so much to the stranger in a new country.'

In another letter to the Overseas Settlement Office, dated 3 April

1925, Simons stressed the importance of after-care:

'My League realises that a great many intangible schemes have been proposed in regard to boy migrants but that most of the plans lack practicability because of the absence of the human touch in the aftercare of the youths.

'To interest English boys in Australia and to induce them to leave their own country represents but two phases in the work of boy settlement. The third and most important factor [is] the welfare of the boy after arriving in the new country [and] is not, in our opinion, sufficiently stressed.

'It is thought that many boys are prevented by their parents from going overseas because of the lack of a sense of security regarding their welfare after landing. We believe that if the Young Australia League stands as a sort of joint sponsor for the wellbeing of the boy settlers, then a feeling of security would be created.

'We believe that the machinery of the League would be readily adaptable to the needs of the boys... In addition to a strong membership in Perth, where the headquarters are situated, we have groups of members – parents of our young boys – in almost every town of the State where British boys would be likely to be located.'

The Overseas Settlement Office agreed in principle to Simons's proposal. The State Government also agreed, but demanded that the League give priority to helping local lads leaving school to find similar rural employment. A Boy Settlers' Department (operated by the League), was established for the latter purpose, and received an annual Government grant of £900.[19]

According to documents in the Australian Archives, the number of 'local lads' seeking help proved fewer than expected, hence permission was given to reverse the priorities. It is unclear just when the first batch of British boys arrived. It appears that red tape delayed the start for at least three years. A file in the Archives indicates that by July 1932, 192 lads had been brought in, most of them in the period 1931-32.

The file also notes that 22 of the 192 boys had subsequently returned home to Britain – a point seized upon by opponents. The role of 'after-care' was considered very important. The files record letters of gratitude from parents in England thanking parents of League members who had undertaken this role.

With youth and child migration there was an assumption, as previously stated, that the source country should be Great Britain. The Young Australia League broke the 'rule' a little by gaining permission (in the late 1920s) for the immigration of a small number of youths – of white British extraction – from South Africa, India and Malaya.

The YAL's involvement with youth migration ceased when Government grants for such purposes were axed in the Depression. Involvement was only half-heartedly resumed in later years.

The Young Australia League remains active in Western Australia, where it runs a school holiday camp and has a girls' marching team. It also survives modestly in Queensland, but no longer operates in other States. The League's centenary year (2005) has been marked by a bands festival, reunion dinner, the laying of a time capsule and the launch of a history of the movement.[20]

## 'MASCOT' RECALLS BRIDGE OPENING

Les (Martin) Waddington, of Berkeley Vale, on the NSW Central Coast, marched across the Sydney Harbour Bridge in March 1932, only minutes after Captain de Groot had illegally cut the ribbon.

The boy, who was 10, was at the front of the procession as a mascot with the Young Australia League's Sydney-based brass band. He recalls: 'There were five of us. We were all in the junior band and marched as mascots ahead of the senior band. Thousands of people were watching us. It was a great honour.'[21]

He did not see de Groot's famous protest, but feels his own father, who was among the spectators and was a member of the New Guard, would have approved. 'We were on the Bradfield Highway, not very far from the southern pylon, and we came to a halt. We just wondered why. We were there for up to half an hour possibly, just cooling our heels.

'It wasn't until we'd actually walked back into Sydney again, back over the bridge, that we found out what had happened. Of course, there were no mobile phones or portable radios around in those days. Then later on in the afternoon the newspapers appeared with the story about de Groot all over the front page.'

Les Waddington's main memory of that day is of the uniform. 'It was nice to look at. All cream, with long trousers and a uniform jacket, buttoned up to the neck. There was gold fancy lacing sewn all over the front. I looked like a miniature commissionaire outside a leading hotel.'

The clothing had been sent across from either Western Australia or South Australia, and arrived only the day before the ceremony. 'It was a disaster. Many of the uniforms were too small; we just had to cram ourselves into them. We had white boots, which everybody found too tight, and white gloves which were also too small. It was torture for all of us.

'We had peaked caps like an officer's cap or a tram driver's cap, only in cream. They were quite smart looking for those days. The caps, too, were ill-fitting.'

As a boy of 10, he and his friends were unaware of any 'political links', but he does not rule out – given his own father's right wing connections – that this may have been the case.

'It's a curious business. The bridge opening was a NSW Government turnout and the Government was headed by Jack Lang. It would be surely an anomaly if a left-wing Labor Premier were to invite a right wing group to head the procession.' (As stated previously, Simons had strong Labor Party connections, which were probably the deciding factor.)

Young Les, then living at Hurstville, had joined the YAL, at the instigation of his father, a year before the bridge opening. The carrot was the opportunity for band training, which appealed to many at that time. Band practice took place weekly at an old cinema in Mortdale. 'It was a pretty tatty sort of place, by that time being used for boxing and other activities.'

The junior band comprised about 15 to 20 boys, aged about eight to 12. Transfer to the senior band was based on competency. Les believes some of its members were, in fact, young men. The bandmaster for both senior and junior bands was Bert Caton.

The experience was to provide good grounding. Les Waddington went on to study music at the Sydney Conservatorium.

In July 2001 he marked his 80th birthday by crossing the bridge again – this time climbing the arches and central span, 134 metres above sea level – with his three daughters.

# 15

## The Millions Club

███████

*'This Club is called the Millions Club.*
*I understand it has nothing to do with filthy lucre.*
*It has to do with something finer and better. Men of commanding position*
*in the great city assemble, not merely for social intercourse,*
*or to increase the greatness of an already great city, but to encourage men*
*[and boys] in their millions to come and help them pioneer this country...'*
Speech by British MP, Ian Macpherson, member of an Empire
Parliamentary Association delegation, 1926.

I T WAS CALLED THE MILLIONS CLUB, and its logo – *Patriotism,*
*Immigration* – superimposed on a map of Australia, says it all.

It was founded in 1912; a blend of gentlemen's club and lobby for an
astonishing variety of causes. These ranged from improvements to the
State railway system, and the eradication of rabbits and mosquitoes, to
expansion of irrigation , secondary education for country children, and –
most importantly – the promotion of immigration.

The name has interesting origins. Basically, a handful of citizens saw
the good which could come from bringing together men of goodwill who,
while enjoying each other's company, could at the same time work
towards the progress of the city of Sydney and its attainment of a population of one million.[1]

An exploratory meeting was held at the Hotel Australia. It was called
by Percy Hunter, a Sydney identity, who, according to a report in the
*Sydney Morning Herald*, got the idea while visiting the US, where similar
clubs, promoting individual cities, had been formed.

A man of limited schooling (though with a reputation, later in life,
for learning and erudition) Hunter, like others associated with the club's
birth, was larger than life. Beginning his working career as a cub reporter

on a Victorian country newspaper, he moved to the *Sydney Daily Telegraph*, where he achieved fame for his many scoops and dedicated approach to newsgathering. He was also a sports promoter, organising professional boxing (including a world title fight at Rushcutters Bay) and the famed Sydney Thousand cycle race. This had the then astronomical prize of 1,000 guineas.

A passionate supporter of immigration, Hunter was persuaded to quit his sporting activities to become (in 1915) first Director of Immigration for the Australian Government, based in London. The idea was that he should prepare for the flood of migrants that was expected to follow the Great War. Incredibly, he also found time, quite unofficially, to do his bit in France as an ambulance driver. His stays in London as Director of Immigration were quite extensive and lasted well into the 1920s. At this time, he also made several visits to Geneva as an Australian representative to the League of Nations.

Hunter's concept was not universally acclaimed. Decentralisation had just become an 'in' word and the critics claimed that Sydney was already overgrown at the expense of the rural districts. The newspaper *Smith's Weekly*, in particular, was hostile towards a body dedicated to a narrow concentration on the city alone. The club's originators, nimble on their feet from the outset, changed their stance. The name quickly became the Millions Club of NSW. The goal was to be achieved by immigration – British, of course.

The club was formally incorporated on 16 October 1912, following a second meeting on the stage of the Theatre Royal. This unusual venue is explained by the presence of Hugh J. Ward, chief executive of the theatrical company, J.C. Williamson's, who was an enthusiastic supporter.

The club from the start was concerned with design and planning concepts – namely, building a city (and State) fit for a million people – as much as the mere gaining of numbers. The club's first president was Mr (subsequently Sir) Arthur Rickard, merchant, entrepreneur and, later, real estate agent, who also became (in 1921) the first chairman, then president of Dr Barnardo's Homes[2] (as the organisation was then called) in Australia. He remained at the helm of both organisations, as well as taking a close interest in the affairs of the Big Brother Movement,[2] until his death in 1948.

Another inaugural member was the retail magnate, Sir Samuel Hordern, who had been closely involved, a year earlier, with the arrival of the first party of Dreadnought Boys.

In its first year the club began arranging for a proposed Great Australian Exhibition, to be staged in London in 1916, also the publication of a periodical, *The Glad Hand*, to provide 'information to newcomers and tourists from overseas'. According to the annual report for the year ending 31 December 1914, the first edition was 'almost ready for publication when the outbreak of war made it impractical'.

The club immediately turned its attention to projects of a more pressing kind, including a fund for Belgian widows, Christmas Cheer for soldiers' and sailors' dependants and the gift of 22 horses to troops serving in the Middle East and the Dardanelles.

With the end of the Great War the club decided to seek permanent headquarters (until then meetings were held in restaurants). Although it was a men's club, the decision was taken – somewhat daringly – to allow members to 'bring their ladies' for two hours daily to partake of afternoon tea.

Another early decision was to re-launch the aborted journal, this time under the title *Newsy Notes*. The mundane masthead was soon replaced by *Millions* – a proud title which survived for over 50 years. Its first edition announced the lease of premises at the corner of Pitt and Moore Street (later renamed Martin Place), an arrangement which was not, in fact, consummated. Instead, the club took up premises at 118 Pitt Street (on the northern corner of the junction with Rowe Streets), within spitting distance of its later, longer lasting headquarters building..

Membership of the Millions Club quickly became a 'Who's Who' of Sydney society. Just about any male person of importance seemed to belong.[3] Guest speakers included Sir Arthur Conan Doyle, Dame Nellie Melba, and opposing cricketers Douglas Jardine and Don Bradman.

The Australian Prime Minister Stanley Bruce visited the club, as did the Prince of Wales, later the (uncrowned) King Edward VIII, who also supported Barnardos. The Prince was intrigued by the club's name, and asked the meaning of the word 'Millions'. 'Population, not pound notes,' he was told. 'Oh, I understand,' he replied.

The Great War had the effect of heightening a sense of insecurity linked to Australia's small population. 'Filling the empty spaces' became an important feature in the club's philosophy. In 1919, a Miss Cameron, representing Barnardos in the UK, came to Australia on a fund raising drive. On the ship was a member of the Millions Club who was a supporter of this cause. He suggested that the visitor call at the Millions Club.

At that time Barnardos had an active migration program to Canada, but had not (yet) considered formal migration to Australia. Miss Cameron explained to club officials that the money would be used to help orphaned and disadvantaged children to make new lives in Canada. Would the club help her? To which the reply was given: 'Yes, we can gather support for you, but only if it is applied to sending young migrants to Australia.'

In 1921 the Sydney Millions Club sponsored the arrival of the first official group of Barnardo Boys. This party of 40 youngsters – average age 16 – arrived in New South Wales on 16 October, on the SS *Berrima*. Being older than later groups of Barnardo arrivals, they were able to enter directly into the workforce.

They had been given a send off from Buckingham Palace and were welcomed in Sydney like heroes. According to a report in *Millions* magazine: 'Many a heart swelled in sympathy for the little strangers who had come here to become good Australians. They bring something like a lump to the throat of many a careful father and mother, these gallant little men who have come a venturing among us.'

## ORPHANS WANTED

This initiative by the Millions Club – in particular its president, Arthur Rickard – led directly to the decision of the UK organisation to establish a branch of Barnardos in this country. It would seem Australians did most of the decision-making. A cable from Sir Arthur (in April 1921) to the Barnardo parent organisation in Stepney read: 'Branch home established here. Can take 50 boys immediately. Particularly want orphans.'

It seems the London body initially had misgivings. The minutes of the executive meeting on 11 January 1922 record that 'Miss Cameron appeared to have agreed to the Australians obtaining money in that country for the work of the local home, which had been subscribed for the general work of the Barnardo Homes [in the mother country].' This is described in the minutes as 'disastrous'. Subsequent minutes reflect an easing of these tensions.

Concerning immigration, the Millions Club's magazine quickly entered the fray. The 1 January 1922, issue of *Millions* carried the slogan on its cover: 'Millions of people are wanted urgently to fill Australia's empty spaces.' Underneath were balloons reading 'Immigration our only salvation' and 'Help your club'. The accompanying photograph showed a suitably Anglo-Saxon looking mother and child, above the caption 'Two new Australians. Just in time for Christmas.'

During the early 1920s, every movement which was in any way directed towards stimulating migration had its most tangible support from the Millions Club and its indefatigable president. In January 1923, the New Settlers' League was formed and, yes, Sir Arthur was its president.

On 15 April 1925, according to the club's records, the Big Brother Movement was 'launched at the Millions Club' at a meeting convened under the presidency of Sir Arthur Rickard.[4] According to the same records: '...a large number of club members were already wearing Big Brother buttons.' For the next 75 years annual general meetings of the Big Brother Movement were held at the club, which for a time also served as the movement's central office.

Later in 1925, Rickard and Sir William Vicars wrote to *The Times* in London in eloquent strain under the heading 'Boy and Girl Settlers', stressing the desirability and opportunity for successful settlement of many thousands of boys and girls in Australia and Canada. The newspaper published the letter prominently in its issue of 26 August.

In the early post-war years the interests of returning servicemen were a prime concern, and one of the club's first drives – overshadowing the question of immigration – was that of securing employment for the returning men. Members were active in offering such jobs in their own businesses or in finding employment for the 'diggers'.

Similarly, home-building for soldiers was pushed. A body known as the Voluntary Workers' Association was the co-ordinator in this work and its executive substantially comprised club members. Several Millions Club members were chairmen of branches of the association. Governments were prodded along to move faster with state-sponsored schemes to settle returned men on their own farms. In September 1921, *Millions* enthused about the prospect of 'a million farmers on a million farms'. Later, this theme was changed to '600 acres wheat farms to replace 10,000 acres pastoralists', and in 1924 the catch cry was 'Break up the estates'. The club membership had in its ranks a sizeable sprinkling of owners of large pastoral holdings. Incredibly, they didn't seem to mind their own threatened downsizing!

Expansion of the state's fledgling irrigation schemes was pushed, as were projects to take branch railway lines to remote parts.

Rabbit infestation quickly grew to plague proportions in the early 1920s and *Millions* asked the question: 'Will Australia eat the rabbits or the rabbits eat Australia?' A little later: 'If politicians chased rabbits the way they chase votes, bunny will soon be counted out.' Again, there is no sign of the club's many parliamentarian members having been greatly upset.

The club demanded improved secondary education opportunities for country schoolchildren, and also called for action to 'stop the decay of country towns'. The Australian Made Preference League was strongly supported, as witnessed by this exhortation to Australian women: 'Australia wants her women, from the cities and the woods, To praise, to buy, to use, to wear, our best Australian goods.'

The Spanish flu' epidemic darkened the life of Australia and Sydney in the immediate post-war period and the Millions Club had its own Influenza Administration Committee. A troopship arrived in Sydney Harbour carrying 2,000 returned soldiers, some of whom had been absent from their homes for five years. Blundering officialdom had allowed these men ashore at an influenza-infected port en route. The ship steamed into Sydney Harbour with a hospital full of influenza patients. It moored in sight of the homes of some of the men. All those on board had to be quarantined, the ship itself becoming a kind of floating prison.

Because of the quarantine homecoming celebrations were thwarted, and friends and relatives unable to make contact. The Millions Club stepped into the breach, becoming a clearing house and conveyer of messages and parcels to the quarantined men. Goods poured in. The task was managed with efficiency and despatch.

Improved main roads, streetscapes, and the rescue of the NSW State

Orchestra were also among the club's interests. The club was an early supporter of the Rev John Flynn's Australian Inland Mission. *Millions* showed a map of Australia marked with 16 points for frontier aeroplane depots, captioned 'Eventually, why not now?' The point was reinforced with: 'There's no alternative but the aeroplane.'

From 1922 onwards the club took quite a high profile in what must have been the precursor of today's campaigns to sell Australia to tourists. 'See Australia First' was the catch-cry and the club did everything possible to back it up.

In the late 1920s the club linked up with Rotary to promote the development of young people, both migrant and Australian-born. A 'Boys' Week' was organised in September 1926.

In early 1926, the British Government acquired Lynford Hall, a 1,000-acre farming property in Norfolk, with the intention of using it as a training establishment for young people who were to migrate to Australia and other distant lands. This cut right across the Millions Club philosophy that the successful settlement of migrant boys and girls into farming situations was heavily dependent on their being trained under the local conditions of the destination country. The club considered the sense of its position abundantly clear and strongly criticised the Lynford Hall concept.

In 1927, the club acquired its own freehold premises at 9, Rowe Street, on the corner with Pitt Street, at a cost of £65,000. The building was previously the NSW headquarters of the Royal Bank of Australia (later absorbed into the English, Scottish and Australian Bank Ltd).

During the next decade immigration remained a prime subject for club support, with the club acting through other agencies – notably Barnardos and the Big Brother Movement – rather than under its own auspices. But there were murmurings that the club should have been doing more. Government zeal for immigration diminished as the years went by and some within the club thought it should have been doing more to rectify this situation. Rickard, while in London, was forthright in attacking what he considered to be the ineptitude of the NSW Government in failing to organise the necessary shipping when there were some 5,000 applicants waiting in Britain.

The purchase of the new headquarters building occurred on the eve of a calamitous event – the onset of the Great Depression. Annual reports show that a profit of £793, in 1927, had turned to a loss of £1,159, in 1930. By 1934, the club was reporting a balanced budget and recovery seemed to be on the way. According to the annual report of that year: 'Now that the Depression is passing there must be a comprehensive plan for lobbying the Prime Minister and the State Premier on new plans for the resumption of immigration and stimulating healthy, productive settlement of the land.'

In 1929, the Millions Club participated in the scheme to purchase Mowbray Park, near Picton, as a rural training centre for Barnardos. One of several residential cottages – appropriately named the Millions Club Cottage – was opened a decade later.

In 1930, *Millions* reported that the club's Immigration Committee was seeking Big Brothers for a group of Little Brothers that were on their way to Australia. This was swimming against the tide at a time when there was unease about immigration. Strong notes of dissatisfaction were issuing, particularly from Victoria where the British Overseas Settlers' Association wanted a curb in migration, fearing that at a time of Depression it was merely creating extra mouths to feed.

Throughout the 1930s, the immigration theme was not allowed to rest, with many practical manifestations by the club and its members. Its utterances were frequently laced with scathing criticism of what was perceived as the ineffectiveness of the Government and its 'costly' immigration commissions with their 'high-handed' appointees. Each month *Millions* carried its 'Migration and Settlement Summary'. Almost on the eve of the outbreak of the war there was a comment by Rickard about the flow of migrants: 'We should be getting them in thousands and they are only coming in tens.'

In July 1939, yet another migration lobby group, the Millions for Australia League, was set up, and held its inaugural meeting at the club. The principal speaker at the luncheon was the former Prime Minister (and Millions Club member), Billy Hughes. An interesting remark by Rickard to this reflected a possible change of thinking concerning immigration. He said that, while it preferred British migrants, the league would welcome migrants of any nationality.

## ON HOLD

The Millions Club's immigration objectives were put 'on hold' (but not forgotten) during World War II. Rickard said in his 1940 report to members: 'Whilst it is not practicable in war years to carry out the primary object for which the club was founded, namely the encouragement of desirable immigration, the constitution of the club is sufficiently elastic to enable it to function usefully in other directions.'

In October 1942, the Rt Hon (later Sir) Robert Menzies – who had been Prime Minister and would be so again – attended a club gathering to launch one of its more novel schemes. This was the Millions Club Patriotic League. Its objects were to strengthen the hand of the British and Commonwealth Governments, to inspire the public generally to encourage pro-British sentiment, to discourage the spread of rumour and defeatist statements and to 'combat subversive activities of all kinds'.

In the aftermath of World War II the club again turned its attention to migration. However, this role weakened as the direct involvement of government increased. Post-war problems were acute in Britain and in June 1947, the Millions Club Food for Britain scheme was inaugurated and received immediate support. Thus, for a while, it found itself supporting Britons in Britain rather than in Australia.

In November 1946, the club officially welcomed the re-emergence of the Big Brother Movement. The club's emphasis gradually changed from bringing migrants over to a concern for how they settled once they got here. The regular Migration and Settlement Summary in *Millions* contained write-ups on individual migrant families, often accompanied by photographs. One which created much interest featured Harold Larwood, the celebrated English fast-bowling cricketer, his wife and five daughters. There were six pages of such write-ups in the July 1954 issue of *Millions*.

By September 1954, the club was actively working towards the promotion of a Co-operative Building Society as a means of assisting migration. In November, the club gave an address of welcome, and a presentation, to Australia's one millionth migrant.

In 1962, by which time migration had ceased to be a major public issue, there were suggestions that the name 'Millions Club' was no longer appropriate. In November of that year the name was changed to the Sydney Club. The old name survived in various ways; the building itself was officially 'Millions House', and the dining room was 'The Millions Room'. In 1923, members who were also Masons formed a Millions Lodge, which, at its peak, had 110 members.[5] It lasted until 1973. The club's journal, *Millions*, noted for its wealth of information and strongly held opinion about so many topics, ceased publication in 1976.

By the late 1960s juvenile migration was running down,[6] but the relationship with organisations that had brought out and nurtured young migrants continued. In 1967, for instance, no less than seven Sydney Club members were office bearers in the Big Brother Movement. The club continued to support Barnardos.

Percy Hunter, the man who called that first exploratory meeting, died in May 1970, aged 96. In 1973 a 'special membership' arrangement was instituted with the Royal Prince Alfred Yacht Club with benefits for both parties.

In 1977, widows of deceased members were allowed to become associate members. The walls did not crumble. In 1984, 'in line with the general liberalising of attitudes and conventions in club life', women were granted full membership.

Migration – juvenile migration in particular – ceased to feature among the Sydney club's aims. The club compensated for this by an increased interest in child welfare. In 1987 – 75th anniversary year – it was decided to increase club support for charities geared mainly or exclusively towards children. The first donations were directed to the Sydney City Mission and the Royal New South Wales Institute for Deaf and Blind Children.

Difficulties which had forced the closure of so many city clubs were for many years bravely weathered by the Sydney Club. Of all the entities – residents, small businesses, studios and the like whose addresses at one time or other had been in Rowe Street (originally Brougham Place), only the club and its tenants seemed able to survive.

To some outsiders the image it conveyed – of wealth, privilege and establishment connections – appeared no doubt anachronistic. Others saw it in a very different light. Barnardos in Australia might not have survived without the practical assistance of members of the Millions Club.

Lois Butcher, who was the longest serving employee of Barnardos, recalled how, in the late 1920s, as an office junior, she was sent to the Millions Club with a request to 'pass the hat round to pay the staff.'[7]

In the late 1990s the club adopted various measures to survive in modern times. In 1999 it relaxed its dress code that members must wear jackets, although it still required that they wear ties. It also reduced the membership fee from $500 to $250 a year and opened the ground level to temporary members who paid just $5 for three months.

Clearly these changes did not work. In November 2000, the Sydney Club merged with the University and Schools Club. The old building was sold to an investment company for $7.6 million and faces an uncertain future[8]. As a heritage building it cannot be demolished. A plaque honouring Little Brothers killed in World War II was relocated in the former training farm. Ways of keeping alive the connections between the University and Schools Club, the Sydney Club and (indirectly) the Millions Club are under consideration.[9]

## CRUSADER FOR IMMIGRATION

The obituary of Sir Arthur Rickard, published in the *Sydney Morning Herald* of 14 April 1948, noted that he was 'one of the most enthusiastic advocates of immigration'. It was actually an under-statement. He pursued this interest, particularly concerning young people, with crusading zeal.

His many causes included the Millions Club, Big Brother Movement, New Settlers' League, British Empire League and the Australian branch of Barnardos. Most of these he either fully or partly ran.

He was born at Currawang, near Goulburn, in 1868, son of a Cornish miner, William Rickard, and his wife Mary. He left Bathurst public school at 13, and worked for a local hardware merchant.

Moving to Sydney at 17, he worked for Tillock and Company, wholesale grocers, as a commercial traveller. By 1893, he was acting as a mercantile broker and agent for Chaleyer Fisher and Co Ltd, East India merchants, of Melbourne.

In about 1899, in a change of tack, he entered the wholesale grocery business with a partner, S.A. Joseph. They gained some Government contracts but had trouble with imported foodstuffs infested with weevils. A controversy arose when, in 1904, Governor Sir Harry Rawson objected to Rickard's proposed appointment as Portugese Consul because the pair had been found supplying goods 'unfit for human consumption' to asylums. The same year the partnership broke up in financial difficulties.

A natural salesman, Rickard then turned to the world of real estate. In 1904 he registered his own company, quickly developing a (for its day) highly innovative approach to gaining custom. His strikingly illustrated advertisements urged families to buy rather than rent, availing themselves of 'Rickard's Easy Terms'.

In 1905 he subdivided 152 acres (61 hectares) at Woy Woy into waterfront residential sites, poultry farms and orchard blocks. He undertook further subdivisions – becoming wealthy in the process – and was named by the *Sun* newspaper as 'Sydney's subdivision specialist'. An excellent self-publicist, he launched a magazine, *Rickard's Realty Review*, which appeared until 1927. Its most novel feature was 'Rickard's Solar System' – a map of Sydney with a series of arcs and dots pinpointing the extent of his land offerings. By 1916 the 'Solar System' extended to Wyong, the Blue Mountains and Port Hacking.

Rickard used his money and influence to promote his views on immigration. In 1915 he published a pamphlet, 'Population: the cash value', in which he argued that the State's population should be increased to nine million. He also campaigned in support of the Government's war bond scheme, for which (largely) he was knighted in 1920.

On returning from overseas the following year, Rickard stressed his preference for the white Australia policy and also praised the US for having 'wiped out' saloons, horse racing and gambling. Like others of his day, he saw immigration as a means of expanding the 'British race', benefiting the new country as well as the old.

Rickard warned against complacency and laziness among the newcomers. The cover of the 15 January 1924, edition of Millions carried the banner headline: 'White Australia Certainly! But.' Underneath was a grossly insulting drawing of representatives of various Asian races, with their populations displayed. Just in case anyone hadn't got the message, a white Australian is shown (with this country's paltry population figure displayed) sleeping under a tree.

Such tactics did no harm to his image, and in 1926 he was made a member of the Australian delegation to the League of Nations.

In what some would have seen as a contradiction, he was elected vice-president of the Defence of Australia League and (in the same year) president of the Japan-Australia Society. He considered the Japanese 'unsuitable' as immigrants, but admired their ambition and social welfare system.

By the late 1920s, Rickard's business activities had expanded to include an impressive array of directorships or part ownerships including leading hotels in Sydney and Melbourne.

A member of the Sane Democracy League, he worked for several taxpayers' associations, advocating public economy and opposing taxes on mortgages. One of his advertisements proclaimed: 'We are in business for all time'. However, he did not foresee the effects of the Depression, and his company went into voluntary liquidation in 1930. He sold his luxury mansion, Berith Park, in Wahroonga, and moved with his family to a more modest home in Killara.

Rickard was married twice. His eldest son, Lieut-Colonel A.L. Rickard MC, DSO, served with distinction in both world wars. His youngest son, Douglas, was chairman of the Australian Postal Commission in the 1970s.

In a city preoccupied with real estate Rickard was the outstanding land developer of his era. His crusade for immigration helped shape (as well as secure support for) Government policies for the first half of this century.

Sir Arthur Rickard died in the Scottish Hospital, Paddington, on 13 April 1948 – a few months short of his 80th birthday. He left a modest estate of a little over £12,000. His portrait by John Longstaff hung in the Sydney Club, successor to the Millions Club, and now hangs in the University and Schools Club. Streets in a dozen suburbs are named after him. A memorial of another sort is in the ornate floral clock – between the seals and the spider monkeys – which he donated to Taronga Zoo in 1928.

# 5

## The Big Brother Movement

# 16

## Big Brothers and Little Brothers

---

*'...however brave and sensible a young fellow may be,*
*he is subjected to a very severe test when,*
*separated from all the friends of his boyhood,*
*he is thrown into a new environment on the other side of the earth...'*
Extract from 1928 promotional article, explaining the need
for the Big Brother Movement.

A TWEEDY MAN, looking rather like the actor Basil Rathbone, stands on a map of Australia, extending the right hand of friendship and support. It is grasped by an earnest youth, on a map of the British Isles, who seems determined to succeed.

The 1925 poster – a variant of the familiar 'Hands across the sea' – says it all. 'Put it there, lad!,' says the caption. Above is the slogan: 'The Big Brother Movement. Bringing together British Boys and Australian opportunities.'

The Big Brother Movement, nowadays known by its initials BBM[1], was the biggest and most successful of the various migration movements for young Britons of working age. In terms of organisational skill and follow-up procedures it was the model for others to follow.

The movement owes its existence mainly to the enthusiasm and dedication of a distinguished Victorian, Sir Richard Linton.

Sir Richard (he was knighted in 1936) was born in New Zealand, settled in Melbourne and became a member of the State Parliament in 1927.

In 1924/25 he and other prominent Australians travelled to Britain to attend the British Empire Exhibition[2] at Wembley. Whilst touring the country they were delighted to discover a number of lads seeking to settle in Australia, particularly on the land. However, parents were reluctant to let their sons go so far afield without guidance or help.

Linton conceived the idea of a migration scheme for boys in which well-established men in Australia would 'act in lieu of parents'. The idea was that each adult should act as a friend and adviser to one lad – not quite as a father but more as an elder brother.

An early promotional article explained the rationale in quaint but compassionate terms:

'...however brave and sensible a young fellow may be, he is subjected to a very severe test when, separated from all the friends of his boyhood, he is thrown into a new environment on the other side of the earth, where the climate, the people, the customs, and manners are different from what he has known.

'Unaided he may fail, may shrink from lonely, laborious years on the outskirts of settlement, and be drawn into the maelstrom of city life, no longer a pioneer and coloniser, as his first enthusiasm had urged him to be.

'If, however, there is someone to whom he may turn in a crisis of doubt and despondency – someone older and more experienced than himself, who knows what is best for a young man in a new country – the temptation to drift will be mastered, and the State will be the richer for another yeoman, another strong, self-reliant tiller of the soil, a producer of real wealth.'

The terms 'big brother' and 'little brother' sprang from the above concept and provided a name for the proposed organisation.

Linton's plan was well received both in Australia and in Britain. What appears to have been a  steering committee met informally at the Royal Colonial Institute, Bligh Street, Sydney, on 16 June 1924. General William l'Estrange Eames, a prominent immigrationist, took the chair. Linton himself, also Sir Arthur Rickard, chief backer of Barnardos, were listed as absent.[3] A report by General Eames, which was well received, said 'the future of the Australian people' depended on six factors, which were organisation, co-operation, immigration, decentralisation, and comprehensive policies on finance and defence.

It seems there was no early follow-up, perhaps because of the exhibition in London. Records of the Millions Club point to a meeting of interested parties in the club on 15 April 1925. Rickard, club president, presided. The club's history describes this as the inaugural meeting.[4] The following day a committee was formed under the chairmanship of Sir Robert Anderson. The term Big Brother Movement was used officially for the first time at a further committee meeting on 25 August.

From the start the BBM saw its role as a patriotic one – cementing the link between Australia and the mother country – rather than as a 'welfare' or charitable body such as Barnardos.

It was unabashedly in support of empire building, and pooh-poohed the notion that 'the colonies of Britain [are] a burden which us not worthwhile carrying'. On the contrary, according to a promotional bulletin: '...no one today has any hesitation in declaring that the Empire is a magnificent reality, the bonds of which are strong and effective. It is the strength of these bonds which provides such clear justification for the modern policy which lies behind the relationship established between the people of the homeland and those who have gone forth to settle at the extremities of the Empire.'[5]

Views such as the above were considered in those days to be statements of fact rather than political utterances. Hence the movement could claim to be 'non-political, non-commercial, and non-sectarian', which position still stands. Ironically, its very links with Britain came to be seen, during a period in its history, as a 'political' statement.

The movement regarded itself as essentially 'different' from the many other bodies then promoting immigration. A history cum handbook, the issued by BBM in 1987[6], says migration schemes already 'existed for adults, families and orphan children but ... Linton and others saw the need for an organisation to help youngsters of working age'.[7]

Within a few weeks of that inaugural meeting, it was announced that 125 Little Brothers were ready to come to Australia. The number would be augmented by the inclusion of some Dreadnought Boys and others who had competed successfully for what were called Wembley Scholarships to attend agricultural colleges in Australia.

In the public mind, and even among the 'lads'[8] themselves, a degree of confusion arose concerning the Big Brother Movement and the older Dreadnought Trust. In an interesting development, the Prime Minister's Department suggested that 'all future Dreadnought boys may be enrolled as Little Brothers'.[9]

The honour of being the first Little Brother belongs to Arthur John Shenton, who arrived in Sydney on the *Sophocles* on 7 October 1925.

Little is known about him, except that he was 19, and came from the town of Letchworth, in Hertfordshire. He was the only Little Brother on the ship, and travelled with a group of Dreadnought Boys. As with later arrivals, he was sent to Scheyville (probably with some Dreadnought Boys), and later worked at Bogan View and Peak Hill. The last entry on his record card states "Gone to Western Australia 16 April 1930."

The first organised party of Little Brothers, numbering over 200 lads, sailed from England in the *Jervis Bay* on 6 November 1925. The ship arrived in Fremantle on December 4 1925. In Perth the boys were given a civic reception organised through the New Settlers' League and the Ugly

*Hands across the sea. Big Brother Movement (NSW) recruitment poster (1925).*

Men's Association.[10] The vessel reached Melbourne a week later, and Sydney on 14 December. About 100 of the young passengers were to make their homes in Melbourne,[11] and 85 in Sydney. A smaller number were to be looked after – though not by the Big Brother Movement – in Fremantle. Each newcomer to the two major capitals had his own 'big brother'.

By mid 1926 Little Brothers were arriving at the rate of 100 monthly and the NSW committee, assisted by organisations such as Legacy, had over 500 suitably qualified citizens, many of them eminent, willing to serve as Big Brothers. Most took their duties seriously; a few did not. In Melbourne, in particular, there was a hint of snobbery about it all. There were complaints, for instance, that some Big Brothers asked their charges to visit them in their city offices, but were reluctant to visit the newcomers in their place of work, or invite the newcomers to their homes.

Such a situation, if true, sat uneasily with the Victorian branch's pledge that 'everything will be done, from first to last, in order that the Big Brothers may carry out to the letter their promise [to parents] to keep watch and ward over their sons...'

The Big Brother Movement, like Barnardos, enjoyed the patronage of 'well-connected' people (with a preponderance of military men) including royalty. Its literature contained scouting terms, references to cricket and – particularly in the early days – an implied praise of all things British.

After the initial push the rate of intake slowed a little, but by 1930 the movement had welcomed 1,806 lads (1,069 in Victoria and 737 in NSW). The world-wide economic crisis had an immediate braking effect on the movement's work and only 10 Little Brothers arrived between July 1930 and June 1931.

BBM, even more than similar organisations, applied fairly demanding standards of health, physique, character, disposition and education to its young 'clients'. These were further tightened as employment became harder to find.

The Great Depression crippled the Big Brother Movement's activities, as it did to other migration bodies. The 1931 annual report of the Big Brother Movement noted wryly:

'The [past] year has proved in consequence more full of difficulty than any period we have experienced. Numbers of Little Brothers have been thrown out of work month by month through no fault of their own, and the task of finding re-employment has been a strenuous one; so much so that there has not been a single day during the last 12 months that all our lads were in jobs.'

The report went on to say, under the heading 'Arrivals and Departures': 'During the year only ten Little Brothers arrived from Great Britain, while we have for the first time had the unusual experience of 29 of our boys returning to England, because of the depressing prospects in Australia. On the whole, our lads are standing up well to the disappointing conditions now prevailing, and are exhibiting a sturdy courage, which augurs well for their future as colonists.'

A committee report dated February 1931 expressed concern that 32 of its lads were unemployed. Within two months, with help from supporters and 'by dint of advertising freely', this number had been reduced to eight. By December the committee was able to report that there were no boys known to be unemployed 'except one lad who has proved to be completely impractical, his only wish being to go on the stage'. He was Harry Dearth,[12] later to become a well-known theatre and radio personality.

At about this time there were articles in the British press about the growing strength of left-wing political movements in Australia, and their equally extreme right-wing counterparts. Lord Inchcape, chairman of the Orient Shipping Line, which brought many migrants to Australia,[13] was anxious that Australia should receive migrants who identified with 'the Imperial school of thought' and thus combat 'powerful Bolshevist and Sinn Fein elements'.

Things got worse when Captain Francis De Groot disrupted the Sydney Harbour Bridge opening ceremony, on 19 March 1932,[14] rushing through on horseback, slashing the ribbon with his sword. Sections of the British press reported that Australia was heading for rebellion. Consequently, parents of some 70 lads already in Australia under the BBM and similar schemes demanded that their sons be returned home.

In 1933, Linton was made Agent-General for Victoria in London. During his three-year stint he was an ex-officio member of the Big Brother Movement's London executive committee. It was hardly a fruitful period, because of the Depression and its aftermath, though things could have been a lot worse.[15]

During this period the committee's thoughts turned towards the creation of a more centralised organisation with greater financial backing and some sort of centre to house the youths on arrival and in emergencies.

Migration resumed in 1939, when about 70 lads arrived in the early months of that year. For the first time, a subsidy of up to £750 a year was provided jointly by the Australian and British Governments. Arrangements were made for the lads to spend a short period at the Dreadnought Scheme's training farm at Scheyville, before being placed on farms and stations.

'Little Brothers', like their counterparts in the Dreadnought Scheme, were volunteers, who migrated with the full support of their parents. No formal educational requirement was set. Ken Johnstone,[16] the movement's current chairman, states: 'I think you just had to be a person who they thought would work hard and make a good citizen. I know in my own case I had to get references from my school and the local church. It was quite thorough.'

Initial selection was by the London office, under supervision of the Australian Department of Immigration, which had the final say.[17]

## WAR SERVICE

The advent of World War II brought an abrupt halt to the recruitment of Little Brothers. Plans for the departure from Britain of 50 lads in September and October 1939 were cancelled. The 14th annual report in September 1940 noted proudly that 31 (more than half) of the 1939 intake had joined the Australian Armed Forces within a year of their arrival.

A group which arrived on the *Ormonde*, in April 1939, achieved the commendable 100 per cent recruitment rate. Most of the younger lads continued working on the land, joining up as they reached 18.

Though migration was interrupted, the movement did what it could to keep the spirit and work of the organisation alive.

'Bigbro Farm' was established on a property at Baulkham Hills, near Parramatta, owned by the honorary director, Captain G.S. Millar, as a centre 'for Little Brothers coming to Sydney for re-employment, on leave from the Services or to join up.'

The 1942 annual report records: 'The decision of the council to keep the office open with skeleton staff has been fully justified. Lads call constantly regarding mail, to store personal effects, etc. The office [has been] passing information to relations through the London office and seeking information for the boys. Comforts parcels are being sent regularly to Little Brothers on active service, the cost met by the movement and the work carried out by the Baulkham Hills Patriotic Committee.'

At the 1942 annual meeting the NSW Premier, William McKell, praised the patriotism of the Little Brothers fighting with Australian Forces and said: 'This war has underlined the need for populating Australia, especially with good British stock'.

Cases of particularly distinguished service, with year of arrival in brackets, include:

Flight Lieutenant Leslie Kilvington (1939). He joined the RAAF in 1941, was awarded the DFC for operations over Germany, POW 1944, returned to Australia 1946.

Major B.H.G. French (1929). AIF, awarded MC in Middle East.

Wing Commander H.F. Slade (1928). RAAF. Served in Europe and Pacific, awarded DSO, DFC and BSM (US).

In 1943 the council reported sadly that two Little Brothers were known to have been killed, seven were missing and nine were POWs. By the end of the war there were 30 confirmed deaths among the movement's nominees. There were probably others, particularly among those who returned to Britain to enlist.

The early Allied losses and the consequent threat to Australia brought benefit to the movement in that it reinforced the beliefs already held by many that a larger population was necessary. The wartime Prime Ministers, Ben Chifley and (Sir) Robert Menzies, on opposite sides of the political fence, both supported BBM. Chifley, Prime Minister 1945-49, took a particular interest, serving on the movement's council from 1942 to 1947.

The support of such an influential Labor figure as Ben Chifley is noteworthy in view of the perception that BBM had an affinity with the 'conservative forces' in Australian politics. From the 1930s until the 1950s several other working class Labor figures also supported BBM. They include William McKell,[18] NSW Premier 1941-47, and Governor General 1947-53, and, of course, Arthur Calwell, Immigration Minister 1945-49, Labor leader in Federal Parliament 1960-67, and Deputy Leader 1951-61.

Such support also appears to contrast with the subsequent stance of the Labor Government of Robert Hawke.[19]

## LITTLE BROTHERS POST-WAR

*'Why did I come? I think it was the lure of the great outdoors.*
*England was just recovering from the war; there was rationing still,*
*and a form of inertia about the place. You could go all the way to Australia*
*for 10 quid. Five if, like us, you were under age. I thought*
*What an opportunity! You could come back after two years if you wanted to.'*
Ben Mohide (Asturias, August 1949)

By 1946, the Big Brother Movement's UK committee was again receiving applications. The committee reported 'heartfelt joy and relief' at the termination of the war and recorded thanks 'to all who had fought and worked for victory, including many of our Little Brothers'.

With the restoration of activities, it was accepted that greater emphasis on after care was needed. Clearly, this could not adequately be performed by Big Brothers, who might only see their particular Little Brother two or three times a year. To overcome this, three district superintendents were appointed with wide-ranging responsibilities.[20]

As stated previously, post-war juvenile migration formally resumed with the arrival of the *Empire Star.* in Melbourne, on 19 August 1947, with 17 'Little Brothers' among an assorted group of adult migrants, refugees and latecomers returning from the war. It was followed by the arrival of the *Asturias*, in Fremantle, on 22 September 1947, with supposed 'orphan' children to be raised by religious charities.

However, unaccompanied juvenile migration – using the term in its broader sense[21] – had recommenced earlier than this; the honour of being 'the first' going to one Geoffrey Alan Moore, a school leaver from Petts Wood, Kent, sponsored by the Big Brother Movement, who travelled unaccompanied on the *Stratheden*, arriving in Sydney on 31 July of that year.

The pace of post-war youth migration increased with the arrival in Sydney of the *Ormonde*, on 17 November. The ship brought, in addition to its cargo of 'orphans',[22] some 20 youths under the aegis of the Big Brother Movement.

In the case of the early post-war arrivals the role of the 'Big Brother' was taken very seriously. For instance, the lads from the *Empire Star* were brought to Sydney from Melbourne by train, commencing the long journey on the very evening of their arrival. Upon arrival at Sydney's Central Railway they went straight to a reception in their honour, at which each was introduced to his 'Big Bro'. According to the Movement's 1947 annual report, the boys went from the reception to the 'home of their Big Brother for a few days.'[23] No doubt they slept soundly.

Some long term relationships were formed. Barrie Dennie, who came out on the *Asturias* in 1949, recalls: 'My big brother was a jeweller in Bexley called Mr Smith. He and his wife took a strong interest in me until I was 21. I'd have my holidays [from the bush] with them; they took me to the beach and other nice places. I wrote to them from wherever I was working. I'd say they were not so much substitute parents, but friends who were very giving.'

Sadly, the BBM did not again take up roots in Victoria, whose State structure had folded.[24]

In 1947 the NSW Council of BBM decided to buy a 640 acre (256 ha) property, known as Karmsley Hills, at Bossley Park, near Liverpool. The cost of £15,000 pounds was financed by a successful fundraising appeal. The Commonwealth and State Governments made grants of one-third each to the cost of accommodation and facilities to house up to 40 lads at a time. It was dedicated as a memorial to the Little Brothers who lost their lives in the war.[25]

According to a history of the property John Jamieson, who received the original grant in 1806, called it 'Coulmesly Hill Farm'. A later occupant changed this to 'Calmsley'. The owner prior to 1947 called it 'Karmsley Hills', which name was adopted by BBM. To most Little Brothers it was simply 'The Training Farm'.[26]

# 17

## Farmers Galore

∎

**T**HE WAR MEMORIAL TRAINING FARM played a big role in the lives of post-war Little Brothers; in particular in the years when farm training was compulsory.

Ken Tubbs, who came out with the first post-war group in August 1947, had worked on farms in England for two years before coming to Australia. 'I could milk and ride and shoe and do most of the things that are associated with the land. Because of this they thought I didn't need training, and they sent me direct to work on a property at Moss Vale.'

He was 16. A mere 12 months later Ken – remarkably young for such a role – was sent to the newly-opened Karmsley Hills Training Farm as a member of the training staff. His official title was junior overseer.

'There were new kids coming out all the time. I taught them how to milk, ride, fence; the practical skills of the property. I thoroughly enjoyed the work and didn't have time to be homesick.'

He recalls the manager of the farm at that time was Bill Waite, an original ANZAC who had won the Military Cross in World War I. He was admired for his hard work in training the lads and in developing the farm operations during the early difficult years.[1]

Overall control was in the hands of G. Simpson Millar ('Captain Millar'), director of the Big Brother Movement, who visited the farm about once fortnightly from his Sydney office. Ken recalls him as 'a raw-boned , big fellow. A man's man and a terrific guy; a real country-type Australian.'[2]

According to Ken Tubbs: 'I reckon the young guys who came here had a great time. They were good, regular kids who fell in with the system. I can't remember a single misfit.'

Ken spent about a year in that role then went to work on a large sheep and cattle station near Cowra. After a further 10 or 11 years in various jobs on the land, his career path took an abrupt change when he successfully applied for training as a Qantas air steward. 'I enjoyed the work, just as I had done in farming. The main reason why I made the change was that it enabled me to get back to England regularly to see my family.'

During his time with Qantas the rule was dropped that had made it compulsory for all newly-arrived Little Brothers to work on the land. Ken has mixed feelings about the change. 'In my view every kid should spend time on the land. It teaches them to be versatile; how to put their hand to anything.

'Learning how to fence and shoe, ride a horse and do general activities around a farm – it's a wonderful start for young people, whatever they choose to do later in life. It toughens them up, a bit like national service, and enables them to cope.'

## SOUNDS, SIGHTS AND SMELLS
For many Little Brothers the sounds, sights and even smells of the training farm remain in collective memories to this day.

Len Rushton, who came out on the *Orion* in 1951, recalls that his first impression was of shock. Not at his surroundings but the heat.

'I came from Sway, near Lymington in Hampshire. It was freezing cold when we left England; my mother couldn't get to Tilbury to see us off. We got here in January and arrived at the farm at about four in the afternoon. The temperature was about 40 degrees C. (104 deg F.) I couldn't believe it was so hot. I thought I was going to die.'

Ben Mohide (*Asturias*, 1949) was luckier. 'We arrived at the farm late August. It was still cool and very pleasant. The first thing that happened was we were allocated to our various dormitories. About four beds in each room. To our amusement above each bed was a mosquito net; something which I'd never seen before.

'Blankets had to be rolled up Army style during the day. You could lie on the springs if you wanted but not on the mattress. Only the dairy boys were allowed to go to bed as they had to get up so early.'

'Early' meant around half-past three. Ben soon found himself performing dairy duties. 'You'd round up the cows, start to milk. You'd finish about eight o'clock, have breakfast, and start again at four in the afternoon. I think later on in the year they were milking three times a day.

It was a fairly modern dairy by standards of the day. They had milking machines. You didn't have to milk by hand.'

Ben confesses that before coming to the training farm 'I had never seen a cow in my life.' I reminded him that some of the Dreadnought Boys were taught to milk on an artificial cow.

'Well, ours were real cows and if you pulled the thing the wrong way something else would come up besides milk. They'd wet all over you, shit all over you. They were not well trained cows at all.'

> Author: 'Did that happen to you?'
> Ben: 'Constantly. You'd have to hose them off.'
> Author: 'Hose you off too, I should think.'

Ben recalls that hygiene was good and conditions 'very strict'. 'You had to scrub everything; soap and water, it was all steam cleaned. This included the utensils you put the milk in. It wasn't like today, when a tanker takes it. The milk was put into churns and when the guy took away those churns they were emptied and brought back. All had to be sparkling clean in time for the next inspection. You couldn't even have mud on your boots. And it was good fun – I liked the life.'

Ben Mohide stayed on the farm three months. This was longer than usual, but there was a good reason.

'It happened about a week after I arrived. I'd been on dairy duties, but didn't feel like going to bed. There was a team of guys cutting down trees. I grabbed an axe and joined them. I got hit on the hand and lost two fingers.

'One of the fingers was cut off at the hospital; the other we buried and played *The last Post* over it on a comb and paper. Actually, I lost three fingers, but they stitched one back on again.'

Then followed a routine of visits to hospital, seeing doctors, penicillin and other treatment. When his time was up, Ben got work on another farm, but found the injuries he had sustained a handicap. 'I could never really get a good grip. In those days farm work was hard work and there were bags of wheat that weighed about 200 pounds. It's not easy picking it up with a crook hand.'

Ben quit farming and decided to go into the city. 'I got a job in sales and have been in that ever since.' He has, in fact, launched and operated a number of successful business endeavours. He is modest about this, preferring to state: 'I got involved in lots of things.'

He is now retired and, true to form, was chairperson of a group known as the Central Coast Active Retirees and Mentors. 'What we did is take high school students in Year 10, and guide them through a school to work program. We can help them to get the job they want, persuade them to do a course at TAFE or maybe stay on and take their HSC. In other words, we try to steer them into the right areas.

'We're all volunteers. About 80 per cent of our students have got a job which they might not have got otherwise. We also help them prepare their résumés, their CVs. We look at their attitude to employment and general deportment – eye contact, dress and so on.'

Ben came to Australia, in the first instance, through wishing to emulate a cousin, John Roche, who had migrated through the Big Brother Movement a year before. He disagrees with the view that only those who became 'city dwellers' were successful. 'The opportunity for boys to do well in the bush is evident by the fact that my cousin did just that, as have many others. It just didn't suit me.'

Ben Mohide has had other brushes with fate, the most dramatic being the occasion – on 24 February 1989 – when he and his wife, Barbara, were passengers on United Airlines Flight 811, in which nine people lost their lives, when a cargo door of the giant Boeing 747 blew off 85 miles south of Honolulu Airport.

Only superb thinking by the captain and senior officers prevented total calamity, including the deaths of the remaining 346 passengers and crew on board the aircraft, which was bound initially for Auckland. Ben subsequently wrote and self-published a book, *Hawaiian Nightmare*, about the drama in the sky.

Never one to let the grass grow under his feet, Ben has spent much of the past decade studying for a Bachelor of Education degree at the University of Technology (UTS), Sydney. He graduated at 71, majoring in Language, Literacy and Numeracy, and was awarded the University Medal in the process.

He became a full-time student at UTS after becoming involved, from 1997, with Year 10 students at various high schools on the NSW Central Coast, in a new mentoring programme known as Plan-It-Youth. The object was to assist students to go from 'school to work' or to encourage them to stay on at high school and seek an HSC (Higher School Certificate).

## FREEDOM OF CHOICE

From 1949 Little Brothers arriving in New South Wales were free to choose any type of employment for which they were suited. A large two-storey house in Broughton Road, Homebush, a Sydney suburb,[3] was purchased in 1950 and named Gunning House in honour of Tom Gunning, whose bequest made it possible. The house, with accommodation for up to 30 lads, was intended as a temporary residence for Little Brothers who wished to take up careers other than farming.

In addition to accommodating newcomers, there was an 'understanding' that Little Brothers on holiday from the country, convalescing from illness or accident, or on study courses, could stay without charge at Gunning House.

Though the scheme of having personal Big Brothers was maintained, by 1951 it was obvious that the number of volunteers was inadequate. An effort to rectify the problem met with only partial success, and by 1953 the arrival rate of Little Brothers far exceeded the enrolment of Big Brothers.

It was felt that unless every lad could be allocated a Big Brother the concept would be unworkable. The system of personal Big Brothers was therefore abandoned in favour of a district Big Brother system. By August 1954 102 honorary welfare officers had been appointed.

1955 marked the 30th anniversary of the Big Brother Movement. The annual report for that year noted that the movement had been responsible for some 85 per cent of all post-war British youth migration. By arrangement with the autonomous London committee, Ernest Cooper, a former Dreadnought Boy, was sent to Britain in 1957 to assist Commander John Spence, general secretary of BBM in the UK, in the work of promotion and selection.

The London committee, the recruiting arm of the movement, later changed its name to British Boys' Movement for Australia, believing that this would have greater meaning.

According to contemporary documents the intention of the London office was not to 'glamorise' Australia, but rather to make the movement and its services more widely known throughout the United Kingdom. The new drive was successful and 2,600 Little Brothers were received in the period 1956-64, with a record intake of 476 in 1964.

Despite claims such as the above, the Big Brother Movement and similar bodies "sold" Australia to young, would-be migrants as a place of fun, excitement and adventure.

David Paris, a Londoner, aged 16, was among those snared.[4] 'I used to subscribe to a paper called *World Wide Magazine*. It was full of stories of adventure in far away places. I initially tried to get to Canada, but they didn't seem to have any schemes equivalent to that of the BBM.

'My first job after leaving school was as a lab technician at the Regent Street Polytechnic, in London. It wasn't far from Australia House, so I wandered down there and made my application. I then went to my mother and said "Mum, I want to go to Australia. I've passed all the tests and everything." She said: "Are you serious?" I said: "Yes." She signed and I left.

'I've no regrets. It was the best thing I ever did and I've said that to so many people. The Big Brother Movement provided me with an opportunity to enjoy a life for which I cannot thank them enough. The minute I arrived here [in Australia] I knew it would suit me down to the ground. The only thing I have regretted was the separation from my mother, who did come out three times and whom I visited frequently.'

In November 1956 the BBM announced that it would assist Hungarian youths who had fled that country during the ill-fated anti-Communist uprising. Frank Mansell said the movement would 'try to find good jobs and friendly homes' for unaccompanied youths who might be arrive as refugees within the next few months. However, the idea flagged – apparently due to failure of the Government to provide financial assistance.

In 1959 the Big Brother Movement was invited to nominate a representative to the Commonwealth Immigration Advisory Council. Sir

John Pagan (then vice president) was elected as the BBM nominee and gave valuable service in this capacity.

The 100th post-war party of Little Brothers arrived in Sydney in April 1960. The new arrivals were met by the president of BBM, Sir John Northcott, and received a civic welcome. The captain of their vessel, the *Fairsky*, gave a luncheon on board in their honour.

For as long as anyone can remember, Little Brothers travelling by sea were given a shopping list of items to take AND not to take on the voyage. A sample is published as an appendix.

The version issued in 1957 advised: 'If buying new clothes, it is necessary to allow for an overall increase of three inches in the waist, chest and length measurements. This allows for the invariable speedy growth in the first six months or so.' Little Brothers were also urged 'in your own interests', not to bring 'flashy or exaggerated' clothes, such as 'drain-pipe trousers, drape jacket and crepe shoes'.

## THE HANDBOOK

A more detailed general information booklet, known as *The Little Brothers' Guide*, was also issued. The 1955 version of the *Guide* stated, under the heading of Appearance: 'Dress neatly and moderately. A sports coat and well kept grey or fawn trousers will do for almost every occasion in the bush. Anything in the nature of "Teddy Boy" or the Australian counterpart "Bodgie" type of dress is looked upon with contempt by the countryman, young or old.'

Under the heading 'Care of Clothes' Little Brothers were told: 'It is advisable that, before sailing, you learn how to wash and iron clothes, sew on buttons, darn socks, mend tears, press suits and generally care for your own things. You will have to do this for yourself during the voyage and while you are at the training farm or hostel, and possibly after that period. You should also learn how to make your own bed and tidy up your bedroom.'

The *Guide* had much to say about personal hygiene. 'Keep yourself clean and tidy. Always wash on rising and before each meal. Bathe or shower every day and wash out your socks and underclothing every day. Teeth and nails should also be given regular attention. See that your working clothes are washed at least every week – a few patches, tatters or stains don't matter much, but keep them clean.

'...many boys seem to get the idea that "anything goes in the bush", but this is not the case and from our experience, country employers are just as much concerned about this aspect as city residents.'

The eight-page *Guide* was intended as an all-purpose document, deliberately pocket size, a blend of passport and Bible. According to the introduction: 'The advice given [in this document] is based on our experience and knowledge of thousands of British lads who have come to Australia since 1925. Large numbers of these Little Brothers are now successful men who occupy responsible positions in the community. It has, therefore, been possible for us to find out just why some young men succeed and others fail...'

The booklet had candid advice concerning homesickness. 'Most lads are homesick at one stage or another, but it is like seasickness in that it passes off after a while. The important thing is to recognise it for what it is and not to blame your job or those around you for the "gloom" you feel.

'So many lads have said in later years: "I was silly to leave the first job, which I now realise was the best I have had. The trouble was that I was homesick and fed up at the time." The cure is to keep your mind occupied with your work and try to take part in local church, sporting and social activities...'

The *Guide* offered practical advice on manners. 'Be a gentleman and don't think it "sissy" to stand up when a lady comes into the room. Open the door for her and observe all those small courtesies which will earn you the good opinion of those with whom you live.

'Be careful of your manners at the table, as this is one of the things about which we do occasionally receive unfavourable reports. Avoid using bad language, as though many country men are not greatly concerned about swearing in the paddocks or yards they deplore it around the homestead or within earshot of the women folk.'

The *Guide* had a detailed section on personal finance. It urged Little Brothers to try to save at least £100 by the end of their first year in Australia. 'The best way to accomplish this is by drawing your wages monthly, banking half of the amount and making the balance "do" until the next pay. Stick to this as a hard and fast rule – "half capital and half income", and your savings will soon grow.'

Little Brothers were cautioned not to change jobs without good reason. 'Never lose sight of the fact that you came to Australia to better yourself and don't let temporary difficulties put you off the track. Be a sticker and stay at your first job at least one year. You may hear talk of higher wages elsewhere or in seasonal work[5], but our records show very clearly that it is those lads who showed perseverance and patience in their first jobs who now have their own properties or are in highly paid positions of responsibility.'

PEARSE HILL FARM

In the 1950s the BBM briefly owned and ran a training farm of about 150 acres in Orange. It had a picturesque location, near the foot of Mount Canobolas, known to local wags as 'Cannibal arse'.

It was purchased from a local farmer in November 1950 for £11,000, the bulk of which (£8,000) was donated by an English retired ship's surgeon, Dr W.H. Pearse, after whom the farm was renamed.

During a visit to Australia, earlier that year, Dr Pearse had been a guest at a BBM board meeting, where he commended the movement for doing 'excellent work in promoting the emigration of British youths to New South Wales'. He said that he was rewriting his will in favour of the movement.

It was decided that a percentage of each new intake of lads should go to the farm, detailed operations of which were to be left in the hands of a farm sub-committee. A farm manager, Mr W. Waite, who was also responsible for training, was appointed.

Board members were initially supportive. A long time member, Mr F.G. White, stated that he was "very favourably impressed with the property," which he felt could, under careful management, carry over a thousand ewes. He also gave advice on the planting of trees on the property. The then president of the Big Brother Movement, Sir Graham Waddell, was equally optimistic, saying that 'Pearse Hill' (which he admitted not having visited) should ultimately provide 'valuable revenue to assist with the movement's many expenses'.

This was not to be. Within a few months the initial optimism began to dissipate. Mr White, having made further visits to the property, stated that he had been 'surprised to find a very extensive soil erosion problem' which affected a large proportion of the total site.

By January 1952 the situation had worsened, with drought and an 'infestation of grasshoppers' (locusts) as additional factors. Mr White also complained that the farm sub-committee, which was supposed to provide day to day guidance and management, had not actually met. He said in his view the local committee was unlikely to become more diligent as its members were 'all too busy with their own affairs'.

This last piece of news annoyed board members who also received a disappointing report from the farm manager, Mr Waite. He said that lack of proper equipment was making it difficult to instruct the lads and was slowing ploughing to the extent that other essential work could not be done.

On the plus side there were now over 100 ewes on the property, and local farmers had promised to donate 200 sheep, which would arrive shortly.

The July board meeting witnessed a further deterioration in the overall situation, including the resignation of Mr Waite and an unsatisfactory replacement. In addition, according to the board minutes: '…the finances of the movement [have] deteriorated to some extent, due to the drop in revenue from subscriptions.'

After some discussion 'the executive committee considered that as well as the difficulty of administration, the movement really [does] not have sufficient money to develop the property to a stage where it would provide revenue for the Big Brother Movement.'

It was agreed unanimously, with some reluctance, that Pearse Hill should be put up for sale, for disposal 'at the earliest possible time', with a reserve price of £13,500. Later minutes show that the property was sold in January 1953 for £15,500. Livestock were disposed of privately after the sale.

Records of the BBM do not show how many 'lads' lived and worked on the farm during the movement's ownership of a little over two years. One who did was Don McDouall, who was there for about five weeks in 1952.

He writes: "It was close to the base of the mountain and the nearest post office was Nashdale. I cannot remember much about it except that it was run by a couple most likely in their late fifties or sixties.

'There were only three of us Little Brothers there at that time. It would have been from about the beginning of May to the first week in June. We were taken from the hostel at Homebush in a 30 cwt Morris Commercial truck the movement had at that time. I was seated on the back in the rain all the way there.

'One day the three of us had this great adventure. We climbed up Mount Canobolas, which was covered in snow, thinking we were one of the very few ever to do so. Imagine our disappointment on reaching the summit to find many people already there and a road leading right to the top.'

## AIR TRAVEL

The first party of Little Brothers to travel by air reached Sydney in January 1961. By 1966 all BBM migrants were using air travel.

In the 1960s the movement's reputation for 'answering the call' in wartime continued, albeit in another direction. The 30 June 1965 issue of the *Sydney Daily Mirror* carried a story and picture of the first national serviceman to enter the Army's recruitment base at Marrickville. The conscript was Walter Sims, originally from Sussex, who had arrived as a Little Brother at the age of 16 and worked on the land in the Coonabarabran (NSW) district. He later brought out his own parents, who settled near Sydney in 1972.

The 1960s saw a continued decline in the percentage of Little Brothers seeking farm work. The rural recession and other economic factors served to dampen interest in life on the land, together with a general change in the attitudes of young people.[6]

In 1964, the decision was made to sell Gunning House. According to Frank Mansell, then the movement's secretary: 'We just didn't need such a big place.' It was sold to a Catholic Order of nuns, and replaced by a smaller house in Burwood, which was re-named Gunning Lodge.

In its final years, in particular, there had been a free and easy approach about who could stay at 'Gunning House'[7] Frank Mansell enjoyed telling a story about an ex-Little Brother, resident in the country, who was in Sydney partying with friends.

In order to save money the visitor decided to kip down for the night in one of the dormitories in Gunning House. Alas, no one had told him about the property's change of ownership. He entered through the unlocked back door – as hundreds had done before him, and started to climb the stairs. Suddenly he saw 'two shadowy black crows coming along the corridor'. According to Mansell: 'It frightened the life out of the poor bloke. He tore down the steps and out of the place and has never been seen again.'

Child migration, as reported elsewhere, ended in 1967. By this time most of the organisations involved in youth migration also had folded. But not the Big Brother Movement, whose reception of Little Brothers carried on as before.

The Karmsley Hills training farm continued on its familiar lines until 1971. In that year only 41 lads sought rural work. They arrived in small numbers, spread throughout 33 air parties, making it difficult for the farm to operate economically.

By 1972 about 70 per cent of the farm land at Karmsley Hills had been zoned 'Open Spaces for eventual public ownership'. Rather than await resumption BBM negotiated with the NSW Government which was prepared to purchase the subject area for $200,000 and lease it back to BBM at no rental other than the payment of rates. It was decided to retain the remaining 80 acres (32 ha) for future eventualities.

In 1973/74 the Australian Government under the Immigration Minister, Al Grassby, introduced a new method for the selection of migrants based on 'national need' and family reunions. At the same time the fare contribution of migrants was increased. Much of this formula was not immediately applied to BBM nominees, but it had a dampening effect upon young Britons and the work of BBM generally.

The Government approved the movement's continued operation 'provided employment could be ensured'. Prominence given in Britain to reports of growing unemployment in Australia reduced BBM applications to a low ebb.

50 YEARS ON
In 1975 special events were held in Britain and Australia to mark the 50th

anniversary of the Big Brother Movement. Members of the London committee flew to Sydney for the Australian celebrations, highlight of which was a rodeo-picnic at the Karmsley Hills training farm. The chairman of the London committee, John Lowther, a Northamptonshire farmer, subsequently wrote to the organisers: 'Any time I have given to this movement was made more than worthwhile when I started talking to a cross-section of the five decades of Little Brothers who had come [to the reunion] from all over Australia.'

The emphasis on skills and the tighter immigration criteria demanded by the Federal Government meant that BBM now had to use greater selectivity – based on employment records, training and experience – in recruitment. In the latter years the movement would only accept migrants who had completed their indentures, which led to an increase in the age of Little Brothers.

There were also strict character, health and attitude requirements. The net result was that only about one applicant in every 18 finally made it to Australia. There was dismay and a degree of ill-feeling at the rejection of so many excellent candidates.

Despite tugs in other directions, the movement continued to stress the value of its links with Britain and felt no shame in such an attitude. At the 1975 annual meeting, the then president of BBM, Sir Denzil Macarthur Onslow, wrote in his report: 'Healthy British lads of good character are among the best migrants Australia can obtain from a simple practical viewpoint. Australians who value the British tradition, the Common Law and the tie with the Crown will see a deeper implication.'

In June 1978 the autonomous London committee wound up its activities. The enforced change from an organisation helping 'boys' to one of selecting well trained 'young men' was blamed for a decline in financial support from individuals and institutions in Britain.

There were also disagreements between the Australian and the UK organisation – just as there had been between the States – and suggestions of incompetency and mismanagement. The then executive director of BBM, Frank Mansell, visited London in September 1978, to establish the new branch of the re-vamped Big Brother Movement [of Australia] and to confer with Immigration Department officials. He confirmed reports of hostility from some London-based staff of the Immigration Department, including an attempt to cancel the Movement's 50-year occupancy of limited office space in Australia House.[8]

The late 1970s saw continued difficulties for BBM. A tightening up in the Government's immigration requirements was coupled with a decline in applications. Adverse publicity in the UK media along the lines that 'the lucky country had run out of luck' was partly responsible. The closure of some regional offices of the Department of Immigration was another factor. There were only 80 BBM arrivals in 1979 – the lowest since World War II.

Probably 50 per cent of BBM nominees over the years had heard about the movement through being given one of its leaflets when making general inquiries at one of the UK migration centres maintained by Australia House. It was found that this practice, too, had ceased – no one is certain on whose orders.

In the mid-1970s the BBM started to receive applications from coloured youths, born in Britain. According to Ken Johnstone, who was treasurer at the time: 'We put up two or three West Indian boys. My recollection is that they didn't make it. I don't think it was because of their colour. At least I hope it wasn't.

'The people at Australia House checked their credentials. My recollection is that the particular category they wanted to go into didn't have jobs available. It would have been difficult to place them. When I came out here [in 1957] things were different, but down the track the BBM's operations became very specialised. You had to have qualifications, some sort of recognised training. You had to be a person who could get a job easily and fit into the community.

'I must stress that every single candidate that we put forward had to get the [Australian] Government's blessing. As I have said, the immigration authorities in London, not us, gave the final go-ahead.'

By about 1980, responding to social pressures, the movement allegedly took an interest in sponsoring non-UK residents from 'coloured' Commonwealth nations. According to Frank Mansell about a dozen lads were sponsored directly from Kenya, Malaysia, India, Mauritius and the Seychelles. Others say this is incorrect, and that the youths – like the West Indians – were already living in Britain.[10]

Even if they were recruited, it is not clear if they actually got here. Ken Johnstone recalls: 'I do believe we took a very small number from India or Sri Lanka. But there would have been a prior contact from London. Of course, our resources were limited.'

(Records held by the Big Brother Movement show merely name, address in Britain, type of school attended and religion. They do not specify 'colour' or racial background.)

In 1980 the Big Brother Movement brought out 166 young British tradesmen. Another 192 tradesmen were brought from the British Isles in 1981/82. A further 100 young BBM migrants were approved for 1983. However, they never got here. Shortly after the election of the Hawke Labor Government in March 1983, the Big Brother Movement's sponsorship role was abruptly terminated, one of the grounds being – as put to BBM – that it discriminated 'in favour of white Anglo-Saxons'[11]

# 18

## The Axe Falls

━━━━━

*'They did the right thing. They brought the right people out; I'm no racist.*
*But they did. They brought people out here that wanted to be here*
*and they kept an eye on them, they didn't just turn them loose.'*
Brian Bywater (Otranto, 1956)

N THE ENTIRE HISTORY OF YOUTH MIGRATION only one organisation involved in this activity suffered official Government displeasure. This was the Big Brother Movement – the longest-running and most successful operator in this field; and, ironically, one of the few such bodies to emerge 'cleanskin', without a taint of moral or other scandal.

The first sign of trouble emerged in September 1982, during the final months of the Liberal-National Coalition headed by Malcolm Fraser. At that time the Department of Immigration's office in London advised that no further BBM applications could be processed pending a decision from Canberra.

The Big Brother Movement sought advice from Canberra but obtained only a vague statement to the effect that there was no suggestion of targeting the organisation in any way, rather that migration policy generally was being reviewed. The then Immigration Minister, John Hodges, twice met a delegation from BBM. At the second meeting (on 17 January 1983) he praised the manner in which BBM had adjusted its work to current conditions and issued a directive to the Department to resume processing the movement' applications in the UK.

By mid February this instruction had not been conveyed to the Department's officers in London. On being so informed, Hodges sent an emphatic telex on the subject (from his Queensland electorate) to the Secretary of the Department in Canberra.

(Much later the movement discovered, by means of the Freedom of Information Act, that the Minister's directive did not reach London until after the March 1983 election and change of Government.)

On 5 March 1983, a Labor Government was elected under the Prime Ministership of Robert Hawke. Just three weeks after the election the BBM received a letter, dated 24 March, from the First Assistant Secretary, Policy and Secretariat, of the Department of Immigration, Mr K.A (Tony) Harris. The letter said the new Minister for Immigration and Ethnic Affairs, Stewart West, was 'reviewing a number of migration matters' and had looked at the arrangements for processing the movement's nominees in London.

The letter said the minister had decided that 'nominees of the movement should be subject to the same criteria and processing arrangements as other applicants for migration. Our officials in London have been notified of this decision and will be discussing its implementation with your officials.'

The letter angered Frank Mansell,[1] formerly secretary, executive director, and (during the tense period which followed) chairman of BBM. He told colleagues: 'To the uninitiated this sounds fair enough but I am fully aware that the requirement amounts to a ban.'

He said the decision was made at a time when British migration had already been reduced by 50 per cent, and ignored the fact that the movement's quota formed only about one thousandth of the proposed annual intake of migrants.

The move came amidst a wider debate on immigration policies. At a time when Australia's ethnic mix was being broadened, the Big Brother Movement's clear pro-British stance was considered anachronistic by those out to sell the new multicultural Australia.

A political rumpus quickly arose. The new Immigration Minister said in Parliament that the BBM had enjoyed 'a favoured position' as the only remaining private group with the right to select[2] and process its own immigrants'. That position was now 'inconsistent with a non-discriminatory immigration policy.'

According to Stewart West, if the Government continued to grant concessions to the Big Brother Movement it could lead to a view among migrant communities that the country's immigration policy 'is weighted in favour of white Anglo-Saxons'.

The speech and others (some of which are published as Appendix3 to this volume) met with a mixed reaction. BBM and its supporters were furious, and considered the organisation to have been a victim of racism in reverse. Frank Mansell described the decision as 'extraordinary and illogical'.

He responded: 'It would appear that the Government believes the reason why previous Governments, both Labor and non-Labor, encouraged and helped BBM was simply because the great majority of the lads were British.

'We believe it was the good results achieved by the movement which earned the approval of all Ministers from Arthur Calwell to John Hodges, and including that champion of anti-discrimination Al Grassby.'[3]

In a letter to the *Sydney Morning Herald*,[4] warming to his task, Mansell said these and other Government Ministers of all parties had encouraged the work, 'not because the boys came from Britain, but because BBM by its careful selection and organisation in Australia has achieved the highest percentage of successful settlement of any form of migration to Australia.'

Car stickers were issued reading: 'Current immigration – putting Australians last'. A letter was circulated which said in part: 'As you are no doubt aware, the Big Brother Movement opposes many aspects of Australia's present migration program. Labor's migration programme appears to be the most anti-British and anti-European in Australia's history. The successful migration program followed by successive Governments from 1946-83 has been abandoned....'

Support was offered by Liberal leaders Andrew Peacock and John Howard, who pledged that 'when the Coalition is returned to Government we will restore the situation [of BBM] to that which existed prior to the Labor Government bringing the movement's activities to a close.'

The Hawke Government denied – and continued to do so for several years – that it had implemented any formal ban.

Mansell and others found this disclaimer unconvincing. He said the Immigration Department's new selection criteria included a minimum 'five years in the workplace after completion of an apprenticeship'. This, as the Department, later acknowledged, meant that an unaccompanied immigrant would have to be about 25, thus effectively excluding BBM youth migration.

A few weeks later West said in a media interview that BBM was free to continue to sponsor young people, though 'special concessions' had been withdrawn. Other comments gave the impression that BBM was unable to continue due to the cancellation of Government funding.

This further infuriated the movement. According to Mansell, at the peak of its activities Government subsidies formed only about five per cent of the movement's budget. Since the cancellation of assisted passages and other ancillary benefits for all migrants in 1981, BBM had received no Government assistance whatever.[5]

The reference to 'concessions' was taken up by Stewart West's successor as Immigration Minister, Chris Hurford, in 1985. Hurford stated in a letter that 'involvement by private organisations' in Australia's migration program would contravene 'Principle No. 1 of Australia's immigration policy, which is that it is fundamental to national sovereignty that the Australian Government alone shall determine who will be admitted to Australia'.

According to Frank Mansell, the BBM had neither sought nor obtained a dispensation to operate outside these principles. The movement's 61st annual report had the following to say about this issue:

'Does Mr Hurford really believe that, until the end of 1982, BBM had been given or had assumed the right to decide whether any particular young person entered Australia and also the total of such young people to come? In fact until our group nominations and annual forecasts were approved by the Department we could not sponsor anybody.'

The theme was taken up in the 1986 annual report, which noted: 'Each applicant had to complete an individual application to the Department and could not migrate until he was interviewed and approved by a departmental officer and issued with a visa or "consent for entry for residence".

'Until the assisted passage scheme was abolished in 1981 all those we had offered to sponsor had to make individual applications for such assistance. Therefore the Government, quite rightly, had full control over our migration work at all times.'

The report noted: 'There appears no lack of energetic organisations representing ethnic minorities in Australia and we applaud their work. On the other hand, there is a clear lack of a rallying point for the ethnic majority who are concerned to retain all that is good in the Australian tradition.'

(In a letter to the *Sydney Morning Herald*,[6] Mansell said that other national groups, had they so desired, could have formed organisations directed towards the immigration of their fellow countrymen. That they had not done so, did not render the work of BBM 'discriminatory'.)

For about five years the Big Brother Movement attempted unsuccessfully to have the effective veto overturned. In 1988 the movement issued a statement conceding that it would probably have to 'await a change of Government' before its 'historic and beneficial youth migration work' could be resumed.

By the time this occurred, with the election of John Howard as Prime Minister in March 1996, the movement had branched out into new directions, and no serious attempt was made to revive BBM youth migration.

Publicity engineered by the dispute had an unexpected, but welcome side effect in that it encouraged some hundreds of former Little Brothers to resume contact. This resulted in the formation of a Little Brothers' Association and, in 1986, the creation of a Friends of the Big Brother Movement. Regretfully, the interest engendered gradually dissipated. Currently about 600 people are on the movement's combined mailing list.

## POLITICALLY CORRECT

*'I was terribly disappointed when the Government of the time [1983] put the kibosh on it [BBM youth migration]. It was a wonderful scheme. The country was getting the right type of people for God's sake. Why put an end to it?'*
Ken Tubbs (Empire Star, 1947)

While former passions have dimmed, many of those associated with the BBM continue to feel it was unfairly attacked and made victim of an extreme form of political correctness which favoured all those other than of British descent and affinity.

These views have received support from both expected and unexpected quarters. Jim Samios, former MLC,[7] a Greek-Australian, married to a Scot, has attended several BBM functions. He told me:

'I believe that in a truly multi-cultural society all strands of that society should be able to articulate their cultural and social needs within the framework of our legal and constitutional framework, which obviously relates to our common language, British Westminster heritage, and a written constitution.

'Having said that I would note that in recent years whilst the communities of non-English speaking background have been able to relate their needs to the community as a whole in a significant manner, the same cannot be said of English speaking groups, and it is pivotal to success and the social cohesion of our multi-cultural society that they should be able to do so.'

Ken Johnstone expresses much the same sentiments, but in blunter fashion: 'They called us sexist, racist, and said we were discriminatory. Now in those days and even today, in terms of Australia, our resources are limited. The argument against us was absurd. You may as well say that if you're helping the deaf you're not helping the blind. I mean we were a specialist organisation; we were selecting young people from all over Britain.'

With the passage of time, some are wondering if the dispute might have been avoided. Eddy Steele, the movement's current executive director, says: 'I think it was avoidable. It was just unfortunate. I was in and out of the country at the time.[8] I remember I came home from a flight and already the signals were passing to and from Canberra, and phones were ringing. I think there were too many players. They were all taking entrenched positions when the issues could have been quietly settled. Sir John Pagan, our then president, was also high in the Liberal Party. It was the start of this multicultural thing and there we were, blatantly promoting British migrants.'

According to Steele: 'I think somebody started complaining. It might have been Fraser,[9] it might have been Grassby,[10] I don't know. But I think what happened there is that push came to shove. Michael Hodgman played a big part; they called him "the mouth from the south". And Stewart West was coming in as the new Minister for Immigration under Labor. If some of these people had kept their mouths shut it would have been quietly defused and we would have been allowed to carry on, maybe in a slightly different way.

'When the issue was brought up in Parliament, people sniffed the wind and thought there were votes in it Various petitions were put around; how we should target certain seats, and so on. The new Government dug in its heels. Then they brought in the race thing. I remember Professor Blainey[11] came in on our side. All these different people were having their input; they just painted each other into a corner, and we were in the middle.'

'So each one came in with his own fuel to put on the fire. Of course, Frank's first approach was to the RSL, and he got letters into *Reveille*[12] He started looking for people to support us. Why stop a good thing like this? The multiculturalists and others hit back.'

Politicians opposed to BBM's migration efforts noted the fact that few, if any, of the young 'Britons' brought to Australia had dark skins[13]. The absence of girls was also highlighted; one parliamentarian[14] mockingly stating that in all its (then) 60 years' history, only one 'Little Sister' had been brought to Australia by the Big Brother Movement.

Actually, he is wrong. It appears there were none, though, according to Ken Johnstone: 'We did have a girl on our books. She was scheduled to come, but the axe prevented it. The reason we never brought out young women in those [earlier] days was because it just wasn't a practical situation. It's different today. Women are totally emancipated.'

Eddy Steele, though he was not involved, confirms that a policy change was under way. 'It [bringing in girls] was being mooted. We'd come to the stage of "Why not?" One reason why it hadn't been done before was that it would have meant buying another hostel. I mean, the thought of 12 young ladies and 12 young men sharing a big house in Homebush. It goes down well with backpackers and others today, but attitudes used to be different.'

## A 'PERK' IN LONDON
During the dispute about the 'banning' of BBM migration much was made of a 'special', and by implication unwarranted privilege given to the

movement – namely the provision of office space in Australia House, in London.

It was implied that BBM had formally sought this concession which had been wrongly granted by a previous Government.

The origin of this now vanished 'perk' is, in fact, quite different. Frank Mansell compared it to a 'pedestrian right of way established by long precedent'. It also brings to light an interesting story of someone who played a significant part in BBM's early history.

During World War I a young woman called Ida Wallis joined the staff of the Australian High Commission and worked in a section dealing with the welfare of the many thousands of Australians serving in France and elsewhere. Later she assisted Australian servicemen who had become engaged or married in Britain – culminating in the 'wives' boats' of 1919/20.

This was in effect her introduction to migration. From 1925 to 1939 she undertook general duties, assisting the migration of unaccompanied youths under both government and non-government schemes. In this capacity she became a good friend and associate of the Big Brother Movement.

The renewal of youth migration after World War II attracted the financial support of individuals and institutions in the UK. Ida Wallis left the Australian Government service and accepted a position with the British branch of BBM. It appears nobody suggested that she should move out of her existing office or that the interviewing of young applicants should take place elsewhere!

Ida Wallis proved a capable administrator with enthusiasm for BBM ideals. She contributed greatly to the successful operation of the movement over the following 16 years. She retired in 1962, having given some 45 years of her life to 'things Australian'.

BBM gave her a small pension, which was continued until her death in 1980. The London office closed in May 1983.

# 19

## Still Going – but Role Reversed

**'W**e brought the Pommy kids in...Now we're sending 'em back.' It's a good-humoured jest, which, though untrue, has a certain ring to it. Actually, the 'kids' are near adult, and, though some were born in Britain, all are dinkum Aussies.

There is a widespread belief, even among those who came out under its auspices, that the Big Brother Movement folded when its immigration activities ended in 1983. Not so! It carried on (and still carries on), but with a marked change of direction. It now sends young Australians to Britain – a reversal of its former role – but as temporary visitors rather than as migrants.

It does this through a BBM Awards Scheme which gives travel grants to help talented young Australians gain additional experience in Britain and Europe. In one sense it reverses the original idea of 'bringing out' young Britons. In another sense it is following the same path. When announcing the scheme in 1984, the then BBM President, the late Sir John Pagan, expressed the hope that it would fulfil one of the movement's original aims of helping to preserve Australia's historic links with Britain.

The BBM scheme also aids a number of charities. (More about that later.) By early 2005, as this chapter was being written, some 800 young people had received awards totalling $2.6 million, while $1.6 million had been awarded to the various charities (including rural scholarships).

Travel grants are divided into 15 categories, covering music and drama, sport, dancing and technical. Terms are broadly defined. For instance, dancing includes ballet, ballroom and highland. Music includes classical, Scottish piping, and jazz. The movement does not itself select the individuals who will receive grants. This is done by a number of educational, sporting and cultural associations and individuals with specialist expertise.

Those nominated are expected to have reached a standard of excellence in their chosen fields (commensurate with their ages) and are likely to enhance their career prospects by the UK experience. Currently most grants are for $7,000. Grants are given on the basis that it would not be possible for recipients to finance their project without BBM assistance.

Recipients of grants must be not older than 23 (25 for 'technical' awardees) and – in a departure from the original role of sponsoring only migrant boys and young men – may belong to either sex!

Classical music awards have been given to young people with an interest in piano, oboe, violin, cello, organ, flute, singing and bagpiping. Many are students at the Sydney Conservatorium of Music. Benefits include opportunities to hear a wide range of concert activities not available in Australia, and to attend lessons and classes at the major music institutions in London.

British organisations which have taken young music award recipients under their wing include the Royal College of Music, Royal Academy of Music, Guildhall School of Music and Dance and the London Opera Centre.

Modern music (including jazz) is also represented in the awards scheme. Thanks to Ken Johnstone's[1] contacts, budding jazz musicians have met top English performers and been invited to play at leading London clubs. Awardees also include members of (Australian) Scottish drum and pipe bands, an interest of one of the scheme's founding architects, former BBM chairman, Jock McAusland.[2]

In January 2003 Sydney teenager Steven McRae, among the previous year's crop of 31 awardees, stunned the dance world by winning the prestigious Prix de Lausanne scholarship in Switzerland. He had also scored a place in the Royal Ballet School in London.

McRae, 17, faced stiff competition from more than 100 European and American competitors to reveal his versatility in contrasting pieces of classical and tap dance. It is unusual for a competitor to perform a tap dance in the Prix de Lausanne, but that did not stop McRae.

In a climactic scene echoing the wish-fulfilment dance movie, *Billy Elliot*, the audience erupted with wild cheers for the boy from Plumpton in Sydney's west. According to the *Sydney Morning Herald's* report: 'Everyone from teenage girls to cynical 'seen it all before' dance critics whooped and whistled to make it known that McRae was the clear favourite. The judges were left with no choice.'

Other ballet awardees have been accepted for training with the London Festival Ballet and Sadlers Wells.

As stated earlier, highland and ballroom dancing also feature in the dance categories. Eddy Steele says proudly: 'One of our awardees, a young female highland dancer, performed solo at the Edinburgh Tattoo. We've also had a piper who played solo on the battlements of the castle.' Two ballroom dancing recipients, Karen Rufus and Paul Green, subsequently became Australian national champions.

Awardees in the technical category come mainly from engineering and allied skilled occupations. Awards have also gone to people employed in catering, hairdressing, horticulture, jewellery and clothing design.

In most cases the additional knowledge sought by technical awardees is gained from commercial undertakings rather than training institutions. British firms have offered their facilities readily to the young Australians.

Horticulture recipients have been welcomed in such centres as the Royal Botanic Gardens, Kew; Royal Horticultural Society Gardens, Wisley; and the Queen's own gardens at Sandringham.

Some technical awardees have received more than the standard grants. In 2002, in a departure from tradition, the BBM sent a group of young trades people from the Hunter Valley to a leadership training college run by the Royal Navy. The course includes dealing with emergencies (a simulated ship's fire, flooding, responding to a missile attack), confidence building skills, and fitness training from forced marches to orienteering in the Welsh mountains.

According to Eddy Steele: 'Our idea is to give these young technical awardees the opportunity to move outside the square they live in, and place themselves in a totally different environment. When they've finished the course they go on to do a period of work for British companies in their own field. This varies from a month to about a year.'

## GOOD SPORTS

Soccer and cricket are the major sporting activities represented in the awards scheme. Swimming, rugby union and golf were added recently.

There have been some stunning successes. In 1989, 17-year-old Adam Gilchrist, from Goonellabah, rural NSW, applied for a BBM travel grant to improve his skills at cricket. He later wrote to Frank Mansell: 'The [UK] experience broadened my personal game and provided me with great opportunities...'

It was a marked understatement. In that year, in the Middlesex County Cricket League competition, he scored a total 1900 runs, including 13 centuries and three innings in the 90s.

Upon return from England, he was almost immediately chosen to represent NSW, from which he relocated, in 1994, to Western Australia. Since then he has achieved a reputation as one of the world's greatest players. Arguably, no Test wicketkeeper in the history of the game has batted as well as Gilchrist, which is why he has become a regular choice in all-time world elevens.

It is Gilchrist's ability to hit freely without appearing to take risks which sets him part. Indeed, recent research showed that in terms of runs scored per balls faced – the ultimate measure of a batsman's scoring ability – Gilchrist is the fastest Test batsman of all time.

Gilchrist has been appointed Australian vice-captain. He continues to excel with the bat. It is likely he will be one of the stars of world cricket for years to come.

## KEWELL THE JEWEL

Other sporting champions, too, have been helped in their formative years by BBM. Possibly the jewel in the crown, as this book was going to press, is Australian soccer legend, Harry Kewell,[3] followed by his co-star and fellow awardee, Brett Emerton.

The two Sydneysiders were awarded BBM grants in 1994, when both were 15. They were nominated by David Lee, then director of coaching for the NSW Soccer Federation.[4] He had first seen them play when both were in primary school. The two youngsters travelled to Britain together, having received the (then) standard grant of $4,500 each.

Kewell was snapped up almost immediately by the northern English club, Leeds United, and quickly made his mark. In 1998 he became involved in an imbroglio when a clash of dates produced a tug-of-war between the club and the Australian junior national side as to which should have priority for his services. It was a shade of things to come.

Emerton, who plays for Blackburn Rovers, having been transferred in 2003 from the Dutch club, Feyenoord, has captained the Australian under-23 team (the Olyroos) and skippered this team in the 2000 Sydney Olympic Games. He, too, has faced difficulties over club and ethnic loyalties.

It is as senior players that the pair now have renown. At the 2002 World Cup showdown with Uruguay, Harry Kewell was on the left wing for the Socceroos[5] and Brett Emerton was on the right wing. At the much-publicised "friendly", in which Australia beat England 3-1 in February 2003, Kewell[6] (the undoubted star of the match) and Emerton scored one goal each for the Socceroos. As on previous occasions, there were doubts about whether or not Kewell would be released by his club to play.

Both men are the subject of constant rumour about transfers and bidding wars. Kewell moved to the top ranking club, Liverpool, in July 2003, for a transfer fee of around £6 million (A$15 million). His weekly income is said to be around around £60,000 (A$140,000).

Eddy points out that the scheme would be worth little without the active support of British sporting clubs. An awardee wrote to Frank Mansell: 'On two occasions I was fortunate enough to train with the first division team (Manchester United) mixing with world class players.' Other clubs offering their services have included Aberdeen, Burnley, Norwich City, Luton Town, and, of course, Leeds United.

In less high profile sports, too, awardees have become champions. Tracy Brook, nominated for ice skating in 1984, subsequently represent-ed Australia in the 1988 (Calgary) Winter Olympics. She is now a profes-sional coach.

Media reports about these sporting personalities' successes rarely, if ever, mention the role of the Big Brother Movement. Not that the BBM is complaining. Publicity resulting from such exposure might well have created a flood of requests which the movement would have been unable to fulfil due to its policy (now under review) of providing alone the fund-ing for all its projects and awards..

INWARD TRAFFIC

Whilst nowadays chiefly involved in sending young people *out* of Australia, the movement does have a small involvement in what might be called 'inward' traffic.

In 1999 the BBM extended its award scheme to include young Britons chosen to represent their country in the so-called World Skills Olympics. From this group every two years 10 young skilled people are selected by UK Skills for a BBM grant which enables them to work and travel in Australia for a period ranging from one month to a year.

The recipients cover a wide field of trades and occupations – engineers, hairdressers, IT specialists, mechanics, plumbers, stonemasons, painters and decorators, among others. Whilst the movement has long since given up the idea of a direct role in the immigration process, it feels its expertise and many years of experience could be used to benefit young Britons who may wish to migrate.

In addition to having a grants system, the BBM also directly supports a number of youth-oriented activities.

The movement contributed financially to the initial setting up of the Slingshot program, which is operated by the Melbourne City Mission. It aims to help young people who have a business idea, but lack the money and experience to see it through. Rotary clubs supply the mentors, and successful applicants, chosen after a thorough grilling, will receive appropriate training.

Another project assisted by BBM is Stepping Stone. This Sydney-based activity, which BBM helped to establish, has provided accommodation for more than 150 disadvantaged young people since its foundation in 1989.

Its main facility, Stepping Stone House, in the inner Sydney suburb of Dulwich Hill, accommodates six to seven homeless teenagers for up to 18 months, depending on their need and maturity level. The centre is staffed 24 hours a day. The program includes the teaching of life skills, with counselling to develop positive relationships at school and at home. The residents, both boys and girls, progress to three privately rented three-bedroom homes. Outdoor activities include camps and ocean voyages.

Charitable and youth enterprises currently assisted by BBM include

NSW Children's Week, Variety Club Bash, the Shepherd Centre, Sydney Children's Hospital, PACT Youth Theatre, Kidsafe, Giant Steps, Tocal Agricultural College, various Lions and Surf Life Saving clubs, and the NSW Sports Council for the Disabled.

Since 1986 the BBM has provided tertiary education scholarships in agriculture. These are scholarships with a difference. The continuing decline of the rural economy has forced an increasing number of students to withdraw from agricultural courses for financial reasons. It is hoped these grants to selected colleges will prevent such withdrawals.

The directors of the Big Brother Movement are well pleased with all aspect of the awards scheme and related projects. Jock McAusland, chairman from 1985 to 1996, noted in a report: 'These talented young Australians enhance their career prospects by the training and experience they receive in the UK. They are good ambassadors for Australia and they contribute to maintaining our links of kinship with Britain.'

These thoughts are echoed by Jock's successor, Ken Johnstone, who told me: 'The opportunities that these young people get when they go across to Britain is tremendous. The value and experience – you can't put money on it.'

The total sum approved for distribution in 2005/2006 was $403,000.

## BIG SISTERS

One of the more novel schemes acknowledged by BBM is the Big Sisters Big Brothers program of the Sydney YWCA. The similarity in titles may seem like plagiarism, but such a suggestion would be incorrect. In any case, the BBM doesn't mind, and in fact is rather flattered.

The program operates under the theme 'Having a big sister or big brother makes a difference'. Promotional literature describes it as 'a professionally run mentoring program that provides young people who lack adequate adult role models with support and friendship through a trusting relationship with an appropriate adult volunteer'.

The program was brought to the Sydney YWCA from Canada, in 1978, by the Sydney YWCA's present chief executive officer, Jocelyn Murphy. A Big Sister herself, while involved with the YWCA in Canada, she saw first hand how the program impacted on the lives of young people.

She says the program aims to develop the self-worth and confidence of the young person through the experience of having 'a positive adult friend in their lives who listens, understands, accepts and respects them'.

Back in her native Australia, she introduced the program into the work of the YWCA. Rather like the original concept of its Australian counterpart, each young person is matched with an adult mentor and they agree to spend a few hours together each week. The match is made taking into account the young person's needs, interests, temperament and location, and the skills and qualities of the volunteer.

According to Jocelyn: 'We cater for children from all sorts of backgrounds, and what all of them need are good adults in their lives. Whether male or female they need adults who are consistent, caring and trustworthy, and who are not there to constantly be telling them what they should and shouldn't be doing.'

The program, as its name implies, embraces both sexes. 'The path from childhood to adulthood: is increasingly difficult for boys and girls, and to make the journey, they need a good friend by their side.'

The program's roots are in the US, where the New York Big Brothers was founded in 1904. A parallel Big Sisters organisation was formed in 1909. The movement rapidly expanded as more branches were formed. In 1977 the male and female organisations combined to become the Big Brothers and Big Sisters of America (BBBSA). The movement now has 500 agencies in all 50 states, plus affiliates in 34 countries and territories. An umbrella organisation, Big Brothers Big Sisters International (BBBSI), was formed in 1998.[7]

The impact of the program has had far-reaching effects in North America. Even Bart Simpson has had a Big Brother, and the 'Bigs' and 'Littles' relationship is a theme which regularly features in popular entertainment, such as Seinfeld and ER.

As stated earlier, the program was brought to Australia, under the umbrella of the YWCA[8] in 1978. In Sydney and Perth the women of the 'Y' – as a women's organisation – have reversed the order so that the title now reads Big Sisters and Big Brothers instead of the more usual Big Brothers and Big Sisters. The counterpart in Darwin is called Big Sisters and Little Sisters.

In Melbourne, where the program is run by the (male) Jesuit Social Services, the program is known as Big Brothers Big Sisters. A Jewish equivalent, run by the organisation, Jewish Care, is called simply Big Buddies.

## WHERE IS THE MONEY FROM?

These projects cost money – a lot of it. Where is the money from? It's a reasonable question which many have asked.

According to Ken Johnstone, chairman and former treasurer: 'It hasn't been easy – the way the BBM has grown in assets and resources from those early days. Luckily, we have had some very strong financial people on the board. Today we've got fairly healthy resources.'

Unusual circumstances have helped. In 1983 the remaining portion of the former 'Karmsley Hills' training farm was gazetted for residential use and was sold to Landcom for $2,500,000. This windfall, added to BBM's earlier investments provided the income to finance these new undertakings.

A lesser windfall was gained from the sale of Gunning Lodge,[9] in November 1982, for approximately $102,000. By the time of the sale new arrivals were being accommodated in private lodgings in Sydney's eastern suburbs.

Receipt of the money from the Landcom sale was not without controversy. A letter dated 16 October 1983 from the Immigration Minister, Stewart West, to an inquiring Senator said the land sold for $2.5 million 'had been purchased shortly after World War II with the aid of a Government subsidy [and] has provided BBM with substantial assets'.

The accuracy of the above is challenged. According to the movement's records neither the Commonwealth Government nor the Government of NSW contributed 'one penny' to the purchase of the original land. BBM staff and supporters found the claim particularly hurtful as implying that the movement's community work was made possible only through past Government generosity.

The sale of what was left of the original Karmsley Hills training farm meant that there was no longer any memorial to the Little Brothers who died in World War II. To compensate for the omission a plaque was erected in the Sydney Club.[10]

The inscription stated: 'The Sydney Club's founder, Sir Arthur Rickard,[11] initiated the formation of the Big Brother Movement in 1925 to foster British youth migration. About 1,000 British lads were settled in NSW prior to 1939. This plaque commemorates those known to have lost their lives in the Australian Armed Forces during World War II. Since then Big Brother sponsorships have grown to more than 12,000 and the close relationship between the Club and the Movement continues.'

In January 2001, following the demise of the Sydney Club, the plaque was relocated in the revamped (and renamed) Calmsley Hill City Farm, also known[12] as the Fairfield City Farm.

The land obtained from BBM together with an area of additional land is now the township of Abbotsbury. Little Brothers who passed through the training farm between 1947 and 1970 would hardly recognise this new outer western suburb (population about 8,000) of large, impressive homes on the traditional 'quarter acre block'. The newcomers include Vietnamese and Cambodian refugees, who have intermingled with European migrants (primarily Italian and Maltese) who settled in the adjoining areas in the 1950s and 60s, and have made good. Two large European sports clubs (Italian and Croatian) and a Buddhist temple are interesting examples of this changing migrant face of Australia.

The City Farm, on the western side of the township, is a community-based project,[13] formed with the intention of helping people of town backgrounds gain an understanding of farm life, and to become involved 'with growing and living things'.

The main farmyard is home to sheep, goats, cows and horses. There are activity areas, a playground, working pottery, cafe (whose fare includes once crocodile and kangaroo steaks) and souvenir shop. An annual event is the presentation of community volunteer awards on Australia Day. The BBM's annual get-togethers are held here.

The City Farm was the venue for the mountain bike events during the Sydney 2000 Olympic Games. Regrettably, some of the more ambitious regular pursuits – including mountain bike and horse riding – have had to be curtailed for financial reasons.

The office and souvenir shop was formerly a dormitory used by Little Brothers, evidence of whose presence is still visible. The lads' former games room became the pottery room[14] and their refectory is now a communal hall.

In 1990 a group of former Little Brothers put together a photo montage in the farm's pleasantly furnished cafe-restaurant. In collaboration with Fairfield Council and Friends of the City Farm, the conservatory was subsequently converted into a 'heritage room', devoted exclusively to the history and memorabilia of the Big Brother Movement.

The room's main feature is a large mural, painted by Queensland artist, Vincent Smith, in 1998. The mural was commissioned by BBM. It measures 24 metres long by three metres high, and depicts a farm scene, with a horse rider, blacksmith, and others laying fence posts, chopping wood and going about their daily chores. It is not clear if any of them are Little Brothers.

The mural then turns a corner, where the artist has painted a different scene. This shows a passenger ship, with people walking along the wharf. In front of this little group someone has placed a (real) and slightly battered suitcase, complete with P&O labels, thus bringing the scene to life.

Bolted to another wall is a 'mural' of a different kind. This is a table top, formerly in the refectory, on which boys had once carved their initials and towns of origin in the UK. The heritage room contains another photo montage, also the war memorial plaque, removed from the Sydney Club, on which 17 names are inscribed.[15]

Fairfield Council takes pride in the fact that it leads NSW in regard to the numbers of countries of origin of its residents.[16] Charles Vella, the Friends' vice-president, believes the existence of the City Farm, and the moves taken in the past decade, will 'keep the flame alive' and ensure that the presence of some 4,000 young Britons will not be forgotten.

## NEW NAME, NEW DIRECTIONS

From time to time the suggestion has been made that the Big Brother Movement should change its name. This was carried out in Britain, where, from 1964 until its eventual demise, the UK-based operation became known as the British Boys' Movement for Australia.[17]

The main reason for the change was fear that the popular, but slightly scary TV drama series, *1984*, based on George Orwell's futuristic novel, had given sinister overtones to the words 'Big Brother'.

In Australia, as in Britain, the phrase 'Big Brother is Watching You' was on everybody's lips. Patrick Milligan, then an illustrator with the Fairfax newspapers, heard about the Big Brother Movement and asked a reporter what it was. The journalist, who should have known better, said he thought it was 'some sort of communist group'. The response caused Milligan to want to find out more.[18]

The name 'Big Brother' has now re-surfaced as the title of a highly popular TV 'Survivor' show.[19] The program, which is not everybody's cup of tea, has created a degree of confusion, with fans occasionally telephoning the BBM to ask who will be evicted this week.

However, more important issues are at stake. In recent years the movement, like similar organisations, has sought new directions and activities in addition to maintaining contact with hundreds of ex-Little Brothers?

In 2002 the board expressed a desire to expand its current grants programs and activities. Limited funds restricted this aim. In late 2003 the decision was made to approach the corporate world with a view to joint sponsorship – perhaps on a dollar for dollar basis – or other forms of collaboration in youth assistance programs.

As this book went to press several major firms had expressed interest in such a scheme, but it is too early to pass judgement.

As part of the 'new look', and to avoid repetition of previous misunderstandings, the name Big Brother Movement was formally changed, in 2004, to BBM Ltd.[20] This name is seen as particularly useful on the movement's website, the desire being to avoid confusion with the TV series, various porno sites and the Big Brothers Big Sisters organisation in the United States.

# 20

# BBM Inter-State. 'Not Plain Sailing'

## ▬

*'No social gathering in Melbourne strikes a happier note
than those reunions at the nerve centre of the movement,
when a new batch of fresh-faced youngsters from the Motherland
are taken into the family and made to feel that their future
is a matter of deep concern to hundreds of the best citizens
of their adopted country.'*
From publicity material issued by the Victorian Big Brother Movement.

THE BIG BROTHER MOVEMENT, contrary to common belief, was not confined to New South Wales. 'Branches' – actually autonomous bodies which were sometimes in conflict[1] – existed at various times in Victoria, Tasmania and Western Australia. All had chequered histories.

As previously noted, the movement itself is thought to have formally come into being at a meeting in Sydney's Millions Club on 15 April 1925. It is not clear if, at that time, the intention was to create a branch system to cover the various states.

At any rate, within three or four months of that meeting a structure of some sort was created in Melbourne. Details are vague, due to the loss of records, but when the *Jervis Bay* arrived, on 11 December, en route for Sydney, more than half that first contingent of some 200 Little Brothers had elected to stay in Victoria, with jobs arranged in rural communities.

### VICTORIA – CALLS OF EMPIRE

The BBM in Victoria functioned independently of its NSW parent, and made its own migration arrangements with the BBM 'branch' in London. The Victorian BBM, like its Sydney counterpart, took boys from all social classes, but had a preference for the products of English public schools[2] for reasons which will be explored.[3]

Even more intently than its NSW counterpart, it promoted what it described as 'The Calls of Empire'. There were three such calls – The Call of Adventure, The Call of Opportunity and The Call of Service.

The Call of Adventure[4] stated in part: 'Young Englishmen have been ever ready to respond to the call of adventure. Is it because they still possess the native qualities of their distant ancestors of Saxon and Norman days? However that may be, we find them today in every corner of the globe.'

In other ways, too, the Victorian branch was more extreme than its NSW counterpart. An interesting example is its adaptation of the 'Hands across the sea' poster,[5] used by the NSW Big Brother Movement for recruitment purposes.

In Melbourne, though not in Sydney, the same drawing was used as cover picture on the magazine, *The New Australian*, with the slogan: 'Keep Australia White' replacing the non-threatening 'Put it there, lad.' A leaflet issued by the Victorian BBM cited four 'good reasons' to support the Movement. They were (in order of priority) 'Get more Population; Increase Production; Reduce Taxation; Keep Australia White.'

Between 1925 and 1929 the Victorian BBM brought out over 1,000 lads, but adverse economic conditions caused it to cease recruitment in 1930. In 1938 Colonel H.N.M Clegg, a vice-president of the Victorian BBM, returned to the United Kingdom and was appointed general secretary of the Big Brother Movement there.

Recruiting was resumed in 1939 and about 120 Little Brothers were brought in (a similar number going to New South Wales). At some stage disagreement arose between Colonel Clegg and the Victorian branch, the cause of which is obscure.

Following the outbreak of war in September 1939, the Victorian branch wound up its activities – or so it was assumed – and handed its assets and records to the Boy Scouts Association of Victoria. The NSW branch took no part in the above matters, of which it was only dimly aware, but decided to maintain a small organisation during the war years.

In 1946 the council of the Big Brother Movement in NSW, in consultation with the London office, decided to resume youth migration and to do so as soon as possible. At this time a report appeared in Australian and British newspapers to the effect that the BBM in Victoria considered this premature.

This piece of journalistic enterprise surprised the folk in the Sydney office, who were unaware that a Victorian branch still existed. Contact was immediately made with the general secretary of the Boy Scouts in Victoria, Frank Sanders, who denied being the author of the statement, but indicated that he agreed with it.

The Big Brother Movement was not the only charitable body at that time to face internal division. Frank Ronald Gladstone Sanders, 'Sandy' to his friends, was a legendary figure in Victorian scouting, of which he had been general secretary since 1924. When he first took up the helm the movement was hopelessly split to the extent that two rival bodies claimed to represent scouting in the state.

Record keeping was haphazard. He had a male helper (rural organiser), and part-time typist. Equipment and stock were valued at less than $200. His strength of personality and no-nonsense approach proved a unifying force, which benefited the movement but did not endear him to people – such as the the committee of the New South Wales BBM – with whom he disagreed.

Sanders' opposition to the resumption of migration annoyed the Sydney BBM committee, which was even less enchanted when the letterhead of the Boy Scouts Association showed it also to be the BBM of Victoria.

A few frosty letters were exchanged, the Sydney committee having decided to go ahead with its migrant program and to 'keep Mr Sanders advised of our progress'. Relations began to improve and 'letters were received from Sanders expressing interest and complimenting us on our efforts'.

In 1954 the New South Wales BBM decided to extend the placement of Little Brothers who wished to go on the land to North Eastern Victoria, from where a considerable degree of interest had arisen. Honorary welfare officers were appointed in various townships and employment given to about 50 lads.

Again, it was not plain sailing. The Boy Scouts Association of Victoria (wearing its hat as successor to the BBM) protested to the director of the Child Welfare Department of Victoria. The director in turn telephoned the BBM in Sydney to say that in the light of the objection, 'transfers' from Sydney could not be approved.

The Sydney committee found this new situation intolerable. As recorded in an internal memorandum: 'As neither the Boy Scouts Association nor pre-war members of the old Victorian BBM had taken action to resume the intake of Little Brothers in the previous seven years we were unable to understand the attitude of those concerned.'

The situation was resolved in Sydney's favour when, after intervention, the then Immigration Minister, Harold Holt,[6] issued a ruling that provisions of the Immigration (Guardianship of Children) Act no longer applied to Little Brothers over the age of 17. In other words, they were no longer wards of the state and could live and work where they liked.

In 1959 – after 35 years as general secretary – Frank Sanders retired and took the records of the Victorian BBM with him.[7] He told colleagues that he was 'writing a book about the Big Brother Movement'. When he died in November 1971, his daughter – not realising their significance – threw them on the tip.

In the early 1950s the combined Boy Scouts Association/Victorian Big Brother Movement did bring a number of British youths to Victoria,[8] but later abandoned the scheme. The headquarters of the Boy Scouts Association in the UK then advised the London branch of the BBM that scouts who wished to migrate to Australia would be referred to them.

## WESTERN AUSTRALIA

In October 1961 four youths, aged 17-18, disembarked from the *Orion* at Fremantle to become the first Little Brothers officially sponsored[9] by the BBM for settlement in Western Australia. The twelve others in the group sailed on for Sydney.

In 1962 another four youths followed suit, after which the traffic fizzled out. The youths had little or no contact with the Sydney office. There was at that time no branch office in Western Australia, and all prior contact had been with London. In order to provide farm training, arrangements were made for the lads to come under the wing of the Fairbridge Farm School, at Pinjarra, where they apparently benefited from the experience.

In 1966 the Sydney office began a correspondence with Herb C. Elliott,[10] president of the Geraldton Regional Promotion Committee, which had a scheme to advance 'farm labour opportunities' in the state's north-west.

The entrepreneurial businessman, who was also prominent in Rotary, gained the support of various community organisations, including Apex, Jaycees, and the Junior Farmers. His idea was to form a branch of the BBM through the auspices of Fairbridge, Pinjarra. This did not entirely please BBM board members in Sydney, who feared loss of influence in the new movement.

Notwithstanding these fears, the Sydney office endorsed the plan and in early 1969 a branch of the BBM was formally established in Western Australia. Following the London example, it called itself the British Boys' Movement of WA Inc.[11] An office was opened in Perth, with Mr F.V. Summerfield as executive director. However, the prime mover – according to local sources – remained Herb Elliott himself.

On 13 May 1969 nine youths,[12] aged 16-17, arrived by air in Perth, where they were met and taken to Geraldton. They received a warm and enthusiastic welcome. A reception, attended by (among others) the mayor, state MP and Bishop of North-Western Australia,[13] was held in their honour.

The local *Geraldton Guardian* gave the newcomers star treatment, reporting – with a degree of exaggeration – that they were 'the first Little Brothers to arrive in Western Australia' and that their presence represented 'a pilot scheme for the Big Brother Movement in the State'.

Elliott, who was no mean publicist, used similar 'pilot scheme' terminology, and ensured, through his contacts, that jobs and accommodation – not all the lads chose to go on the land – were quickly found.

During the following six years, a further 160 BBM-sponsored youths migrated to Western Australia. Many – but not all – undertook farm training at Pinjarra. The numbers,[14] despite the original optimism of the scheme's backers, were hardly impressive. The last West Australian migrant[15] was received on 9 December 1975, soon after which the Perth office closed down.

Varying accounts have been given to explain the West Australian scheme's failure. According to Ken Johnstone: 'It fell apart due to rivalry and just didn't work. The fact is that we're eastern states and they're western state, and ne'er the twain shall meet. My experience is that organisations with separate structures in each state don't really work. It's better to have an executive officer who runs the whole thing.'

Correspondence in the National Archives, in Canberra, and in the files of the Sydney office, support this view. An appeal brochure, initiated in Perth, gave one brief reference (only) to financial assistance received from Sydney; adding salt to the wound by showing the names of only those office bearers based in London and Perth.

The role of the London office was the subject of much confusion. An internal Department of Immigration memo, from one F.C. Castle, states: 'I spoke to Mr Mansell [BBM executive director]. He told me that the BBM in Sydney regards itself as an organisation independent of the one in the UK, which is in fact a recruiting body for it.

'The UK organisation is not a "parent" body and does not give any orders or financial support to the Australian movement. In fact, it was necessary at one time for the movement in Australia to send money to the London organisation to enable it to continue its recruiting activities.'

## TASMANIAN STORY

Possibly to compensate for the loss in Victoria the Big Brother Movement established a branch office in Tasmania – then considered ideal territory for youths contemplating a career on the land. It opened in 1948, and lasted until 1964.

As with BBM in Victoria, records of the autonomous branch appear to be missing. Files in the Tasmanian Tourist and Immigration Department, a few press clippings and a University of Tasmania Honours history thesis by Laura Williams provide most of the information now available.[16]

The first group of 10 Little Brothers arrived on 9 November 1949. According to Williams the delay in their arrival – some 18 months after the branch was established – was due to difficulties in ensuring the selection[17] of lads 'of the right stamp'.

A photograph in *The Mercury*, Hobart – the individuals are not identified – shows a somewhat bedraggled bunch, wearing raincoats; except for one youth, smiling broadly, wearing a kilt. The newcomers received a formal welcome, slightly marred by the fact that someone had forgotten to invite a representative from the Department of Social Services, the body primarily involved in their welfare.

The lads spent their first week at a training farm at Taroona, during which they were allocated places of employment. Problems arose when two of the group wanted to leave their employer. They received a stiff letter from the Department, reminding them of their contractual obligations.

According to Laura Williams: 'Tasmania's post-war enthusiasm to become involved in this scheme was closely linked to rural labour shortages simultaneously being experienced in the state. This raises the question of whether the Movement's stated philanthropic intent of giving young British lads the opportunity to establish themselves as farmers was actually a front to acquire cheap labour for Tasmania's rural community.'

She says funding for the new branch 'was derived primarily from donations made by farmers and pastoralists, these being the same people who benefited from the labour of the Little Brothers'.

The movement in Hobart was under the wing of Walter Loney, Company Secretary of the Royal Agricultural Society in Tasmania. It appears that he looked after the interests of BBM as a sideline.

John Morris was recruited by Loney as office boy. He recalls: 'I was 17, the same age as many of the Little Brothers, so had a natural affinity with them. My duties were not very arduous; I would do things like send on their mail.'

One of his duties was writing up the minutes of board meetings. 'I remember one meeting well. A Little Brother had put a farmer's daughter up the duff. I can't remember what was decided, but I do recall them discussing it. All these old men – at least they seemed old to me – seated round the table. It all seemed so incongruous.'

The BBM was to face far worse difficulties. In 1950 two youths 'ran away' and were officially listed as missing. A stink arose about the selection criteria in Britain. It was claimed these and other lads had used the Big Brother Movement's London office merely to gain access to Australia, and had no intention of farming as a career.

Problems of another sort arose when a branch of the RSL alleged that a farmer had left a 'sick boy' alone in a small hut for three to four weeks without company or supervision. While the committee took action after it had been notified, critics claimed it was too little, too late, and that the BBM itself had been negligent.

## A TOUCH OF BIGOTRY

Religious bigotry was a feature of Tasmanian life in those days, usually – but not always – with Catholics at the receiving end. The island itself had an image as a 'bastion of Anglo-Saxon Protestantism'.

Problems arose regarding mismatches between migrant boys and employers of a different religious persuasion. While a choice of religion was given to an employer (and a Big Brother) upon application to the scheme, religious preferences – by accident or design – were sometimes overlooked or ignored.

Such was the case with one Protestant farmer,[18] whose negative attitude towards his particular Little Brother (whom he referred to as lazy and in need of constant supervision) appears to have been based on the youth's Catholicism. Believing that the lad had not been given 'a fair chance' the Department intervened and the youth was transferred to a Catholic employer. His work record was thereafter deemed satisfactory.

(In a reverse of the above situation, a youth brought out under South Australia's Barwell Scheme, recalled how a Catholic farmer, from whom he was seeking employment, asked for his views on the Immaculate Conception – which question left the lad suitably foxed.)

Not all farmers were 'unkind', still less exploited their charges. The lads' needs were basic, and their desires modest. One youth expressed gratitude that his employer had supplied him with a small wireless set in his bedroom. Another was thankful to have been introduced by the farmer into the social life of the community. In general, the farmers – even those inclined to be stingy – appreciated the efforts of those who worked for them. One youth was considered so highly skilled that he went from one farm to another, as each employer offered him more pay. Strictly speaking, this was frowned upon. But the Department praised his acumen.

By 1950-51 the BBM in Tasmania found itself in further difficulties. There was a shortage of volunteers to act as 'Big Brother' combined with accusations that existing Big Brothers were 'getting slack' in regard to their duties. It was said that one Big Brother, for instance, had never visited his Little Brother's place of employment in three years of their association. However, the man had shown kindness in other ways, and was not reprimanded.

Arguments also arose between the BBM and the state's senior public servants. The (Tasmanian) Department of Social Security actually put a block on BBM immigration, but lifted it when promises were made to 'do better in future'. Complaints began again. The BBM argued that most of the allegations were 'pin pricks', and relations once again deteriorated.

In the midst of this continuing saga, however, a change occurred in the BBM's Tasmanian leadership, when Donald Von Bibra, previously vice-president, took over the branch's presidency. Controversy subsided, and branch affairs ran smoothly for several years.

Unfortunately for the movement, by the late 1950s technological advances in farming and a decrease in the number of adults employed in primary production led to a drop in demand for 'boy' farmers.

In 1933, one-third of all Tasmanians had been categorised as primary producers. By 1961 – when the Big Brother Movement was winding down – it had fallen to 11 per cent. The Tasmanian branch ceased recruiting in1964.[19] In the 16 years of its operations, it had brought out just 161 young migrants – a hardly impressive figure – yet had been the second longest running juvenile migrant recipient organisation in the state.[20]

## POMMY JACKAROO

Sixteen Little Brothers from all over the British Isles met for the first time in London on the morning of 13 September 1961. Of those 16, four were the first BBM migrants bound officially for Western Australia.

One of the four was 18-year-old John Weaver, from Farnborough, in Hampshire. He recalls: 'Following the completion of formalities we travelled to Tilbury Docks by train, before embarking on the SS *Orion* for our journey to a new land "down under".

'We sailed mid afternoon, leaving behind apprehensive family members in the gloom of an English autumn day. There was still sufficient daylight to see the white cliffs of Dover as we sailed in a westerly direction through the English Channel. That was to be the last time I saw England for many years.'

The group's first landfall was the port of Piraeus in Greece. 'We made the most of those few hours on land to visit the sights of Athens. Next stop was Port Said, then through the Suez Canal to Aden, then on to Colombo, before heading south, passing the Cocos Islands, before reaching Fremantle on October 10.'

At this point John and his companions – Gerald Holden, David Lowe and David Pryde – farewelled the other 12, and were not, in fact, to meet again. The four were met by Tom Brain, then deputy principal of the Fairbridge Farm School, Pinjarra, which was to be their home for the next six weeks.

Training was not particularly arduous and John enjoyed the experience. 'We were introduced to the sheep, also to billy tea and blowflies. I didn't get into the milking shed, but I already knew how to milk a cow from visits to my grandparents' farm in Cornwall.

'It was hay making time and we spent much of our time turning these great bales of hay over, or assisting the regular farm workers cuttings the oats or barley.'

John and his companions were older than the other young people at Fairbridge, who had come to Australia as British child migrants. 'Everybody treated us very well, and that included the other Fairbridge kids. We were put into dormitories, whereas the regular Fairbridge kids were in cottages, which were within walking distance.'

Fairbridge, Pinjarra, unlike the BBM's own training farm in New South Wales, had girls as well as boys. 'We didn't see much of them,' he says disappointedly.

With their training over, the four split up and found jobs at various properties throughout the state. 'David Pryde and I went south, David worked on a property east of Ongerup and I went to a property near Borden, north of Albany.'

Here John learnt to drive cars, trucks and operate farming equipment 'the likes of which I had never set eyes on in England.' He was also introduced to the shearer's 'hand piece',[21] and became quite proficient in its use. 'However, my back didn't like this type of work, and neither did the sheep.'

The cricket club in Borden quickly recruited him as a 'pom'. 'It was considered that I must have played cricket in England, whereas nothing could have been further from the truth. However, with some coaching from the locals I soon became a regular member of the team.'

After a few years in Borden, John moved up to Geraldton, in the state's north-west, where he made a dramatic switch – from the land to the sea – working an 'island' season on a crayfishing boat between Geraldton and the North Island of the Abrolhos group. There were 'hair raising moments', especially one day when – convinced he was about to drown – he removed his watch and handed it to the skipper, whose predicament was equal to his own.

In the spring of 1964 the land called again, and he moved further north to join his friend, David Lowe, on Warralong Station as a jackaroo. It was an interesting choice. Warralong is near Marble Bar – reputed to be the hottest town in Australia. The station itself covered an area bigger than his home county of Hampshire.

At Warralong John was given a station horse, saddle, and sent on his way to muster sheep for several weeks at a time. After a year or so of this he tired of these duties and returned to the Borden area, where he again worked on the land and in a number of shearing sheds as a roustabout and wool presser.

As a result of a farm accident he spent a few days in the Gnowangerup Hospital, where he fell in love with a nurse, Margaret Buckingham, who was attending him. 'We were married in February 1967. In April 1968 our first daughter, Ann-Marie, was born. Our second daughter, Helen, arrived in June 1970.'

By this time John had been joined in Western Australia – though not in the outback – by his parents[22] and a sister, who subsequently returned home, but remained a frequent visitor.

In March 1969, John Weaver decided on a complete change and joined the Western Australia Police. Following his three months initial training he spend the next two years on the Fremantle wharfs, where he had first set foot on Australian soil. The couple then spent 11 years in various bush towns before before returning to Perth, where John became a police prosecutor, based mainly in the Central Law Courts.

One case, in particular, sticks in his memory. It involved a committal hearing for a sexual assault matter in which both the complainant and offender were 'of the itinerant nature'. As John tells the story: 'I was leading her through her evidence. It was like extracting hens' teeth; it was that difficult. We established that they were both in the park, and he had got her down on the grass.

'I said: "What happened?" "He pulled off my pants." "And then what happened?" "He pulled off his pants." "What happened then?" "He unscrewed his wooden leg." So I said: "Yes, go on. And then what happened?" "The sprinklers came on."

After 10 years as a police prosecutor, another move occurred in 1993, when he was given charge of a large suburban police station at Morley. That lasted five years. From January 1998 until his retirement in September 2003 he was attached to the Communications branch at Police headquarters, with the rank of senior sergeant

In 1989 John was elected to the council of the Western Australia Police Union, from which he retired in June 2000. In 1991 he was made chairman of a committee, which subsequently formed Police Legacy in Western Australia. The organisation supports widows, widowers and children of deceased police officers in that state. He was chairman from 1992 to 2003.

# 21

## A Better Class of Boy

---

*'There is no better guarantee ... that the bonds of the Empire*
*will remain for ever strong, than the guarantee which is afforded*
*in a continuous stream of young manhood*
*from the great [Public] Schools of the British Isles*
*setting out to swell the ranks of pioneers...'*
From *The New Australian* (see below).

**T**HERE IS A COMMON BELIEF – one of many facets of the famed Sydney-Melbourne rivalry – that Victorians see themselves as a cut above the convict-tainted citizens of New South Wales

It is not entirely myth. On my first visit to Melbourne, in 1971, having lived in Australia less than a year, I was asked by an elderly lady in a restaurant how I liked the southern city. Impressed by my polite but favourable response (though she was aware I had chosen to make my home in Sydney), she whispered conspiratorially: 'You see dear, we're descended from free settlers here.'

The Big Brother Movement, as previously noted, began simultaneously in Sydney and Melbourne. Both the Victorian and NSW branches operated on similar lines, but there were ideological differences – the Victorian branch being, as noted previously, more passionate in support of Empire causes.

The board of the Victorian BBM comprised pillars-of-establishment types, as did the London committee, which had 61 titled people[1] out of a total 124. The Big Brothers, who took on responsibility for the lads' welfare after their arrival in Australia, were similarly upper crust. A 'Personal' page in the Victorian publication *The New Australian* lists four titled people and describes Generals Sir John Monash and Thomas Blamey as 'enthusiastic Big Brothers'. All were anxious to recruit what they considered to be 'the right type' of boy.

---

As previously stated, the *Jervis Bay* on which this first party of Little Brothers sailed, reached Melbourne on 11 December 1925. *The Argus* had this to say of the Victorian contingent: 'The boys are probably the finest batch of new settlers, physically and mentally, that has stepped off an overseas liner in Melbourne. Most[2] of them are from [English] public schools[3] and their ages range from 15 to 19.'

The desire to recruit youths from the higher social classes was found among several organisations promoting youth migration in the early years of the 20th century. And not merely migrants for Victoria. This situation is interesting in view of the common perception of youth migrants as working class lads from humble backgrounds.

An early example involved the formation, in Norfolk, England, of a body calling itself The Australian Farms Training College. Its prospectus, issued in about 1912, claimed an alliance with the Queensland Government in preparing boys from (English) public and grammar school backgrounds, who hopefully would 'form a College Guild to uplift antipodean life'.[4]

Another body,[5] Australian Farms Ltd, had broader aims. This land-development company, formed in 1913, had considerable support in the early post-war years when it sought young farmers and investor-settlers, chiefly among ex-servicemen. Among its backers were Victoria's Agent-General and many big names of Australian capitalism. According to the eminent historian, Professor Michael Roe,[6] it recruited mainly among 'ex-officer and public school types'.

A small but similar scheme had a brief run in Tasmania, 1919-20, consequent upon an Anglican idealist persuading 30-odd ex-officers there to establish an elitist farm commune.

In London, Lord Clarendon, chairman of the (British) Overseas Settlement Committee, shared with others a desire to improve the standard of men and youths migrating to the colonies. In a letter to a colleague he opined that 'if the right type of public schoolboys could be induced in sufficient quantities to emigrate [to Australia] they will, if they make good – as a proportion of them should – enter public life and so raise the whole tone.'[7]

In support of these aims the Public Schools Emigration League was formed in Britain. One of its aims, according to Thomas Sedgwick, was to 'recruit better class boys for the colonies'. Among the movement's supporters was James Darling, famed headmaster of Geelong Grammar School, who was anxious to cultivate an English public school ethos down under.[8]

## PLAY UP – PLAY THE GAME

From the magazine of the Victorian Big Brother Movement.

*'The open field of sport plays no small part in this matter of character. Self-reliance and a sense of fair play are at once noticeable in the contests between house and house, or school and school. The British [public school] boy knows the value of teamwork. The school has taught him to play for his side, and to estimate his own importance in the light of his usefulness to the school or house team of which he is a member.*

*'Here, then, is the source of the material which has proved so valuable in building up British prestige and in the great work of laying the foundations of the overseas Dominions.'*

In 1924, the Headmasters' Conference, a body representing most of Britain's more famous schools, circulated among its members a notice suggesting that school leavers might like to consider agricultural work in the Dominions. The argument was that there would be benefits for the Dominion Governments as much as for the boys themselves.

The suggestion received support from some schools and was ignored by others. Among its sponsors was the governing body of Christ's Hospital, popularly known as the 'Bluecoat school', a quasi-charitable foundation with a long history of good works.

The clerk to the governors told officials of the Oversea Settlement Committee that he wanted 'to secure for the Empire the valuable type of migrant which schools like Christ's Hospital can produce for the Dominion Colonies... A leaven of well-brought up boys from public schools, who would teach them how to play the game in society and in commerce, and provide a very strong link between the dominions and the mother country.'

There remained problems in finding suitable arrangements for such boys. Schemes put forward to employ public school boys as jackaroos on sheep stations in NSW and Queensland foundered on arbitration rulings restricting the numbers to a proportion of one to every three station hands.

Overall the large pastoral companies remained reluctant to upset the labor movement and were doubtful if enough English public school boys would come forward anyway.

Certainly, the very wealthy were not attracted to Australia. As the Secretary of the Public Schools Employment Bureau pointed out: 'Our experience seems to show that boys who are likely to have considerable capital seldom seek an agricultural career overseas.'[9]

It seemed therefore necessary to devise ways of attracting the middle strata of the not so wealthy professional and business class and to do it in a way that offered both guidance and some prospects.

The idea was 'sold' through newspaper articles and by word of mouth. By a happy coincidence while these matters were being discussed Richard Linton was in London promoting his concept for the Big Brother Movement. Linton produced a pamphlet headed 'Parents, Give Your Son A Chance.' It was not primarily geared at upper middle class families but had a relatively strong response from this quarter. The pamphlet stated:

'Let your boys join their fellow Britons beyond the seas. They will be welcomed by people who speak the same language, share the same traditions, and are heirs to the same history, literature, ideals as the citizens of the mother country. The flag above them will be the same old Union Jack, plus the five stars of the Southern Cross – the symbol of Australian nationhood. Your boys need Australia: it is their opportunity. And Australia needs them.'

Ex-public schoolboys were considered particularly suitable. According to a promotional article:

'The atmosphere in which these young men [public schoolboys] have spent the most impressionable years of their lives, the manner in which they have learned to make use of the opportunities and to carry responsibilities ... will mean much in fitting them for the claims and duties of Imperial citizenship'.

After the arrival of the first group of Little Brothers, Linton, now back in Melbourne, took every opportunity to promote the new arrivals. He said that all who had talked to the boys were impressed by their 'manliness and physical appearance'.

The press in Melbourne supported these endeavours, though later it was to make fun of them. It was claimed the London office of the BBM was receiving 10 or 12 applications every day, but only accepting one in every three. A report in the *Argus*[10] said that in the course of a few weeks '47 public school boys have been accepted at an aggregate prospective capital of £60,000 pounds.'

An article, 'Public Schools and the Empire', in *The New Australian*,[11] gave the raison d'etre for public school migration.

'There is no better guarantee ... that the bonds of Empire will remain forever strong, than the guarantee which is afforded in a continuous stream of young manhood from the great schools of the British Isles setting out to swell the ranks of pioneers, statesmen and captains of industry in the oversea branches of the British Commonwealth of Nations.'

The article, which bore the sub-heading 'Secret of the Empire's solidity', went on to state:

'Many of the leading pioneers of the last century, as well as many of the leading citizens of today, whose names will be remembered in the annals of oversea development, are sons or grandsons of men who received their education in the great schools of England and Scotland.

'Carrying with them the best ideals of the race from which they came, they sought to find expression for them in their new environment to the general good of those amongst whom their lot was cast. Such young men must find it hard indeed to resist the call of the great open spaces of Australia, with their abundance of sunlight, fresh air and freedom.'

By 1930, 1,059 boys had, indeed, answered the call and entered Victoria under the auspices of the Big Brother Movement. Of these 60 per cent had received a secondary (grammar school) education, while a further 10 per cent had attended a British public school. The ratio of public school boys, aged 17 to 19, dropped somewhat in the following two years, but remained – in Melbourne though not in Sydney – never less than about six per cent.

## GENTLEMAN FARMER

The premature demise of the Victorian branch of BBM has meant that the scheme to import 'young gentlemen' farmers has not been well documented.

I was fortunate in making contact with Mrs Helen Vellacott, widow of Geoffrey William Vellacott, who was one of this 'happy breed' of English public school migrants.

Geoffrey Vellacott, son of a Presbyterian minister, was a student at St Paul's School, the long-established day-boy public school in London,[12] where his brothers had also been. He was approaching 17 when his father died. He would like to have gone on to Cambridge University, as his brother had done, but was conscious of the strain this would put on the family finances.

He decided to leave school and migrate to Canada. For a period he went to a relative's farm in Essex and learnt to milk. He then chose Australia after his mother read of the Big Brother Movement in a newspaper and suggested he apply.

Geoffrey sailed on the *Jervis Bay* leaving England on 29 March 1927. His letters to his mother, during the voyage and for the first eight years after his arrival in Australia, are still held by his family who supplied copies to me. His Big Brother in Australia was Sir Robert Knox, a captain of industry and director of BHP.[13]

Clearly a dutiful son, and certainly a voluminous correspondent, his first letter, written while the ship was still in port. It begins: 'I am writing now in the hope of being able to find where to post it. I'm not sure…'

There is family chit chat. He uses schoolboy phrases such as 'topping'. He is touched by a letter given to him by his mother to be opened, presumably after the ship sailed. He apologises for having left his sponge bag behind, and asks her to send it to him at Port Said. He describes his fellow passengers: 'The crowd in my berth are quite a decent lot. I think certainly not quite the roughs we saw [earlier], and I think we shall have a good time.'

He apologises also that 'the amount of news accumulated so far is not very great'. He describes the food: 'The grub for dinner wasn't bad until sweets – boiled rice and dried peaches [arrived]. However, I suppose they won't have that every day.'

There are two letters from Port Said, one of which, written over three days, is 19 pages long. The first begins with a more detailed description of his cabin mates – mostly 'very decent fellows'. He has made friends with the crew: 'a jolly crowd if you don't fill in the –'s in their conversation'.[14] He describes the voyage so far – some rough weather but not enough to put him off his food. He describes a church service on board ship and the view along the African coast.

Concerning money, he had 'started off with resolutions about economy', but could not resist buying trinkets and other items, presumably from the peddlars who came alongside. He now had just £1 left of his original pocket money. At Port Said he and other Little Brothers buy a 'community tea pot' in order to 'have a decent cup in the afternoon'.

Geoffrey is fascinated by the process of 'haggling' at which he and his friends soon consider themselves expert. He has 'a scrap' with a fellow in the next cabin who 'comes into our cabin whenever he likes and [starts] smoking'. He complains about the weather, which is so hot that he is now 'sleeping out on deck'. He has taken several photographs which he and his friends develop and print on board. His £1 is now reduced to 7/6d. 'I've got to stop all expenditure from now on.' During the remainder of the trip he wrote three more letters to his mother – each of more than 15 pages.

Geoffrey's first letter from terra firma is dated 2 May 1927. Whilst still on the ship the lads were allocated their Big Brother. He says everybody on board congratulated him 'as Mr Knox is a wealthy man of English blood, a member of society, but withal extremely nice. [They said] I couldn't have done better.'

On the Melbourne wharves, Geoffrey was the only one to respond affirmatively to the query 'How many of you milk?' At the BBM office in Melbourne prospective employers lined up to interview the new arrivals. A British ex-officer, in his thirties, was the first to arrive and thus had first choice. He picked Geoffrey, who said later: 'I hope he didn't regret his punctuality'.

That same day Geoffrey took a train to Red Cliffs, a small township about 20 km from Mildura. With public school optimism, he was

# THE BIG BROTHER MOVEMENT

## BRITISH YOUTH MIGRATION

NON SECTARIAN    NON POLITICAL    NON COMMERCIAL

Head Office: 33 MACQUARIE PLACE, SYDNEY

Telephone: BU 3627

THIRTY-SEVEN TYPICAL "LITTLE BROTHERS" ARRIVE IN AUSTRALIA (S.S. Otranto, 20th January, 1955)
EIGHT SIMILAR GROUPS WERE RECEIVED BY THE MOVEMENT THIS YEAR

## THIRTIETH ANNUAL REPORT
### OF THE COUNCIL OF THE MOVEMENT

*Little Brothers arrive on the Otranto, January 1955.*
*Eight similar groups were received by the movement that year*

*Otranto group (April 1955)*

*Before and After: Little Brothers at Australia House reception before departing for Australia (March 1956)*

*The same group a few weeks after their arrival*

*The right image: Smile for the camera.*
*Little Brothers at training farm (1949). Peter Sargent on horse*

*Down on the Farm. Little Brothers get used to rural life*

*New arrivals on the Strathhaven, March 1955*

*Frank Mansell (then) general secretary
and the Big Brother Movement's guiding light,
with unidentified Little Brother
(probably late 1940s)*

*Singalong on the Farm – late 1950s. Note the contemporary hair styles*

*Gunning House – later to become Divine Mercy convent*

*One of the last groups of Little Brothers to arrive by sea (1965)*

*No longer by sea. An early 1970s group is welcomed at Sydney Airport*

*'Kewell the Jewel'*
*Harry Kewell, Soccer Superstar,*
*as teenage awardee.*

*Adam Gilchrist,*
*later to become Australian*
*Cricket vice-captain*

*Ken Johnstone, chairman of BBM,*
*with music awardee, Naoko Miyamoto*
*(November 2000)*

**Still going...but role reversal**
**BBM Awards Scheme under way**

*Patrick Milligan (left), head of drama awards panel, with*
*Ken Johnstone, chairman of BBM*

*John Weaver*
*Pommy Jackaroo*

*Harry Kewell in action*

*'A Better Class of Boy'*
*Geoffrey Vellacott, third from right, having a last look at England*

*Ready to go*
*Geoffrey Vellacott in 1930*

*Geoffrey Vellacott in Army service*

*Michael Abney-Hastings: Milord of Jerilderie.*
*Top: as 'Farm Lad (age 18)*
*Left: 'Rightful King of England'*
*Right: With Australian 'royal' grandchildren Isabella and Caleb*

*Frank Mansell ,' A lifetime of active service'*

*Above: Leslie Kilvington,
war hero*

*Left: Eddy Steele,
executive director, BBM*

*On parade in Cyprus.
Major-General Prem Chand passes
Chief Inspector Michael Coyle (far right)*

*Ben and Barbara Mohide*

*Michael Coyle, Anzac Day (2002)
at Commonwealth War Graves Cemetery, Oslo, Norway*

Down at the Farm.
The future noted author and scriptwriter
Ron (Maslyn) Williams

Maslyn Williams in 1973

Harry Dearth
broadcaster and entertainer

Brian Bywater
enthusiastic Little Brother
(Note car registration plate)

*Brian Bywater*
*Spirit of the Cooees*

*Group Captain John Ward (2002)*

*John Ward as fighter pilot – Darwin 1977*

*Wally Pare (centre rear)*
*with wartime special forces*

*Wally Pare (2000).*
*Nottingham Evening Post photo*

*Norm Smith*
*Very Able Seaman*

*Norm Smith with Danna Vale,*
*Minister for Veterans' Affairs*
*at Ktangi Cemetery, Singapore (2002)*

*Archdeacon Howard Ellis (second left) and Norman Radcliffe (far right),
members of the original 1925 Jervis Bay group, with Tom Nicholson,
Pat Maguire and Paul Botto, who arrived in 1982*

*Big Brother Movement reunion (1993)*

intrigued rather than disappointed to find Red Cliffs consists of 'a half-dozen concrete buildings and a few shacks by the railway station'.

His new home turned out to be a soldier settlement block, between Red Cliffs and Cardross, another small town. It encompassed 20 acres (8 ha.), 'which is as much as one man can work alone'.

Typically, almost the lad's very first act is to write to his mother. He is anxious that his mother should have his address, and is obviously excited about the job. He describes his employer, Major G.A.B. Hooper, as 'a tall, lean, typical soldier, and, I think, an awfully decent chap. He has only been out three years, so he hasn't yet made his fortune.'

The 'Major' and his wife provided him with 'a nice little room, which is beautifully cool. It is only wooden and there are no coverings on the walls, but I have a little furniture, a bed, a table and a rough wooden box which serves as a dressing table'. He reassures his mother that 'I've got a bed and sheets which is more than a great many people have out here'. He tells her that a cow is to be purchased the following day.

## COW TROUBLE

A letter, written about a week after his arrival, describes the ensuing drama: 'On Monday morning we went to fetch the cow. After grim struggles down the road, pulling the animal on a chain, or being hurled along after it, we managed to tie it up among the vines, where we left it.

'At five in the evening we went to get it up for milking. Directly we undid the chain it stampeded for home, pulling the horse and me behind it. After heading round the block it gave a final lunge and I was sprawling with my nose in the sand. It charged towards the house and Mrs Hooper, seeing it, rushed indoors.

'We caught up with it by the gate and got hold of the chain again. But I had been slashing all day and my hands were reduced to pulp, and a chain being pulled through blistered hands  isn't pleasant. So the cow got away again. However, it was the last time and we eventually got her tied up against one of the drying racks.'

It was not the end of Geoffrey's problems. 'Having fed her I proceeded to milk her. After 10 minutes hard labour I had got about a half pint, and by this time the cow had finished her feed and got restless. She charged forward, turned round and struck an attitude of defiance.

'We beat her around again, but got little further result. After two or three more charges we decided to go and fetch one Neil Gray, her former owner's milker, who came down and finished the performance which had taken two-and-a-half hours and had been finished by moonlight. This sort of thing went on for four or five days, but now we have made a proper stall and she is getting used to me.'

In another letter he explains what he means by 'slashing'. 'The slasher is a long handled thing like a golf club with a double blade knife at the end, which is used for cutting the weeds between the rows. It is rather heavy and the weeds are young trees, so an afternoon of it was enough to start with. We did three days of it and then started clearing a bit of the reserved bush for the new horses which came on Friday.'

Geoffrey was pleased to receive a visit from the local Presbyterian minister, but apologised to his mother that, on his first Sunday in Australia, he was unable to go to church. 'The only service is at 7 pm. I can't go this evening, I am afraid, because I don't feel up to walking five miles each way on the loose sandy road and I don't know the way well enough to do it in the dark.'

In a letter on 30 May 1927 he describes other farming implements. 'The rake we used [he enclosed a crude drawing] is designed for raking the cuttings from the vines and not for weeds. It reminds you of the instruments of torture out of the Chamber of Horrors. It is like a huge toasting fork. The prongs are each one and a quarter inch thick and the handle is bent upwards slightly.'

The letters continue in similar vein, with a variety of employers – not all of whom are as 'decent' as the 'Major'. After some unhappy job experiences, he thought it would be wise to continue with his interrupted studies with a view to seeking entrance to university. He was assisted by an Anglican Bush Brother, and – though rising at dawn to milk cows – succeeded in this aim, gaining a scholarship to the University of Melbourne, where he got arts and theology degrees.

While at university he got embroiled in a major battle, which ended in physical violence, over freedom of speech. The BBM office in Victoria wrote him a letter saying his behaviour was 'disgraceful' and accusing him of being a Communist. His name was expunged from the organisation's records.[15]

On a happier note, also while at university Geoffrey Vellacott met and married his wife, Helen, a fellow student, returning briefly to England where he completed his theological training, becoming, like his father, a Presbyterian minister. Back in Australia he had postings at St Andrew's, Canberra, and then at a remote church at Bingara, near Moree, having been persuaded to go there by the Rev John Flynn (Flynn of the Inland).

World War II intervened and he volunteered – not as a chaplain but as a non-combatant medical person. He left for active service on 6 January 1942, going straight to Singapore, which fell within a few weeks to the Japanese. Geoffrey Vellacott died in December 1943, as a prisoner-of-war on the notorious Burma-Thailand Railway. He had given away his food, carried other people's packs, nursed cholera victims, and was regarded as a hero. He died without seeing his younger son, who was born after the fall of Singapore.

When the war ended, and news of Geoffrey's death finally reached Australia, his widow, Helen Vellacott, took their two small sons over to Cambridge, where they were now residing, so that they would grow up knowing their father's family. She herself did further study and was awarded a Nuffield research grant. When the boys left school, the family returned to Australia. After retiring as a social worker Helen turned her hand to writing, and had four books published, the last at the age of 84, in 1995.[16]

# 22

## 'Milord' of Jerilderie

▬▬

**T**HOUGH IT DID NOT DO SO INTENTIONALLY, and was deliberately unsnobbish, the NSW branch of the Big Brother Movement, like its Victorian counterpart, acquired over the years a fair number of youths who might reasonably be considered 'upper crust'

A jubilee publication of the Big Brother Movement (in NSW) claimed, in a light-hearted article, that one Little Brother was an Old Etonian, and another a fully fledged 'Lord'.

The 'Lord' was said to be a youth of 18, who inherited, in the 1950s, an ancient Scottish title. The aristocratic Little Brother was in fact Michael Abney-Hastings (Lord Mauchline), one of 40 youths, aged 15 to 19, who travelled in the 100th post-war party, which arrived in Sydney on 22 October 1960.

Lord Mauchline, interviewed by the *West Australian* when his ship, the *Fairsea*, berthed in Fremantle, stated that it was his preference to be known and treated simply as Abney-Hastings, or Michael.[1]

He said that he had 'wanted a change' and thought Australia was 'a good country to come to'. He had attended Ampleforth College in Yorkshire, but had left at the age of 16 to attend an expressionist school in Hastings.

He told the paper's reporter: 'You just do what you like there – you go to school when you feel like it and so on. I think that I did better there than anywhere else.'

He said that he intended to stay permanently in Australia and would stick with his friend Ralph Sherwin-White (17) from Great Yarmouth, Norfolk, whom he had met aboard the ship and who was a fellow migrant under the Big Brother scheme.

An escort officer, Bill Pollitt, was quoted as stating that all 40 Little Brothers would be seeking jobs on the land.

The BBM long ago lost contact with Lord Mauchline, whom I

found via an entry in *Debrett*. Yes, he had kept his word about 'staying in Australia', and has 'absolutely no regrets' about his original decision to migrate. He had also kept his word about not using his title, though not about sticking with his friend Ralph, nicknamed 'Chalky', whom he had not seen since they left the ship.

After three years as a farm worker, Michael 'travelled around for a while', one of his first jobs being to sell the *Encyclopaedia Britannica* in Sydney.[2] 'It was mid-summer and we had these samples. We never got through a door – we were told to piss off by everyone. It was hot, and so every pub we passed we had a couple of beers and by the end of the day we were so drunk we'd forgotten what we'd done with the samples and we never went back again.'

After this dubious start, he returned hastily to the bush, working first as a jackaroo, then as a stock and station agent. He married his Australian wife, Noeline, and settled in the NSW-Victoria border town of Jerilderie (population 1,100). Interestingly, for someone who was first motivated by travel, Michael has spent all but the first five-and-a-half years of his time in Australia in the one country town. 'I moved in on 14 February 1966, the day the Aussie currency was decimalised. It's only a tiny place, but I love it.'

The next 16 years were spent as a ranger with the local Pastures Protection Board, followed by work – which he still performs – for a rice growers' co-operative. He explains the work as 'doing whatever needs doing'.

The couple raised all five of their children in Jerilderie, where community interests include the 'footy club' (Australian Rules, of course), the St Vincent De Paul Society and Jerilderie Historical Society. Michael is president of the latter two organisations.

As stated earlier, Michael has not used his title, which is just as well, since there is more than one. 'It's a bit complicated,' he says matter-of-factly, 'Actually, there's a heap of titles in the family, but the main two are like this...'

The head of the family was until recently his octogenarian mother, who had the title (dating back to 1601) of Countess of Loudoun. The ancestral seat used to be Loudoun Castle, outside Kilmarnock. Unfortunately, it was burnt down in 1942 and became a ruin. The grounds were subsequently turned into a theme park with a fun fair and rides.

When all this occurred his mother moved to Ashby de la Zouche, in Leicestershire, which was also the seat – together with Jerilderie – of the (slightly lower ranking) Mauchlines.

The year 2002 was an 'annus horribilis' for Michael Abney-Hastings. His sister died in June; his wife, Noeline, died in August, and his mother died in October. Michael, an easy-going man with brawny forearms and suntanned face from decades of working in the Australian bush, has taken these and other vicissitudes in his stride.

A complicated situation has arisen concerning his present title (actually titles). According to genealogical sources in London, Michael has inherited his mother's title, and is now the Earl of Loudoun. 'Yes, that's true. My eldest son, Simon, has become Lord Mauchline, and so it goes on. The system perpetuates itself. The whole thing's not worth two bob.'

The new Lord Mauchline, who is 30, is a service station manager in Wangaratta, Victoria. He shares his father's lack of interest in rank and status. Despite self-disparagement by both men, Michael has enjoyed the occasional privilege during his infrequent holidays in Britain.

In 1998, Michael, accompanied by Noelene, two of their five children and a son-in-law, went to the House of Lords, where Michael took his seat on the cross-benches. He cannot remember much about the debate. 'The kids thought it a great joke. We had lunch in the peers' dining room and all that.'

He says his late wife shared his love of Australian rural life – and in the situation in which they lived and worked, talk about 'titles' seemed irrelevant. 'It's not really appropriate out here, is it? It's common knowledge around town. I've never tried to hide it, but I've never thought about it much.'

## YOUR MAJESTY

It is possible that Michael Abney-Hastings may have more than a mouthful of 'Lords' to his name. A British television programme, screened in Australia on 23 May 2004,[3] concluded that the humble farmer from Jerilderie was nothing less than the rightful reigning monarch – King of England and, therefore, King of Australia.

Roll over Elizabeth II. The real royal family has been robbed of its inheritance. The extraordinary claim was made in the feature documentary, *Britain's Real Monarch*, produced by Spire Films for Britain's Channel 4.

The programme – only ever so slightly tongue in cheek – was the brain child of producer, David Willcock, in collaboration with the historian, archaeologist, writer, funny man and (in this case) presenter, Tony Robinson.

Robinson is probably best known for his acting role as Baldrick in *Blackadder* and as the Sheriff of Nottingham in *Maid Marion and Her Merry Men*, which he also wrote. A British website, feigning annoyance at his 'crowning of an Aussie bloke', has called it 'Baldrick's revenge'.

Robinson himself is no cultural redneck. He is president of the Young Archaeologists' Club, active in several historical societies and was, until the last election, a member of the National Executive Committee of the British Labour Party.

The programme, which rewrites 500 years of history, has an interesting background. While researching the life of Richard III (for another Channel 4 TV programme) fellow historian Michael K. Jones uncovered what appeared to be proof that the 15th century English monarch, Edward IV (born 1442), was, in fact, illegitimate, thus throwing the legitimacy of all the kings and queens who followed into question.

According to this theory, the royal line should have extended, not through Edward, who reigned 1461-1470, but through his brother, George, Duke of Clarence, and his heirs. At this point Tony Robinson came onto the scene, tracing the 'true' heirs through subsequent centuries.

What follows is a complicated but highly entertaining web, occupying 47 pages of typescript. The search for Britain's 'real monarch' is conducted in the manner of a detective story, dissecting families high and low throughout the British Isles, with locations from the Tower of London to ruined castles and family vaults.

Their verdict, revealed somewhat dramatically in the latter half of the programme, is that Britain's present day 'true monarch' does not actually live in Britain at all, but – you've guessed it – in the small NSW country town of Jerilderie.

All of which means that Michael Abney-Hastings, Earl of Loudoun and before that Lord Mauchline, can now add King Michael, last of the Plantagenets, to his pedigree[4].

## FLOREAT ETONA

The mystery Etonian – mentioned frequently in BBM lore, was harder to identify, though several Little Brothers claim to remember him. It is thought he came out in the early 1960s. One version of the story has it that his uncle was an aide to the then Governor General, Lord De Lisle and Dudley. Some sources say there was not one Etonian but two.

A paragraph in the *Sydney Morning Herald's* Column 8, seeking further information, led to calls to me from two former Little Brothers, both pointing to a lad called 'Terry'. Neither could remember his surname.

Tom Wilson, who arrived on the *Fairsky* in March 1961, thought 'Terry' was one of his own group of 16. 'I remember him well. He didn't actually say he was from Eton. He was about 19, and had the poshest accent you ever heard.'

It was not just his accent that was memorable. 'He was about 6 ft. 10 in. tall, thin and gangly. You could see him a mile away; he stood out like a sore thumb, and he was aware of that. But he had a great sense of humour and was able to take himself off, which he did very well.'

It appears Terry made a name for himself on the voyage out. Though travelling in economy class, he would sneak off to the first class section, where he would play cards with and accept drinks from first class passengers. Did they know he was travelling with the peasants? 'I asked him that and he put on a pained expression, and said: "Oh no, no. I'd certainly never tell them a thing like that".'

According to Tom, Terry's 'grand plan, or rather the grand plan of his family, was that he should see the real world. So they thought that sending him out to the antipodes, especially economy class on a migrant ship, would be a starting point.'

Upon arrival members of the group were accommodated at Gunning House. Tom recalls: 'It was Good Friday when we arrived and on the Saturday a group of us decided we'd go into the city to look around. We went to Homebush station. I remember the train was supposed to arrive at, say, 9.30 and at 9.31 it hadn't arrived.

'Another two minutes passed and still no train, so Terry took himself off to one of the station staff and in his best upper class accent said: "I say, my good man. Where is this train that was due at 9.30?" The bloke on the platform just looked him up and down and said: "Well, if you just hang on a minute mate, I'll run up the track and have a look for you".'

At weekends the young migrants would meet around Hurstville way, where many of them had taken lodgings, and go to the cinema or ten pin bowling. 'One night at the movies there was a shot of a car passing down a road, and Terry leapt out of his seat screaming "That's my home, that's my home." It was a large palatial mansion somewhere on the outskirts of London.

'I have often wondered about what happened to Terry. He was a real character, an eccentric, a great guy. I know that at one stage he was working for David Jones as a buyer. I remember him saying or someone telling me that one of the perks was that he'd be able to get free trips back to England when he was doing his buying sprees.'

Other sources say Terry did not become a David Jones buyer but 'went bush' and became a jackaroo. The Old Etonian Association in Australia knows of at least two Etonians, none of them sponsored by the BBM, who became (temporary) jackaroos. There is a story, probably apocryphal, about how they met and recognised each other by the tie each wore to support his trousers.

According to Tom: 'I would assume Terry eventually went back for good, though possibly a little after the others. I recall he wasn't over enthused about the place. He was doing his duty by his family, by leaving the family mansion or wherever, haring off into the boondocks with the peasants, to learn something of the real world.'[5]

## HOMESICK BRITONS

Tom Wilson came to Australia with the Big Brother Movement in March 1961. He enjoyed his voyage on the *Fairsky*, but many of his companions did not.

Of the original 16 Little Brothers in his group, he believes all except himself, and possibly one other, returned to the UK after the minimum two years. 'The problem was basically, I guess, that as soon as the ship left

Southampton we were homesick. Then by the time six weeks later we had reached Australia, we were all convinced we were coming to the end of the earth.'

After a few days in the hostel Tom went to live with an aunt in Stanmore. 'Most of the others shared flats together, and it seems they all got jobs in places where there were lots of English people. Then when they came home at night they sat down and watched English TV shows on the ABC which made them even more homesick.'

Several evenings a week the newcomers would go ten pin bowling, where the conversation would again be about 'home'. Tom found the overall situation depressing. 'I gradually extricated myself from the others, because it was really getting me down. All they talked about was how wonderful England was and how awful Australia was. And I thought to myself, If I'm going to survive here then I'm going to have to get away from this.

'Of course, in those days you could come to Australia for £10, and if you were under 21 it didn't cost you anything. If you waited two years you did not have to refund your passage money, and that's just what they all did.'

Tom found himself a job with the old CBC Bank. 'It was good for me in that I met all kinds of people all day long, and it helped me to integrate.' After about three years Tom left to join the staff of the Child Welfare Department, where he stayed 27 years. He currently has a senior management position with the Australian Red Cross.

MISSED THE BOAT

Bill Hudnott, another *Fairsky* voyager,[6] had no time to be homesick. He had been raised in an orphanage, unlike most Little Brothers, and 'fell in love' with the Australian Bush. His adventures in Australia – which began within moments of his arrival – would fill a book

As he tells it: 'We lined up on the rail looking at the town of Fremantle and couldn't believe what we were seeing. The sky was simply blue – endless blue sky – which went on forever. The town was made up of short, squat, long, low small buildings and the ground seemed orange in colour and it looked like something out of Texas.

'We honestly felt like pioneers. Our Aussie escort officer was rapt to be home. So what do you do with a bunch of teenagers? Well, it was easy; the good ladies of Perth were to take us for a tour of the town and we would visit Kings Park.

'We drove around until we reached the park, where we got off for a picnic lunch. Our downfall was assured when we met up with some blokes who said that they were boxers from the Eastern States. This was an expression which had no meaning until it was explained that this included Victoria, NSW, Queensland and Victoria.

'We had no money and they seemed to have heaps. So I think we tended to be all over them like a rash. The next you know we had a lot of laughter with the ladies and with the boxers and a good time was had by all. By the time the ladies had got this bunch of louts back onto the bus and back to the wharf, the ship had sailed!

'There we were, a bunch of 17 happy vegemites, an escort officer who couldn't give a damn, and three lovely ladies, all enjoying the same adventure, all watching our ship receding into the distance.

'There was no way in the world that the ship would stop for us and there was no boat available to take us to the ship. We were therefore doomed to be illegal immigrants. I bet the Captain heaved a lovely sigh at seeing us left behind. He was glad to see us gone.

'The police were called and we were taken to the Subiaco migrant hostel to await our fate. We turned up with a police escort, no identity papers and no money. We were to stay there until somebody figured out what to do with us.

'We didn't mind – we were being fed and we were here. Next thing you know we were being told that we were very lucky migrants as Ansett Airlines being told of our 'plight' would fly us to Sydney in time to meet the ship.

'So there we were, a whole bunch of no-hopers flying across the huge expanse of Australia, all red and empty.

'So when we arrived at Sydney we were all pretty smug and pleased with ourselves and were enjoying the whole scenario. Until after we met the ship to get our gear off, as we had nothing than the clothes we were standing in.

'We went to the BBM headquarters only to be told very sternly by the BBM guys that we were the first migrants in the history of the movement to arrive in debt, as we had to pay Mr Ansett back for our plane rides. That took the gloat from our faces, but we were here in Australia. It was our new home and it was great. Thankfully a few months later the BBM advised us that the debt had been forgiven.'

# 23

## 'What You Take Out Please Give Back'

*'I always try to think what can you offer to something,*
*rather than what will you get out of it?*
*It's no good being part of something if you can't put something back.*
Eddy Steele, executive director, BBM.

EDDY STEELE was born in July 1940. It was a week after the start of the Battle of Britain. A wartime baby? 'More or less, but I can't remember anything about it,' he says with a hint of apology. What he does remember is a poverty stricken background in a group of workmen's cottages near the Scottish mining town of Bo'ness.

The estate was called Miller Pit, an unattractive name denoting an unattractive area. 'There were 24 little houses, six to a block. There was a front room and a back room. No electricity; we used paraffin lamps. The water tap was outside, shared between the houses, as was the toilet. My job on a Saturday morning was to fetch the paraffin from a little shop about two miles away. I did it summer and winter. In the winter I had a sled. The shopkeeper loaded the paraffin on, and I'd drag it home.'

Eddy would sing to himself whilst hurrying back with his burden. A popular song of the day was *Ghost Riders in the Sky*. He liked the tune, but the words frightened him.

He had another reason for hurrying. A 'wireless' addict', his favourite program was *Dick Barton Special Agent*. On Saturday mornings there was an omnibus edition, a repeat of each of the 15 minute programs earlier in the week. 'That was my reward. I loved it. The radio was powered by an old-fashioned wet battery. I always feared it would break down.'

When he was about 11 the family left Scotland, where unemployment was rife, to go and live in Coventry. Work was plentiful, though, because of German bombing accommodation was scarce. The city centre was still in ruins. For a few months the family lived in one room. 'We considered ourselves lucky. There were folk living in tents and buses.

Eventually dad got a house which had been condemned in about 1900.'

Their new home was in a typical working class terrace, very similar – apart from the benefit of electricity – to the house they had occupied in Scotland. Again, there was no running water, and toilets were shared with neighbours.

Eddy had a normal schooling, then at 15 was apprenticed to the Singer Motor Company. His section folded soon afterwards and he and other apprentices were farmed out among the many other motor companies then based in the area. Eddy found himself working for a major garage which acted as service division for the Rootes Group.

At about this time he started to get itchy feet. Why did he choose to emigrate? 'People of my generation had brothers and uncles and fathers who'd been in the Merchant Navy, Army and Air Force. Our grandfathers had served in World War I when they were as young as 16 and 17. We were surrounded by people who had done things when they were young. Also in those days half the map was painted red. It was the Empire.'

Through a friend he met Geoff Silman, slightly older than himself, who had been to Australia as a Little Brother, and had worked for a time with BBM in Victoria. He had returned to Britain for family reasons. One evening Eddy, Geoff and a handful of friends were walking home after visiting a youth club. It was a cold night; the wind was whistling in their ears. The older youth talked about his experiences in Australia. The others listened intently.

Eddy thought about his own working day – lying on the ground, underneath a customer's car, with slush from melted snow going down his neck or up his trouser leg. Australia suddenly began to appeal. 'We had no real sense of either distance or time. We knew we had to stay for two years minimum, but that meant nothing. It was actually six years before I got home again.'

Parental attitudes to the proposal were mixed. 'I think my father didn't mind at all. He'd been a prisoner of war when he was just out of being a teenager. His attitude was "Get out while you can and see the world". My mother of course was a different kettle of fish. But I don't recall any arguments. I think their approach was "You'll just be going for an extended holiday and you'll be coming back again".'

The Big Brother Movement handled all arrangements smoothly. An interview and medical examination were held at Australia House in London. A few months later came a notice that he was to sail on the *Orontes*, departing July 1957.

Goodbyes were said in Coventry, which eased the actual departure. He travelled down to Tilbury with two mates, Ken Foster and Stan Grantham. 'We were still the Coventry lads, all emigrating together.' There was the first sight of the *Orontes*. And all else was forgotten.

Eddy enjoyed the voyage, which he regarded then, and still considers 'a fantastic adventure'. As a bonus he celebrated his 17th birthday on board.

'Aside from not having any money we had a great time.' Most of us started out with about £10 each. By the time you'd bought a musical box or whatever in Naples to send back home, there was not much left. We played cards. Luckily the food was free. I don't think any of us were drinkers, so we didn't spend money on alcohol.

'There were quite a few migrant families on board ship, and many of them had daughters, which provided company at the dances. There was boxing, swimming; a highlight of the trip was the crossing the line party ceremony. We made friends with the crew and visited them in their quarters. There always seemed something to do. We had PT every morning. Our escort, a Mr Carlton, was not much older than we were.'

'Of course, there were a few bad times. We had a typhoon, I remember. The *Orontes* was 20,000 tonnes. But it was sitting down in a valley with the waves higher than we were. I was terrified. Then we went to Ceylon (now Sri Lanka). Our escort was not impressed when, out of 24 of us, 16 ended up with the same tattoo.'

The ship stopped at Naples, Aden, Perth, Melbourne, and finally Sydney. 'It was cold and wet when we arrived – a bit of a disappointment really. Funnily, I can't remember anything about the city. But I do remember coming in to the harbour and we were all looking out for the Bridge.'

## SPIDER WELCOME

The bus trip from the quay to the Gunning House hostel is also 'blurry', but the first night at the hostel remains crystal clear. 'Australians on the

*Orontes* had been filling our heads on the way out with stories about sharks and spiders and man eating koalas. Enough to give you nightmares.

'A rule in the hostel was that you had to have a shower before going to bed. There was a shower block with plastic curtains across each shower stall. I pulled the curtain back, and stepped into the shower. Then I noticed on the wall, right above my head, the biggest spider I had ever seen in my life.

'I stepped back and it seemed to move with me. I thought it was about to pounce. I tried to attract the attention of the other fellows. I didn't dare move, didn't want to shout. I finally got the attention of somebody and he ran into the house to get the guy who was in charge. He was a real bushie; I think he lived in a pair of shorts and bare feet. He sauntered over, pulled the shower curtain across. He said: "Oh, it's only a bloody so and so," and flicked it into the shower stall with me. I beat a very hasty retreat.'

Eddy, like others who passed through its portals, has other, happier, memories of Gunning House. 'We'd get off the train at Homebush station. Close by was this little pie shop. It did a roaring trade. Our first Aussie meat pies.'

The next day – their first full day in Australia – Eddy and other new arrivals trekked into the Big Brother Movement office, located in what is now Chifley Square, to begin the important task of job finding.

Eddy found that his papers, including references, were already on an employment officer's desk, and a job interview had been arranged. 'It was very well organised. The Big Brother Movement was our legal guardian, and a lot of companies were used to dealing with them. So if the employment officer rang a firm and said 'We've got a lad here looking for a job', it would be taken seriously.

'My papers said I was an apprentice motor mechanic. So they got me a job with York Motors in Sussex Street.' Eddy found himself once more lying on the ground, looking at the underside of cars. But this time there was no melted snow coming down his neck.

He served a full apprenticeship of four years. 'I started by staying at the hostel, and went to tech a couple of nights a week. That's where I first discovered bean sandwiches. I didn't know you could put cold baked beans in a sandwich. Then I got a room with full board in Marrickville. Again, it was organised by the BBM.'

Still only 17, as his work experience advanced, his social skills stagnated. Or so it seemed. He was to spend the next few years in Marrickville, spending most of his leisure time playing snooker and hanging around the Rosella milk bar with 'cowboy' mates.

This situation changed when he came into contact with the YMCA. Eddy now believes membership of the 'Y' changed his life. 'I came to realise there was another world outside Addison Road. Being so poor was part of the trouble. You never had any money, so you tended to knock around with people who were in the same boat. But with the "Y" things were different. They were very decent. Several of my mates joined with me. Because of this they actually formed a separate club within the club, just for us.'

During his apprenticeship Eddy served two years in the CMF, reaching the rank of Corporal. He served in a bomb disposal group of the Royal Australian Engineers

In 1960, through the joint activities of the YMCA and YWCA, he met Pat Hutchinson, who – six years later – would become his wife. Meanwhile there were other diversions. In 1961 Eddy finished his formal apprenticeship and decided that being a motor mechanic was not for him.

'For a couple of years I sort of bummed around and hitchhiked. I'd never seen anything of Australia. It was quite easy in those days to hitchhike. Huge semi-trailers would leave Zetland daily, laden up with cars. You'd just turn up and say "Where are you going mate?" Adelaide, Brisbane, or whatever. It was great because you'd climb into one of the top cars, just sit there and survey the scenery.

'During that time I did odd jobs, all sorts of different things – night shift, day shift, car washing, you name it.' It was now 1963. He was 23, and still uncertain about a career. I was then living in a boarding house at Coogee. I told another fellow there that I was looking for a job, also that it was five years since I had left home.

'This fellow had worked for British Airways, or BOAC as it was then. And he said to me: "Why not try for a job as a steward, with Qantas or another airline?" I'd never heard of Qantas, but I'd worked in pubs so

I knew a little about waitering and all that. By coincidence, I saw an ad in the *Herald*, about vacancies for jobs with Qantas. As it happened the man who interviewed me was an officer in the CMF.

FLYING HIGH

Eddy got the job, and was signed on as a trainee flight steward. He loved the work, particularly the travel opportunities. 'It was fantastic. I got back to the UK at least once a month. Five days in Cairo, Tehran, New York or Bermuda. It was an unbelievable lifestyle, so I stayed.'

It was to be adventurous as well as fun. Always there was the unexpected – riots in Tehran leading to the fall of the Shah, floods in Bombay, rescuing Europeans caught up in fighting between India and Pakistan, and an attempted hi-jacking in Darwin. A distinctly unfunny episode occurred when the aircraft on which he was travelling fell five-and-a-half thousand feet after striking three separate bumps of air turbulence.

Eddy was thrown violently across the cabin, cracking four ribs, and losing consciousness. He awoke to find Sir Malcolm Sargent, the famous conductor, who was travelling first class, holding his head, with someone else 'giving me a sip of brandy'. His troubles did not end at that point. When the plane landed in Calcutta, a nurse, seeing blood on his face and his clothing torn, asked him if he was alright. He replied in the affirmative, at which point she squeezed him on the back and he promptly passed out (for the second time) in pain. He was to spend the next two weeks in a hospital in Calcutta, where 'we were treated like royalty'.

There were pleasanter interludes. For a while he was based in London. Pat was already planning a European holiday. So they married in Coventry in 1966. In 1967 Eddy was promoted to senior steward, and in 1974, after the introduction of the Jumbos, became a flight services director (equivalent to purser).

As befits his later role with the Big Brother Movement, Eddy struck an easy rapport with passengers, ranging from foreign diplomats to Cypriot brides, married by proxy and flying nervously to join their husbands in Australia. Not all his 'passengers' were human. From time to time he had to escort horses from Australia to the US, via Tahiti, Acapulco, terminating in New York. The aircraft was a converted Boeing

707. The animals, partially drugged, were placed in stalls. 'To get from the rear galley to the flight deck you had to run the gauntlet of horses' heads, protruding from the stalls. Some of the beasts were still fairly lively: You had to duck your head or receive a love bite.'

In 1965, when Australia's role in the Vietnam War was upgraded, a shortage of military aircraft meant that Qantas became involved in troop carrying. The role was to last until 1972. Only male volunteers participated – Eddy among them. 'It was a little hair raising. The aircraft were still fitted out as commercial carriers complete with the flying kangaroo on the tail. One wonders what the Vietnamese thought on seeing these aircraft coming in to land.

'On the flights to Vietnam the troops were all quiet and sombre. When we were bringing them home it was the reverse.'

In 2001 – many years after the event – Eddy and all the Qantas crews who worked on these Vietnam charters, including Alan Wilkinson, a fellow Little Brother, were awarded the Vietnam Logistic and Support Medal and the 1945-75 Australian Active Service Medal. In April 2003 these present and former Qantas staff marched as an entity for the first time in Sydney and Melbourne ANZAC Day parades. They did so under the banner 'Skippy Squadron'.

When off-duty from the airline Eddy often went to the Sydney Club to play snooker. There he met Ken Johnstone, whom he had known previously when they were together at Gunning House. Ken was by this time already treasurer of BBM, and an active committee member. 'So I got involved again with the BBM. I went regularly into the office in Sydney, and in 1981 I was invited to join the board.' He and Ken initiated the ex-Little Brothers' contact scheme. Starting with just six names, there are now over 600 on the BBM mailing list.

In Eddy's own words: 'I always try to think what can you offer to something, rather than what will you get out of it? It's no good being part of something if you can't put something back. Because I was flying I was able to go to the BBM office in London. Like a courier, I could go and see how they were getting along and report back.'

A difficulty faced by the Big Brother and similar movements was that, unlike the organisations which brought out child migrants, there was no long term point of contact. Ties were closer when all newly-arrived youths went to a training farm, thus spending an enforced period of time together. For the later air travellers, lacking even the contacts made during a sea voyage, the sense of 'belonging' was further reduced. As Eddy admits: 'Once you were settled in a job the BBM meant nothing unless you had a reason to stay in contact.'

Eddy has spent much of the past two decades trying to reverse this situation and create a sense of 'bonding'. He discovered that at least three other ex-Little Brothers were Qantas flight attendants and on some journeys from Britain he actually met new migrants who were sponsored by the BBM. He retired from Qantas in 1991. The custom of having an annual reunion was revived in that same year. Meetings are held in the attractive surrounds of the Fairfield City Farm.

In 1994, following the retirement of Frank Mansell, he was appointed full-time executive director of the Big Brother Movement. For many years, with assistance from others, Eddy has produced a 24-page newsletter which is sent yearly, free of charge, to all known Little Brothers.

Locating ex-Little Brothers who came to Australia over so many years, and who have had little or no contact since, requires patience and the skills of a detective. Contacting these, according to his friend, Ken Johnstone, is a major headache. 'They're scattered all over the place.'

The records maintained by BBM also supply ex-Little Brothers with legal proof of their arrival in Australia when applying for citizenship or passports. Sadly, it is probable that many 'Old Boys' are unaware of the movement's continued existence.

### FRANK MANSELL – A LIFETIME OF 'ACTIVE SERVICE'

In 1925 young Frank Mansell stood at Tilbury Docks with his parents and brother farewelling his oldest brother Bill.

Bill was one of the boys leaving Britain in the first party of Little Brothers to begin a new life in New South Wales. Little did Frank realise that the best part of his own life would be given eventually to the Big Brother Movement in Australia.

Four years later – when Frank was 15 in 1929 – Frank Mansell, his parents and his other brother migrated to Australia too. This was one of numerous instances of families following a Little Brother across the world.

Frank was born in Harrow, Middlesex, where he spent his formative years. His father was a policeman and the boy's life seemed set upon an English path. Destiny was to dictate otherwise. The lad was not quite 15 at the time of his arrival, and the financial depression was just beginning. He found work on rural properties around NSW, gaining farm experience and a network of connections that would prove useful later.

In 1940 he joined the 8th Division, 2nd AIF, travelling on the Queen Mary with about 12,000 others to Singapore. Following the fall of Singapore, he spent three-and-a-half years as a POW in the notorious Changi camp and in Japan.

As with so many returned servicemen, Frank rarely spoke about the hardships of POW life. He returned to Australia ill and emaciated. It took him years to build up his health again.

Part of that process was his marriage to June Dorothy Dodwell, a nurse from Wagga. They would have a daughter, Christine, and a son, William. They bought a house in the Sydney suburb of Burwood and became well-known identities.

In 1946 Frank worked for a few months for the then Country Party as a campaigner and organiser in the Goulburn and Eden-Monaro districts, raising funds for the party and organising meetings for candidates for a looming election. His was a brief stint in the political arena because that year he began working for the Big Brother Movement.

The BBM was expanded in 1946 by the appointment of three district superintendents. Their duties were to secure honorary welfare officers in country areas, find suitable positions for the boys, visit them at their workplace and generally to raise funds and promote the movement.

One of the three men appointed was Frank Mansell. He was made secretary of the movement in 1949, and executive director in 1966. Appropriately, also in 1966 he was made an Officer of the Order of the British Empire (OBE).

The Big Brother Movement, nowadays regarded as financially 'comfortable', was not always thus. In the early days – when resources were slender – Frank was literally going around the bush soliciting donations.

According to Ken Johnstone: 'Frank had to personally raise money to pay wages and keep the place afloat. He was a very hard worker for the movement in those early days. That's the hardest part, to get the thing on the road. Once you've got it up and running it's a piece of cake.'

Frank retired in 1980. However, when the Government effectively stopped the movement's immigration work in 1983 Mansell was 'recalled to active service', prevailed upon to rejoin as a director and at the first meeting in January 1984 was elected chairman.

According to Frank, the dispute with the federal Government had one advantage in that he had more contact with Little Brothers after the Government wielded the axe than before. 'They all rallied to the cause.'

He retired as chairman in 1985 to comply with the Companies Code age requirements but in an effort to retain his invaluable knowledge and to utilise his experience the board of directors reappointed him secretary.

He retired from that position – a second time – in June 1994. In a sense Frank Mansell *was* the Big Brother Movement – having been associated with it officially for all but the first 21 years of its existence.

For most Little Brothers their most vivid memory of Frank Mansell is of presenting themselves in his office – usually the day after their arrival, or if they have been to the training farm, at the end of their period of induction – to begin the important process of job finding. Most were struck by his huge range of contacts, and his skills at what might now be called 'networking'.

Michael Loftus, now of Queanbeyan, arrived in Sydney on the *Himalaya*, in April 1954. He recalls being called in to see Frank, who put his finger on a tiny dot on a huge map, and said: 'This, son, is where you'll be going.' It was a small township called Burrumbuttock.[1]

Tom Wilson, who came out on the *Fairsky* in March 1961, was less impressed. 'The arrangement was that we would all go in each day to see Frank Mansell and he would organise job interviews for us. Well, this consisted of us reading the *Sydney Morning Herald* and picking out jobs for which we wished to apply.

'We figured there was no point in trekking all the way into Macquarie Place every day just to read the *Herald*, when we could read it at home. So we just gave it away and didn't go near the place [the BBM office] any more.'

Frank had a fund of anecdotes, like the one about the youth who was pursued by 'ghostly' nuns.[2] However, his favourite anecdotes were about the experiences of Little Brothers when job seeking.

One story concerned a youth at Gunning House who agreed to accompany another Little Brother to a job interview – the idea being to provide moral support. However, when they arrived at the offices of IBM, the escort not only sat in on the interview, but decided he would like to have a go himself. He did just that and came top. It is not known if he actually took up the position.

Another newly arrived Little Brother came to Frank Mansell and said he was a 'snake milker' and wanted a job working with snakes. Ken Johnstone, who was then assisting Frank, telephoned Eric Worrall, the well known snake expert who had a reptile farm on the NSW Central Coast. Ken asked if Worrall could take the lad on.

This approach proved unsuccessful. Undeterred, the youth went hunting snakes on Sydney's upper North Shore, then turned up at Frank's office with a sugar bag full of slimy creatures, which he wanted to pour over the desk. The youth, who was then living at Gunning House, was made to promise not to introduce snakes there.

Frank and Ken were somewhat relieved when, after a short interval, he moved into private lodgings. According to Frank the lad soon afterwards eloped with his landlady – a woman well over twice his age – and was not heard of again.

As a follower of the old school, and a man who had suffered a few knocks himself, Frank Mansell saw the physical demands of rural life as a plus rather than a negative factor in youth migration.

Homesickness, however, was a different matter. 'It's a physical thing,' he told me. 'It's like seasickness. I used to tell them that when they came off the ship. It's like love sickness. They can't eat, and they lose their appetites.

'People talk about all these damn farmers treating them harshly. I knew a lot of them – some of them were a bit tough on the lads, but they were tough on themselves. They were used to working all the time, their sons worked all the time. They don't feel happy if they're loafing.'

Frank Mansell died on 13 January 2001. He is remembered for his gruff, cheerful though occasionally prickly manner, informality, down-to-earth wisdom and practical foresightedness. He is remembered most of all as counsellor and friend to countless post-war Little Brothers, to whom he was always accessible.

Many Little Brothers continue to regard him as a hero. Brian Bywater, who came out on the *Otranto* in 1956, is among the more vocal. 'I think the Big Brother Movement and especially Mr Mansell, whom I'll always call Sir, did more for Australia and emigration than anyone else has ever done.'

It has been estimated that some 550 parties of Little Brothers were personally welcomed by him at the wharves and airport. Individuals personally welcomed by Frank at the docks include the present chairman, and former treasurer, Ken Johnstone (arrived 1957); his predecessor as chairman, the late Jock McAusland (arrived 1963); and the current executive director, Eddy Steele (arrived 1957).

# 24

## Scot with a Flair for Figures

K EN JOHNSTONE has no hesitation in claiming 14 as his lucky
number. He arrived in Australia on 14 May 1957. His two daughters were born on May 14, two years apart, and a son was born on
January 14.

'Numbers' have interested him in other ways, determining the
choice of his career as a professional accountant.

He was born in Dumfriesshire, in Scotland, on 25 February 1940 –
just five months after the start of World War II. He describes his childhood as 'mobile'. 'Dad was a saw miller. He went wherever the timber
was, and we went with him.' The family moved to England when Ken was
about six. But the transient lifestyle remained. By his early teens he had
attended 14 schools in as many parts of the British Isles.

At school – through his favourite subject, geography – he developed
an interest in Australia. 'I knew about the various states, where they were
located and what their industries were.' His interest extended to sport. 'I
used to admire the Australian cricket team and still do. When England
played Australia I used to barrack for Australia because I regarded myself
as being from Scotland.

'In the school leaving certificate English exam we had to write an
essay on the country where we would most like to live. I wrote about
Australia. At that stage I didn't know I'd ever go there.'

After leaving school – the family were then living in Norfolk – he
worked briefly with his father in a saw mill, but could not decide on a
career. One avenue he pursued was meteorology. 'I had an interview at
the local met office. They sent me all this paper work; how I'd earn £3
and 10 shillings as a cadet, leading to £8 a week as a fully blown weather
man. It didn't sound all that encouraging.'

'I couldn't find anything else that suited. So I went to the local
employment office. The woman there was helpful. She said: 'Why don't

you emigrate? You could go to Canada or Australia".

'I said there's no way I would go to Canada, it's just too cold, I didn't fancy the severe winters. Australia was different. She gave me this pamphlet on the BBM plus a few other brochures. I was so excited. I could envisage myself on the back of a horse in the outback herding cattle and sheep. From that second onwards I just went hammer and tongs to get to Australia.'

Ken's eagerness was rewarded. Within three months of applying he found himself – one of a group of 33 Little Brothers – en route for Australia on board the *Orontes*. He had travelled down to London a couple of days before the ship's departure, giving him time to attend a jazz concert at the Stoll Theatre. 'I'm a jazz fanatic. There was a New Orleans clarinet player called George Lewis. He was one of my idols. That was probably the greatest send-off I could have had.'

The journey out was uneventful. Some pretty girls travelling with their parents were disappointingly well chaperoned. 'In those days a girl of our age would be unlikely to be allowed to travel by herself.' There were two escort officers. 'They used to pull us out of bed early every morning, run us round the deck and make sure we didn't drink or misbehave.

'The Suez crisis was on at the time. We had only two stops, Las Palmas and Cape Town, which is a magnificent place. We sailed in during the morning, just at sunrise. The whole harbour was a blood red colour, a sight I will never forget.'

At the time of Ken's arrival, the Big Brother Movement was easing its policy that all new arrivals should spend at least a couple of years in farming. 'When I came [in 1957] people were beginning to move away from the country to the city and to industrial areas because that was where the jobs were.

'My original intention had been to go on the land, but five weeks on the ship had given me plenty of time to think about my future, and I had decided I would like to pursue something in the city.'

On the day after his arrival, he went to the BBM office, where an interview was arranged with someone from a manufacturing company for the following day. 'That interview was on a Friday. I started work on the

Monday. I'd been in Australia only four full days. The unemployment rate was about two per cent at that time.'

The 'something in the city' was not very grand. 'I was assistant to the cost clerk, a very mundane job. First thing in the morning I used to sharpen the boss's pencils and turn his calendar to today's date.'

After he had been in the job a few months, good fortune struck. Ken and other Little Brothers were befriended by a local doctor, John Coles, honorary medical officer to Gunning House. 'He used to take us to his property at North Rocks. We would ride horses bare back, chop trees and clear land for him. He told us that to get on in Australia you had to have either a trade or a profession. So not long after that I started studying at Granville Technical College doing accountancy.'

One day Ken saw an ad in the paper for an accountancy position with Qantas. 'I was 18, with boyish enthusiasm, and thought this is the job for me. They were actually seeking a mature, middle aged manager, which I definitely was not. So when I went in for the interview they just looked at me and said "Next!"

'That afternoon I went and saw Frank Mansell.[1] I told him what had occurred. Of course, I was not very pleased, but as it happened, it was my lucky day. He said to me: "Our treasurer, Edward Marriott, a City accountant, is looking for a young bloke to start training. Would you be interested?" Would I, indeed?

That same evening Ken drove to Marriott's house in Killara. 'He sat me down in his lounge room and spoke to me like a father. It was one of two turning points of my life. He took me completely under his wing. He gave me sound advice and was very supportive. When there wasn't enough work to keep me going, he said "Just go and sit by yourself and study".'

Ken left the Granville Tech and began a course at the Australian Accountancy College in the City. 'Being able to study at times during the day was a great plus. I had no extracurricular activities in those days; I played cricket with the local church team and that was about it. So virtually all I did was study, including at weekends. Because of this I went through the course fairly quickly.'

A few months later Ken experienced his other 'turning point'. At the

Sydney Jazz Club, in the old Ironworkers' building in George Street, he met his future partner, Wendy Woolley. In addition to sharing his tastes in music she was an accomplished athlete, who had run with Betty Cuthbert and Marlene Matthews in the NSW state relay team.

By that time the custom of appointing a 'big brother' to look after a 'little brother' was no longer observed. In Ken's case Edward Marriott effectively performed this role. 'He was a great influence on me and I would say he replaced my own father. I named one of my sons after him.'

Ken and Wendy were married in St Paul's Church, Canterbury, on 17 December 1960. A jazz band performed during the ceremony. 'There were Negro spirituals and gospel music. It was just wonderful.' The minister had been 'horrified' when the request was first put to him, but Ken won him over by playing a record of *Jazz At Vespers*, recorded in the US.

Ken qualified as an accountant, gaining a degree in 1963. 'As soon as I qualified, he made me a partner.' Marriott, who was then in his seventies, retired in October 1965 and Ken took over the practice. He remained as treasurer of BBM for a further year. His intention to retire from that post was submitted to the October 1966 board meeting. He died eight weeks later on December 10. At the board meeting on December 13 Ken formally succeeded Marriott as treasurer of BBM. He held the post until December 1996, when he replaced the late Jock McCausland as chairman.

Collectively, Ken Johnstone and Edward Marriott had created a unique record in that the movement had been served by only two treasurers in 71 years. Ken now runs his own accountancy business in partnership with another ex-Little Brother, Eric Haines. He was for many years (1983-1997) treasurer of the Sydney Club, now merged with the University and Schools Club, and was its president from 1997 to 1999.

Despite heavy pressure of work, he manages to find time for his two leisure interests which are golf – he tries to spend two afternoons a week on the golf course – and (as previously mentioned) jazz music. He is an avid collector of records, tapes and CDs of jazz music world-wide, with particular interest in New Orleans and Chicago style, which he believes is no longer adequately preserved.

A great sadness in the lives of Ken and Wendy Johnstone occurred in 1978 with the death of their eldest son, Garfield, in a train accident. 'We named him after Garfield Sobers, the West Indian cricketer. When we came back from our honeymoon we saw every ball bowled at the Test in Sydney. It was that famous series with the West Indies, and Sobers scored 163 – one of the finest batting displays I've ever seen.'

The choice of name proved appropriate. 'He was a brilliant sportsman. He won the State primary schools' 100 metres, clearly taking after his mother; and represented the State in junior rugby and cricket. He was more a bowler than a batsman, and just so fast. If he had older boys taking the catches, they just couldn't catch the ball at that speed. If he had lived longer, I'm sure he would have represented Australia in cricket or athletics.'

PRIVILEGED

Ken is very proud of the work now being done to steer the movement along paths appropriate to changing circumstances. He says without a trace of selfconsciousness: 'I feel very privileged to have been accepted as a migrant by the BBM.'

'Of the 33 in my own group there were a couple of fellows with whom I really had something in common. It's nice when you run into such people. Had we stayed together longer, we could have formed lasting friendships. But we separated almost as soon as we landed. I think the whole emphasis of the BBM was to assimilate young people into the community, so that they'd find their own way of life as quickly as possible.'

He admits there have been a few 'bad apples' among Little Brothers. He knew of two who had been in jail. 'If you bring in 12,000 young people from anywhere, a few have to slip through, don't they? We've had a few rascals. One fellow in our group finished up, as they say, up the river. He was a bit of a kleptomaniac. It manifested itself on the boat. He was knocking off clothes from the cabins; he just couldn't help himself.'

Frank Mansell[2] had a theory that homesickness, not physical hardship, was the biggest hurdle faced by Little Brothers.

Ken Johnstone agrees, and speaks from personal experience. 'There wasn't one person I spoke to in those first weeks after our arrival who wasn't adamant about saving up the money to go back. There were no exceptions. I felt that way myself.[3]

---

'My own problem was exacerbated by the fact that I never had any letters from home until I'd been in Australia two months. Something went wrong with the mail or maybe the stamps were for the wrong amount. Then suddenly I got about 16 envelopes all at the same time. It was like reading a book. And that made me feel a lot better. I remember, even in recent years, that if I got on the phone to my elderly father in Scotland it was a great feeling. Quite uplifting, in fact, just to hear his voice.'

## CONFLICT RESOLUTION AND 'THE PRODIGAL COW'

Michael Walter Coyle arrived in Sydney, as a 17-year-old, on the *Orontes* in August 1953. He was part of a group of 40 Little Brothers.

After a month at the BBM training farm he was sent to work for a John and Ruth Heyworth, who ran a sheep and wheat farm at Tullibigeal, a fairly remote spot about 100 km north-east of Griffith.

'It was quite an adventure. There was no electricity, telephone or fresh water at the farm. Work was from first light to dusk six days a week. I considered it not bad for £2 10s. a week and keep. After all, I was only getting £1 2s. 6d. in London before I departed.

'The Haworths were good Christian people; that's why Sunday was was our day off. It was all hard physical work; it did me no harm later in life.' In 1955 his parents also migrated, for a while living in a house on the property.

The two families remained friends. Michael continued to visit the couple for various periods long after he had left their employ.

In 1957 Michael switched to share farming on a wheat property in the same district. During this period he completed his full-time National Service, performed with the 19th Training Battalion at Holsworthy, NSW, followed by further training at Leeton, NSW, with the Citizens Military Force.

He returned to Britain in 1960, where he was a prison officer in the maximum recidivist prison of Pentonville. He undertook special duties training, which served him in good stead when he returned to Australia, in October 1962, and joined the Commonwealth Police (now the Australian Federal Police).

He performed both uniformed and plainclothes duties, dealing with such matters as fraud, VIP security, and the investigation of serious crime. In May 1970 he was seconded for two years to the Australian civilian police serving with the United Nations Force in Cyprus. It was the first of four such postings.

At the time of his first tour of duty the island was not partitioned. The Turkish Cypriots lived in enclaves dispersed throughout Cyprus. Michael's duties were to investigate complaints that arose between the local Greek and Turkish communities.

Some of the complaints received would appear petty to those not familiar with the ongoing Cyprus 'problem'. Small incidents could boil over into actual shootings or other physical violence. Typical problems might involve a complaint that a Greek Cypriot village was receiving less irrigation water than a Turkish Cypriot village; the alleged theft of water melons by Turkish Cypriots from a Greek Cypriot farm; and complaints that Turkish Cypriots were stealing antiquities from graves in areas under their (illegal) control.

One morning Michael was called to the local Greek Cypriot police station where it was alleged a cow that had gone missing from the village of Kritou, south west of Polis, some four years previously, had been found in the possession of a Turkish Cypriot in the hills surrounding Kritou.

'In company with a member of the lawful Greek Cypriot police and (illegal) Turkish Cypriot police we went to the site where the cow had now been fenced in. We held long discussions with respective parties claiming ownership to the cow; in fact it went on for most of the day.

'We were still getting nowhere, when a Greek Cypriot farmer appeared on the scene. He examined the cow very closely then stated boldly that this cow was in fact his. Bearing in mind that the cow was not branded nor earmarked, all of us were surprised to now learn that ownership of the cow had now been resolved and the animal could be handed over to its lawful owner.

'As I would need to submit a report clarifying ownership, I asked the Greek Cypriot how could he possibly know it was his cow after not having seen it for the past four years? He replied: "How does a father know his own son?" That was that, everyone was happy, and as is the Cypriot way everyone adjourned to the local coffee shop for drinks. The last we ever saw of the cow was it being led away by, what one could only describe as its Greek Cypriot father.'

His return to Australia did not herald a quiet life. On 27 December 1974, just two days after the devastation of Darwin by Cyclone Tracy, Michael was sent to that city as part of the Interstate Police Contingent involved in relief work and reconstruction. This led to important – and sometimes delicate – security duties at the Australian Embassy in Peking.

Whilst in Peking, he met Signe Marie Vatne, who was on the staff of the Norwegian Embassy in the Chinese capital. They were married at Volda, in Signe's home country of Norway, two years later.

Promotion to sergeant was followed by crime intelligence duties, much of it concerned with organised crime and the activities of minority groups. Increasingly important security and intelligence duties followed, for which he was promoted to Detective Senior Sergeant.

In 1978 Michael had another tour of duty in Cyprus. Then in November 1979 he was seconded to the Organised Crime Task Force, formed in Sydney under the code name 'Operation Safeway'. Its main purpose was to target suspected leaders of drug-related crime. The following year he returned to Canberra to investigate the feared 'Yugoslav connection' to terrorist activity. Duties as a trainer followed.

In 1982 and 1984 he returned yet again to the United Nations in Cyprus, with the brevet rank of Chief Inspector. This time as Police Operations Officer at the United Nations Force in Cyprus (UNFICYP) Headquarters in Nicosia.

In late 1984, back in Canberra, he was appointed to special duties, reporting to the Assistant Commissioner.

Michael Coyle retired from the AFP in August 1992, with the Police Commissioner's commendation. In a 30-year 'stretch' he had performed almost every form of police and security activity from cheque fraud to preventing hijackings.

Looking back on his very active career, he recalls times which were hair raising, times which were humorous, and times which were a blend of both.

In this category is an incident from his Cyprus days when a complaint was received that a forestry worker using a bulldozer in the hills near a Turkish Cypriot enclave was involved in a suspected military enterprise. The man claimed he was shot at but not injured.

Michael accompanied a Major of the (British) Winchester Regiment (The Royal Green Jackets) to investigate. The driver claimed that he was only performing work as delegated to him by the Greek Cypriot Forestry Department.

The British officer decided it would be a good time to test the freedom of movement, accorded by law to the United Nations Force. As Michael tells it: 'The Major, two of his soldiers, a Greek Cypriot interpreter and I – none of us carrying firearms – lined up and advanced up the hillside towards the ridge where the Turkish Cypriot fighters were entrenched.

'On reaching a point some 200 metres from the fighters a message was called out to us. The interpreter advised that we were being told to stop and return down the hill. The Major decided we should continue forwards. At 100 metres we were again called to stop or they would open fire on us. The Major decided once again to move forward. On reaching 80 meters from the fighters a final warning was called out that they would open fire if we did not immediately leave the hillside.

'At this point I found it was true that one's life flashes before you just before you are about to die. The Major called a message to the fighters to the effect that we were UN personnel, wearing the Blue Beret, and were free to move anywhere on the island. We then heard rounds being fed into weapons and could in fact see the fighters work their action to load.

'We all paused and said nothing for a while, then the Major addressed us saying: "Gentlemen it appears our Blue Berets are not bullet proof, we shall now make a strategic withdrawal." We about turned, moved down the hill then drove away and entered Yalia village and lodged a protest with the Commander of the Turkish Cypriot Fighters.

'The commander apologised and said we must have misunderstood what his men said. We then, as is the Cypriot way, adjourned to the village coffee shop for drinks where undying friendship between the Turkish Cypriot, British and Australian people were toasted.'

Following a brief return to Canberra Michael and Signe took up residence in the Norwegian Capital, Oslo where Signe was employed at the Royal Ministry of Foreign Affairs. This resulted in a short posting to Athens whilst Michael took a short term contract acting as security consultant with a British businessman who had interests in Marbella, Spain. In 1995 the couple were posted to the Norwegian Embassy in Tokyo until 2000. This was followed by a further posting to the Norwegian Embassy in Amman, Jordan.

For personal and medical reasons their posting to Amman had to be terminated, they returned to Oslo early in January 2004. Unfortunately Michael's medical situation deteriorated, as a result of which he was admitted to Aker University Hospital in Oslo where he underwent a serious operation for aortic aneurysm.

The most recent contact with Michael in July 2005 revealed that he was still in rehabilitation mode but had not lost his sense of humour. He advised that the previously mentioned operation required complete removal of his aorta and replacement with an artificial one. His surgeon has assured him the artificial aorta is guaranteed to last 500 years, Michael finds this a very comfortable assurance of a long life.[4]

# 25

## Some Success Stories

### CINEMATOGRAPHER, WAR CORRESPONDENT, AUTHOR

Ronald Robert Williams, later to be known as Maslyn Williams, had three 'careers' – farm lad, cinematographer, author – in all of which he left his mark.

Ron arrived in Sydney on 3 March 1929, on the *Largs Bay*, with 29 other "Little Brothers". He was then 18. His early movements are obscure, but it is known that he worked on a farm near Bowral, and at least one larger cattle station, where he enjoyed his time as a jackaroo. His card in the BBM office shows that he received praise from his employers. He also enjoyed the support and patronage of his Big Brother, a local doctor,[1] who played a role in shaping his future.

After a little over three years Ron went back to England, working his passage as a seaman, to spend six months with his mother. He returned to Australia in July 1932. The timing proved opportune. The friendly doctor, who had by now moved to Sydney's Double Bay, helped to obtain a job for him as a trainee film editor with the fledgling National Studios at Pagewood.

Here he enjoyed the company of Damien Parer, later to achieve fame as a wartime movie and still photographer. Others in his immediate circle included the budding cinematographers Eric Hinds and John Heyer.

Film making in the 1930s was still somewhat of a novelty. None of Ron's new circle of friends were very experienced. One of his first jobs, with Parer, was to shoot close ups of letters being opened, door knobs being turned, and similar overlooked inserts necessary to achieve continuity.

According to Parer's biographer, professional film historian, Neil McDonald,[2] Ron was escapist by nature, and sought to create for himself the image of a languid, romantic intellectual, epitomised in the 1930s by the screen persona of the British actor, Leslie Howard. His clothes were elegant but elaborately casual, his tie loosely knotted and a lock of wavy hair hung over one eye.

In conversation with his friends[3] he was inclined to be vague about his origins, dropping hints about family property in England and Ireland. On other occasions he would casually allude to studies in music and a period at the Sorbonne in Paris. His companions treated these and similar claims with justifiable scepticism.

In 1938 Ron joined the Cinema and Photographic Branch of the Department of Commerce[4] in Melbourne as a writer and editor. It offered a rare opportunity for documentary film making at that time. Parer, whose enthusiasm and obvious expertise fascinated the young Englishman, joined him a few months later.

In September 1939 Australia joined Britain and France in declaring war against Nazi Germany. The Cinema and Photographic Branch was taken over by the newly formed Department of Information. Within a few months Ron was appointed scriptwriter.

The war was, in fact, good news for Parer, Ron Williams and others whose work now assumed national importance. They were now officially re-employed as war correspondents, accompanying Australian troops to Palestine, Egypt, Greece, Syria, North Africa and Papua New Guinea, where they were exposed to the same dangers as the men they were filming.

Ron Williams, Parer and Anglican padre, Fred Burt, who joined them on many of their assignments, formed a particularly closely knit group that earned them the nickname "The Trinity". In addition to cinema newsreels the group, joined by Captain Frank Hurley[5], Chester Wilmot, and other famous names, made longer films to boost morale and help the war effort.

Ron remained particularly close to Parer and was best man at his wedding to Marie Cotter in March 1944.

About this time disagreement arose over the ownership of a Hollywood Academy Award in respect of the now classic film, *Kokoda Front Line*. This was a newsreel compilation produced for Cinesound, then led by the veteran Australian film maker, Ken Hall. Ron Williams wrote the script. Parer, then employed by the Australian Department of

Information, was not only camera operator, but generally acknowledged as having done most of the work! To further complicate matters he was working out his three months' notice prior to taking up a similar job with the American company, Paramount.

Many saw irony in the fact that Australia's greatest wartime cinematographer should now wish to serve the interests of the Americans. His explanation was that he switched employers to be free of what he regarded as the restrictions and jealousies he had experienced at the hands of the Department of Information.

It was a decision that cost him his life. Sadly, the marriage of Damien and Marie Parer was to prove of short duration. On 17 September 1944 Parer, having joined Paramount, was killed while filming US troops in the battle for the Japanese held island.

Ron, who was in Australia at the time, was at an official function in Canberra when told by (then Opposition leader) Robert Menzies of his friend's death. The former (and future) Prime Minister had seen a report earlier the same day and remembered Williams and Parer were friends. Marie's child, Damien Robert Parer, a future award winning film maker, was born on 15 February 1945.

Ron Williams stayed with the Department of Information as it transformed itself into the Australian National Film Board, later to be known as the Commonwealth Film Unit, and now Film Australia. He initiated and wrote the scripts for many fine documentaries, becoming one of the unit's most gifted producers.

Possibly his best known effort was *Mike and Stefani*, about Australia's reception of refugee migrants. Though filmed mainly in 1949, political pressure delayed its release until 1952. The reason, allegedly, was the tough, gruff manner in which immigration officers were portrayed.[6] Harold Grant, an immigration officer then based in Germany, said this was true to life and was how they were expected to conduct themselves.

Grant, a key contact person in the making of the film, was interviewed many years later for the making of a modern film about immigration.[7] He was to say of his old acquaintance: '...Williams came across as a lean, laconic, experienced person. He absorbed situations quickly and sized up people in a masterly way. He was an artist in what he did and most dedicated. As was Reg Pearse, the cameraman who was with him. He [Williams] had virtually only his book and his brain with which to develop a scenario, which he did in an extraordinary way.'

Ron Williams himself, interviewed in 1978, told film researchers that the film came about as an attempt to counter the opposition within Australia to immigration from Europe.

'I think if you show the Australian people, who are an emotional and sentimental people, that these Balts, wogs or dagoes are human beings who've had a terrible time, you'll find that most Australians will be on their side. But you've got to get down to the guts of the thing and show them reality. It's no good telling them that they've had a bad time, you've got to show it.'

In 1962, after a conflict with Stanley Hawes, the director of the Commonwealth Film Unit, Ron Williams resigned from the unit. In the years which followed he largely abandoned film making for writing, choosing to be known as Maslyn Williams.

He produced some 20 books in as many years, all based on his personal experiences. They included *Stone Age Island, The Far Side of the Sky, The Land In between, The Benefactors, Five Journeys from Jakarta: Inside Sukarno's Indonesia, Dubu, The Phosphateers, Seven Years in New Guinea, The Opposite Earth*. Probably his best known work was *The East is Red*, an account of a journey to Communist China.

Ron Maslyn Williams's last book was *His Mother's Country*, a fascinatingly oblique memoir of his early life. He died in August 1999.

## DEATH IN BALIBO

The Balibo Five were a group of Australian journalists based in the town of Balibo in the then Portugese Timor (now East Timor), who were killed in October 1975 by Indonesian troops mounting incursions, prior to the full-scale invasion of the territory in December that year.

One of the five was UK-born Brian Peters, a cameraman with Channel Nine, who had migrated to Australia with the Big Brother Movement in 1967.

Brian, 26 at the time of his death, was born on 17 February 1949 in the British port town of Bristol. Rationing was in force and there was not much food on the table of the modest council house where the family lived. Brian's mother, a chronic TB sufferer, was frequently hospitalised, which blinded her husband, a kind, gentle person, to her abusive nature and acts of physical cruelty towards her offspring. From the age of five the lad was effectively raised by his teenage sister, Maureen.

Brian left school at 15. A teacher who had taken an interest in him employed him in a photographic studio, and then in 1967 he got a post as a darkroom assistant on the Bristol *Evening Post*. Following a military tradition (his father had been a sergeant-major in the Gloucester Regiment), Brian next applied to join the RAF as an aerial photographer. Though his application was successful, he thought the several years' training was too long, and decided instead to emigrate to Australia.

He left England on November 16 that same year, travelling by air. He was accompanied by two friends, also Little Brothers, making a lively and optimistic trio. His sister Maureen described the leave-taking: 'There was no money to go and see him off in London. A friend and a friend's girlfriend came to take him to London by car. They came at 4 am and we all cried on the doorstep.' The pair were to correspond until the eve of Britain's death.

He found work in a photo printing laboratory, where he stayed only a few weeks. He spent the next few months (in his own words) 'bumming around', including a spell selling daffodils in Woolworths. In May 1968 he obtained a job as a news cameraman with Channel Seven. He had not been there long before he was approached by rival Channel Nine, which he joined in November 1969.

During the next six years Brian Peters grew in both expertise and reputation, and was regarded as one of the finest news cameramen in Australia. He volunteered for the assignment in Timor, and realised the risks involved.

Though aware of a pending attack by Indonesian troops on the town, the Balibo Five, as they were to become known, believed that as Australian journalists, they would not be considered military targets. One of the five, Greg Shackleton, was filmed painting an Australian flag and the word 'Australia' on the wall of a house where they had taken refuge.

First reports said that the five were killed in crossfire on October 16, the first full day of the occupation operation. Accounts of the event differ, with one holding that the newsmen were killed accidentally in the heat of battle and others that they were deliberately sought out and 'executed' by the Indonesian military.

Some Indonesian military personnel have attempted to justify the killings on the grounds that they were 'communists' and sympathisers with the Fretilin party in Portugese Timor. However, most historians think they were killed to prevent them exposing the Indonesian incursions.

Thirty years on, controversy still surrounds the Balibo Five. It became clear, when official documents were released in 2001, that the Australian Government of the time not only knew about the imminent invasion of the town, but failed to warn the journalists of the likely danger they were in.

Many believe the then Labor Government of Gough Whitlam virtually assured the Indonesian annexation of the region by indicating to Indonesia's Suharto administration that it would not oppose such an action. While Australia supported a United Nations general assembly resolution condemning the Indonesian action, Canberra, it is claimed, had quietly told Jakarta it did not want to get involved in East Timor.

Several relatives of the Balibo Five became active supporters of the fight for independence in East Timor. Others were traumatised. In 1994 Brian Peters' sister, now Maureen Tolfree, became involved with the East Timor issue, having heard of a demonstration in Bristol against the sale of British-made fighter jets to Indonesia.[8]

## THE ENTERTAINER

In the 1920s, when the Big Brother Movement was in its infancy, youths who migrated under its auspices were found jobs on the land and, by and large, were expected to stay there.

Most did as they were bid. But not Harry Dearth, who migrated, at the age of 18, in 1926. He told those who would listen that he wanted to 'go on the stage', and that's precisely what he did.

The path was not easy. In his own words: 'I left school at 17 and seemed faced with a career in the City [of London], which prospect I found rather appalling. My father had come out here on a concert tour in

1919. It was apparently a most successful one, and he always spoke very highly of this country.'

(Harry Dearth senior was a well known baritone singer in London in the early years of the 20th century. He appeared on stage with his wife, Edith Bristow.)

'The spirit of adventure helped me eventually to persuade dad and my mother into letting me try my luck abroad. The Big Brother Movement provided the way and assurance to my parents that I would not be left to battle alone. So I came out here, full of the pioneering spirit, and all set to make my fortune.

'For the next four years I tried my hand at everything from clearing, fencing and lamb-marking to milking, slaughtering and breaking in horses. My success, I believe, was varied.'

A 'break' occurred during this time when Harry's sister arrived in Australia as Enid Adair, of the dance team Gerardo and Adair, under contract to J.C. Williamson's. Unwisely, her brother turned down an offer to join the pair for an American tour.

After a couple more years on the land, Harry moved to Sydney, which he described as a 'cold-hearted' place in the grip of the Depression. For a year he struggled as a shop salesman, then took a job as an usher in a picture theatre. 'All this was leading one step nearer the inevitable end, and I eventually joined the chorus of J.C. Williamson's production of *Dearest Enemy*.'

For three or four years he did chorus work, small parts, and understudying – admirable training, he found, for the radio work he undertook later, and which gave him fame, if not fortune.

In about 1935 Harry Dearth had the first of several auditions with the ABC. 'That keenness was needed before the end of the auditions – there must have been about 400 of them, but in the end they took me on as a staff announcer. After another six months I joined 2GB, which was my real break.'

After a short period he joined J. Walter Thompson (Australia), increasing his scope in commercial radio. He combined announcing with work as a radio actor and producer, returning to work with 2GB.

During the war he served in an entertainment unit. Then, in the boom days of radio after the war, he produced the *Amateur Hour, Lux Radio Theatre, Leave It to the Girls*, and *Harry Dearth's Playhouse*. He was also associated with other radio shows.

In the late 1950s he moved into television work and was appointed program manager for Channel 7, with overall responsibility for live programs.

In 1963 he went overseas to study drama production for television. He had begun to put new ideas into practice for a proposed new drama series when he became ill and was diagnosed with cancer. He died, aged 56, in July 1964.

## THANK YOU, SIR DON

Stuart Harris grew up in Tottenham, North London, where he was first attracted to Australia through meeting two RAAF servicemen billeted at the homes of friends from school.

Don Bradman and Keith Miller were greater influences. 'Of course, we all knew about the prowess of the Australian cricket team, which was probably more influential than anything else. I saw an ad for the Big Brother Movement and it seemed like a good idea.'

His parents gave qualified approval. 'Parents don't easily like their children to go off into the wilds, and to be miles away from them. But they accepted it and eventually came out themselves anyway.' (Stuart sponsored his parents in 1952.)

He came out, at 16, with the first post-war contingent of Little Brothers. It was August 1947. The training farm was not yet set up, so he was sent to a farm at Temora. There was a misunderstanding about his identity. 'They thought I was an orphan, a Barnardo Boy; or a wayward child.' He declines to elaborate. 'It was not a happy period.'

After a few months the BBM found him work on another farm, where his reception was more welcoming. 'The family I worked for were very nice; in fact, I've met them once or twice since then and we kept in touch.

'They did not exploit me, rather the reverse. They had a number of cows and said I could milk them if I got up earlier, sell the cream and keep the money for myself.' The posting also allowed him to see a fellow Little

Brother, Vic Bartlett, whom he had befriended on the ship, and who was on a nearby property. They have remained friends to this day.

After about 18 months at the second farm Stuart switched to doing contract work – harvesting, tank sinking and fencing. It was typical heavy farm labour. Then at 18, a little over two years after his arrival, he decided on a change of career.

'I didn't want to stay on the land. It was not for me. Before leaving England I had matriculated. Part of the reason why I came out, I guess, is that I had wanted to go to university, but realised this was not going to be possible in Britain. I was looking for alternatives and thought perhaps I could eventually go to uni in Australia.'

Stuart did just that, joining the staff of the Taxation Department whilst studying, part-time, for an economics degree at Sydney University. It was the first of several academic qualifications.

He moved with the department to Canberra, then transferred first to the Department of Trade and then to the Bureau of Agricultural Economics, where he became senior economist (1962) and (in 1967) director. He returned to the Department of Overseas Trade as deputy secretary (1972-75). He then took up an appointment at the Australian National University as Professor of Resource Economics (1975-84), subsequently also becoming Director of the Centre for Resource and Environmental Studies.

Taking leave from the university, he returned to the public service in the key roles of secretary of the Department of Foreign Affairs (1984-87), and of the enlarged Department of Foreign Affairs and Trade (DFAT) (1987-88).

In 1988 he returned to the ANU, this time as a professor in the Department of International Relations. He formally retired in 1996, and is now Visiting Professor in the same department.

In both his academic and public service roles he has chaired or co-chaired a number of important national and international councils and committees. (The list occupies some 20 lines in the Australian edition of *Who's Who*.) He is the author of several publications on key issues of foreign and economic policy. He was made an Officer of the Order of Australia (AO) in 1989.

Stuart Harris married in 1958. He and his wife Pamela have five adult children and seven grandchildren.

He is modest about his achievements and describes his migration to Australia with the Big Brother Movement as 'a very good step. I have no regrets and am grateful to the BBM.' Of the time he spent digging post holes and other labouring jobs, he says: 'It was a very good experience. It was obviously helpful when I was in the Bureau of Agricultural Economics. It was a rough time, but it gave you knowledge of the outback, or at least the rural areas and the problems rural people face.'

Stuart Harris differs from most other Little Brothers in that he considers the disbanding of the movement's immigration program as 'reasonable'.

'While I have not followed the issue closely, I know that it was in response to a change in immigration policy which the new Government said should be non-discriminatory.

'It was felt that the BBM was inevitably discriminatory as it was for British migrants. I personally strongly support the non-discriminatory aspect of immigration so I couldn't really object to what was happening to the BBM.'

# 26

## In the Spirit of the Cooees

━━━━━━━

*They are coming from Gilgandra, our soldier men to be.*
*They sing along the western tracks who'll come and fight with me.*
*On the country roads they're coming, can you hear the distant drumming,*
*Can you hear the message humming over long long miles of bushland*
*from Gilgandra to the sea.*

**B**RIAN BYWATER apologises for having been born 50 years too late. 'I should have been born around 1890, he says only half jokingly.

It's a valid observation from a tall, lean, Chips Rafferty-type figure, a ringer for the classic rural ANZAC depicted in films and old newsreels. Though far too young to have fought in either of the two major 20th century conflicts – picking up shrapnel was the closest he got to actual combat – his name is commonly associated with Australia's contribution to World War I.

All this from a man who isn't even a native born Aussie, but a 'Pom' who migrated to rural NSW with the Big Brother Movement at the age of 17 in 1956.

Gilgandra (population 2,739) takes pride in its reputation as 'the best little town in New South Wales'. Nobody recalls who conferred this title, which has stuck. There is acceptance in neighbouring communities that 'Gil' people are special. And for one event in particular.

In late 1915 the mood in Australia was grim. ANZAC forces were struggling in Gallipoli. There was no conscription; Turks appeared to have superiority in numbers and likewise the Germans in Europe. Posters declared: 'Your country needs you.' Newspaper editorials pleaded for 'men and more men'.

From the mid-western farming town of Gilgandra, a group of patriots, loyal to God, King and mother-England, set off to march to Sydney

━━━━━━━

and join the Army, gathering volunteer recruits along the way.

They called themselves the 'Cooees'. They answered the call, as seen in the poster of the time depicting a Digger coo-eeing for men to come and help.

Twenty-seven marchers left Gilgandra on that fateful day, 10 October 1915, and 263[1] would-be recruits arrived at Liverpool camp, Sydney, on November 12. By that time Gallipoli was no longer a destination – the ANZAC forces withdrew in December 1915 – but there were plenty of other opportunities.

By the war's end half had paid the supreme sacrifice. Several of the survivors were decorated. Leslie Greenleaf, an English lad of 17, won the Military Medal at Villers Bretonneux. 'Fighting Tom' Turvey won the same award at Pozieres.[2]

Sadly, the man said to have thought up the idea, local identity and 'pied piper' Bill Hitchen[3] – who deducted eight years from his true age (of 50) to enlist – never made it to the front. 'Captain' Bill[4] died of a heart condition and various complications in a military hospital at Harefield, in southern England, within months of arriving in the UK.

The Cooee marchers earned local renown – many of the veterans attending a golden jubilee reunion in 1965. But time marches on and the wider community largely forgot about those men of the bush and their footnote in history.

At this point along came Brian Bywater, newly married and employed as overseer on a property in the Warrumbungles. 'Me and some mates were having a smoko one day, when some of the shearers started talking about the Cooees. I said: "Cooees! What's that?" They told me a bit about them and I thought how great. I'd have been one of them had I been around.'

Not long afterwards Brian joined the Army Reserve, where weekend route marches formed part of the training. He met two other reservists, Kym Templeton (now a senior officer) and Rob Maclean, and suggested a Cooee re-enactment march as a way of stimulating recruiting.

Neither had heard of the Cooees, but were enthused. 'We put it to the Army, who said "No, it's a bloody waste of time". This was just as Bill Hitchen was told in 1915. So we thought we'd do it as civilians. Just the

three of us; we'd march along the road. But after I told one or two people, they wanted to be in it and the idea just grew.'

In 1987 Brian Bywater's 'idea' became a reality – a full-scale Cooee
re-enactment march from Gilgandra to Sydney, recorded by Film
Australia as an award-winning documentary.

There were fewer participants – 29 marchers and a dog – than in
1915, but all finished the course. Their ages ranged from 17 to 64. There
were also three or four part-time marchers and a support team of 13.

They stuck as far as possible to the original route, covering the 330
miles (Cooees do not think metric) in 21 days instead of the 33 days taken
by their forebears.

As with the first Cooees, the re-enactment marchers made a stirring
sight. Drummer Rob Maclean beat out 528,000 paces between 'Gil' and
Sydney, hitting his drum, in the approved military style, as the left foot
passes the right. Truck drivers honked in respect as they passed the column, schoolchildren gave lollies and ran between the marchers' legs in
scenes that made Bywater and his companions weep. At the head of the
procession was Bywater himself, carrying a huge Red Ensign flag donated by the Catholic parish of Enfield.

Brian's own story is almost as eventful as his 'Cooee' hobby. He was
born in the dock area of Liverpool, in 1939, from where his parents
moved soon afterwards to Wolverhampton. Both cities were enemy targets. As Brian puts it: '1940-42 were busy times up there.'

His desire to emigrate to Australia began when he was about eight.
'My mother told me I used to pester her and dad from then on.'

He was perhaps a little confused about destinations. 'I wanted to be
a cowboy, ride on the range and be free. Maybe I was confusing it with
America. But I'd seen a couple of Chips Rafferty films at the local flicks
and we all thought he was great.'

He left school at 14 and worked on farms. At the age of 16 his parents gave in to his demands to go to Australia. 'Dad said "OK. Get the
paperwork and we'll have a look at it." He didn't know that I already had
the paperwork. I remember he said "OK, we'll let you go." I remember
he said to mum, "We must let him go; if we don't he will resent us for the
rest of his life".'

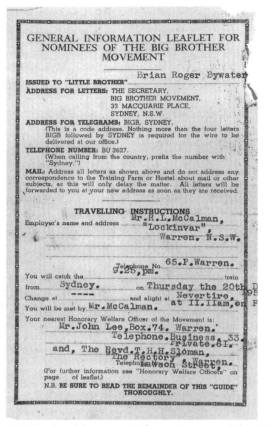

*Big Brother Movement information provided to Brian Bywater.*

In November 1956 Brian Bywater and former school chum Peter Anderson, whom he had talked into making a similar application, sailed together on the *Otranto*. There were some 35 Little Brothers altogether. There was war in the Suez Canal and the ship had to travel via the Cape, adding a few weeks on to the journey.

'It was very nice – we stopped at Cape Town and Durban – but it was a long time at sea, and on an ocean liner with no money it isn't awfully entertaining. There's not much you can do except walk around the ship.'

Upon arrival in Australia Brian – unlike so many of the others – settled in immediately, and cannot recall ever being homesick. 'I loved it, out in the country, in the bush. This was what I'd always wanted; what I had been demanding of my parents.'

The training camp was overcrowded, as a result of which, and his previous farming work in England, he was sent within days to his first employer, a certain Ron McCalman, of Lochinvar, Warren. They were of Scots descent, kind-hearted, and 'aristocratic minded'.

'Your table manners had to be perfect. I thought I'd been raised right because, I mean, I came from a good family too. But table manners were a big thing with this lady and I got my knuckles rapped a couple of times for doing the wrong thing.

'Actually, I should be grateful I was allowed to eat with the family. At the time I just wanted to sit under a tree with a frying pan and some bacon and beans.'

Brian stayed at the property about 18 months and then went to work, in turn, at other properties, all with Scottish names, owned by the same family. He left their employment when one of their sons came home.

The procedure for job seeking was then somewhat different to what it is now. 'I remember going into town, into the pub, and someone met me at the door. "They say you're looking for a job. There's a place going at so-and-so. Right'o, you're on".'

Several short-term jobs followed, one of which involved working for a family called Fletcher. 'They were down to earth, worker type of people. Old Tommy Fletcher was a real old type Aussie. He never said much, but the nicest bloke imaginable. His wife treated me like the son she never had.' One day – proud of his newly acquired Volkswagen car – Brian offered a ride home to their guests.

From Warren to Dubbo was a fairly long journey and they suggested he stay the night. He agreed, at which point 'this really good sort walks in – it was the lady's eldest daughter – and I thought Wow. From then on I was driving between Warren and Dubbo almost every weekend.'

Brian and Ann (his 'good sort') were married in January 1966 and – in time – became the parents of 'seven little Australians', four boys and three girls. A talking point in the family was Brian's uncanny knack of predicting, correctly, the sex of each new arrival.

Soon after their marriage Brian obtained a permanent job with Dubbo City Council, where he was to stay the rest of his working life. When I first met him about 15 years ago he was noxious weeds inspector. In his final eight or nine years they promoted him to Landcare Services Manager – 'It sounds much nicer than the weeds man.'

Did he ever become a landowner? 'No, I never did get around to buying my own place like I'd always intended. Perhaps I set my sights too high. I wanted 10 million acres out in the middle of nowhere.'

Brian retained his interest in the Cooees. On 30 September 1990 he played a big part in Cooee 75th anniversary celebrations, and followed this up with a Cooee march to the battlefields of France. In July 2005 (wearing a World War I officer's uniform and with the Australian flag held high), he led the leading A Company in the smaller scale 90th anniversary re-enactment in Gilgandra and Sydney. Just one pace in front was the parade commander, John Gallagher, a descendant of Bill Hitchen.

Surprisingly, in view of their association with the Cooees, Brian and Ann Bywater did not live in Gilgandra – at least until recently – but in Geurie, about 70 miles away. The omission was rectified in 1998, when, after retirement from Dubbo City Council, Brian heard via the grapevine that a house in 'Gil' was to be auctioned.

It was not just any house, but the cottage in Miller Street, which had been Bill Hitchen's home. Brian bought it at a bargain price, since when he has been converting it into a museum of militaria. For good measure he subsequently bought another house four doors down in which he and Ann now live.

There have been other changes. The couple's 'Seven Little Australians' are now Seven Big Australians – having married and left home. A reminder of the old days occurred recently when a coach load of tourists pulled up, unannounced, and visited his museum. One of the pensioners recognised him. It was Mrs Joyce McCalman, from Warren, the grazier's wife who had taught him etiquette at the dinner table 45 years ago.

In 1998 Brian was awarded the Order of Australia Medal (OAM) for services to local military history. He has also received the Reserve Force medal with two clasps and a Chief of Staff's Commendation for Reserve service and relief work during the 1990 Nyngan floods.

## VERY ABLE SEAMAN

*'We were slaves really. Just 15 bob a week and keep.*
*But that's what was paid in those days. I suppose we weren't much use*
*for a while. But I've got no regrets, though I did lose my finger,*
*or part of it, on my first job.'*

Norm Smith is what people politely call an 'identity'. He is one of nature's enthusiasts who gets carried away about almost anything.

Naval veteran, diarist, raconteur, a compulsive chronicler of people and events. He is also a BBM stalwart and, in everybody's view, a 'thoroughly nice bloke'.

To enter Norm's modest flat in the Sydney suburb of Summer Hill is to enter an Aladdin's cave. Walls, corridors, almost every inch of floor space are covered with books, newspapers, dolls, memorabilia of every kind.

He admits to being a 'holic' æ workaholic, 'bookaholic', 'collectaholic', but not 'alcoholic'. 'No, I don't drink at all; I don't smoke and I've run out of women.' But at my age [Norm is 83] it doesn't really matter.'

On a shelf behind him I spotted two little bears; a token of affection from his partner, who died a few months previously. On another shelf was a duck; on a third what seemed to be reindeers from a discarded Christmas decoration. Down the other end of the room were two painted papier-maché birds', seated on an indoor plant which look as if it had been there from World War II.

There were books galore, with several trunk loads in the bedroom, and piles of yellowed newspapers and magazines. On the floor were three briefcases, each representing a different interest. The idea is that when he's due for a meeting he just picks up the case and off he goes. Has he ever picked up the wrong one? 'Not yet,' he says. 'That's why they're clearly marked.'

One of the cases reflects his involvement in the Fellowship of Australian Writers. He's no shrinking violet and has sent some of his verses to the Queen. The second relates to his membership of the Ashfield-Burwood branch of the Association of Justices of the Peace. The third has personal finance records and material concerning the ANZAC Day march. On a shelf is a stack of material pertaining to the building's body corporate. 'Are you the secretary?,' I ask politely. 'I *am* the body corporate,' he replies.

The body corporate role also feeds his 'collecting' habit. He explains meekly: 'People are always putting things out the front they don't want and I tend to rescue some of them.'

He's also involved in the affairs of St Andrew's Church, Summer Hill. He describes his role as 'doing the garden and lending a hand'. All this activity isn't counting his Naval interests. 'I'm a member of the RSL, the Naval Association of Australia, the Corvette Association, the Fairmile Association...' He rattles off a list.

He says these activities are less time consuming than they seem. An example is the Fairmilers, 'There's just an annual general meeting, with lunch afterwards, usually at Parliament House, and a church service at Garden Island.'

Which explains how he still finds time to prepare cross-words for *White Ensign*, the magazine of the Naval Association.

Norm was born in London, and – his parents having separated – raised initially by his mother and grandparents in Sheffield. After a family conference he was sent to live with an old lady at Baslow, in Derbyshire. He was then sent to a Christian Science children's home in Richmond, Surrey. 'It was a strange place. Some of the children were mentally handicapped. Not that it worried me. I wasn't unhappy there.'

After another family conference his grandparents, who were comfortably off, removed him from the children's home and sent him to a private boarding school, Sibford, in Oxford, where he stayed until he was 15. The decision was then made – he is not sure by whom – that he should seek fame and (perhaps) fortune in Australia.

'I think the Big Brother Movement had advertised for young chaps in a newspaper and my relatives saw the ad. I did what they told me and applied. I was the chattel. But I didn't really mind. In fact, it seemed like a good idea.'

He sailed on board the *Strathallan* in January 1939. He enjoyed the voyage. 'Apart from the Newhaven to Dieppe ferry I'd never been to sea before. Seeing those cities and ports around the world was quite impressive. We were like little lords with the run of the ship. I've no complaints at all.'

On arrival in Sydney he and his mates were sent to the Government training farm at Scheyville. 'It was pretty basic, just to give us an idea what farm work was like. We called the man in charge desert head. His head was shaven. We were terrified of him. I remember his bed was a concrete slab. I can't remember his real name. He was probably a decent bloke.'

Whilst still at Scheyville the BBM made contact with farmers and property owners who wanted boys. He was sent to a farm at Ballengarra, near Telegraph Point in northern New South Wales.

'He was a tough Irish bloke called Ken Tubman. He worked us hard and I was only there for a few months. One of my jobs was to milk the cows. One night he didn't come home until late and I was still milking the cows at midnight. He said: "Oh, you should have left them." But what could I do.

He was contracted to the Big Brother Movement to pay me 15 shillings a week. But after a couple of months, he said: "I don't think you're earning 15 shillings, I'll try you on 7s 6d for a while". He wasn't allowed to do that, but of course I didn't know any better. He'd just bought himself a new car. Whether there was any relationship I don't know.'

Shortly after his arrival Norm lost a finger, or part of it, in an accident. How that came about is as follows: 'It was on a Sunday and I was having a bit of a ride on the horse that was allocated to me. I came to tie it up on a railing fence. I was putting the rein through the hole when suddenly there was thunder and lightning and the horse panicked and pulled back. My finger was caught in the rein. It was severely fractured and I had to go into Port Macquarie [the nearest sizeable town] to see a doctor.

'Unfortunately the doctor who owned the practice was on holidays and he had a locum, whom I think was drunk. He put a bandage about three inches in diameter round the finger and sent me away. It went gangrenous. Later the doctor who owned the practice said I should have gone to someone else, but I was green, just out from England, working in the scrub, and didn't know anything better. Anyway, I had to go back again and they put me into Port Macquarie Hospital and they took the top off the finger.

'Mind you, the farmer himself wasn't very caring. The unfortunate part was he had two people working for him and the other man had run a plough over his foot the week before. But he only had one person insured, so I was the unlucky one. He also said to me: "It's your day off, so you're not entitled to insurance cover anyway." Of course, I took his word for it.'

Another 'finger' incident led Norm to quit. 'One of the man's little boys caught his fingers in the hinge of the door and went and told his father I'd hit him. Of course the dad wanted to beat me up, but I hadn't been near the lad. It was unfortunate because the accusation was quite untrue.'

Ever forgiving, Norm still thinks of the farmer as a 'fairly decent bloke'. 'Anyway,' he ruminates. 'It all happened a long time ago.'

Norm left his first employer after about six months. By this time war had broken out. He wanted to join up. Being only 15, he was too young to join up. The BBM found him work at Gunning, between Goulburn and Yass.

'It was a sheep station. I was supposed to be learning, but all they did was make me a kind of houseboy. I seemed to spend most of my time digging holes and burying the toilet refuse, so I shot through.' To facilitate his departure he took a makeshift cart belonging to the man's son. 'It was just a couple of boards with wheels on it. I used it to shift my trunk to the railway station. They were not amused and accused me of theft. The Big Brother

Movement made me write a letter of apology to the farmer about it.'

Norm's next job was on a dairy farm at Grenfell. 'I milked the cows daily and delivered milk into Grenfell. I forget why I left there.' Now 16, he decided to try his luck in the big smoke. He scraped the fare down to Sydney, found a room in Annandale and a job in an engineer's shop making screws. However, he found that until pay day he had insufficient money to buy food. 'So after three days of not eating I contacted the Big Brother Movement and they rescued me.'

His fourth and final farming job was at Geurie, between Wellington and Dubbo. From here, in February 1941 – just 17 and four months – he joined the Royal Australian Navy.

NAVY LIFE

The first weeks of Naval life were spent in the civilised surroundings of Beach Road, Rushcutters Bay. 'They paid you 30 shillings a week to live ashore while you did your initial training.'

He believes that at that point his life was literally saved. 'I had a very bad ingrowing toenail and they put me into Prince of Wales Hospital and took half of it off. The class that I was in went on to Flinders in Melbourne to continue their training, and I had to join a newer class. Of the group that went to Flinders, half went on to *HMAS Sydney* and half to *HMAS Perth*. They were both sunk.⁵ And I came through the war unscathed, so I reckon the toe saved my life.'

There were, in fact, some near misses – 'All ships have their moments,' he says drily. He served mainly in corvettes, including a harrowing time in *HMAS Toowoomba*, which had a role in events preceding the fall of Singapore on 15 February 1942.

The *Toowoomba* had reached Singapore three weeks earlier, on 22 January . War clouds were on the horizon. 'The place was bombed while we were actually in harbour, but none of them dropped close to us, thank God. But when we were out mine-sweeping or patrolling, five Japanese planes attacked us directly. The bombs fell 30 or 40 feet away, and we were very lucky they missed, resulting in only superficial damage.'

The *Toowoomba* was one of seven corvettes involved in minesweeping, escorting convoys and rescuing people off bombed and crippled ships. It left Singapore waters on 2 February, 'but we weren't idle. We went up to Palembang, in Sumatra, refuelled and helped take a convoy to what was then Batavia. We were still in South Java when the Japanese landed in North Java.'

After leaving the *Toowoomba* Norm served in the *Geelong*, engaged in convoy duties around the Australian coast, and in the *Gympie*, escorting troopships to New Guinea. While still in the *Gympie* a call was made for volunteers for other form of service. Norm 'felt like a change' and found himself serving in fairmiles (patrol boats) in New Guinea, operating frequently behind enemy lines. He later volunteered for air sea rescue. After appropriate training he was back in New Guinea once more, also New Britain, this time as coxswain in the rescue vessel *HMAS Airspeed*.

As a single man Norm was among the last to be demobilised and did not leave the service until late 1946. 'When the war ended they had post-war training programs for ex-servicemen. A lot of people did university training, went on other courses and probably made a very nice living in due course. But I was still up in New Guinea, well into 1946, and nobody knew or told me about these opportunities.

'All the officer said when I went for my discharge was "What are you going to do?" Not "What *could* you do?" I said truthfully that I had only ever worked on farms, so he put down farming. And when I came back to Sydney they sent me out to a chook farm the other side of Liverpool. But after a couple of months of that I thought I'm not going to get anywhere. By that time I was a man. I'd had five and a half years of Naval service and wasn't a fool. I had a girlfriend then. She worked in the city and she encouraged me to work in retailing, which I did.'

Norm spent the next 15 years in the retail industry, specialising in home decorating and furnishings. It included four years at Beard Watsons, and a period as group buyer at Waltons. He then spent 25 years as service manager for Woodweev, a woven timber blind manufacturer. He retired in May 1992. Since then all his activities have been 'unpaid and voluntary'.

Loyalty and mateship are qualities Norm has exhibited throughout his life. They are indicated by his practice of keeping photographs of his wartime commanding officers on display in his home. He has documented their subsequent careers and writes to those who are still alive – an interesting display of friendship between men of the upper and lower deck.

In February 2002, Norm was one of a group of veterans – including four war widows – chosen by the Australian and Singapore Governments to take part in an official visit to mark the 60th anniversary of the Fall of Singapore.

By coincidence, the offer was confirmed a few weeks after the death of his long time friend and partner, Jean Badman. Norm decided to go. 'In essence it was a blessing to me in that I had something to distract me from my worries.'

Norm regarded the journey as a 'pilgrimage'. When visiting the official war cemetery he decided, not having any relatives or immediate comrades buried there, to 'adopt' a departed serviceman. He deliberately chose someone with the same surname as himself – the idea being to seek information about his family, and perhaps send them a copy of the photo he had taken of the headstone.

# 27

## Military Men – 'Z Special'

**R**ECORDS OF THE BBM show that by 1942, when Australia faced a threat of military invasion, almost every Little Brother – past or current – within the accepted age limits, was serving in the Australian armed forces. This is the story of one of them.

Wally Pare, from Beeston, Nottingham, arrived in Sydney on the *Strathallan*, in March 1939. He was then 15. His card in the BBM office says he had £2 'landing money' and a background as a boy scout.

His group of 20 Little Brothers were given a farewell at the Mansion House by the Lord Mayor of London, who put half-a-crown in each lad's hand and offered the advice: 'Don't buy a car or a saxophone; always wear a hat in summer.'

Wally and his Henry Mellish Grammar School chum, Don Cooper, who accompanied him, received a promise from their fathers of £500 (each) if they lasted five years 'in the bush'. It was an incentive in the hope that they should open their own farm and forge a successful life in their new country.

Wally, at any rate, never got his £500. The Japanese saw to that. He got a job on a dairy stud, but three years later – having volunteered for military service immediately he was of legal age – found himself in surroundings that were considerably less tranquil.

As a bright lad, with a high IQ, Wally was initially put into Signals. It was there he heard about Z Special Units, commando-style undercover groups being trained in jungle warfare, sabotage and espionage, and decided to join 'their show'.

The 'Z Specials', originally known as Allied Intelligence Bureau, were developed from the Special Operations Executive (SOE) and were at one time called Special Operations Australia (SOA). To avoid confusion, and to put people off the scent, the name was changed to Services Reconnaissance Department (SRD).

Wally recalls with wry amusement: 'It was just a cover. If you went into an Aussie pub and someone called out, "What are you doing, Digger?" you would smile and reply "Service Reconnaissance Department" or "SRD". It was a nom de plume.'

In small units the Z Specials would be inserted behind enemy lines – sometimes by flying boat or submarine, sometimes by parachute from 3,000ft. It was their job to get information on Japanese positions and cause as much damage as they could in the process.

To achieve their objectives, they recruited the help of jungle tribes – often headhunters, armed with poison darts and blowpipes. The Z Special Units were singularly successful in what they did. But it came with a price. During a raid on (Japanese held) Singapore Harbour, some of the Z men were captured. They were beheaded with a samurai sword.

Wally goes silent for a moment as he recalls such horrors. 'There was an op in Timor, a bit of a disaster really, and I had a close friend on it who was captured. We heard after the war that the first thing the Japs did was to cut his hamstrings. He died at the age of 21 and I think he was glad to die.'

Wally's feelings for the Japanese, even today, need no fuirther explanation. 'We didn't take prisoners. If we caught any of the Japanese we gave them to the headhunters.'

When they clashed, the fighting was fierce and merciless. Yet, like so many veterans, it is difficult to draw specifics from the ex-sergeant. 'We had one or two hairy moments,' said Wally – a chess fanatic who carried a pocket set with him on ops.

'We set up an ambush along the banks of a river. There were eight of us with bren guns and when the Japanese came we made a bit of a mess, but they hunted us with planes and we had to get out a bit sharpish.' It was as much detail as he was prepared to offer.

Wally had to return to Nottingham after the war when his mother died and never got the chance to take up his life in Australia. But he has never lost touch with the comrades who survived. He is a member of several veterans' associations and has made numerous trips for reunions.

'Sadly, there are so few of us now that the 2000 reunion, held in Tasmania, was the last official get-together,' he said.

As for Wally's school chum, Don Cooper, who was also a Little Brother, the story has a remarkable postscript. They split up when war came, Don joining the RAAF, and were not to meet again.

Wally always wondered what had happened to his mate, and in 1999, having discovered Don had come back to England to run a dairy at Long Bennington, a country town, approached an ex-Royal Marine in the area to ask around.

The ex-Marine approached the local postwoman. 'Have you come across any Coopers in the area?' 'Which Cooper would that be?,' she asked. 'Don Cooper', 'Really, he was my father,' was her reply.

Alas, Don Cooper had died some 13 years earlier. Wally and the daughter of his old school chum now meet regularly. 'I am so glad to know her. I have tied both ends of the circle now,' he said.[1]

## FIGHTER COMMAND

In more recent theatres of war, and in the peacetime military forces, Little Brothers have served their adopted country well.

John Ward, who retired from the RAAF with the rank of Group Captain in 1998, is an excellent example of this.

In January 1963 – three months after his arrival in Australia – John joined the RAAF as a trainee electrical fitter. Following his training, he served at Richmond, near Sydney, but was soon posted to Butterworth, in Malaysia, serving with Nos. 3 and 77 fighter squadrons. In turn, he was sent to Ubon Air Force Base in Thailand with 79 fighter squadron. The squadron gave fighter protection to the base while the American Phantom squadrons bombed North Vietnam.

Although happy at being an aircraft technician he had always wanted to be a pilot in the Air Force. In following this path he qualified as a commercial pilot in his spare time, while waiting for selection by the Air Force. Acceptance came just one week before he was due to be discharged.

He came second in the course, was commissioned, and selected for duty on Neptune maritime reconnaissance aircraft. This was not entirely to his liking; his first choice had been fighters, for which no courses were running at that time. This was particularly disappointing for John as he had wanted to fly fighters to enable him to qualify as a Forward Air Controller (FAC) and to return to Vietnam in this role.

Two years later (in 1972) he got his way and was flying Mirage fighter aircraft from Williamtown. After a further three years he undertook an instructor's course, which led to an 18 months' posting at RAAF Pearce in Western Australia followed by a two-year posting to Singapore, training pilots for the Republic of Singapore Air Force.

Back in Australia, he was posted to the F-111 Strike Reconnaissance Force at Amberley and after an operational tour with No. 1 Squadron he then became an instructor with No. 6 Squadron. In 1983 – by now a Squadron Leader – he was made Operational Flight Commander of No. 1 Squadron. A posting to the Australian Joint Warfare Establishment followed (1984-87), where he taught Joint Operations to Australian Defence Force officers and overseas military officers. Promoted to Wing Commander, he returned to fly F-111s as Commanding Officer of No. 6 Squadron. He filled a number of further interesting staff officer appointments, culminating in a return to the Butterworth base in Malaysia.

This time it was not as a non-commissioned aircraft fitter, but as senior Australian representative (with the rank of Wing Commander) at the Integrated Air Defence System, responsible for the air defence of non-communist Malaysia and Singapore.

In 1996, having been promoted to Group Captain, he was posted back to Australia as Officer Commanding the RAAF Tindal base in the Northern Territory. This was his last posting over a career that had spanned 35 years. A tranquil existence was shattered by the devastating (January 1998) Katherine flood. He was placed in charge of the relief program, for which he had 800 Air Force, 400 Army and 18 RAN personnel under his command. For that he was awarded the CSC (Conspicuous Service Cross) in the same year's Queen's Birthday honours.

Though now officially retired, John Ward is still on call as a very active member of the Air Force Reserve. In 2001 he planned and commanded the Defence Forces' participation in the Melbourne International Air Show. He was assigned to plan a similar spectacle to mark the 80th anniversary at the Amberley RAAF Base in Queensland. Unfortunately – just 10 days before the event when all was in place for an outstanding show – the attack on the New York World Trade Centre occurred and the Air Show was cancelled.

## A BICYCLE AND A REUNION

John Ward (see above) was one of 15 Little Brothers who arrived in Sydney on 19 October 1962, on board the *Canberra*. He had few possessions but brought with him one link with home – his cherished Raleigh push-bike.

John obtained a temporary job at Central Railway Station loading parcels onto trains. He had a free railway pass so didn't need to use his bike, which he loaned to another Little Brother.

For 30 years, almost from the very day of his arrival, John Ward had not met any of the lads from his intake. In 1993 he felt it was time to rectify the omission, and with this in mind attended that year's BBM reunion at Rawson Park, Mosman.

He was disappointed to find no one there from his intake. Positioning himself by the list on which people wrote their year of arrival, he saw someone write down September 1962 – a month before his own arrival.

He struck up a conversation. 'I told him my story of lending my bike to an apprentice and finally giving it to him. A roar went up from both of us when he said that he was the apprentice and had kept the bike for 15 years and used it extensively until it was stolen.'

The two now keep in touch. According to Mike Barker, the former apprentice: 'Every time he rings me, he begins the conversation by saying "Where's my bloody bike?"'

## NO 'BOREDOM' IN VIETNAM

Chris Webster, from Macclesfield, Cheshire, arrived in Sydney in September 1962 and two months later joined the 1st Battalion, Royal Australian Regiment (RAR) as a regular soldier. He was then 19. He had been in his English school cadets, finding the experience 'very enjoyable', and enlisted for three years.

After two-and-a-half years – by which time he was a corporal in an infantry section – his colleagues were told they were to be sent to Vietnam. The normal period of duty was one year. With only six months left to serve, he would have been excused the posting.

Instead he volunteered, signing on for a further three years, in order that his wish could be achieved. I asked him why he did so. He replied: 'Well, you couldn't really spend three years training to do something, and then the minute you get the opportunity to do it properly, disappear.'

According to John Ward, also mentioned in this chapter, his friend's war experiences were harrowing. Chris is modest about this: 'It wasn't specifically me. It was the same with all of us. Every platoon, the entire battalion, had a fairly interesting time. Things started to buzz, which was what we expected.

'As always, for most of the time nothing much happened – though I wouldn't call it boredom. Then that one per cent comes along, and you get extreme excitement.'

'Excitement' in his vocabulary meant fierce fighting against an unrelenting fore. In the course of his year-long tour of duty three members of his 30-strong platoon were killed, and about a dozen wounded. Chris himself escaped injury.

The young soldier returned to Australia still with a couple of years to serve. He was posted to the Holsworthy base near Liverpool, and promoted to sergeant, as a result of which he was now second in command of his platoon.

A little over a year later the battalion was again required for combat in Vietnam. Chris had 10 months to serve. Again he volunteered. 'I guess they [his superiors] felt the more experienced NCOs were valuable to them even if, in my case, I couldn't do the full 12 months.'

The second tour was as eventful as the first, but Chris missed much of a major battle, about which he still feels considerable angst, having been sent to Saigon to take charge of a security guard protecting visiting VIPs.

The 'action', as Chris calls it, came to be known as the Battle of Fire Base Coral, and is commemorated annually by the regiment. It occurred when the artillery base of that name was attacked by a large number of North Vietnamese regular troops, and very nearly overrun.

The platoon of which Chris was normally second in command faced decimation, but was saved by the bravery and astuteness of the young commander, Second Lieutenant Neil Weeks, who received the Military Cross. The substitute platoon sergeant, Bruno Flematti, received the Distinguished Conduct Medal.

Chris himself returned to the war zone a few days later, and participated in the final stages of the battle. When this interview was conducted, ex-Sergeant Chris Webster had just returned from a visit to Townsville, where he had met up with the ex-platoon commander, now retired from the Army with the rank of Brigadier.

## THE FIRST 'NASHO'

Walter Sims, a Little Brother, who came to Australia as a 16-year-old, in April 1961, earned a footnote in history by being the first person inducted in the national service call-up, when conscription was re-introduced in 1965.

The call-up, operated on a ballot system, was specifically to provide troops and the necessary back up for service in the Vietnam War. The length of service was two years. An earlier scheme, consisting of 98 days full-time and two years' service in the reserve, operated in the 1950s, in the time of the Korean War.

Walter, originally from Midhurst, Sussex, was one of a group of 700 who arrived on the same day – 30 June 1965 – at the Army training depot at Marrickville.

Interviewed at the time by the Sydney *Daily Mirror*, Walter told a reporter: 'I came from England to get some adventure. But this is more than I bargained for.'

Michael, then aged 20, said he had worked mainly on sheep stations in the Dubbo area since his arrival four years earlier. He had recently joined the railways as a trainee engineman.

'I don't mind being called up. I didn't try to get out of it,' he said. 'My only complaint is that two years seems a bit long.'

Asked how he would feel if he were sent overseas, he said: 'Someone has to do it, and, anyway, I won't be the only one on the boat.'

As it happened, Walter did not go to Vietnam. He was injured in a car accident and served the bulk of his time with a bren carrier unit at Puckapunyal.

## THE OLDEST AND THE SENIOR

The question is sometimes asked: Who is the oldest (in years) or senior (in terms of arrival date) Little Brother?

Loss of some interstate records and the failure of so many Little Brothers to maintain contact with 'head office' makes this a difficult question to answer.

For many years the most 'senior' Little Brother in NSW, and probably in Australia, was thought to be John (Jock) Bone, born 9 December 1909, who arrived in Sydney, in the *Balrandald*, on 12 February 1927.

A convivial fellow, he liked the company of younger ex-Little Brothers, one of whom, Alan Wilkinson, would share a few beers with him at the Sutherland United Services Club, of which Jock was a founding member.

Alan assisted him with shopping and other errands. One day, soon after his 90th birthday, Jock asked for a lift to 'the centre'. Alan assumed this to mean the local health centre, but after a few minutes Jock claimed they were going in the wrong direction.

'Don't you want the health centre?' Alan asked. 'Oh no,' came the reply. 'I meant the driving test centre.' Jock duly took his driving test – at age 90 – and passed. Jock died, just short of his 91st birthday, in July 2000.

### 'TRUANT' BECAME LUTHERAN PASTOR

Just behind Jock in the seniority stakes was Ken Sarson, whom I discovered[2] in a residential community home at Freeling, near Gawler, in South Australia.

Ken, originally from Sheffield, the Yorkshire 'steel town', arrived in Australia in April 1927, two years and two weeks after the BBM's official foundation meeting.

Ken had a novel background, having been expelled from the school at which his own father was a teacher. His offences involved truancy. In Ken's words: 'I was not dedicated. They [the local education committee] tried various schools, even putting me in my dad's class, but I just stayed away.'

He recalled one day when another teacher was calling the roll. When his name was announced, there was no answer. A voice piped up: 'He's down the street, looking in shop windows.' As Ken told it: 'Two of the bigger boys were sent to find me. They frogmarched me back to the school. My dad gave me four sticks [strokes of the cane] and took me to see the headmaster.

'The headmaster made me sit in the corner of his room. He went out frequently, and every time he came back in he gave me four sticks. Then, when I went home, my father gave me another four sticks.' With an impish chuckle, Ken adds: 'Next day I played truant again. That's how effective the cane was.'

Expulsion followed. Adults – including his teachers – thought he was 'high spirited' rather than bad. Nor was he stupid. Educationally, he had been considered suitable for grammar school. Emigration was the answer! The newly-formed London committee of the Big Brother Movement was approached, and agreed to sponsor him.

Ken Sarson, by now 15, travelled out on the *Jervis Bay*, which arrived in Adelaide, en route for Melbourne, on 1 May 1927. The timing was auspicious, coinciding with the presence in Adelaide of the Duke and Duchess of York (later King George VI and Queen Elizabeth). The royal couple, whose visit included every mainland state, were on their way to open the first Parliament House, in Canberra.

The royal visit slightly delayed the onward journey. Ken stayed on board and disembarked in Melbourne, where he was supposed to be met by his Big Brother, a civic leader in Box Hill. Alas, his 'greeter' was not there, having left for Canberra to represent that municipality at the Parliament House ceremony on 9 May.

However, the man's wife was there to meet him, and said she would put him on a train to the Victorian country town of Rainbow, where he would be met by the farmer who would be his employer.

Confusion reigned. Ken missed the train; a telegram was sent that he would be arriving two days late. Though he is now old and frail, and his memory is fading, he still vividly recalls his eventual arrival at Rainbow:

'It was about half past nine in the evening, and already dark. I was the last one off the train, and pulled down my trunk and two cases. I looked around for someone to meet me. There was a chap about my own height – I was five foot 10 inches. Only he was much stouter and wearing a slouch hat. He came up to me and said: "Have you seen a little boy about?" I said: "That's me".'

The farm was about three miles south of Rainbow. On their way the dray hit a mound of earth, and the lad and his luggage were nearly thrown out. Ken got on reasonably well with the farmer, but disliked his son. 'He had a vile temper and tongue. You could hear him on a cold morning swearing at the horses.'

The area was in a period of drought. One of his first tasks was to kill sheep. 'The boss had too many sheep around the bare paddocks. Some of the sheep were in a bad way, so weak that if they got down they couldn't stand up. My job was to look for those in this condition and end their misery by slitting their throats.'

Other farm workers called him a 'new chum' and were amused at his ignorance of farm ways. He recalls the boss's wife showing him how to milk cows. She said: 'If you want them to be happy make sure that your fingers are warm in the winter time.'

One day an argument developed between Ken and the boss's son. It came to blows. The boy was 15 and the son 27. When the farmer separated them, he gave Ken the sack, depositing him the next day with the local Baptist minister.[3]

Through the New Settlers' League Ken found a job with a Lutheran farmer named Koop, about 10 miles west of Rainbow. The pay was £1 a week, whereas the previous farmer paid him 15 shillings. Ken was delighted, but not so the Baptist minister, who wished him to stay with his 'own kind'.

As part of the arrangement, Ken had to work alternate Sundays. But when the first 'working' Sunday came along, the farmer asked if he would like to down tools and accompany them to church. Ken considered this the pleasanter option and came along. This sparked an interest in Christianity, and – at the farmer's suggestion Ken began to attend Baptist services one Sunday and Lutheran services the next.

Eventually, the Lutherans won out, and Ken – by now almost part of the 'German' community – asked to attend confirmation classes. For the next year, every Friday, after finishing his farm duties, Ken would cycle into Rainbow, along the unmade roads, to attend instruction from Pastor G.A. Leske, who became a close friend.

This friendship led ultimately to Ken's decision to become a

Lutheran minister. After his graduation from Concordia Seminary in 1939, Ken had temporary pastorates at Coonalpyn, South Australia, South Melbourne, and Warrnambool, before getting a permanent posting in 1942 to the tough and isolated NSW mining town of Broken Hill.

At Coonalpyn, Ken met and courted Margaret Klitscher, a member of the local Lutheran community, and they were married in 1941. In Broken Hill, Ken suffered a breakdown in health, resulting from emotional strain, and this forced him to quit the active ministry in 1946.

He moved south with his wife and three children, and took a variety of jobs to support the family. In the half-century which followed, he was first the employee of a rural roadmaking contractor; since then he has been schoolteacher, shop keeper, diesel mechanic, and finally marine engineer. His wife died after a drawn-out illness in 1970.

In his retirement years Ken took up swimming at the urging of his daughter Rosalie, herself a champion, and swam one to three km daily. In fact, he won championship awards at consecutive Masters Games. Ken Sarson died, age 93, on 10 August 2004.

## LIFE IS WHAT YOU MAKE OF IT

At the time of creation of the BBM's database, Tom Moffett, then aged 90, was number one on the veterans' list of (known) Little Brothers in NSW. He died on 10 August 2004, thus making that information obsolete.

Tom, who lived in a Uniting Church retirement village in Nowra, was proud of his longstanding connection with the movement. 'It's nice to know where you are in the seniority stakes,' he told me modestly.

Tom was born on 7 July 1914, in the border town of Berwick-on-Tweed. He came from a broken home and was raised by his mother.

How did he come to migrate to Australia? 'It sounds silly but it was through geography lessons at school.' Australia 'seemed exciting – it was all about going to a new land'. The Church of England minister in Berwick was a representative of the BBM, and smoothed the path for emigration.

By that time Tom had already left school and was working for a laundry, delivering and returning bundles of washing. For this he was paid eight shillings a week.

He travelled out on the *Moreton Bay*, arriving in Sydney on 3

October 1929. He was 15 and three months.

The journey itself was uneventful. He and some mates volunteered to work in the galley (kitchen). 'It was unpaid, but they gave us apples and other fruit. It helped to pass the time. We were too young to break the bar. Six weeks at sea can be a bloody boring.' He enjoyed the comradeship of the other Little Brothers. 'They were good fellas all.'

In Australia his first job was with a family at Singleton. They too were 'decent fellas', who worked him hard, but treated him kindly. He was disappointed at the low pay of 10 shillings a week – 'just two bob more than I got with the laundry' – from which three pence was deducted in tax.

'From then on if anybody offered me a penny more, I'd take it and be off like a shot.' Consequently, he had six jobs by the time he was 18 or 19.

The Depression struck hard. In 1934 he quit farming and joined the NSW Police, in which he spent 32-and-a-half years, serving in Nowra, Milton and Sydney. He retired in 1966 with the rank of senior sergeant.

In 1939 he brought his mother and two sisters to Australia. He lost his wife, Vida, to cancer in 1986. He has a married daughter, Wilma Sims, and two grandchildren.

In 1990 he went back to England for the first time in 61 years. He found the experience 'disappointing'.

He was proud of having been a Little Brother, and had 'absolutely no regrets' about coming to Australia. He said his motto was 'Life is What you make it'. It served him in good stead.

Tom Moffett was the last of the 1920s' arrivals with whom the BBM had contact. If others are still alive, the BBM would like to hear from them or their families. Because of the economic depression there was a brake on the movement's immigration activities from 1930, when there were a mere 10 arrivals, until 1 March 1939, when a small group arrived on the *Strathallan*.[4]

## THE LAST LITTLE BROTHER

Craig Stuart Wright arrived in Sydney on 27 August 1982. Craig, from Shipley, Yorkshire, was the last Little Brother and – in a manner of speaking – Australia's last juvenile migrant.

He heard about the Big Brother Movement through an advertisement in the (British) Sun newspaper, and thought: 'I'll give this a go. Why did I do it? I don't really know. Perhaps for a bit of adventure.'

He was at the time of his application an apprentice plater welder at Henry Barrett, Engineers, in Bradford. He was then 19. The gap between applying and being accepted took about 10 months. 'They gave me a flight date two days after I was due to finish my apprenticeship, but they brought the date forward because of the problems in Australia. So in theory I didn't really come out of my apprenticeship.

'When I got there [Australia] I was supposed to have been promised a job. I went to this place with about 10 others, but the man in the office said there was no work for us. We were put in a hostel, I can't remember where. A couple of days later I went to Garden Island Dockyard on spec. I asked the bloke on the gate if there were any vacancies, and it fell lucky for me as they were looking for someone that day.'

Craig worked at Garden Island Dockyard, as a boiler maker and welder, for four years. They were happy times. He made 'lots of friends', and shared flats with his mates in Bondi and Maroubra. After four years he got the wander bug and decided to see more of Australia. 'I went to Darwin, had a bit of a look around and worked for a Greek fellow up there.'

He then returned briefly to Sydney, working for Kelloggs at Botany Bay. He met a girl and went with her to her native New Zealand, with the idea that they should get married. 'I didn't particularly like it there, at least not as much as Australia.' The relationship broke up and he returned to Sydney. 'I found all my old friends had gone; they'd moved on. It was like starting from scratch. I think I was also a bit homesick, so I decided to come home.'

Craig Wright returned to England in 1988. He now lives in the Yorkshire village of Baildon and is still working as a welder. When I telephoned him from Australia, he said he was aware of his unusual status in Australia's immigration history and remembered his time here with great pleasure.

'In the past I've looked into the possibility of going back [to Australia], but obviously things have changed. It's much more difficult to migrate now, and of course you have unemployment problems as we do.'

# 6

# Youth Migration – Other Players

# 28

## Scouts, Guides and Friendly Girls

**A**S NUMBERS OF YOUTH MIGRANTS INCREASED – including those sponsored directly by State Governments – more elaborate arrangements had to be made for their reception.

In the early years of the 20th century some 30 groups, in addition to major players such as the Dreadnought Scheme and Big Brother Movement, had a hand in welcoming and settling in newcomers, and sending them on their way to farm schools or direct to places of employment.

Bodies which involved themselves in youth migration included Barnardos, the Boy Scouts, Girl Guides, British Dominions Emigration Society, Board of Guardians for Relief of Jewish Poor, Fellowship of the British Empire Exhibition, Girls' Friendly Society[1], Travellers' Aid, Victoria League, Lions Clubs and both the YMCA and YWCA.

The Barnardos organisation, as previously stated, took in both child and youth migrants, and operated a training farm to assist boys of school leaving age find jobs.

Bill Moverley (1934) was one of those. He writes:[2] 'When I went on the land after Mowbray Park farm school, at 14, we were treated like chattels. One Sunday, I took the pony over the paddocks to the next property to see young John Buxton. He was sitting alone with his head in his hands. He told me that the boss was working him to death, doing 18 hour days. I knocked on the boss's door and asked him why. "Are you a Communist?" he replied.

'One boss only banked two shillings a week for me, which I didn't find out for a long time. Another boss was so disagreeable that I shot a bucket of milk over him and walked off without even changing my clothes. I thought I'd go fruit picking in the next state, but the police always brought you back.'

Even British counties became involved in youth migration. A file in the Australian Archives records (30 April 1929) a scheme by the Kent

Association for Empire Settlement 'for providing passage assistance, out-fits and incidental expenses for certain migrants who proceed overseas under the auspices of the Association.' A group of public-spirited students at Oxford University sponsored youth migration to Australia. It centred on Balliol College, and was helped by the Rhodes Trust.

The degree of involvement by these and other public spirited organisations varied. Some large, international bodies took up youth migration as a sideline. The Scout movement briefly sponsored youth migrants to Victoria[3] and South Australia. Cyril Bavin, general secretary of the Migration Department of the English National Council of YMCAs, saw a role for the Council in assisting Australia House in screening general applications, also in 'solving the difficult problem of assimilating settlers into the life of a new country'

Three representatives were appointed by the YMCA for this duty – one each in Victoria, NSW and Australia. Additionally, the YMCA assisted modest immigration programs of the Methodist and Presbyterian Churches, and directly sponsored an unknown number[4] of 'British boys', aged 15 to 18, into the care of 'private persons whom we guarantee'.

Some major religious denominations were involved in youth migration through affiliates with recognised social welfare agendas.

The Church Army, a uniformed Church of England body, loosely modelled on the Salvation Army, arranged the migration of about 200 British boys, and a similar number of ex-servicemen, for farm work in Australia in the 1920s.

The work was in the hands of two innovative social activists, J.H. Stanley and T.S.P. Pughe. It seems they got on well together, while being temperamental opposites. Pughe was 'fatalistic' and Stanley a man of 'hearty cheer'[5].

Pughe, an Anglican cleric, believed that migration to Australia had become 'the last throw – the last desperate chance.' He wrote: 'It [emigration] is an expediency, not an expectancy. It is an act of despair, and not of hope.'[6]

The Church Army, which was not at that time represented in Australia,[7] offered to act as a 'recruiter' for the Anglican Diocese of Melbourne, which would have responsibility for the young people when they got here. According to correspondence in the Australian Archives the plan, which had the approval of the Archbishop, involved bringing out a monthly quota of 30 lads, aged14 to 18 years; an unspecified smaller number, aged 18 to 20 years; and 30 female domestic servants.

'The lads will be drawn ... from the rural districts of Great Britain and will, therefore, have had some little farming experience.'

A memorandum from the joint Church Army/diocesan committee states: 'Upon arrival it is proposed to again medically inspect these new-comers in order to ensure their physical fitness for the positions allotted to them... Positions will be found for them in various parts of the State, and the Church hopes by this means to assist the Imperial Government in settling her surplus population overseas.'8

The reference to 'surplus population' depicts a common view of Australia as a suitable vessel for Britain's poor and unemployed. A report by the Rev David Garland for the Queensland Church of England Immigration Council takes a more cautious approach.

According to Garland: 'The prosperity of the Empire depends upon the transfer of this excess population to where there is unoccupied land; but it is no use bringing the unemployed from where they belong, to remain unemployed where they do not belong.'

His solution – similar to that proposed by most other bodies includ-ing the Church Army itself – was 'that land should be prepared and farms got partially ready for those who, having had experience, would be suit-able for taking up land immediately on arrival, or for those who, after some testing in England, would be willing to undergo training on their arrival in Australia'.

References to 'surplus' or 'excess' population raise another difficulty in that the groups promoting youth migration faced an understanding sensitivity on the part of the British Government to a perception that the mother country 'could no longer cope' and wished to 'dump' its 'surplus' population elsewhere.

In post-war Britain those anxious to resume child and youth migra-tion faced a similar difficulty, although the diminishing enthusiasm was probably based on genuine ethical considerations.

A letter to Australia House from the Church of England Advisory

Council of Empire Settlement, in September 1949, makes the complaint: 'In spite of the fact that post-war child migration has been in operation for nearly three years, we are of the opinion that Great Britain is not reconciled to the great opportunities and advantages which Australia offers to the children.'

This issue re-surfaced during the child migration controversy a decade ago. The criticism was made that the sending of 'orphan' children to other countries of the British Empire seemed rather like 'depositing refuse in someone else's backyard'[9].

## FAIRBRIDGE

The Fairbridge Farm Schools, though expressly for child migrants, provided a degree of trade training, as suggested by the name, with at least nominal concern for after-care. Some youth migrant organisations – notably the Big Brother Movement in Western Australia – regularly made use of its facilities.[10]

Leon Nelthorpe-Cowne – 'Len' to his friends – was a pre-World War II student at the Fairbridge Farm School, at Molong, near Orange. Len, who now lives in Britain, recalls his entry into the workforce.

'When my turn came to leave Molong as a 16-year-old youth, Ted Heath was the principal, and his remit was as laid down by Kingsley Fairbridge. His question to me was not 'What do you want to do now?' but 'What kind of farming do you want to do?' I didn't really want to do any kind of farming, but 'dirt farming' was out, which left me with cattle or sheep.

'Still romantically thinking of riding the range like my schoolboy heroes, I chose cattle. I was then sent to a cattle breeding stud, where riding the range had never been heard of.

'After about a year of being a slave to pedigree cattle in the cattle yards, where the beasts were more valued than the workers, I realised two things. The first was that I would never aspire to being able to afford a farm of my own; the second was that my parents were being bombed night after night by Germans – a race that I had been brought up to dislike intensely, since my father had served in the Royal Flying Corps in World War I.

'So I joined the RAAF, and after a bit of pleading and wangling, managed to train as an air gunner and be posted to the UK, where I served in Bomber Command on Lancasters.'

When the war ended Len returned briefly to Australia, then decided to settle in England with his English wife. The journey on a tramp steamer took six months.

After unsuccessful attempts to settle into a civilian career – 'having been trained for farming in the wide open spaces of the Australian bush towns' – Len 'gave up', and re-joined the RAF as a qualified air gunner, volunteering for pilot training.

After gaining his wings he qualified on many aircraft, including the various types of Meteor, but was eventually forced to quit with sinusitis, being unable to cope with the high descent speeds. Ted then went into Air Traffic Control, serving in Uganda, Bahrain, and Saudi Arabia, among other countries.

On a recent visit to Australia Len made a nostalgic trip to the old Fairbridge Farm School site at Molong. He was not amused:

'It brought tears to my old eyes to see the floors that I had so assiduously polished on my bare feet until they shone like a french polished table, now covered in chicken manure and rotting away; the huge kitchen, with its anthracite burning stoves, and its floor, scrubbed daily by half-day trainees, until it was clean enough to have been used by a surgeon as an operating table, now covered in filth. All the three original cottages [boarding houses], Green Brown, and Red, have gone – sold off to people who realised the standard of construction, and their current market value.

'My sons have been at me for several years to write it all down for the benefit of my descendants.[11] It may have wider appeal, I don't know. But I have good reason to remember Fairbridge.'

(At the time of writing approaches were being made to the NSW Government to have the main building and some outhouses restored as heritage items. A previous approach was knocked back on the grounds of cost and 'insufficient interest'.)

## CATHOLIC YOUTH MIGRATION

Youth migration, as already stated, was the preserve mainly of secular patriotic or broadly based community organisations, the best known being the Dreadnought Scheme and Big Brother Movement. The major religious denominations generally favoured child migration.

The reasons for this state of affairs are varied. Children from orphanage backgrounds presented an obvious need, whereas school leavers did not. Orphanage children were young enough to be malleable, and, hopefully, raised in the basics of the faith.[12]

If the Australian and Canadian Governments needed teenage farm workers to 'fill the empty spaces', then this, too, was a worthy motive but hardly a pressing pastoral need. On a practical level, many church bodies already had children's homes in which *child* migrants could be put. In the case of the Catholic Church, there were nuns and religious Brothers with experience in childcare.

Caring for the needs of teenagers posed different problems. Trade training, the creation of work programs and hostel facilities were expensive to provide and outside the realm of normal church-related activities.

This is not to say that the major denominations were totally without interest in youth migration. The Westminster Roman Catholic Archdiocese, through its 'Crusade of Rescue', had been involved in child migration to Canada since 1874. In the 1920s Father George Hudson,[13] founding secretary of the Catholic Child Welfare Committee,[14] began corresponding from Birmingham with leaders of Catholic organisations in Australia.

It is said that Father Hudson – influenced by the Dreadnought and similar schemes – initially favoured youth migration, but changed his mind when he realised the almost total absence of the required facilities.

There was support also from the Catholic Emigration Society and one of its key figures, Father C.C. Martindale, a disciple of social justice on the lines advocated by G.K. Chesterton and Hilaire Belloc.

Within Australia an early supporter of both youth and child migration was Brother Paul Keaney,[15] then newly-appointed director of the Christian Brothers' Clontarf orphanage near Perth. Motivated by the success of the West Australian Fairbridge Farm School, Keaney, in association with the local Knights of the Southern Cross, canvassed the possibility of establishing a similar school, mainly for sub-teens, but with the possibility of it being available to older youths, at Tardun, near Mullewa, west of Geraldton.

Financial and other difficulties – notably the refusal of the Federal Australian Government to grant a subsidy – delayed the establishment of the Tardun project.

Meanwhile other players (notably another Christian Brother, Aloysius Conlon) had arrived on the Catholic migration scene, and the mood hardened in favour of child migration.

In reality, there was to be no organised youth migration under Catholic auspices for another 25 years, and then on a limited scale only. The first such effort came after World War II, when Father F.W. Lombard, chaplain to the Young Christian Workers (Victoria), visited the United Kingdom with the assistance of the Australian Government to assess the possibilities of bringing young British Catholic workers to Australia on lines similar to that of the Big Brother Movement.

The Young Christian Workers, generally known by the initials YCW, was founded in Belgium in 1924. The founder, Canon (later Cardinal) Joseph Cardijn,[16] who was himself from a working class background, believed that the dechristianised masses could be reached by deeply committed Catholic laity rather than by priests whom many workers saw, all-too-often, as remote and alien. Workers would witness their faith to other workers and by extension over time Catholic doctors would witness to other doctors and so on.

The YCW was also involved in various facets of Catholic 'social action', in which it clashed with the more politically-oriented *Movement* of the late B.A. Santamaria.

In a letter to the Immigration Minister, Arthur Calwell, dated 28 July 1948, the YCW's national secretary, Ted Long, set out the organisation's immigration goals. They were:

'**Objects**: To foster immigration of suitable young workers between the ages of 15 and 19, and to ensure that each immigrant will be given every opportunity to become a good Australian citizen.

To establish a hostel in or near Melbourne as a well organised clearing house for such immigrants.

To house immigrants at this hostel for a period of up to three months, and during that time help them to become accustomed to the Australian way of life by providing necessary education, to find them suitable employment, and to find them suitable accommodation when they are ready to leave the hostel.

To provide a well-established "Friend"[17] who will take a personal interest in each new arrival, and, as far as possible, take the place of absent parents and friends.

To provide, through our YCW branches, activities that will enable young immigrants to quickly find new friends and practical interests in their new country.

**Method**: The National Executives of the YCW Movement in other countries will set up selection committees, which will recommend to us potential suitable immigrants. Our Executive will consider the recommendations received, and nominate through normal immigration channels those young workers chosen.'

A property in Hawthorn was bought as a hostel, the idea being that it should house some 25-30 youths, mainly apprentices, for a three-month settling in period. There was an 'understanding' that the purchase would qualify for a two-thirds building subsidy. In order to gain the subsidy, the YCW had to gain acceptance as 'an approved organisation to bring youth migrants to Australia'.

Lombard was optimistic that the movement could take in up to 150 youths per year. The Immigration Department was more sceptical, but eventually £12,000 was made available to prepare the hostel, and a further £16,000 awarded to support the British youths.

According to files in the Australian Archives, 49 young British migrants had arrived in a two-year period ending May 1951, and 30 more were awaiting berths. These figures, though presented in an optimistic light, were clearly far lower than the target declared by Lombard. Another six youths (only) arrived in 1952.

The files show that within a few months of their arrival nine of the youths had been apprenticed, nine (others) had jobs with the PMG, and five were working on farms. However, with staff costs and other unexpected factors the Hawthorn hostel was running at a loss.

A letter to the Immigration Minister from the Federal Catholic

Immigration Committee says the YCW was experiencing difficulty in placing youths in suitable employment. Consequently, they were staying in the hostel for a much longer period than was anticipated. Additionally, those who did have jobs were receiving very small wages and could not afford much money for board and lodging.

Because of these problems the YCW announced that it planned to withdraw from youth migration. The decision provoked a certain amount of recrimination, mainly from the Department of Immigration, which thought its money had not been well spent.

Despite a protest from Monsignor George Crennan, director of the Federal Catholic Immigration Committee, who considered the Government mean, the situation resulted in the forced disposal of the Hawthorn hostel (which the YCW wished to use for other purposes) and repayment of a sizeable part of the original Government grant.

Catholic organisations at various times sought to sponsor unaccompanied youths from non-British sources, including the Republic of Ireland. The Government response was unenthusiastic. Only one such scheme – involving young people from Croatia (then Yugoslavia)[18] – received formal approval.

## THE SALVOS – UNDOING SATAN'S WORK

*Migrants: '…the flower of the country that had never had a chance to bloom.'*

One religious body which gave wholehearted support to youth migration was the Salvation Army. The movement, with its highly developed work ethic, saw 'idleness' (arising from poverty and unemployment) as a tool of Satan, and espoused emigration almost in missionary terms.

The Army's founder, General William Booth, had been deeply concerned about the grinding poverty in London. In a book called *In Darkest England and the Way Out*, published in 1890, he found in emigration the solution for the problems of what he called the 'submerged tenth' of the British population.

According to Booth, young unemployed people should be given agricultural training and then sent out to the 'colonies'. These, he said, were 'pieces of Britain distributed around the world'. Hence the emigrant would be quite at home.[19]

The Salvation Army established an 'emigration department', in London, in 1908.[20] The 'Salvos', unlike some other organisations, thought people sent to 'the dominions' should receive training before they left Britain. The Army's existing farm school at Hadleigh, in Essex, was considered ideal for this purpose.

(The Hadleigh farm colony[21] was known as the 'country elevator' – indicating that those who attended were enabled to 'elevate' themselves. The first such centre, the 'city elevator', which taught manual trades, had been established by Booth in Whitechapel.)

In the period 1908-1914 the Salvation Army directly assisted 50,720 people (adults and youths) to emigrate to the Dominions. Regrettably, detailed records – of specific interest to Australia – were destroyed in the London Blitz.

An article in *The Age*, Melbourne,[22] published in 1913, had this to say about the Army's migration activities in the early years of the 20th century.

'It is 10 years[23] since The Salvation Army entered into emigration with characteristic thoroughness and mastery of detail. A special bureau for co-ordinating the system was established under Commissioner Lamb, and the first decade bears witness to the fact that 70,000 Britishers have emigrated under Army auspices. Most of these people have gone to Canada, for the reason that it is much easier and cheaper to cross the Atlantic – and it is not such a wrenching of home ties – than to make the journey of 12,000 miles to the Commonwealth [of Australia and New Zealand].

'[However] many have come out to [these countries] under the same vigilant protection in the confidence that the Army would be able to remove many obstacles in the path of the settler or help him to remunerative employment.'

The article goes on to state: 'It is strenuously denied that these emigrants were in any sense the residuum of civilisation, or that they were recruited from the undesirable class. In many respects they were the flower of the country that had never had a chance to bloom.'

After World War I the Salvation Army's emigration programme resumed on an equal, if not grander scale. It was decided that training should be conducted in the receiving country, in addition to the sending one. In line with this dictum a new 'training camp' was established at Riverview, near Brisbane.

Whilst the emphasis was on men and 'boys' (lads of working age) attention was also paid to the provision of girls and young women for domestic service.[24]

A welfare officer (a non-Salvationist) on the ship, *Manilius*, taking a group of lads to Australia, commented on the difficulties of turning 'cockneys into cowboys'.

He wrote in his report: 'A large proportion of [these] boys[25] are below the standards of weight and height for [their] age...they droop, slouch and smoke too much...for them farm training is desirable.'

The 'new start in a new land' concept has been mentioned before in connection with youth and child migration. To the 'Salvos' this had a special quality. As stated previously, four times in as many years the Salvation Army chartered a ship, the *Vedic*, to bring young migrants to Australia[26].

On all four occasions the departing passengers were given a send-off worthy of royalty. In fact, junior members of the royal family and Government ministers were at the various functions to bid them adieu. The chartered ship departed, for the first time, in November 1925. On board were 90 youth migrants and about 300 adults.

On the day of the day of the departure, according to the Army's newspaper, the *War Cry*, the boys 'marched triumphantly through the heart of London's West End to Paddington Station'. From there by special train to Liverpool, where, following another reception, a brass band accompanied the travellers to the quayside. 'Surely [this] will remain an indelible impression,' the *War Cry* exclaimed.

The newspaper offered the following advice to the young migrants: 'Lads make good! Choose the right, do the right...Serve God – and serve your boss, too!'

According to the *War Cry*, work for the newcomers was guaranteed on farms which had been selected by the Salvos, and an agreement made with farmers for 'a fixed and fair rate of wages'.

(The *War Cry* had a penchant for colourful prose. It wrote of 'Charlie', a 16-year-old passenger on the 1927 departure of the *Vedic*: 'Charlie's heart was gay with hope and strong in the knowledge of sin forgiven.')

The Army insisted on receiving half yearly progress reports on those under its wing, and as part of the deal, agreed to 'stand by' each migrant until he or she was happily settled, and to retain guardianship 'until the boy or girl reaches 21 and has made a suitable start in life'.

After World War II the Salvation Army was eager to re-introduce youth migration. However, the British and Australian Governments were by this time more interested in child migration. In the end only a handful of youths – fewer than 100 – passed through the Riverview training farm during the 1950s. By the mid-1960s the Army was using the place for other purposes.

In the early years of youth migration the Salvation Army is generally considered to have been the leader in its field, in terms of numbers and organising ability. It was also subject to criticism.

According to social historian, Professor Michael Roe, author of the in-depth study, *Australia, Britain and Migration 1915-1940*, there was suspicion in Government circles that the Army was wangling grants from the British and Australian Governments for the same work, and was also exacting from its clients more than pay-back of loans. That the Salvation Army – alone of all philanthropic societies – continued throughout the period to garner commission as a shipping agent intensified such odium.

This arrangement was common in the early years of youth migration. It is said the YMCA was the first philanthropic body to disclaim agent's commission.

## BRIGADIER FRED

Fred Chambers came to Australia, from the Irish Republic via Belfast, in 1927. He was 19 years old. In his own words: 'They were difficult times, work was hard to get.

'From my home I ventured out to Belfast, managed to get a job, but it was not very profitable. The pay was 7s. 6d. a week and I had to pay 10 shillings for board and lodging. Things didn't brighten up, so I applied from Belfast for the emigration scheme offered by the Salvation Army.'

He went to the farm college at Hadleigh, where he was well received. 'In fact, they wanted me to remain there to teach the other fellows.' He persuaded his masters otherwise, and embarked for Australia, with about 60 others, on the SS *Ormonde*.

Fred Chambers remembers his send-off from Northern Ireland. 'I was the only lad leaving from Belfast. The idea was that I should join the rest of the party at Liverpool and board the *Ormonde* there.

'I made the crossing to England in a small boat. When it came to pick me up, the whole of the local Salvation Army Corps and band came down to the wharf and gave me a farewell that I shall never forget. Never, as long as I live.

'It was an ordinary cargo boat, with very little accommodation. When the boat moved off, and the strains of "God Be With You Till We Meet Again" sounded, a gentleman standing alongside me said, "I've never in all my life seen such a tremendous occasion."

'He said to me, "Where are you camping tonight?" I said, "I haven't got anywhere. I've only got a night to last." He said, "You come in with me." He dossed me down with him, and asked: "What sort of a sailor are you?" In fact, I'd never been on a ship. Anyway, when morning came he said, "You're not too bad; you slept throughout".'

The long journey to Australia on the *Ormonde* proved exciting. By coincidence a large group of youngsters had left, about a fortnight earlier, on one of the voyages of the *Vedic*. They were able to make what seemed like a race of it – the first ship to leave going by the slower Cape route, and the second (faster) ship via the Suez Canal. The two vessels arrived almost simultaneously in Melbourne.

On arrival in Australia, Fred was sent to Riverview Farm, the Army's 300-acre training farm, near Ipswich, Queensland. 'We all had to do three months there, but they again wanted me to stay on, and teach the boys. They made me a sergeant, to give me status. They paid me, our meals were good, the Army was very kind. You get people everywhere who complain that this or that doesn't satisfy them, and that's natural, I guess. As far as I was concerned I never had any complaints.'

In Queensland, Fred Chambers worked for two-and-a-half years on the land. By this time he had embraced the religious beliefs of the Salvation Army, which was to change his life.

'My idea originally was that I wanted to have a farm of my own. But I got a call from God that He wanted me. I put forward all the reasons why I couldn't be an officer. Eventually, I thought, Well, if I turn against

God I'm on the losing side; I can't win. I took it as His will that I become an officer. And from then on I had peace. And I've never regretted taking that step.'

Fred began officer training in 1934. Soon after commissioning, he found himself, as a lieutenant, back at the farm college. Several years later he was to return there again, as manager. Several years in children's work and institutions followed. It included service in Salvation Army homes at Dee Why, Bexley and Goulburn, NSW. From 1945 to 1950 he was manager of the Salvation Army boys' home at Indooroopilly, Queensland.

As he became more senior, Fred Chambers managed the accommodation centres known as 'People's Palaces', and became a prison and courts welfare worker in Rockhampton, Brisbane, Sydney and Newcastle. His final position – by which time he had reached the rank of Brigadier – was as manager of the Weeroona Retirement Village, Bass Hill.

His retirement, in 1974, was marred by the death of his first wife, Edith. He subsequently re-married a well-known retired Army officer, Brigadier Enid Lee, a former missionary in Indonesia. Since he migrated in 1927, he has returned only once to the British Isles – to see his parents and to act as escort to another party of British kids bound for Australia.

When I interviewed him he was 'gratified' that most of his professional life had been spent among migrant lads, like himself, and young people generally. 'I wanted to help. It was the thing I felt I could do. I didn't count myself as a preacher.'

He said he was disappointed at the bad publicity given to juvenile migration, and thought there was a misunderstanding in modern minds about discipline. 'Whom the Lord loves He disciplines. And I'm a believer in that.[27] You don't have to be cruel to discipline people; it can be done in a kind way.'

He also regretted the fall in moral standards. 'Things that were frowned upon are now an everyday occurrence. There's no "sin" any more, neither is there proper love in the home.'

Fred and Enid Chambers moved to a Salvation Army Retirement Village, When interviewed for this article he was 92.[28]

# 29

# Europe's 'Tragedy' – Plea for Non -Britons

REFUGEE – in Australian post-war parlance 'reffo' – is an ill-defined term suggesting immigration through circumstance rather than choice.

Unaccompanied (supposed orphan) British children had long been made welcome. Australian institutions were full of them, the idea being that a favour to the mother country[1] would simultaneously help build a white Australia.

When peace resumed after World War II, fears of Asian expansionism and Australia's perceived vulnerability led to a renewed 'push' for migration. Unaccompanied children, teenagers and young adults would again be part of this scene.

The bid to boost population coincided with the desire of thousands of refugees and displaced persons (DPs) to find a new home – preferably far removed from the fighting.

Continental Europe, with its huge number of orphaned children and young people without means of support might have seemed – particularly to those who had visited war zones – an excellent source of recruitment.

It was, in fact, a hard struggle. The Government's attitude, like that of the general Australian population, was ambivalent.

At a meeting on 18 November 1946, the State Premiers had stated their opposition to 'large-scale group settlement of foreigners'. The Immigration Minister, Arthur Calwell, and federal colleagues, while taking note of this, actually produced much milder legislation, although the policy towards unaccompanied juveniles remained conservative.

In an important policy speech[2] shortly after the Premiers' meeting Calwell raised what he called 'the tragedy of Europe's army of displaced and persecuted people'. He suggested that 'on humanitarian grounds' a 'limited number of these people' (refugees) should be accepted as immigrants.

The Minister made clear that he was referring to juveniles as well as adults, and said the Government would pay the cost of their fare.

His reference to refugees was taken up, in an unexpected way, by Rowland James, Labor MP for Hunter (NSW), who suggested that German[3] children might be brought to Australia as child or youth migrants.

It was not the first such approach. While the war was still in progress L.S. Amery, British Minister at the India Office, had suggested that Australia set up more schools on the Fairbridge model,[4] and that they should take in a number of German orphans.

Rowland James, a self-admitted 'sentimentalist', described a visit to the once mighty industrial Ruhr where 'little children now descend into dangerous caverns in the ruins to retrieve what scraps of foodstuffs may remain in wrecked shops.

'I saw children crawling from ruins with blackened dust-covered scraps of sugar, which they licked while they returned to the end of the queue. A man is an inhuman monster if such sights do not move him.'

He said that after previous wars victorious nations, by being harsh instead of generous towards their defeated enemies, had sown the seeds of new wars. 'We may be doing so now.'

Anticipating a hostile reaction, James continued: 'Frequently I allow my heart to run away with my head, but I believe that I voice the sentiments of all British[5] people when I say that we should assist those children. Many of them are homeless, and we need migrants. Our immigration authorities should take action to bring some of them to Australia.'

## YOUNG NAZIS IN GEORGE STREET

Other MPs were predictably irate. There were references to the Hitler Youth and 'young Nazis parading in George Street'[6]. James responded with an anecdote about German children mucking up to British soldiers by goose-stepping behind them. An Australian, he said, would have countered such cheek with 'a good kick in the pants'.

Winton Turnbull, MP for Wimmera (Vic), thought his colleague from Hunter was well-intentioned but his sentiments misplaced. 'Why should people from an ex-enemy country receive preference to people of British stock?' Instead, the honourable member should be welcoming 'our own kith and kin'.

The debate led Leslie Haylen, MP for Parkes (NSW), to suggest a better idea. He said that in Norway there were some 9,000 children who were 'particular victims of German aggression' – the offspring of German soldiers and Norwegian girls. The children were 'ostracised ... unwanted and could be brought to Australia.'

(An Australian Parliamentary committee, headed by Haylen, visited Norway in November 1945, and was allegedly offered 8,000 children[7] The offer was not taken up.)

By coincidence, within a few weeks of the debate in Parliament, an international representative of the Religious Society of Friends (Quakers) made an enquiry to the Australian Mission in Bonn regarding the possibility of supplying German orphans for adoption in Australia. This led the mission to request relevant Adoption of Children Acts from each state in the Commonwealth.

Long delays followed while copies of the Acts were sent from Australia. The mission finally responded: 'In such matters as this in Australia, the states alone are competent'.

Meanwhile, the Department of External Affairs had made similar enquiries to the Australian Military Mission in Berlin and was told: 'Very few German orphans are available who are not properly cared for.' In November 1948, the Immigration Department advised that, in principle, Australia was willing to admit German orphans. In practice nothing came of the proposal.

## GOING DUTCH

It was not the first time a case had been put for non-British juvenile migrants. In 1938 the Territorial Commander of the Salvation Army in Holland, Commissioner Vlas, raised with his British and Australian counterparts the possibility of extending the Army's existing migration program (intended for UK residents wishing to go to Canada and Australia) to include young adults and youths from Holland.

The suggestion was passed to officials of the Department of the Interior, in Canberra, where it was well received. A memo on the relevant file states: 'The Minister indicated that under the migration policy the Commonwealth would welcome the introduction of Dutch people of non-Jewish race.'

In a letter to the Army's Australian leadership, dated 10 June 1938, the Minister of the Interior, John McEwen, formally approved the Dutch request, repeating the unflattering reference to Jews. The letter said the Salvation Army was to be 'responsible for the reception, placement and after-care' of an unspecified number of Dutch youths, 'between 15 and 18 years of age for farm work'.

Permission was subject to a proviso that any youths who proved unsuitable during their first five years in Australia would be repatriated to Holland. World War II intervened before the proposal could be implemented.

In early 1947, Australians were horrified by a report that 12 young children had died in the Bonegilla Camp near Albury, NSW. The deaths illustrated the condition in which some young people had survived the war. The Immigration Minister, Arthur Calwell, said the children had suffered from malnutrition which was 'too far advanced' to heal.[8]

The incident may have had a negative as well as positive effect on the desire to welcome refugees. According to an Immigration Department memo: 'Large numbers of orphans available in Europe probably would be medically unacceptable owing to disease, malnutrition, tuberculosis, mental instability, neurosis and other incapacities of a permanent nature. Many have been uncontrolled waifs on the streets for so long that from the circumstances in which they have been placed they would be problem children unresponsive to authority.'

### GREEKS, IRISH, MALTESE

In February 1950, by which time normal immigration patterns were being renewed, the Greek Consul-General in Australia approached the Department of Immigration to see if Greek teenagers would be acceptable as unaccompanied migrants. A correspondence followed, in which the matter appeared to fizzle out.

Also in February 1950, E.J. Long, Victorian president of the Young Christian Workers, wrote to the secretary of the Department of Immigration, Tasman Heyes,[9] seeking permission for the YCW to sponsor youth migrants from the Republic of Ireland.

The letter stated: 'These are lads between the ages of 14 and 21 years [who are] anxious to come to Australia from Southern Ireland and to whom sponsorship by a recognised Australian organisation would be of considerable assistance. We are in a position to guarantee accommodation to such lads per means of a property we possess in Weatherall Road, Cheltenham, Victoria.'

No number was specified, but the letter suggested a target of 'up to 12 lads every few months as they become available'. The letter promised that 'after a settling down period we will find them suitable permanent accommodation and will arrange satisfactory employment.'

In a less than enthusiastic reply, Heyes knocked back the suggestion on the somewhat technical grounds that, under current legislation, Irish youths – not being British citizens – would be ineligible for assisted passages and, therefore, would have to contribute 'a substantial sum depending upon the type of passage obtained'.

In a separate approach the YCW had also sought permission to bring out youth migrants from Malta. The letter of application stated: 'These young men are English speaking and are prepared to work hard in our country'.

The reply is not on file, but an internal memo, relating directly to the issue, states: 'This department is not desirous of expanding the [existing] scheme under which Maltese are introduced into Australia.' The memo notes that a scheme already existed which allowed the introduction of some 300 Maltese child migrants, aged nine to 14 years, to Catholic institutions run by the Christian Brothers in Western Australia.[10]

## 'ESCAPEES' FROM TITO

In the mid-1950s there was a new interest in assisting refugees, only this time Soviet Russia and her allies were perceived as the threat.

In April 1955 the Federal Catholic Immigration Committee sponsored the immigration of 25 youths, average age 16, from refugee camps in Italy.

All were Catholic Croats who were said to have 'escaped' the oppressive Tito regime in Yugoslavia. The migration took place on the initiative of the committee's director, Monsignor George Crennan. The Immigration Department readily gave its approval.

It was agreed the young people should be settled in Adelaide, where they would be apprenticed or found suitable employment as soon as possible. They were welcomed on arrival by church officials, fellow countrymen and representatives of the Good Neighbour Council. The manager of the Adelaide Catholic Immigration Office, Father Luke Roberts, coordinated arrangements for their welfare.

The presence of 'escapees' from communist regimes in Eastern Europe fascinated the local media, resulting in headlines such as: 'Yugoslav boys for Adelaide'; 'Yugoslav youth seek haven in Australia'; 'Escape from Tito' and (later) 'Croatian boys settling down happily now'.

The young migrants spent their first few days at the Woodside Army camp, while the Good Neighbour Council and the Croatian Catholic Club assisted Father Roberts in arranging jobs and accommodation. The newcomers settled in well and today many are prominent members of Adelaide's well-established Croatian-Australian community.

Some 30 years after the representation by Commissioner Vlas, the possibility of Australia taking youth migrants from Holland was raised again. The setting was unlikely – a citizenship ceremony, in Sydney, attended by Brigadier Sir John Pagan, then president of the Big Brother Movement, and P.R. Heyden, Assistant Secretary of the Department of Immigration. The conversation took place in January 1966.

Pagan told Heyden that the BBM was interested in recruiting young migrants from other than the British Isles. Holland and Germany were mentioned as prospective sources.

It is not known if the conversation was intended to be private, but a note was made by Heyden, who subsequently sought the views of others within the department.[11] Heyden's view, according to documents now publicly available, was that the BBM should be assisted 'in its broader aims', but that 'certain difficulties' arose with Pagan's suggestion.

One of these was that migrant recruitment must, generally, be conducted in conjunction with the overall migration policies of the countries concerned. Migration applications usually resulted from advertising, and some countries might not take kindly to any campaign 'outside the auspices of their own authorities'.

Heyden noted that the BBM sought 'young' migrants, which could cause problems in countries that had restrictions against the emigration of unaccompanied minors. In the department's view permission was only likely to be given if the young person was migrating to join a family member rather than participate in a group scheme such as that organised by the BBM.

The department considered prior knowledge of English important. Although Dutch applicants were likely to have some knowledge of English the knowledge of English amongst other would-be young migrants was 'likely to be negligible'.[12]

A desire to emigrate could also be construed in some countries as a bid to 'avoid compulsory National Service'.

For many years nothing more was heard of the proposal that the Big Brother Movement should take in unaccompanied non-British youth migrants. It appears to have been raised again – though nothing came of it – to help counter Labor claims that the movement's immigration practices were 'discriminatory'.

# Postscript

## YOUNG AND ALONE

*'We left our homes so long ago,*
*To reach a land we did not know.*
*Our hearts were young, our hopes were high*
*To live beneath the Southern sky.'*

VERSE AND SONG are powerful means of expression. The above forms part of a poem which I received, unsolicited, when I first began this project. There was no covering letter, and the sender remains unknown.

The man who penned those words was A.V (Tony) Kibblewhite, now deceased, who came to Australia as a Dreadnought Boy in 1923. The remaining verses, printed below, are also worth reading in that they so vividly capture the essence and spirit of the early immigration movements.

*'The land was wild, the country rough*
*the wages low, conditions tough.*
*At milking cows, we found employ*
*Most Cockies had a Pommy boy.'*

*'As years went by, for many reasons,*
*and just as varied as the seasons,*
*by change of job, and change of station,*
*We played our part to build this nation.*

*Yet we prize our British birth.*
*Still call it "home" across the earth.*
*I think you'll agree with me*
*these lines, our epitaph should be.*
*We love this land of our adoption.*
*To leave, we know, there is no option.*
*She gave us joy, She gave us toil,*
*God give us peace, beneath her soil.'*

338

As recorded elsewhere, the initial goal of the youth migration schemes was to recruit boys for farm work and girls as domestic servants. A high proportion spent their entire working lives on the land. Even among those who did not, there is a strong affinity with rural life. The following verses, penned in retirement by Eden Thompson, offer another example.

> '*I worked alongside the old Bidgee,*
> *For Cockies of different dreams,*
> *Picked fruit and also sprayed trees,*
> *And sat behind stump jump teams.*
>
> *I lumped the three bushell wheat bags,*
> *And smiled when I shouldered the rice,*
> *Trimmed many the jumbucks' dags,*
> *And other jobs that were not so nice.*
>
> *Whatever it was you could name it,*
> *I gave every thing I could a go;*
> *Every thing that allowed me to fit in,*
> *With the people I came to love and know.*'[1]

There is a tendency in today's society to hold up for admiration primarily those who have 'made it' – the rich, the fashionable, the influential, the powerful. This book includes accounts of achievers and those whose material accomplishments were modest. The Australian term 'battler' comes to mind.

An excellent example of an 'achiever' is Steven Paul Bennett, who arrived in Australia with the Big Brother Movement in July 1970. After a short period on a farm in Baldry, NSW, he persuaded his brother John, in England, to join him, and together they formed Benbro Electronics, which has been in business for several years. In 1998 and again in 2003 the company won the Prime Minister's Employer of the Year award.

Steven himself received the Order of Australia Medal (OAM) in 2001 for service to the community. This was after the two brothers formed an organisation known as Employers Making A Difference, which seeks to encourage employers to take on staff with a disability.

Most of the people interviewed for this book are in 'retirement' years, though you wouldn't know it from their active lifestyles. Former

Little Brother David Paris is a behavioural scientist and management consultant living in Denmark, Western Australia. Two years ago, at age 65, he commenced an 18-month contract as Superintendent of Organisational Development at one of the world's top two iron ore mining companies in the state's 'deep north'.

He celebrated the end of the mining venture by taking a holiday trekking, white water rafting and paragliding in New Zealand, followed by more adventures in Croatia and Italy. Is he retiring? Not on your life. As this book went to press he had just registered a new consulting business, focussed on the mining industry. Additionally, he was recently registered as a Bowen Therapy[2] practitioner and is establishing his southwest property as a health resort.

## NUMBERS

The question is often asked about numbers. Just how many youth migrants were there? As previously indicated, stated, confusion in Government circles about defining 'child' and 'youth' migrants makes a response difficult. The two groups were often lumped together, whereas in reality they were quite distinct.

As already indicated, the oldest and second largest (non-government) importer of British lads was the Dreadnought Scheme. Altogether, nearly 7,500 youths came to Australia under its auspices. To be precise 1,787 lads between 1911-1914, and 5,669 between 1919 and 1939, making a total 7,456. It did not resume after World War II. The youngest 'Old Boys' are in their eighties.

The 'Dreadnoughts' were overtaken by the longer lasting and better organised Big Brother Movement, founded in 1925. The BBM, as it now likes to be known, brought out some 14,000 young migrants in a period lasting 58 years. All told a total of 12,264 Little Brothers came to NSW and about 1,200 to Victoria. According to Eddy Steele[3] some 25 per cent returned to Britain, but many of these came back again.

It will be seen from the above that these two organisations alone brought out nearly 21,000 youngsters – easily eclipsing the 'Leaving of Liverpool' kids who have received the lion's share of attention.

As with the child migrants, many of the young people featured in these pages assumed, incorrectly, that the organisations which sponsored them were the sole players in this field. Thus many Dreadnought lads were unaware of the existence of the Big Brother Movement and vice-versa. Documentation about the Dreadnought Scheme is held in the National Archives, Canberra, and in the NSW Mitchell Library. A list of Dreadnought arrivals is held by the BBM, which receives queries about both organisations.

The training farms of both the Dreadnoughts and Big Brother Movement are etched in the collective memories. As described earlier, the former training farm of the Big Brother Movement is now the revamped Fairfield City Farm, also known as Calmsley Hill City Farm, and sometimes by the earlier name, Karmsley.[4] It makes a most attractive gathering for the annual reunions of the 'Little Brothers'.

Scheyville, where the Dreadnooought Lads and some others did their initial farm training, has had a chequered life. Since its occupation by the Dreadnoughts, it has been used by the Army and RAAF (in World War II); later as a migrant hostel (1948-58) initially for European refugees, and for various community purposes. From 1965-73 it returned to former glory as an officer training unit[5] for selected national servicemen, a high percentage of whom served (and some died) in Vietnam.

Its uses since then have been less auspicious. In the middle and late 1970s, an arms dealer used it to store aircraft parts,[6] including near complete Canberra bombers, which he hoped to sell to developing countries. The deal went bust; much of the equipment was abandoned. Visitors claim it is still lying around in rotting crates.

In the 1980s Scheyville was suggested as a site for a new prison and for Sydney's second airport. It was briefly leased to Hawkesbury Agricultural College, now the Hawkesbury Campus of the University of Western Sydney. A few of the original wooden farm buildings are still standing, but have been damaged by time and vandals.

It is helpful to re-emphasise[7] that 'farm lads', once they had completed their initial training, did not suffer the tribulations of orphanage life which was the lot of the child migrants, but they did suffer extremes of isolation, separation from companions, poor housing and low wages, which was almost as bad.

All in all, the British 'farm lads' and teenage girls who went 'into service' led hard lives – many experiencing the full brunt of the Depression years – but triumphed over adversity in ways that many would consider heroic.

The jingoistic language which characterised many of the settlement schemes in the early days has received attention in this book. This should be judged in the context of history and not according to today's quite different viewpoints.

Fear of foreign invasion and a certain romanticism typified in the verses of West Australian poet, Lillian Wooster Greaves,[8] were factors in the demand for youth migration, which was pursued with religious zeal.

Whereas child migration 'fizzled out' (in 1967) through lack of interest by the participating bodies, youth migration schemes continued for at least another decade.[9] The Big Brother Movement is of particular interest because of the later political pressures[10] – a belief that its policies 'discriminated' in favour of British kids – which forced abandonment of its immigration activities.

I found only one former Little Brother who supported the Hawke Government's standpoint. According to Stuart Harris, formerly one of the nation's most senior public servants: 'I think it was reasonable. It was an unfortunate conflict of two different ideas.'

As readers will now be very much aware, the BBM did not 'die', but has lived to fight another day. It is greatly to the movement's credit that it not only survives, but performs community work second to none. 'We brought them out; now we're sending them back,' is a quip sometimes heard.

During the writing of this book I have received letters and telephone calls from people seeking information about deceased or elderly relatives, as well as enquiries of a general genealogical nature. Conversations usually begin: 'We know that grandpa came out on a ship when he was very young…' Such requests for information are a healthy sign. As previously pointed out,[11] the clock is ticking away. In the case of the pre World War II migrants, in particular, the passage of time will soon make it impossible to get first hand accounts of their experiences.

Some have told their stories before – often in self-published memoirs or by way of tape recorded discussions with family members. A typi-cal example is *Blue's Story*, a 40-page attractively illustrated memoir, which I received recently from William Duncan 'Blue' Young, a former Little Brother who has had more adventures than most people have had hot dinner.

'Blue' came to Australia with the last group of pre-war migrants in May 1939. He was then 16. After two years of farming, he volunteered for war service with the RAAF, where he rose to distinction as a flight ser-geant pilot. When the war ended he almost immediately got a job with Qantas, flying on the Brisbane to Darwin run. His work included flying for the then fledgling Royal Flying Doctor Service. From 1949 to 1962 he was a pilot with Trans Australia Airlines, flying mainly in outback Queensland. During this period he handled the delivery flight of a Fokker Friendship aircraft from Holland. After being grounded for medical rea-sons he transferred to a variety of ground jobs with TAA, from which he retired in 1983.

'Blue' was at first hesitant about putting pen to paper – in this case finger to keyboard – but was 'nagged' into it by a female relative, who dis-covered her own father had died without even the officiating minister knowing his first name.

For many former youth migrants their stories, if they have not been recorded in the above manner, will die with them. One who has interest-ing views on this topic is former farm worker turned Qantas steward Ken Tubbs, who, like 'Blue' Young, came to Australia with the Big Brother Movement.

Ken now says: 'I often talk to my grandkids about my early life. In the past, people like the diggers didn't say too much to their kids. Like my brothers who went to the war against Hitler and my father in World War I. They didn't speak about it, so you didn't know what bloody well hap-pened. But I often have a chat to them and tell them about my early years in Australia and that they were happy. I didn't miss England for Christ's sake. I came out and made the most of it.'

Many Little Brothers and Dreadnought Boys[12] subsequently brought out other family members. It is interesting to speculate how many Australians are their descendants. 'Guesstimates' of between half and one million have been cited. In 1979 Professor Geoff Sherington interviewed one of the first Dreadnought Boys, who had arrived in 1912. The sprightly octogenarian said at the time that he had 61 living descendants in Australia.

## MEMORIALS

Australia has six tablets or memorials marking the contribution of young migrants to Australia's European settlement. Some have received brief mention in previous chapters.

First contender is a plaque in Sydney's historic Rocks area, honouring the Dreadnought Boys. The inscription states:

'This plaque commemorates the 5,595[13] Dreadnought Boys who passed this way on their arrival in Sydney between 1911 and 1939, and their contribution to Australia's development. Many served and some died in two world wars. Recruited for farm labour, they branched into a wide range of occupations. A number ultimately achieved community leadership and distinction. Despite early adversities, we who now survive recall our youthful venture with satisfaction, and here record complete affiliation with our adopted land.'

There is a modest plaque, also to the Dreadnought Boys, at Wollongbar Agricultural Research Station, near Lismore. Attached to it is a leather bound book in which is inscribed the names of all the 'Boys' who were trained at the then Wollongbar Experimental Farm.

Another modest contender is a plaque in Fairfield City Farm[14], where it had been re-located from the former Sydney Club. It commemorates the war dead of the Big Brother Movement.

On 6 October 1997,[15] Fairbridge Old Boy, David Hill, formerly managing director of the ABC and before that head of the NSW State Rail Authority, unveiled a plaque at Darling Harbour, on an outer wall of the Australian National Maritime Museum, honouring both youth and child migrants. Charitably, he invited a representative group to help him pull the ribbon.

The plaque is appropriately headed 'They came, young and alone.' It reads:

'Many thousands of young people made the long sea voyage alone to establish a new life in Australia. Some 20,000 youths of working age arrived between 1911 and the 1980s sponsored mainly by privately funded humanitarian bodies. They were in addition to some 50,000[16] younger children, generally regarded as orphans, brought to these shores by charitable and religious agencies between the convict era and modern times. This plaque recognises the contribution these young migrants have made to Australia.'

A footnote records that the plaque was 'donated by the Big Brother Movement, which sponsored the migration of 12,000 British youths, by sea and air, and their resettlement 1925-1982'.

During the past five years building works have caused minor damage to the plaque, which has now been replaced. Several former youth migrants have recorded their names on the museum's 'Welcome Wall'.

As this book went to press arrangements were being made for a sculpture honouring the British child migrants to be located near the main entrance to the same museum. The memorial has federal government funding

A memorial to former British child migrants was unveiled at the West Australian Maritime Museum, by Fremantle Wharf, in December 2004.[17]

Alan Gill, November 2005.

# Appendix 1

**British Boys** By Lillian Wooster Greaves
(From newsletter of Victorian branch of the Big Brother Movement, 1933.)

*The bush in all its beauty,*
*The wheat lands in their pride,*
*The forest in its freedom,*
*The sand plains far and wide –*
*They are waiting, waiting, waiting,*
*With their struggles and their joys;*
*They are waiting to be conquered*
*At the hands of British boys.*

*Australia, land of promise,*
*A prize the wide world knows,*
*Is envied by her neighbours,*
*Is coveted by foes;*
*But she's waiting, waiting, waiting,*
*With her rich rewards and joys;*
*She is waiting to bestow them*
*On the heads of British boys.*

*Her undiscovered treasure,*
*Her yet unlifted gold,*
*The fleet that waits a Jason,*
*The wheaten wealth untold –*
*They are waiting, waiting, waiting,*
*These gracious gifts and joys;*
*They are waiting to be gathered*
*By the hands of British boys.*

*Australia calls her kinsmen*
*Across the ocean blue:*
*'Come! Join us, boys of Britain!*
*Here's wealth for us and you.'*

*We are waiting, waiting, waiting.*
*Come! Share our toils and joys;*
*For the land that bred the Anzac,*
*Is the land for British boys.*

# Appendix 2

## Clothing list issued to Little Brothers (1957)

1 pair plimsoles.
1 hat, light felt, wide brim
(eg. An old scout hat).
2 pairs shorts – khaki twill for
preference.
Swimming trunks
(Above essential for voyage)
1 sports coat and trousers.
1 working coat.
2 pairs working trousers, or jeans.
1 pair best boots or shoes
(not sandals or suede type).
2 pairs working boots
(not too heavy).
1 pair wellingtons, for rural work.
1 rainproof coat or overcoat.
2 pairs heavy socks.
4 pairs light socks.
3 best shirts.
3 best shirts.
3 working shirts (strong khaki
material) with breast pockets.
4 singlets (cotton).
3 singlets (woollen).
3 underpants (cotton).
2 pairs pyjamas.
1 pair slippers.
Dressing gown (particularly if
undertaking an urban occupation).
Handkerchiefs.
Collars.
Neckties.
Cardigan jacket or pullover.
Rug – if available.
2 strong towels.
Hair brushes, comb, tooth brush,
clothes brush, boot brushes.
Shaving kit – if required.

**Farming only:**
3 single sheets, 2 pillow cases –
unbleached calico is suggested. (Note:
Bedding and blankets are provided by
the employer, under the Rural Wage
Awards).

**Town work**
A light travelling electric iron (220
volts) is very useful when working in a
town.
Padlock and key – suitable for a locker.

Two large, strong suitcases and a
knapsack. Large trunks, boxes, etc are
unsuitable. It is much better to have
two large strong suitcases and a knapsack, which can be carried easily, and
are of much more use to you after the
voyage than a large trunk. Your knapsack should contain the necessities for
a few nights' accommodation.

Sheath knives are not allowed in
Australia and must not be taken
aboard ship.

# Appendix 3

## THE 'POLLIES' SPEAK

**HOUSE OF REPRESENTATIVES  5 May 1984**

Hon S.TEWART J. WEST [Minister for Immigration and Ethnic Affairs, Cunningham ALP] – Mr Speaker, I suggest that I take a few minutes to refute the claims of the Big Brother Movement. I refer to its statements in the community and those it has made through its representatives in this House. I say to that Movement that we are not anti-British. We are not pro-Asian and I am not looking forward, as it seems to believe, to the Asianisation of Australia.

Not at all. As I said at Question Time I do note that there is some element of sexual discrimination in the Movement's activities because since 1925 it has brought into Australia 12,000 young males and only one girl. What it was doing might have been all right in the halcyon days when we were bringing in tens of thousands of independent immigrants, but we are not doing that any more. To allow the Big Brother Movement to be an organisation acting outside the parameters of government, determining its own standards of entry, is just not on in a situation of considerably reduced numbers. The former Minister for Immigration and Ethnic Affairs, the honourable member for Balaclava [Ian Mcphee, Lib], well knows all that. On 19 August 1981, he met with the President of the Movement, Brigadier Sir John Pagan, who, I think, used to be the President of the Liberal Party.

The former Minister said that we would not be able to continue with financial assistance to the movement. He further advised Sir John that, because the movement could be seen as discriminatory in both terms of source and its restriction to males, he did not think that new financial arrangements would be acceptable to the Government. The next Minister, the then honourable member for Petrie [John Hodges, Lib] reversed all that. He had my Department send a cable to London which stated that the Big Brother Movement was to interview and process its own nominees; the standards and criteria to be applied were to be decided by the movement; and the movement was not bound to ensure that the qualifications of its nominees would be recognised in Australia.

Quite frankly, I think that should end the debate. We cannot have any organisation choosing and processing its own migrants and putting them up to the Government on an accept or reject basis. We cannot have that. If we do we will have to give the same facilities, if requested, to many other migrant organisations in Australia, including those that represent the Greeks, the Italians, the Yugoslavs, the Asian countries and so on. I hope that I have answered the assertions of the Opposition. I will not accept that what we have done is an example of anti-British or pro-Asian behaviour. I have simply removed the positive discrimination in favour of the Big Brother Movement. It is not an example of anti-British behaviour or pro-Asian settlement. That is simply nonsense.

**HOUSE OF REPRESENTATIVES  7 May 1984**

Hon Peter MILTON , La Trobe, Lib – Has the attention of the Minister for Immigration and Ethnic Affairs been drawn to complaints by the Big Brother

Movement, an organisation previously responsible for selecting and processing its own British migrants, which allege that because the Minister has terminated the favoured arrangements previously enjoyed by this organisation he is guilty of anti-British and anti- European bias?

Hon Stewart WEST – I hope that the Opposition will listen very carefully to what I have to say. I have been recently quite disturbed at the allegations referred to by the honourable member who asked the question. Perhaps it would be in order for me very briefly to tell the House something about this matter and the history of this organisation.

The Big Brother Movement since 1925 has sponsored, selected and processed approximately 12,000 young British lads and brought them to Australia. It has enjoyed a great measure of assistance from the Australian Government because, particularly since the Second World War, it has been part of a program which has been assisted at times. For instance, in 1980 the Big Brother Movement was receiving 50 pounds sterling as part of the cost of bringing people to Australia . It also received an office in Australia House for 140 pounds sterling per year. That is a very advantageous and subsidised arrangement.

Hon Stewart WEST (Clarification) – Mr Speaker. During the early part of my reply to the first question I took today I inadvertently said that an amount of 50 pounds sterling in 1980 was the extent of subsidy by the Commonwealth Government to the person concerned. It was, in fact, the other way around. That is, the person concerned is required to pay a small fraction-that is, 50 pounds sterling, of the cost of his flight to Australia.

## HOUSE OF REPRESENTATIVES  8 May 1984
Hon William M. HODGMAN, Denison (Tas) Lib – To repeat: Without any mandate this Government, as Professor Geoffrey Blainey correctly points out, has adopted the most anti-British stance which we have ever seen in this country. Without any mandate whatsoever, this Government has brought about, and the figures prove it, a substantial reduction in British and European migration to Australia altering dramatically the traditional proportions of Australia's immigration policies which have been so successfully implemented by governments of both political persuasions over so many years.

Without any mandate whatsoever, this Minister and this Government within 19 days of coming to power, took a brutal stock whip to an Australian charity, the Big Brother Movement, by cutting off its support and putting it out of business, notwithstanding the fact that great Australians such as the late Ben Chifley, a former Labor Prime Minister, served on the board of the Big Brother Movement for years and Labor Prime Minister Gough Whitlam and the then Minister for Immigration and Ethnic Affairs, Mr Grassby, to their great credit, continued to fund and support the Big Brother Movement between the years 1972 and 1975.

The vicious attack on this organisation, an Australian charity, is dramatic evidence of this Government's mean minded paranoia and this Government's continuing anti-British bias. The Big Brother Movement has brought to Australia more than 12,500 young people over the past 56 years. Many of these little brothers have grown up to become outstanding Australians and have made a magnificent contribution to this nation. About 200 a year have come to Australia for nearly six decades. But this Minister, autocratically and without any consultation with the Big Brother Movement put it to death within 19 days of his coming to office.

Worse still, for nearly a year he refused to meet with the representatives of the Big Brother Movement, telling them bluntly and arrogantly that the decision was made and that there was no chance of that decision being reviewed, let alone reversed. When finally an appointment was made and representatives of the Big Brother Movement came to Canberra the Minister was unfortunately unable to meet with them in his office but, in fairness, he did condescend to have a brief meeting and drink with them in the non-members' bar after Parliament had risen that evening.

**HOUSE OF REPRESENTATIVES  5 August 1984**
Hon Wallace C. FIFE, Hume, Lib – Does the Minister for Immigration and Ethnic Affairs consider that the 12,500 young people brought from Britain to Australia under the Big Brother Movement for nearly six decades have made a valuable and worthwhile contribution to this nation? Does the Minister believe that the late Ben Chifley was misguided in agreeing to serve for many years as a member of the Board of the Big Brother Movement? Does he believe that Prime Minister Whitlam and the Minister for Immigration, Mr Grassby, were wrong in giving the Big Brother Movement their full and total support in the years 1972 to 1975?
Hon BARRY O. JONES, Lalor, ALP – Mr Speaker, I take a point of order. The honourable member is seeking merely an expression of opinion as to the Minister's view. It is not a matter for which the Minister is administratively responsible. The question is out of order.
Mr SPEAKER – In the initial stage, the honourable member asked a direct question. I believe, with regard to the personalities involved, that he is out of order on those points because they are matters of opinion.
Hon Wallace C. FIFE – Finally, I ask: Where does the Minister claim a mandate to terminate the outstanding and beneficial activities of the Big Brother Movement?
Hon Stewart J. WEST – I certainly do not want to say in any way that I would dispute decisions taken by any of my illustrious colleague predecessors. I simply make the point, and honourable members opposite should consider it well, that the halcyon days of virtually unlimited immigration, when we took tens of thousands of independent migrants, are virtually over.

Only 70,000 people will come to Australia this year. Most of them will come under the family reunion scheme or as refugees. I ask honourable members to consider how British people who might be rejected and do not get through the family reunion assessment system would feel, when, say, up to 200 people are accepted by the Big Brother Movement, an organisation which is outside government, and they get through under the criteria determined by this organisation.

The decision regarding the Big Brother Movement was a government decision. It was certainly agreed to by one of the former Government's Ministers.

That Minister said that perhaps the Big Brother Movement discriminated against the sexes because there was no mention of the little sisters. In 60 years only one female was ever brought into Australia by the Big Brother Movement.

**HOUSE OF REPRESENTATIVES  7 September 1984.**
Hon William.M. HODGMAN – This Minister [the Hon S.J. West, Minister for Immigration and Ethnic Affairs] relentlessly pursuing his ideological commitment to the socialist Left of which he is the titular leader, has acted in an authoritarian manner against organisations such as the Big Brother Movement, an Australian organisation – I repeat, an Australian organisation – which has had the support of every Prime Minister of Australia since 1930 until the present Prime Minister came to power. This Prime Minister and this Minister have treated the Big Brother Movement in a most unjust and disgraceful manner.

# Appendix 4: Time-line
## YOUTH MIGRATION – A CHRONOLOGY
The following time-line shows key events in the history of youth migration prior to World War II.

In **1908** the Salvation Army established an 'emigration department' in its London headquarters. The idea was to save young people and married couples with families from the 'sin' of idleness through unemployment. Unaccompanied juveniles were included from about **1913**.
In April **1911** the first party of **Dreadnought Boys** arrived in Australia. It was the first government-assisted body of migrants, other than during the convict era, to consist exclusively of minors. Most were apprentices and older teenagers.
**South Australia** was the first state to initiate Government sponsorship and guardianship of youth migrants for farm work. The program was inaugurated in **1913** under the Immigration Acts of 1901 and 1913, The traffic was cut short by the outbreak of World War I.
In January **1913** a party of 13 children arrived in Fremantle from England in an experiment of the social pioneer, **Kingsley Fairbridge**.
World War I **(1914-1918)** brought juvenile migration temporarily to a halt. In **1919 Kingsley Fairbridge** went to London in a successful bid to rekindle support.
In **1921** the **Sydney Millions Club** sponsored the migration of the first official group of **Barnardo Boys.** (They were called 'official' in that arrangements were made for their welfare upon and after arrival. Unofficial groups had arrived in 1883 and 1891.) It is said they carried Bibles and promised to read six verses daily. The 40 youngsters arrived in Sydney on 16 October, on the *Berrima*.
In **1922** the Premier of **South Australia**, Sir Henry Barwell, revived a farm apprenticeship scheme which his government had founded a decade earlier. The claimed aim was to bring in 6,000 teenagers to fill the places of the men who had been killed during the war. The first parties were known as **'Barwell Boys'.**

Youths aged 15 to 18 were eligible, and young women aged 18 to 21. They had to agree to be under Government control for three years.

In **1922-1923** the **Tasmanian Government** briefly operated a scheme to recruit young Britons as 'farm lads' in Tasmania. There were complaints that the boys (average age 15) were too young.

In **1923**, the first group of **Barnardo Girls** arrived on board the *SS Euripides*. They, too, were school leavers, considered old enough to get jobs as ladies' maids and similar capacities. Before leaving England they took afternoon tea with Queen Mary in Buckingham Palace. Also in **1923**, the **Fairbridge** scheme was re-instituted in Pinjarra.

The period also saw an expansion in the migration activities of the **Salvation Army**. The Army newspaper, *War Cry:* reported in its issue of 12 January **1924**: 'For some time, the Australian branch of the Army's great Migration Department has been engaged in the transfer to this land of suitable young women for domestic service, and also of war widows and their families, orphans, etc.'

In **1925** a major milestone occurred with the arrival of the first migrants sponsored by the **Big Brother Movement** in NSW. An autonomous **Victorian branch** was formed at about the same time. The Big Brother Movement quickly became the hallmark against which other immigration bodies were judged.

Meanwhile, in **South Australia**, the Barwell Boys scheme had run into trouble, and the program was again temporarily shelved. A modified scheme was put into operation in **1927**. Conditions of apprenticeship were relaxed. A greater portion (approximately one half of the total wages due) was paid direct to the farm apprentice, instead of being held in trust.

In **1927** the **Christian Brothers** Order raised the question of sponsoring Catholic juveniles from Britain and Ireland. Desultory correspondence ensued for several years until, in 1938, Brother Alphonsus Conlon (known to his colleagues as Brother Louis) was sent to the United Kingdom and spent six months finalising arrangements to bring about 100 Catholic boys to Western Australia. They were child migrants, officially regarded as 'orphans'. The first group of 119 boys duly arrived that year.

## SOME STATISTICS

Between **1921** and **1930**, according to information collated by Professor Geoffrey Sherington, formerly Dean, Faculty of Education, Sydney University, altogether 18,131 juveniles were recruited from the British Isles to work on farms in Australia. By far the greatest number (7,299) went to NSW. Next highest was Victoria, with 4,149, and Queensland, with 4,095.

In **1928**, before the Depression started taking its toll, a total of 2,392 farm boys were recruited to Australia. A breakdown among the Australian States is as follows: NSW 1,105, Victoria 480, Queensland 510, South Australia 125, Western Australia 172. In the same year a total of 3,840 adult farm workers were recruited, the highest score (2,150) again going to NSW, followed by Victoria (830).

Nearly all the farm boys recruited in that year had affiliation with one or other of the patriotic philanthropic groups. In NSW the Dreadnought Scheme led with 960, followed by the Big Brother Movement with 120. In Victoria 300 came out with the Big Brother Movement and 180 with the Boy Scouts. In Queensland 300 came out with the Church of England Immigration Council; in South Australia 125 with the Big Brother Movement; in Western Australia 100 with the Young Australia League and 72 with the Church of England .

Organised youth migration ceased, on account of the Depression, in **1931**. It was resumed briefly in **1939**, then curtailed once more, on account of World War II.

## SCHEYVILLE TRAINING FARM

Scheyville National Park is situated about 45 km north-west of Sydney and six km east of Windsor, New South Wales.

It is named after William Francis Schey, a prominent trade unionist and MP, who was deeply involved in the development and use of the site. The area was originally inhabited by the Aboriginal Dhurug people of the Cattai clan.

Since the dispossession of its Aboriginal population, Europeans have used Scheyville in a great variety of ways.

**1802-1893** Nelson District
Common – community use for
grazing and timber supply.
**1893-1895** Pitt Town Cooperative Settlement, a 19th century utopian socialist experiment.
**1896-1910** Casual Labour Farm;
a refuge for the unemployed and
destitute of the 1890s depression.
**1907-1910** 'Boys Town' project: training for rural employment. Settlement is named Scheyville.
**1910-1914** Agricultural Training Farm: Used by the Dreadnought Scheme for training British youth migrants for rural employment.
**1914** World War I internment camp for German seamen.
**1915-1917** Wartime training scheme for women to replace male rural workers.
**1921-1940** Used (again) by Dreadnought Scheme, but interrupted by Great Depression.
**1930s** Depression agricultural
training scheme and refuge for urban unemployed youths.
**1940-1945** World War II training camp for searchlight and parachute units.
**1949-1964** Camp for post-war migrants to Australia.
**1965-1973** Officer training unit during the Vietnam war.
**1974-1996** Annex of the Hawkesbury Agricultural College. Site also used for police training and community activities.
**1996** to present: Scheyville National Park.

# Appendix 5:

## Commonwealth Migration and Settlement Office.

GOVERNMENT AGRICULTURAL TRAINING FARM,
SCHEYVILLE, near Pitt Town, NEW SOUTH WALES.

*REGULATIONS concerning the Instructional Course for Farm Students under the "Dreadnought" Agreement.*

1. Every person desirous of admission to the above farm under the "Dreadnought" agreement must make application on the special form.
2. The applicant, if approved, will be admitted to the farm, and may remain there subject to good behaviour, for three months. When considered desirable, this term may be extended by arrangement with the Director of Labour Exchanges and Immigration, Sydney.
3. "Dreadnought" Students are conveyed to and from the farm once free, and are also provided with free transport by rail or steamer to the station or port nearest their first place of employment. They must pay for any further journeys they may desire to make.
4. Every student must take with him not less than two full sets of clothing; must change his linen and underclothing not less than once in each week; and must wash such linen, &c., during each Saturday afternoon, or such other time as may be set apart for such purpose.
5. Forty-eight hours work must be performed in each week by every student, apportioned in every case as the Manager of the farm may direct. In cases of necessity, any extra work required must be cheerfully performed. Unless in cases of emergency, no work will be required after 12 noon on Saturdays. Students on dairy work must work such hours as are prescribed therefor.
6. Students must cheerfully and promptly execute any orders given them by the Farm Manager or his deputy. They will, as far as possible, be given a turn at every kind of work afforded by the establishment, and will have opportunities to learn how to ride, harness and drive a horse, kill and dress a sheep, milk, feed and look after cows; feed and care for poultry and pigs, plough, harrow, sow, reap, etc., use an axe, take part in gardening, fencing, ringbarking, suckering, etc., etc., when any such work is available. A brief turn in the kitchen assisting in the preparation of meals is included.
7. Whenever the Manager may consider it necessary he may require the students to do all or any cleaning &c., required in any rooms or buildings used by the students or their overseers.
8. No student is permitted to be in any dormitory or room on the farm set apart for the use of persons other than students excepting by permission of the Manager or his deputy. Any student found breaking this rule will be severely dealt with.
9. Students when not at work must confine themselves to such portions of the farm as may be authorised by the Manager.
10. All students must be in their dormitory and in bed by 9-30 p.m. each night, at which time all lights are to be extinguished. Leave to be out till any later hour must be obtained from the Manager.
11. Students may not leave the farm for any purpose whatever, within thirteen weeks of their arrival there without the permission of the Manager. Should any one do so he will be considered as absent without leave, and will not be re-admitted.
12. The Manager will consider applications from students for leave of absence to visit their friends or for other purposes.
13. While on the farm, every student must observe all rules of good order and discipline there in force. Minor infractions will be met with a caution or a fine, but serious or second offences will entail immediate dismissal.
14. No student is entitled to any payment or allowance of any kind excepting food and shelter during his period of residence. "Dreadnought" students may, however, earn a bonus of £1 by good conduct and compliance with the regulations.
15. No student shall, under any circumstances whatever, bring, or have in his possession while at the farm, any fermented or spirituous liquor or wine. Any firearms must be handed to the Manager immediately on arrival (any person carrying firearms in New South Wales without a gun license is liable to a penalty of £10).
16. Any student who has any fault to find or request to make concerning food, accommodation or work, or matters appertaining thereto, shall do so to the Manager, who will at once decide any point which may be raised.
17. Any student who may consider himself aggrieved by any decision of the Farm Manager may appeal to the Director, either personally or in writing. The decision of the Director shall be final and conclusive in all matters.
18. A certificate of competency and conduct will be issued to every student who completes a satisfactory course, but not otherwise. No certificate will be issued to any student who goes to employment without the consent and approval of the Director. No reason will be assigned for any refusal to grant a certificate in any case.
19. Any student who breaks his agreement will :—
    (a) Forfeit all claim (if any) to any bonus which may have accrued;
    (b) Be called on to repay the whole of the assistance granted by the Government and the Trustees of the Dreadnought Fund towards his passage.

*For further particulars apply to—*

THE DIRECTOR OF MIGRATION AND SETTLEMENT,
Australia House, Strand, W.C.2.

# Notes

## Chapter 1

1 In particular Philip Bean and Joy Melville's *Lost Children of the Empire*; Margaret Humphreys' *Empty Cradles*, and Alan Gill's *Orphans of the Empire*.

2 See Chapter 21.

3 A delightful phrase, whose 'cattle yard' overtones appeals to writers. (See bibliography).

4 'Boys to be farmers and girls farmers' wives'.

5 See Alan Gill's *Interrupted Journeys – Young Refugees from Hitler's Reich*.

6 See Michael Roe *Australia, Britain and Migration 1915-1940* (Cambridge University Press)

7 Kingsley Fairbridge died on 19 July 1924.

8 Often referred to as Dreadnought Lads.

9 About 1,500 Barwell Boys arrived in Adelaide, and were duly moved out into rural areas, in the first two years' of the scheme's revival.

10 The organisation (to the annoyance of some) has dropped the former apostrophe.

11 A difficulty arises over whether migrants brought out as juveniles by the various organisations should be described as 'Dreadnoughts', 'former Dreadnoughts', 'Little Brothers', 'former Little Brothers' etc. On the basis that Old Etonians are called 'Etonians' and former Presidents of the US are still 'President', this book uses both literary styles.

12 As indeed, some of them were.

13 Charles Atlas – 'You too can have a body like mine.'

14 Some sources claim this figure includes the numbers recruited in 1922-23.

15 Now known as Big Brothers Big Sisters of America. See Chapter 19.

16 See Chapters 28, 29.

17 Some sources claim the Depression continued until the start of World War II.

18 They are often confused with child migrants. Their stay was supposedly short-term, but many remained permanently. See Bibliography.

19 A broad term that was often inaccurately applied.

20 A scheme involving the re-settlement of Polish children was particularly successful. See 'Children of Pahiatua', *Orphans of the Empire*.

21 See note 18 above.

22 It is not clear if the Fairbridge (Pinjarrra) Farm School took children from that first voyage.

23 See *Interrupted Journeys*. A solo migrant, Tom Keleman, arrived on 19 July 1947.

24 See Chapter 13.

25 Other records held by Barnardos say there were nine children and two adults.

26 The school struggled on – as a privately funded agricultural school for young Australians – for a further seven years, finally closing its doors in December 1973. The companion Fairbridge Farm School in Pinjarra, by now taking children from single-parent Australian families, closed in December 1981.

27 Optimism proved misplaced. The last Barnardos party, comprising seven boys, arrived in Sydney by air on 9 October 1965.

28 See Chapter 18 and 19.

29 The Immigration (Guardianship of Children) Act (31 December 1946) Section 4 includes the following definition of 'immigrant child'. '... a person under the age of 21 years who comes to Australia as an immigrant otherwise than in the charge of, or for the purpose of living in Australia under the care of, any parent or relative of that person.'

30 In a case known to the author an ethnic communities council successfully sought a grant to prepare a history of 'child migration' based on just such a misunderstanding.

31 Farm School was part of the Fairbridge title.

32 A term beloved of cartoonists, sometimes written as 'noo chooms'.

33 Ivan Visontay, writing in relation to Holocaust survivors featured in *Interrupted Journeys*.

## Chapter 2

1 Producer of *Triumph of the Will* and the official record of the 1936 Olympic Games.

2 Lillian Wooster Greaves was born in Melbourne but spent much of her life in the Perth suburb of Leederville, where she became an authority on the wild flowers which featured in her popular verse. Her poem British Boys is printed in full in an Appendix.

3 J.A. Alexander, a journalist on the *Sun News-Pictorial*, Melbourne.

4 I was touched and a little surprised, when, soon after my own arrival in Australia in 1971, I heard elderly people, who had never been there, refer to England as the 'old country' or even as 'home'.

5 From *The Life Story of J.J. Simons, Founder of the Young Australia League*. (Halstead Press, Sydney) 1961.See also Chapter 14.

6 Considered by many to be a racist and anti-semite, with strong views on immigration issues.

7 Delivered to Federal Parliament on 22 November 1946.

8 See *After Barnardo*, by Ann Howard and Eric Leonard (Tarka Publishing).

9 These experiences of Philip Norton were first recorded by Blanche Charles in Britain's *Family Tree* magazine.

10 The letter dated 24 November 1924 is still in Government archives.

11 Whose name, but not address, has been preserved.

12 Letter dated 22 September 1925.

13 The Government was then taking 15-16 year-olds.

14 The Great Depression is usually dated from the collapse of the US stock market on 24 April 1929.
It ended in 1933, but its effects continued until the outbreak of war in 1939.

15 Wilson and others were upset that when the Dreadnought Scheme folded, as a result of World War II, the trust's remaining assets of about £20,000 were transferred to the Fairbridge Farm Trust, which, ironically, was later the subject of similar complaint.

16 See *Australia, Britain, and Migration, 1915-1940*, by Michael Roe (Cambridge University Press)

17 Ibid

18 Ibid

## Chapter 3

1 See Diane Armstrong's *The Voyage of Their Life* (HarperCollins/Flamingo).

2 See *Interrupted Journeys*.

3 See account in *Orphans of the Empire* of the child who asked if she would be back in England 'for tea'.

4 One Little Brother has dutifully retained his first menu, complete with the word 'sausages' underlined.

5 Veteran escort, see also Chapter 13.

6 In *Orphans of the Empire* David Hill tells how, on their first day at sea, he and other working class lads charged into the dining room, when 'tea' was called, scoffing themselves silly; not realising that another evening meal would be called, some two hours later, known as 'dinner'.

7 Actually there was plenty of both.

8 See *Australia, Britain and Migration 1915-1940*, by Michael Roe (Cambridge University Press).

9 Maxine, who was eight, was not strictly a juvenile migrant as she was travelling with her parents. Her father, Isaac Norman Goodman, was for many years secretary of Sydney's Great Synagogue.

10 See Note 8 (above).

11 See Fred Wolstenholme – A Passiona Romance, Chapter 10.

12 See *Interrupted Journeys*.

13 See *They Passed This Way, Stories of the Dreadnought Boys*.

14 Sir Alan Walker died on 29 January 2003.

15 The Fairbridge scheme (See Chapter 1) took only youngsters below school leaving age.

16 He had been forced to quit, as a Naval flyer, following a back injury.

17 There was a further argument about £300, which David had deposited in the purser's safe (for which he had a receipt) and which had gone missing. It was suggested that he had pulled a scam and had taken the money before leaving the ship at Aden. David pointed out that he was unconscious at the time. He finally got the money after saying that a journalist friend planned to run the story as a "David v Goliath" feature.

18 David Paris subsequently became a successful businessman, teacher administrator, lecturer, and entrepreneur.

19 The *Diomed* left Liverpool on 17 September 1940. The *City of Benares* was attacked and sunk on the same date.

20 Out of 406 people on board the *City of Benares*, 256 died, including 77 of the 90 child evacuees. A graphic account of the incident is given in *Finest Hour*, by Tim Clayton and Phil Craig (Hodder and Stoughton).

21 The *Arandora Star* was sunk on 2 July 1940. The attack is often confused with the

sinking of the *City of Benares* (See above).

22 See *Orphans of the Empire*.

For resource material about the migrant ships see Bibliography. I am grateful for assistance received from Bruce Miller, Peter Plowman, Philip Simpson, Marion Carter and Geoffrey Sherington.

## Chapter 4

1 The committee had about a dozen members.

2 See Chapter 28.

3 See Chapter 18.

4 As previously stated, it is not known what percentage were juveniles.

5 See Chapter 3.

6 Professor of History at the University of Tasmania. His book *Australia, Britain, and Migration 1915-1940*, quoted in this chapter, is a 'must' for any student of migration.

7 Stories abound, on other vessels, of the sexual adventures of stewards, some of whom followed their favourites (male and female) to remote parts of Australia.

8 Correspondence in Sydney's Mitchell Library, cited by Roe.

9 The Big Brother Movement's farm was (as will be explained) for boys only.

10 Assisting youth migrants was not a primary goal. Hence the Fairbridge organisation has received limited attention in this volume. (See *Orphans of the Empire* for information on child migrants.)

11 See *Orphans of the Empire*.

12 The same applied to school leavers brought out initially as child migrants.

13 The Barnardos hostel.

14 From *Emigrants and Empire, British Settlement in the Dominions Between the Wars*, by Stephen Constantine.

15 There was an affinity between Royalty and Barnardos. See *Orphans of the Empire*.

16 Lily Hooper died, aged 93, in 1999.

17 See Chapter 3.

18 Ibid.

19 See Chapter 28.

20 In the 1960s a row arose about a Barnardo girl who did well at school and wished to become a doctor. She got her wish.

21 It is claimed that some girls may have forgotten the custom of holding back a portion of their wages in a compulsory savings scheme.

22 Stan Allen (the first Barnardo Boy to be appointed manager of a facility) and Tom Price are deceased.

## Chapter 5

1 A cart with flaps that could be let down like a trailer.

2 Sir Ronald and Lady Cross were on leave in England, travelling in the wake of Queen Elizabeth, who had just completed her first – and famous – Royal Tour.

3 Sir Ronald Cross (1896-1968) was a British merchant banker, turned Conservative Party politician. He was appointed Minister of Economic Warfare at the outbreak of World War II, and became well known for his efforts to bring about the economic isolation of Germany. In June 1940 he was made Minister of Shipping in Winston Churchill's Coalition Government and at the time of Dunkirk gave a famus speech in which he encouraged anyone with a sea-worthy boat to set out and 'save our boys'.

He was created a Baronet in 1941 and the same year succeeded Sir Geoffrey Whiskard as British High Commissioner to Australia. It was Churchill's initiative at that time to send politicians he knew and trusted to key Commonwealth countries to help liaise with the war effort. Subsequently Sir Ronald started the Food Parcel Scheme, which continued until well after the war. At the end of his term in 1945, he returned to England ahead of his family to fight the election, which he lost due to the huge swing to Labour.

In February 1950 he was re-elected to parliament, but retired a year later in order to become Governor of Tasmania. He held office from August 1951 until June 1958, when he retired and returned to England. He died on 3 June 1968, in London. Mount Ronald Cross in western Tasmania is names after him.

4 She was accepted without an interview, a sign of more trusting times.

5 According to Bridie, she came out with the Queen 'just to make sure everything was run properly'.

6 In 1966 Susanna married Francis Sitwell, public relations executive, patron of the arts, clubman, political networker and (then) younger member of the famed Sitwell 'brood' of literary 'stormy petrels'. The family included Edith Sitwell, poet, biographer and eccentric, her brothers Osbert and Sacheverell (Susanna's father-in-law), all of whom enlivened the London literary and artistic scene from the 1920s until late in the last century. Francis Sitwell died in January 2004.

## Chapter 6

1 Still the preferred term by the majority of those who have been in the organisation's care.

2 They were to correspond for 20 years. To this day Kathleen refers to her as 'my foster mother' rather than 'Mrs Masters'.

3 Her word for being 'put down'.

4 One of two senior superintendents.

5 Now Westpac.

6 Later, as she got older, there was a 2s 6d pay rise which also went back to Barnardos, and was banked. It was this sum put aside which enabled her to take her business course.

## Chapter 7

1 22 October 1995.

2 For a description of this unusual woman, see Chapter 13.

3 Thomas Sedgwick, a good friend to the

Dreadnoughts. See Chapter 13.

4 The first donation recorded was from A. Johnson and Priscilla Johnson of Glebe, for 10 pounds, 10 shillings. The largest single donations were from Sir Samuel Hordern, A.A. Dangar, Walter D. Hall, Sir Samuel McAuchay, and Dame Edith Walker, each of whom gave 10,000 pounds.

5 See note in Chapter 1.

6 See also Appendix 4.

7 See Chapter 21.

8 ie. private schools.

9 Some Old Boys disagree. See comments by Bill Wilson, Chapter 8.

10 In Australian parlance fee-paying private schools.

11 See comment by Bill Wilson in Chapter 8.

12 Resulting from this decision, at dinners and similar gatherings those who came out under the scheme were subsequently referred to as 'Original Dreadnoughts'.

13 Including a page about Dreadnought activities in the movement's journal.

14 George and Edna Oakes, on behalf of the Sydney-based association, handed over books, badges and key rings, plus a cheque for $1,300, representing the association's assets.

## Chapter 8

1 Author of Australian Archives reference book *Good British Stock. Child and Youth Migration to Australia.*

2 At the time of writing (2005) the youngest is 83, the oldest 98.

3 See Chapter 3.

4 A two wheel cart without springs.

5 Two shillings and sixpence. A fine inflicted for failure to perform duties adequately.

6 Wilf's experiences are taken from *They Passed This Way, Stories of the Dreadnought Boys*. Wilf Bennett died in October 2000.

## Chapter 9

1 Jack Easter, Country Party MLA for Lismore from 1953 to 1961. He died in 1978.

2 See Preface and Chapter 12.

3 References: *The Ironworkers - A History of The Federated Ironworkers Association of Australia*, by Robert Murray and Kate White (Hale and Iremonger); and *Laurie Short: A Political Life*, by Susanna Short (Allen and Unwin in association with Lloyd Ross Forum).

4 See Postscript. Eden Thompson died on 21 August 2005.

5 Ralph Wood died on 25 January 2004.

## Chapter 11

1 The phrase, which inspired the title for this book, inspired the title for Norman Monsen's own typewritten autobiography, also textual material by Professor Geoff Sherington, now in the NSW Mitchell Library.

2 His mother visited her son in Australia in 1950.

3 Norman Monsen died on 6 February 1995.

4 Farmer, landowner, boss.

5 Now the Commonwealth Scientific and Industrial Research Organisation (CSIRO).

6 In Earlstone Park, Wallasey.

## Chapter 12

1 Most sources cite 845 Australian servicemen and 208 civilian prisoners. Some sources claim a higher number of military prisoners and a total of 1,503.

2 See description in preface.

3 For the record, 12 Methodists, three Catholics, two Seventh-Day Adventists. For general reading I recommend *Whereabouts Unknown*, by Margaret Reeson (Albatross Books).

4 See autobiography *This Crowd Beats Us All.*

5 Recorded in *Yield Not to the Wind*, by Margaret Clarence.

6 Sydney Beazley, a builder and technical instructor with the Methodist Overseas Missions.

7 He was followed in this role by an Anglican clergyman, Canon Arthur Rawson, then Rector of St Matthew's, Windsor, who shared his enthusiasm for the cause.

8 10 February 1993. He was 86.

## Chaper 13

1 Also known as the ANZAC League of Women.

2 The building was itself a former pub, the Royal Hotel.

3 Material about Dr Mary Booth is housed in Sydney's Mitchell Library. See also *Dr Mary Booth*, by I.L. Marden (1957), and *Biography of Dr Mary Booth*, by R. Mackinnon (1970).

4 I am grateful for information about Sedgwick supplied by Dr Stephen Constantine, of the University of Lancaster, UK. Sedgwick's personal papers are housed in the Royal Commonwealth Society Collection, Cambridge University Library.

5 See also Chapter 21.

6 Of obscure origin, possibly describing a 'rushing' (booming) full-grown kangaroo. 'Boomer' came to be applied to someone very active, or who excelled in several spheres.

7 Companion of the Gold Cross of the Holy Sepulchre.

8 A similar Church of England body established in NSW brought out 700 young migrants in 1924-1925.

9 These figures may be unreliable. In another report, by the same Church of England Immigration Council, Garland claimed to have brought out 4,000 'farm lads' from 1921-1930.

10 Garland ensured that as ANZAC Day was a civilian tribute, the commemoration committee should be made up of civilians. The Returned Sailors and Soldiers Imperial League of Australia under Sir Raymond Hewish only gained control of the committee and thereby of ANZAC Day in Queensland in 1935.

11 He incorporated the wing and the lion of St Mark, because St Mark's Day coincided with ANZAC Day.

## Chapter 14

1 There is some doubt about this. *The Australian Dictionary of Biography* says Simons was apprenticed to a tinsmith.

2 According to a booklet, *Tell Me About It*, by J.J. Simons.

3 He had put on his first 'theatre' production, with his friends as paying customers, in a shed near his home at the age of nine.

4 To close friends, who may have considered the use of initials a mouthful, he was 'Jack'.

5 The present design was approved by the King's father, Edward VII, in 1903, and the Commonwealth Star added in 1909.

6 Including the Rev David Garland (above).

7 A division, with responsibility for the entire Eastern States, was established in Sydney, and later transferred to Brisbane.

8 Old Boys could also become life members or reserve officers, called upon to assist in running tours and other activities.

9 Simons said later that he regretted this had not been done earlier.

10 The American-born designer of the City of Canberra.

11 It is believed Griffin himself never visited Western Australia.

12 Regarded at that time (and possibly today) as the biggest travelling group of boys in history.

13 Subsequently the ill-fated Duke of Windsor.

14 In Sydney some League members had

parents active in the New Guard movement, which drilled in the streets with wooden rifles, and was politically of the far right.

15 Araluen, a holiday retreat near Roleystone, on the Canning River, was built by volunteers in the 1930s. Its main feature is the Grove of the Unforgotten, a memorial to the League's war dead.

16 It is not known if the hapless vendor, who had to wait six months for his money, took the ice cream to them there.

17 See *The Life Story of J.J. Simons, Founder of the Young Australia League*, by Victor Courtney (Halstead Press, Sydney) 1961.

18 By Lyall Hunt.

19 Later reduced to £200.

20 *Love, Service and Tolerance. A Commemoration of 100 Years of the Young Australia League*, by Max Ball.

21 By coincidence a photo of the band, with one of the five mascots, is the cover for the ABC Classic FM CD, *Strike Up the Band*!

## Chapter 15

1 Many within the club, including its first president, Arthur Rickard, wanted an even higher figure.

2 See Chapter 16.

3 In 1920, of seven knighthoods conferred, six were club members.

4 There is confusion about this. See Chapter 16.

5 The Millions Lodge closed in 1973.

6 The immigration of 'orphan' children had actually ceased.

7 Lois Butcher stayed with Barnardos over 50 years. She died in January 1994, having become a legend in the movement's Australian history.

8 Currently (2005) the ground floor and basement are used as a bar, with offices above.

9 The author is grateful for permission to use material from *From Millions to Sydney*, by John Alpen, published privately by the Sydney Club.

## Chapter 16

1 In its earlier days as the 'Big Bros'.

2 The famed exhibition helped launch groups such as the Big Brother Movement and gave a fillip to the 'empire cause' generally. Follow-up material included a *Weekly Bulletin of Empire Study*, which was used as a classroom teaqching aid.

3 Presumably both were attending the empire exhibition in Britain.

4 See *From Millions to Sydney*, by John Alpen. Also chap 15.

5 From *The New Australian*, magazine of the Victorian branch, May 1928.

6 *Big Brother Movement* 1925-1987, an informative 48-page publication, includes a reprint of the Big Brother Movement's golden jubilee booklet, published in 1975.

7 In fact, the Salvation Army, Dreadnought Scheme and some state governments were already bringing out British school leavers and others who went, after a brief period of induction, directly into the workforce.

8 See Preface.

9 Memo dated 15 December 1925.

10 This philanthropic body sought at one time to establish a branch of the BBM in Western Australia.

11 See Chapters 1 and 20.

12 See Chapter 25.

13 The Orient Line was a pillar of WASP society. According to Philip Simpson, interviewed in *Orphans of the Empire*, only two Catholics were employed, one a nephew of the other. Even to be a humble clerk a GPS background was preferred.

14 A political protest, apparently on behalf of the right wing New Guard movement.

15 The 8th annual report in 1934 showed

that, of those still in contact with the movement, 241 were employed on the land in NSW, of whom 17 owned or leased farms, 15 were share farming and 13 were contractors.

16 Ken was himself a 'Little Brother'.

17 It's a touchy point. Ken Johnstone emphasises: 'No one could get through without the immigration people giving it the rubber stamp.'

18 Whose statement of support is quoted above.

19 See Chapter 18.

20 For a description of duties see Frank Mansell, Chapter 23.

21 : ie. with the focus on school leavers and apprentices.

22 See above.

23 The report also noted that five former Little Brothers had recently enrolled as Big Brothers.

24 See Chapter 20.

25 Interestingly, one of those involved in its inspection and purchase was Roland Paxton, farm superintendent of the Barnado's farm at Picton. Paxton was himself an ex-Little Brother.

26 The sign at the entrance said 'War Memorial Training Farm'.

## Chapter 17

1 Little Brothers of the early post-war period also remember with affection Bob Girvan and his wife, Jean, who served effectively as manager and matron for 11 years.

2 Captain Millar retired in 1949 and was succeeded by Frank Mansell.

3 Later revitalised as site for the 2000 Olympic Games.

4 David Paris came to Australia on board the *Otranto* in April 1955.

5 Seasonal work, involving moving from one part of the country to another, and employment in circuses and travelling

entertainment shows was officially forbidden to Little Brothers.

6 The proportion of Little Brothers seeking occupations other than farming rose gradually from 25 per cent in 1955 to 42 per cent in 1964.

7 It is estimated some 3,000 lads stayed there, free of charge, in the 14 years of its existence.

8 See Chapter 18.

9 Also awareness of a decrease in the number of applicants.

10 Mansell himself, being deceased, cannot be questioned.

11 See also Chapters 18 and 29.

## Chapter 18

1 Now deceased. See Chapter 23.

2 This is denied. See reference to 61st annual report (below).

3 It is possible Grassby changed his mind. See below.

4 Published 6 September 1984.

5 Mansell's statement seems to have overlooked a modest Commonwealth Government Equipment Grant, which was $3,540 in 1983 (when it was cancelled). The cost of running the scheme was then estimated at $109,000 a year.

6 See footnote above.

7 Deputy Leader of the Liberal Party in the Legislative Council, and special adviser to the Opposition Leader on ethnic affairs and the arts.

8 Eddy was a Qantas steward. See Chapter 23.

9 Malcolm Fraser, Liberal Prime Minister, who lost to Labor in 1983. Although not then regarded in this light, he is now distinctly left of centre.

10 Al Grassby, former Immigration Minister, at that time Commissioner for Community Relations.

11 Professor Geoffrey Blainey, the eminent historian.

12 The news magazine of the Returned Services League.

13 See Chapter 17. Ken Johnstone is adamant: 'We never looked at it from the point of view of the colour of a person's skin. We're a non-sectarian, non-political organisation.'

14 Stewart West, Immigration Minister.

## Chapter 19

1 Current BBM chairman and former treasurer.

2 Jock McAusland, died in December 2000.

3 Nicknamed, appropriately, by the British media 'Kewell the Jewel'.

4 David Lee now advises the BBM under the auspices of his own company, *NSW Soccer Coaching Services.*

5 The Australian senior national team.

6 One English tabloid, annoyed at the win, suggested that all 11 England players should be 'transported to Australia'.

7 BBBSI is involved in technical support, training and volunteer assistance programs in several countries, including those formerly part of the Soviet Union.

8 Young Women's Christian Association.

9 Successor to Gunning House.

10 Formerly the Millions Club. See Chapter 15.

11 Rickard's precise role is unclear. The BBM credits Sir Richard Linton as having provided 'the inspiration and drive' for the establishment of the Big Brother Movement. Neither man sought membership of the committee formed to run its affairs.

12 Now the preferred term.

13 Sponsored by Fairfield City Council and the Department of Urban Affairs and Planning.

14 Now defunct.

15 Apparently, several names could not be found, and were therefore omitted.

16 Regrettably, it may also lead NSW in a less desirable direction. As this chapter was being written, Fairfield City Council was under a considerable stain following allegations that council members, including the mayor, had maintained connections with former councillor, Phuong Ngo, jailed for life for ordering the 1994 murder of political rival and local MP John Newman, in what was described as Australia's first political assassination.

17 The name, British Boys' Movement, was also adopted by BBM in Perth. See Chapter 20.

18 Milligan's discovery led to a 30-year association with the Big Brother Movement, as a result of which he now on the drama selection committee of the BBM awards scheme.

19 In the genre of 'Reality' television. According to one newspaper description of the Channel 10 show: 'New inmates in the Gold Coast house drink, bum dance and vote each other out.' A *Daily Mail* columnist described watching the British version of the show as like 'ogling the inmates of Bedlam'.

20 Eddy Steele put it thus in a circular to Little Brothers: 'Unfortunately, with the combination of the *Big Brother* TV show, Brother office machines and George Orwell's *1984*, it was [considered] highly unlikely we would get an objective hearing for any presentation we might give to the corporate sector.

## Chapter 20

1 In a letter to Mr P.R. Heyden, Assistant Secretary, Department of Immigration, Frank Mansell said neither Sydney nor Melbourne was 'a branch in the true sense of the word', and that the term was used ' as a matter of facility in writing'.

2 In Australian parlance, private or GPS schools.

3 See Chapter 21..

4 Quoted in *The New Australian*, May 1928.

5 See Chapter 16.

6 Later Prime Minister.

7 In the absence of records, material for this section is taken largely from papers in the National Archives, including a memoir by Frank Mansell, executive director of the New South Wales BBM.

8 A practice it had done in the 1920s.

9 Or so it is thought!

10 Father of the famed athlete.

11 This, too, displeased the Sydney office, which was not consulted..

12 Two youths, presumably travelling independently, had arrived earlier; making a grand total of 11.

13 The Rt Rev Howell Witt, who caused mirth by saying he had been a migrant for 20 years.

14 A grand total of 169 or 171 (the exact figure is unclear).

15 Hamish Guy Valentine

16 Published under the catchy title *Good British Stock*. I am grateful to Laura Williams for her consideration.

17 Just by whom is unclear.

18 Named by Laura Williams.

19 Correspondence with the Sydney office continued until 1968.

20 The longest-running was Tresca, a Fairbridge Farm School, described in detail in Laura Williams' thesis.

21 Shearer's tool with comb and cutter attached.

22 'Dad', a local identity, died in Jauary 2004 aged 99.

## Chapter 21

1 This somewhat overloaded body had 39 people described as vice-presidents.

2 Possibly an exaggeration.

3 ie. private schools.

4 From *Australia, Britain, and Migration, 1915-1940*, Michael Roe (CUP).

5 Possibly an affiliate of the training college.

6 Ibid.

7 R.T. Appleyard and C.B. Schedvin, Australian Financiers, *Biographical Essays*, Melbourne 1988, as quoted by Michael Roe.

8 In 1928 Darling led an (English) public schoolboys tour of New Zealand. An Australian tour was to follow, though it is not clear if it took place.

9 Letter to interested parties dated 28 February 1925.

10 *Argus*, 14 December 1925.

11 May 1928. The writer of the article, W.M. Buntine, was headmaster of Caulfield Grammar School, Victoria.

12 Old Boys include Field Marshal Viscount Montgomery.

13 In practice, like many Big Brothers, he did little to help him.

14 Presumably a reference to their language.

15 Which were lost a few years later anyway.

16 Helen Vellacott died on 28 February 2003, a few weeks short of her 92nd birthday.

## Chapter 22

1 Not everybody was co-operative. Other members of his party, having discovered his identity, called him 'Lord Claude'.

2 Michael's time as an encyclopaedia salesman and other episodes in his life were recorded by Mike Safe in The *Australian Magazine*, 30 October 1999.

3 ABC TV.

4 The producer and presenter turned up at Michael's home unannounced , in order to get a fresh approach to the subject. Michael, who might have thrown them out, took it all in good part.

5 Records kept by the BBM show that a certain Terry David travelled in Tom

Wilson's party. Contact was subsequently lost.

6 Bill arrived in Sydney 1 September 1960.

## Chapter 23

1 Subject of jokes about its name and a comic verse about the Burrumbuttock Boys Brigade Drum and Bugle Brass Band.

2 See Chapter 17.

## Chapter 24

1 Then the movement's full-time secretary,

2 See profile, Chapter 23.

3 In fact, a very small percentage did go back. According to Ken: 'The ones that did were back here again in very quick time.'

4 Depending upon his medical progress, and in company with his wife Signe, he looks forward to visiting Sydney in May 2006 to celebrate his 70th Birthday with family and friends.

## Chapter 25

1 BBM index cards refer to a Dr Ziele (first name unknown), also to a Supreme Court judge, identified only by the initials BJF.

2 Author of *Damien Parer's War*, 2004 (Thomas C. Lothian Pty Ltd), previously published as *War Cameraman: The Story of Damien Parer.*

3 See above.

4 The unit was at various times affiliated to no less than six federal government departments.

5 Best known for his coverage of the Shackleton and Mawson expeditions to the South Pole.

6 A further problem, according to Grant, was the decision of the government, also in 1952, to renew 'normal' migration from Germany. There was concern the film might re-ignite anti-German feelings.

7 Available from Film Australia as a com-

pilation DVD under the title *Immigration*.

8 The above includes material extracted from *Cover Up – The Inside Story of the Balibo Five*, by Jill Jolliffe, Scribe Publications, Melbourne.

## Chapter 26

1 Some sources claim 25 marchers left Gilgandra and 277 arrived in Liverpool.

2 Leslie Greenleaf, the last of the Gilgandra Coo-ees, died in 1980. Tom Turvey died in 1965.

3 Bill's older brother, Dick, who owned a butcher's shop next to Bill's residence in Miller Street, is credited with the actual idea of a recruiting march. It is said he raised the idea with Bill one night after dinner, when it was their custom to sit out at the front of their house and enjoy a pipe and a yarn. Dick took no further part in the march planning, and it was Bill who put the plan into practice.

4 He was known as 'Captain' Bill, owing to being the captain of the Gilgandra Rifle Club. The only rank he was given in the Army was Corporal.

5 In the case of HMAS Sydney, with no survivors.

## Chapter 27

1 I am grateful for permission to reproduce material originally published in the Nottingham Evening Post.

2 Thanks to a tip off from Everard Leske, a retired Luthanan pastor.

3 Ken's registered denomination.

4 The onset of World War II in September 1939 brought all migration activities to a halt.

## Chapter 28

1 Nicknamed the 'Friendly Girls'.

2 As reporteded by Ann Howard and Eric Leonard in *After Barnardo* (Tarka Publishing).

3 Under the enthusiastic leadership of the movement's, general secretary in Victoria, Frank Sanders.

4 Probably no more than 100.

5 See *Australia, Britain, and Migration 1915-1940*, by Michael Roe (Cambridge University Press) 1995.

6 See *The Problem of Migration and Unemployment*, by T.S.P. Pughe, published in London (1928),

7 A group of Church Army personnel came to Australia in 1910-1911, intending to found the work here, but it was unsuccessful and they returned home.

8 The Church Army was established formally in Australia in 1934. It was decided that the emphasis should be on evangelism, hence youth migration was discontinued.

9 As former child migrant, John Hennessey, told me: '...like dumping nuclear waste at the bottom of the sea.'

10 See John Weaver, Chapter 20.

11 Leon Nelthorpe-Cowne is now writing his autobiography.

12 Some Catholic organisations, for instance, saw child migration as a means of increasing the Catholic percentage of the general population. Some Protestant bodies acted in a similar manner. See *Orphans of the Empire*.

13 A giant among British childcare leaders, founder of the Father Hudson's Homes, now the Father Hudson's Society.

14 Combining the 'Rescue Societies' of Westminster, Liverpool, Salford, Southwark and Birmingham, and the Superiors of the various religious congregations involved wih the care of children.

15 Later accused (posthumously) of acts of extreme cruelty towards children at the Bindoon and Clontarf Christian Brothers' homes.

16 The Young Christian Workers (YCW) is sometimes confused with the Young Catholic Students Movement (YCS),

Dorothy Day's (US) Catholic Worker Movement, or the short-lived (French) Worker Priest Movement.

17 Equivalent to Big Brother.

18 See Chapter 29..

19 See Barry Coldrey's *Good British Stock*, National Archives Research Guide (1999).

20 It is believed that even before establishment of the 'emigration department', maybe as early as the 1890s, the Salvation Army had sent a number of young men and youths as farm workers to Canada.

21 Interestingly, the Hadleigh Farm Colony still exists, and continues to perform a broadly similar function, training unemployed people.

22 Reprinted in the *War Cry*, 16 August 1923 .

23 Actually five years.

24 See Chapter 4.

25 The group in question applied to Australia House through their local Labour Exchanges.

26 In a letter to *The Times*, published on 11 June 1927, General Bramwell Booth said the Army had selected, trained and 'transplanted' some 3,000 'boys' (youths of working age) since 1922. This statement is valuable in view of the destruction of records previously mentioned.

27 Fred Chambers' views about 'discipline' have bounced back in an unexpected way. Since the interview was given a former resident of the Indooroopilly home has alleged that he and other residents were subjected to bashings and excessive punishments at the hands of Chambers and another officer. The Salvation Army rejects the charges, but has confirmed that the other named officer was dismissed.

28 Fred Chambers died on 15 September 2002.

## Chapter 29

1 In taking what were generally regarded

as 'abandoned, illegitimate orphans'.

2 22 November 1946.

3 Presumably non-Jewish.

4 The Fairbridge Farm Schools in Orange (NSW) and Pinjarra (WA).

5 It was common for Australians of that period to describe themselves as British.

6 Interestingly, in 1938, a Tory back bencher, A.R. Wise, complained in the British House of Commons about the interest being shown by (adult) Germans in migrating to Australia, and what he feared was an organised (Nazi) plan of settlement. He cited as evidence that 10 per cent of new arrivals were German. (In fact the ratio was greater). In the following year A.C.D. Rivett, head of the Council for Scientific and Industrial Research (CSIR), in a speech supporting growing economic ties between Britain and Germany, remarked that Germans had proved superior to Britons as Australian immigrants.

7 According to Norwegian academic, Professor Lars Borgersrud, who is researching the topic. See also *Children of World War II – The Hidden Enemy Legacy*, by Eve Simonsen and Kjersti Ericsson, Berg Publishers, Oxford and New York.

8 The children had arrived from Poland and the Baltic States via a refugee camp in Naples.

9 Later Sir Tasman Heyes.

10 See *Orphans of the Empire*.

11 See material now in National Archives.

12 This statement, perhaps valid at that time, would be challenged today.

**Postscript**

1 For the first verse of this poem see Chapter 9.

2 A form of remedial massage developed by an Australian, Tom Bowen, in Geelong.

3 Executive Director of the BBM.

4 See Chapter 19.

5 *Sydney Morning Herald* journalist

Malcolm Brown has a double reason to remember Scheyville. He did National Service officer training at Scheyville, and subsequently married Ingeborn Koch, who had lived there with her parents as newly arrived migrants from Germany.

6 Hawkesbury Council's version of events is that it was simply a work site for aircraft restoration enthusiasts.

7 See Chapters 1 and 2.

8 See Appendix 1.

9 An exception being the Dreadnought Scheme which was not revived after World War II.

10 See Chapter 18.

11 See Chapter 1.

12 Some say as high as one in five.

13 An under-statement.

14 See above and Chapter 17.

15 The ceremony was to have taken place on 22 September, 50th anniversary of the arrival of the first post-war child migrants, but had to be deferred because of David Hill's absence overseas.

16 This figure is now thought to have been an exaggeration.

17 The WA memorial (to child migrants only) is in the form of a bronze statue depicting a boy and a girl, the latter holding a suitcase. There is a plaque reading: 'This memorial is jointly funded by the Commonwealth and West Australian Governments and is dedicated to the British boys and girls who left their homelands to brave an unknown future in Western Australia. Hardships were endured, benefits were derived. These child migrants provided valuable contributions to Australian society in diverse ways as parents, workers and citizens. Australia is better for their coming.' Alongside is a similar plaque honouring child migrants from Malta.

# Bibliography

## Books, Videos and Useful Contacts

The following books have a bearing on issues raised in this volume.

Alpen, John (1992) *From Millions to Sydney*, The Sydney Club

Anon (1998) *They Passed This Way, Stories of the Dreadnought Boys*, Dreadnought Association.

Anon (1998) *Windows – Rhodesia Fairbridge Memorial College Autobiographies*, Fairbridge Marketing Co Ltd, Christchurch, New Zealand.

Anon (2005) *These Also Came, New stories of the Dreadnought Boys.* Dreadnought Association. To be advised.

Arnold, John, Spearitt, Peter and Walker, David (1993) *Out of Empire, The British Dominion of Australia*, Mandarin, Melbourne.

Ball, Max (2005) *Love, Service and Tolerance. A Commemoration of 100 Years of the Young Australia League*, YAL, Perth.

Bateson, Charles (1994) *The Convict Ships 1787-1868*, A.H. and A.W. Reed.

Bean, Philip and Melville, Joy (1989) *Lost Children of the Empire*, Unwin Hyman, London and Sydney.

Calwell, Arthur (1972) *Be Just and Fear Not*, Lloyd O'Neill, Melbourne.

Clayton, Tim and Craig, Phil (1999) *Finest Hour*, Hodder and Stoughton, UK.

Coldrey, Barry (1999) *Good British Stock, Child and Youth Migration to Australia*, National Archives of Australia Research Guide. [also Tamanaraik Press, Melbourne].

Coldrey, Barry (1993) *The Scheme. The Christian Brothers and Childcare in Western Australia, 1898-1944*, Anglo-Pacific Press/Christian Brothers Provincialate, Perth.

Constantine, Stephen (2001) *Emigrants and Empire, British Settlement in the Dominions Between the Wars*, Manchester University Press.

Courtney, Victor (1961) *The Life Story of J.J. Simons, Founder of the Young Australia League*, Halstead Press, Sydney.

Fethney, Michael (1990) *The Absurd and the Brave – The True Account of the British Government's World War II Evacuation of Children Overseas*, The Book Guild, Lewes, Sussex.

Gill, Alan (2004) *Interrupted Journeys – Young Refugees from Hitler's Reich*, Simon & Schuster, Sydney.

Gill, Alan (1988) *Orphans of the Empire – The Shocking Story of Child Migration*, Random House/Vintage, Sydney.

Hammerton, A. James and Richards, Eric (2002) *Speaking to Immigrants*, Australian National University Press. One of a series of six books dealing with various aspects of migration.

Henderson, Michael (2004), *See You After the Duration – British Evacuees to North America in World War II*, Britannica, London.

Holman, Bob (1995) *The Evacuation – A Very British Revolution*, Lion Publishing, UK.

Howard, Ann and Leonard, Eric, *After Barnardo*, Tarka Publishing.

Humphreys, Margaret (1994), *Empty Cradles*, Doubleday Division of Transworld, London. Now part of Random House.

Jolliffe, Jill (2001) *Cover Up – The Inside Story of the Balibo Five*, Scribe Publications, Melbourne.

Jupp, James (2002) *From White Australia to Woomera: The Story of Australian Immigration*, Cambridge University Press.

Kociumbas, Jan (1997) *Australian Childhood, A History*, Allen & Unwin, Sydney.

Lack, John and Templeton (1995) *Bold Experiment, A Documentary History of Australian Immigration since 1945*, Oxford University Press, UK.

McDonald, Neil (2004) *Damien Parer's War*, Lothian Press, published previously as *War Cameraman: The Story of Damien Parer.*

Mecham, Frank (1995) *The Church and Migrants*, St Joan of Arc Press.

Monsen, Norman (1989) *One of the Likely Lads*, printed privately.

Palmer, Glen (1997) *Reluctant Refuge, Unaccompanied Refugee and Evacuee Children in Australia, 1933-1945*, Kangaroo Press/Simon & Schuster.

Parsons, Martin and Starns, Penny (1999) *The Evacuation, The True Story*, DSM, Peterborough (originally for BBC Radio 4).

Reeson, Margaret (1993) *Whereabouts Unknown*, Albatross Books, Sydney.

Roe, Michael (1995) *Australia, Britain and Migration 1915-1940*, Cambridge University Press, UK.

Sherington, Geoffrey (1980) *Australia's Immigrants*, Geoffrey Sherington, Allen & Unwin, Sydney. Updated and reprinted 1990.

Sherington, Geoffrey (1987) *The Dreadnought Boys*, Published privately. Now in Mitchell Library, NSW. See also *Journal of the Royal Australian Historical Society* (1995), *Australian Historical Studies* (2002) and textual material *Likely Lads in NSW* Mitchell Library.

Sherington, Geoffrey (1998) Fairbridge: *Empire and Child Migration*, Woburn Press, UK, and University of Western Australia Press.

Sherington, Geoffrey (2002) *Suffer Little Children*, Published privately. Presented as an address to the History of Education Society and Australia and New Zealand

History of Education Society conference in *Swansea*, Wales, Nov/Dec 2002.

Simonsen, Eva and Ericsson, Kjersti (2005) *Children of World War II – The Hidden Enemy Legacy*, Berg Publishing, Oxford and New York.

Stokes, Edward (1999) *Innocents Abroad, The Story of British Child Evacuees in Australia 1940-45*, Allen & Unwin, UK.

Wicks, Ben (1995) *No Time to Wave Goodbye*, Stoddart, Canada.

Williams, Maslyn (1995) *His mother's Country*, Melbourne University Press.

**Shipping**

The following books contain information about the migrant ships:

Baty, Scott (1985) *Ships that Passed*, Reed Books.

Gordon, Malcolm (1985) *From Chusan to Sea Princess, The Australian Services of the P&O and Orient Lines*, George Allen and Unwin.

Maber, John (1990) *North Star to Southern Cross*, T. Stephenson and Sons Ltd, Lancashire, England.

Plowman, Peter (1985) *Emigrant Ships to Luxury Liners*, University of NSW Press.

**Theses and special articles**

Coldrey, Barry. Author of a large number of essays, articles and contributions to learned journals on migration issues (including child and youth migration). Tamaranaik Press, 7/67 Collins Street, Thornbury, Vic 3071. www.barrycoldrey.com

Sherington, Geoffrey. Journal of Royal Australian Historical Society, June 1996. Topic Dreadnought Boys. Also Australian Historical Studies, October 2002. Topic Big Brother Movement

Williams, Laura, University of Tasmania thesis, *Good British Stock.*

A radio series, 'The Child Migrants',

which also touches on youth migration, went to air in Britain, on BBC Radio Four, in 2002. It was produced by David Prest. Presenter was Charles Wheeler. For information on availability contact Whistledown Productions, 66 Southwark Bridge Road, London SE1 OAS, England. Another radio series, '*The Evacuation – The True Story*', was produced in 1999 by the same sources.

## Useful Contacts

Big Brother Movement (BBM ltd,) Eddy Steele, executive director, PO Box N874, Grosvenor Place, NSW 1220. www.bbmyouthsupport.asn.au.

Dreadnought Association (Formerly Far North Coast Dreadnought Association): Contacts Olwen and Gordon, King, 7 Elliott Avenue, Alstonville, NSW 2477. tel 02.662-80522. Norma Wyndham, 14, Kruseana Avenue, Goonellabah, NSW 2480. Tel 662-41027.

This book includes material researched by Professor Geoffrey Sherington, formerly Dean, Faculty of Education, University of Sydney. Professor Sherington has made detailed studies of the Dreadnought Scheme, Big Brother Movement and Fairbridge Farm Schools.

# Index